Frank Sinatra
and
Popular Culture

Frank Sinatra
and
Popular Culture
Essays on an American Icon

Edited by
Leonard Mustazza

PRAEGER

Westport, Connecticut
London

Library of Congress Cataloging-in-Publication Data

Frank Sinatra and popular culture : essays on an
   American icon / edited by Leonard Mustazza.
         p.   cm.
   Includes bibliographical references and index.
   ISBN 0–275–96495–7 (alk. paper)
      1. Sinatra, Frank, 1915– —Criticism and
interpretation.   2. Popular music—United States—
History and criticism.   3. Popular culture.
I. Mustazza, Leonard, 1952– .
ML420.S565F73   1998
782.42164'092—dc21   98–23933
[B]   MN r98

British Library Cataloguing in Publication Data is available.

Library of Congress Catalog Card Number: 98–23933
ISBN: 0–275–96495–7

First published in 1998

Praeger Publishers, 88 Post Road West, Westport, CT 06881
An imprint of Greenwood Publishing Group, Inc.

Printed in the United States of America

The paper used in this book complies with the
Permanent Paper Standard issued by the National
Information Standards Organization (Z39.48–1984).

10 9 8 7 6 5 4 3 2 1

For my parents, Teresa and Joseph Mustazza

Contents

PART II
The Troubadour as Modern Hero

PART III
Personal Reminiscences

Preface

Like my two previous books on Frank Sinatra, this one is, to use an overworn phrase, a labor of love—an expression of my affection for and gratitude toward the greatest popular performer that this century has produced. It is also a labor of poetic justice. Ever since I was a child, I have found myself defending my appreciation for the man and his art to those who chose to regard him as little more than a famous hoodlum. (Others who have shared my affinities for this remarkable performer have reported similar experiences.) Never mind the fact that he produced a vast and glorious body of music and, in the process, preserved one of the few true and distinct American art forms. Never mind the fact that his output and range as an actor, though secondary to his work as a musician, drew the industry's highest honors and the admiration of Hollywood's greatest directors, including Frank Capra and Otto Preminger. Never mind the fact that his fabled generosity benefited countless individuals—benefited them not only materially, but also socially when he championed causes like civil rights long before such causes became fashionable. Never mind all of that, casual observers say. He was chummy with unsavory characters and he had a bad temper . . . or so the press told us.

Now that he has died and the dust has settled on a tumultuous life spent all too much in the distorting glare of media attention, the nature of our cultural interest in and dialogue about Frank Sinatra has changed, decidedly for the better. Time has conspired with the short attention span of celebrity watchers and gossip mongers to render many of his reported exploits irrelevant now, and interest has shifted to what mattered most all along anyway—the art. Serious assessments of Frank Sinatra's contributions to American popular culture have begun to proliferate. Book-length studies, of which there has been no dearth over the decades, are turning away from the lurid tell-alls and toward serious artistic assessments by leading music critics (see, for instance, Will Friedwald's 1995 book *Sinatra! The Song Is You: A Singer's Art* and Donald Clarke's 1997 work *All or Nothing at All: A Life of Frank Sinatra*).

Even more impressive is the fact that academe has begun to pay scholarly attention to Sinatra, including his work in courses on music and popular culture, establishing Frank Sinatra chairs in these academic areas (the most recent at Roosevelt University in Chicago), and featuring discussions about him at scholarly conferences. Not only did the Popular Culture Association include a panel on Sinatra at their annual meeting in 1997, but even that traditional bastion of erudition, the Modern Language Association, featured a Sinatra panel the previous year. More impressive will be the three-day conference to be held at Hofstra University in November of 1998, "Frank Sinatra: The Man, the Music, the Legend," which promises to draw scholars from all over the world. The number of Sinatra sites on the World Wide Web and Internet discussion groups (the best known of which is housed at Temple University in Philadelphia) also continues to grow each year. To say the very least, these developments are exciting and encouraging and long overdue. Perhaps in a very short time, Sinatra will require no more defense by me or others than, say, Shakespeare and Rodin do.

It is my sincere hope that this book will add to the growing dialogue about the contributions of this unique American to our culture. The voices in this volume are informed, impressive, and wonderfully varied. Some of the writers are scholars at leading universities, some knew Frank Sinatra personally and write about their experiences, others are famous personalities in their own right, and still others earn their livings in businesses that are far removed from art and entertainment. Together, they provide a provocative perspective on what Sinatra the man, the artist, and the celebrity has meant to popular culture over the past sixty years.

There are many fine people whose assistance and encouragement helped me to complete this book, and I would like to acknowledge some of them here. First of all, my sincere thanks to Sinatra expert extraordinaire Ric Ross for the assistance and advice he has provided over the years. My colleagues at Penn State University's Abington College have gone well above and beyond anything I could have dared expect. Especially noteworthy are Karen and Peter Sandler for their unflagging support; Margaret Bodkin, Dinah Geiger, and Phyllis Martin for their patient and good-humored assistance; Mel Seesholtz and Harry Felton for their expert aid;

and the magnificent library staff—Patricia Weaver, Binh Le, Missy Manzer, Margaret Hindley, Jeannette Ullrich, Carol Julg, and Linda Kinter—for their tireless and first-rate professional work on my behalf. As always, special thanks to my wife, Anna, and my sons, Christopher and Joseph, for their patience, love, and unwavering support. I would also like to express my appreciation to the excellent staff at the Greenwood Publishing Group for their expert professional work. Finally, my deepest gratitude and appreciation go to the contributors to this volume—thorough professionals one and all.

Introduction

LEONARD MUSTAZZA

From the beginning . . . Sinatra's tremendous appeal stemmed from something more than his singing or showmanship. He has always been a study in myths and images, some of them carefully constructed. He early became the popular symbol of the sensitive youngster in a hostile world, the little guy bucking the Establishment, the insatiable man whose reach always exceeded his grasp, the irrepressible and unpredictable individualist.
—Arnold Shaw, *Sinatra: Twentieth-Century Romantic* (1968).

Over his 50 years of singing, Frank Sinatra has become such a huge and ubiquitous star that his disappearance would leave a vacuum that would be abhorrent to the nature of popular culture.
—John Marchese, *The New York Times*, 30 April 1995.

The scope of this book is perhaps best defined by contrasting it to another book on Frank Sinatra, one published some two decades ago. In the preface to his 1976 unauthorized biography, Earl Wilson grapples with the difficulty of writing about this larger-than-life figure, this human icon. "The Sinatra mythology grows and grows," Wilson asserted, "and the problem of a biographer is to cut through it and find the truth." The intent of this book is the very opposite of the one proposed by Wilson. It is not a biography in the traditional sense, nor does it offer secret glimpses into the private life of the man behind the myth. Instead, it is concerned with those very surface myths and images that Wilson had hoped to cut through, with the fans' perceptions of this public figure, with the factors that led to the sculpting of the iconic Sinatra, and the nature of the changing culture that fashioned it.

Some of these images of the performer as iconic hero are familiar products of the twentieth-century American cultural psyche and its preoccupation with celebrity. As organized religions have declined in influence in America, our religious zeal for the otherworldly and powerful has not. It has simply been rechannelled with the aid of technological "magic" and the high priests of mass media. Much of this public projection was, as Arnold Shaw has suggested, carefully constructed by individuals—not the least of them Sinatra himself—who well understood what it would take to thrive and survive in the age of mass media. Through the manipulation of media images (the only way most of us get to "know" our celebrity-heroes), Sinatra essentially told the world how he wanted to be viewed, and, for the most part, he had it "his way."

Sinatra was the first popular performer to exploit the possibilities in this age of mass media, and the myths and images he managed to trade on are the result of a unique conspiracy—the union of a prodigious talent, revolutionary leaps in communications technologies, a shamelessly Dionysian life lived always in the public eye, a strong middle class with economic influence to exert, and a culture that came increasingly to prize individuality above Apollonian loss of self in community. Regardless of his peculiar talent, the cultural product known as "Frank Sinatra" would not have been possible in the class-conscious and decorous eighteenth century or the industrial nineteenth, when the working class saw precious few rise from its ranks to distinguish themselves. It was only with an emergent immigrant middle class and through technological know-how that his art and antics could be spread worldwide on records, films, live radio transmissions, and, a decade into his solo run, on television, the most democratizing medium of them all. The mass hysteria that met his first appearance at the Paramount in late 1942 would probably have remained a local phenomenon had the press not done its part to spread the "contagion" to other venues across the world, thus creating the first of many teen idols to come.

In this regard at least, it is most ironic that Sinatra and the press did not get along very well . . . or so they claimed. The press complained continually that they "made" the Sinatra image and that they never got anything but grief from the combative performer; Sinatra complained continually that the press was parasitic and disloyal, presenting its own distorted image of him as a fascinating bad boy. The fact is that they were both right . . . and wrong! The press did "make" him insofar as his magnificent vocal art might have been little more than a localized flash in the pop-culture pan without their coverage, and he was wrong to say that his talent alone would have been enough to ensure success. By the same token, however, he understood much better than the ever-conservative press the new undercurrents that were flowing through American life and how his own life and art served as a wellspring of the new America—more individualistic, romantic, ambitious, and free. A decade later, the same conservative elements misunderstood the even wilder forces that young Elvis Presley was unleashing. While the free expression and rebelliousness of youth as expressed through peculiar clothing, behavior, and, most of all, music is a given in our own time, it was not in Sinatra's, and he was the first to exploit its power. Despite their continual unease with each other, the press always found Sinatra a fascinating study, and Sinatra benefited longer than any other celebrity from its fascination. Even a glance at *The Reader's Guide to Periodical Literature* or other reference databases will reveal that there has not been a single year since 1942 that Sinatra has been entirely absent from the news, even during his retirement in the early seventies, even in the years prior to his death on May 14, 1998. (The biographical highlights and bibliography at the end of this book, despite my best efforts and their length, do not even begin to exhaust the catalog of accomplishments and their media coverage.)

In his own way, and often on his own terms, then, he managed to defy the transitory nature of popular culture, becoming the first singer to record in *seven* decades (the thirties through the nineties) and to be considered "newsworthy" throughout that time. To say the very least, such sustained attention is extraordinary. Even at a time when mass media and the popular consumption they effect can create and uncreate super- and mega-stars by the day, when celebrities are so appealing that people camp for days outside the venue of the Academy Awards ceremonies just to get a good spot behind the barricades to catch a glimpse of the glittering movie stars as they enter, when the celebrity factor alone can bring about sales of popular artifacts that outpace the GNP of some nations, when celebrity worship has taken on religious zeal for many (the recent worldwide reaction to the deaths of Princess Diana and of Sinatra himself provide good cases in point), Sinatra holds a special place of reverence and awe. The reasons for this elevated seat in the popular pantheon are as complex as the man himself and the ways in which he so effectively tapped into the American mythos.

Thanks to space-age telecommunications and the worldwide appeal of American popular culture, celebrities in our time are known to and influence the lives of many more people than did their counterparts in centuries past. As a result, many celebrities have become more than well-known people. Rather, they are human icons whose appeal and "powers" far transcend their human attributes or talents. The term *icon* itself is derived from the Greek word for "image," and most people "know" celebrities not as they do ordinary human beings but literally as images—on small screens in their homes and large ones in movie theaters, on millions of mass-produced album and videotape covers, and in newspapers and magazines distributed all over the world. Relatively few people have direct access to these celebrities, interact with them on a regular basis, or get to know them as human beings. While part of the reason for this restricted access is security, a large part is also a studied distancing from the crowd. The less a celebrity is actually seen, the more mysterious he or she becomes and the more he or she can live by a manufactured image that is always grander than reality. Even scandal sometimes has the effect of deepening the celebrity's projection of an uncommon existence on a plane apart. By contrast, those who venerate celebrities often regard their own lives as too ordinary, too predictable, too explicable. As organized religion with its potent deities has lost ground in our scientific age to explicable facts and soon-to-be explained phenomena, people have not entirely abandoned their sense of awe in the gods, their desire for mystery. Modern humanity has simply replaced the cast of characters in the pantheon.

A culture's icons—which may refer to supernatural beings, human heroes, and artifacts—reveal a great deal about its values, myths, beliefs, and desires; and, as noted by Jack Nachbar and Kevin Lause, the connection between religious icons in the past and secular ones in the present is clear:

> The term "icon" stems from the Greek word for "image" and is traditionally used to refer to religious objects developed in late medieval times in eastern Europe as a means of communicating significant beliefs and values of a faith to a largely illiterate population of believers. Traditional icons convert objects into signs that everybody can read. . . . But traditional icons (and their popular counterparts) are more than mere "signs," however, because they express deep-seated, significant messages of faith, bind believers together in a community of belief, and impart magical powers to those who venerate the icon. . . . A sign is just a signal; an icon is also a talisman.
>
> Popular icons perform similar roles in the realm of secular beliefs and values. The analogy with religious icons helps us to appreciate how vital and important popular icons are in giving a tangible shape to a culture's mind set. Like traditional religious icons, popular icons are meaningful objects which unite those who believe in the icon, express the important elements of the group's beliefs and values, and impart magical powers to the group. (171)

The values of the secular "faithful" are often diametrically opposed to those of their religious predecessors, preferring reward (direct and vicarious) in the here and now rather than the hereafter and believing that the ostentatiously rich and famous—and not the meek—inherit the earth. As for the belief in "magic," it is evident in many ways—in the surge of fans trying to see and even touch their heroes at rock concerts or political events; in the sums that a guitar played by Jimi Hendricks can fetch at auction; in the pilgrim's shrines that the houses once occupied by Elvis or Diana, Princess of Wales, have become. Moreover, so prevalent is the iconography of celebrity that it has led to much formal academic study. In April of 1992, for instance, Georgetown University hosted a conference entitled "Icons of Popular Culture I: Elvis and Marilyn." "The jumping-off point," according to a report by Sandy Fernandez in *The Chronicle of Higher Education,* "was a shared belief that both Elvis and Marilyn are so closely identified with American culture that the way they are represented speaks directly of America itself. In the papers presented, purported sightings of Elvis say something about American religion. Elvis's quivering lip foreshadows sensitive 70's masculinity, and the view of Marilyn as a mindless sex symbol reflects limits placed on American women" (A10).

The untimely deaths of Elvis Presley and Marilyn Monroe have deepened the mystery and, therefore, the iconic value of their names, but Sinatra's longevity served to widen his fame and to swell the ranks of the faithful. (In fact, Sinatra will get his own scholarly conference in late 1998 at Hofstra University in New York—a three-day affair titled "Frank Sinatra: The Man, the Music, the Legend.") Perhaps because of their ages or the media in which they worked or the personae they projected, neither Elvis nor Marilyn has inspired the kinds of extravagant iconic labels that Sinatra has. Although unfavorably disposed toward Sinatra in his biography of the singer, Tony Sciacca calls him "a man of Olympian proportions" (245). Pete Hamill defends Sinatra from those who criticized his loss of vocal purity and control in the later years of his career by asserting that "if, as some critics charge, the voice itself is a ruin, well, so is the Coliseum; its power and beauty are not diminished simply because the lines are not as clean and pure as they were when young. Sinatra is loved, he is hated, but it is hard to imagine America over the past five decades without Frank Sinatra as part of its basic fabric" (66). Still another significant icon is that of the lion used by both Murray Kempton in his *New York Newsday* article "Sinatra: The Lion in Winter" and David McClintick, who, in a piece for *Vanity Fair,* asserts "the lion is still roaring, still irrepressible, still feisty, still difficult, and still the most potent singer of songs who ever lived" (64). And in 1973, then President Nixon introduced then-retired Sinatra to the Prime Minister of Italy at the White House by drawing an analogy between the singer and the Washington Monument!

Although it is true that, in popular culture, hyperbolic epithets are not uncommon and that one's sense of history is severely foreshortened, enabling many who manage to remain public figures for a decade or more to be called "legends," Sinatra's fame and longevity are transcendent. Part of the reason for this stature has to do with talent, but sheer talent alone has never made icons of performers. How many people who can sing are waiting tables? How many who record albums ought to be waiting tables? There are also great singers like Jack Jones and Steve Lawrence who have not become icons even though they have worked steadily at their trades for many years. Part of the reason may be luck or opportunity, but luck is not enough to give one a long run in a fickle business, much less a six-decade run. The body of material that Sinatra has left behind is truly extraordinary, as is the quality of most of it. However, that body of material might well have been forgotten by most people, declared dated and obsolete, were it not for the continuing fascination with the man himself. Through his work and his behavior in the public eye, both of them uniquely American in style and outlook, he tapped into the psyche of a nation, and has mined the myths that we subscribe to collectively and those that we wish we could live by individually. In describing those myths, however, I would also like to consider the various types of conventional American icons, all of which Sinatra represented in his dance with fame for sixty years.

THE CELEBRITIES' CELEBRITY

Celebrities are individuals whose principal claim to fame *is* fame. They may or may not possess any special gifts and talents, represent immediate cultural interests, and generally neither defend nor oppose cultural values. Their fame results primarily from media attention, and their following (fans) usually only last as long as they receive such attention. By and large, celebrities are made and broken by media attention, which often deliberately blurs the line between the real and the imagined. Stories about celebrity exploits thus become a type of fiction. After all, what do we really know about celebrities besides what the tabloids tell us? How many times have we heard celebrities deny media reports of their behavior or the interpretations of their motives? We know what the papers and TV announcers tell us. Nachbar and Lause put the matter well: "All celebrities are chimeras—half real, half imaginary. A celebrity is a real person, of course, but in the public eye the celebrity is transformed into a created image which is every bit as imaginary—removed from the celebrity's private life and identity—as any movie or television role. The celebrity as 'real' person is interesting to us only as aspects of his or her life reflect or enhance the celebrity's image" (326). Defined as it is primarily by the media, therefore, celebrity status is the most short-lived and unstable of the iconic labels. An attorney in a high-profile case can become a celebrity for awhile, as can those simply associated with other celebrities (a good example is Marla Maples). Performers are the most recognizable of celebrities, and their stock remains high only as long as they can manage to keep up their appeal to the media and, through the media, to consumers. Relatively few do so for long, given rapid changes in media curiosity, style, and popular taste.

Of course, until his retirement from the concert stage and recording studio, Sinatra kept up his celebrity appeal worldwide, drawing crowds whenever he appeared in public, whether performing or merely going about the business of living. The question, however, is this: would that drawing power have remained so intense had it been only for his recognition as a celebrity? Probably not. Conversely, would his Tin Pan Alley art have appealed for so long without the controversial life spent in the hot media eye? Same answer. In fact, Sinatra's life and art were so closely commingled that they became of a piece. He carried the baggage of an explosive and passionate life with him onstage, and the songs he sang evoked his own alternately lonely and swinging existence. The biographical miniseries that Tina Sinatra produced for television awhile back must have been, at one level at least, easy to make. After all, like his art in various media, his life was nothing short of dramatic, the art and the life at once sustaining and feeding upon each other. "Who could possibly be obsessed with Perry Como's offstage personality, or Barry Manilow's?" Daniel Okrent has aptly asked. "Without the celebrity-mongering iconoclasts who could find fuel in Sinatra's every offstage move, the world might have lost interest in him long ago. . . . Every new headline creates a new audience" (216). Indeed it does, and Sinatra kept the celebrity light glowing far longer than any other contemporary figure, thereby keeping his art alive despite changes in musical fashions. In fact, his death, which drew intense worldwide media attention, will likely lead new audiences to the legend's work.

CITIZEN-HERO

Be that as it may, celebrity status alone cannot account for his six-decade marathon. In order to pass into legendary status, there must be a direct and sustained appeal to values—in this case, distinctly American values— and that is the primary function of "heroes." Traditional heroes are those who do possess exceptional gifts, talents, and achievements. Unlike celebrities, who do not actively promote a set of moral/social values, traditional heroes are defenders of conventional values, often epitomizing such values by their very personae. Moreover, their heroism is commemorated formally through various recognitions and honors, and a cult of admirers carry on these heroes' veneration even after their deaths. Not surprisingly, such heroes are often the subject of legends and myths, which are far more important to their cult of admirers than "the facts." A famous example of such a myth is the apocryphal cherry-tree story told about George Washington. Nearly every American knows that story even though most Americans can't tell you much that is factual about Washington besides his being the first president and having his face on the one-dollar bill. The historians' doubt about the tale of the uncommonly honest lad who, because of his great virtues, grew up to be president hasn't made much of a dent in the myth. Fictions are, after all, more glamorous and appealing than truth insofar as they project a sense of order, justice, and reason—qualities that all too often come up short in real life.

Indeed, it is far easier and more comfortable to create heroes out of fictional characters and remote historical personages than from recent or living celebrities, especially in our cynical age. This century has revealed far too much about the discrepancies between human activities and media projections of those activities, about real motives as opposed to those professed and perceived, to allow us to accept heroism of any stripe at face value. We can react favorably, even sentimentally, to fictional superheroes because, as we suspend disbelief to participate in the fiction, we also suspend disbelief in the probability that such great virtue can reside in one human breast. Once outside the theater, however, our vision takes on a realistic cast.

Hence, to make a heroic legend out of a living personage, one must also do a great deal of fictionalizing, so to speak—projecting values and virtues that they may or may not truly possess, inventing remarkable feats to deepen the legendary aura, and forgiving social excesses and personal appetites on the grounds that talent, compassion, and charisma are excuses in themselves. In fact, it can be argued that only two personalities in the twentieth century have reached such heroic proportions during their lifetimes—Babe Ruth and Frank Sinatra. (Earlier I mentioned the 1998 Sinatra conference to be held at Hofstra University. Ironically, the only other time the university hosted a conference of this sort, the subject was Babe Ruth.)

Like Sinatra, the historical Ruth was hardly a model of propriety and probity, and yet, like Sinatra too, he was idolized by many as a supremely talented man of great generosity, charisma, and compassion. His prowess on the baseball field and his colorful charm off allowed his defenders to forgive his antics and appetites, turning his life and art into the subject of awe-inspiring legend. Ruth was depicted as one who could heal dying children by hitting home runs for them or even just being seen by them. When Ruth visited a dying boy after pounding three home runs in the 1926 World Series, a feat supposedly meant to help heal the lad, the Universal News Service wrote, "Just as natural and casual as if he were mortal, Babe Ruth popped into the little second story room where 11 year old Johnny Sylvester was getting the edge in a fight with death today and seemingly turned death's retreat into a rout" (Lloyd 219). Although there were skeptics at the time, many, particularly those in the working and middle classes, ate up the tale with the help of a story-hungry press. Among these fans at least, there probably wasn't a dry eye in the house.

As for his ability to heal the sick, Sinatra could not compete with Babe

Ruth's reported prowess in this regard because even diehard fans today would not tolerate such stories as Ruth's fans did—until recently, that is. Sinatra's healing activity took the form of his generosity to people in trouble, both celebrities (e.g., Lee J. Cobb and Bela Lugosi) and ordinary people whose plights he learned of. On the artistic side, there have also been many commentaries upon the "healing power" of his music. Two striking examples come to mind. After the Phillies' heartbreaking loss to Toronto in the 1993 World Series, *Philadelphia Inquirer* columnist Clark DeLeon wrote a piece in which he admitted to discovering "the extraordinary recuperative power of Frank Sinatra's voice upon a soul-sick loser late at night. . . . The sound of his voice was a tonic, a wonder drug taken by ear, faster acting than Prozac, without the dangerous side effects" (B2). In a similar vein, a recent article in a medical magazine on recovery from major surgery advises the reader to "take the time to really listen to some of the great music we take for granted. I was mesmerized by the timeless artistry of Frank Sinatra, discovering why 'Old Blue Eyes' is deserving of the title 'living legend' " (Hayes 44). Such stories about the effect of Sinatra's music on people's lives and psyches are legion.

However, Sinatra could even compete with Babe Ruth in preternatural power—at least on the movie screen. The Sinatra legend reached its apotheosis in a 1995 made-for-television movie entitled *Young at Heart*. The premise of the film is simple and, on one level, hokey. A Hoboken woman, played by Olympia Dukakis (who also played Sinatra's mother in the 1992 TV biography), named Rose Garavente (the real name of Sinatra's maternal grandmother), is suddenly widowed, and, to get herself through the shock and grief, she turns indirectly to Hoboken's hometown hero. Not only does she listen to his records (which make for a delightful score for the film), but she actually hears his voice whispering to her in the night, "Rose, do it your way." She does, and, in the end, opens a restaurant on the rebuilt site of her late husband's social club, which was burned down by a mobster to whom her husband owed money. Also burned in that fire was a framed 1940s newspaper photo of herself accepting a rose from the teen phenomenon Sinatra. The film comes to rest on a maudlin scene that actually works, particularly if the viewer has shared her faith in the healing power of The Voice and the larger-than-life myth of the Sinatra persona. (Without this faith, of course, the viewer would probably have changed the channel long before or, hearing the promos, never tuned in.) At the restaurant's opening, when she reunites her family and resolves their difficulties, who should mysteriously walk through the door but Sinatra himself, bearing a rose? As one might expect, the rose becomes the punning prop for a new photograph of Rose and Frank to replace the one destroyed in the fire. But the most curious part of the film occurs in Sinatra's brief speaking part. When Rose asks him what he's doing there, he replies, "Joe sent me," referring to her dead husband. Everyone present is surprised by this response, this encounter with the supernatural, but no one thinks to question it. This is, after all, Sinatra. To say the least, the film is not for the faint of mythic imagination—or the Sinatra basher. Still, what other living celebrity had the cadre of fans willing enough to accept this premise at face value?

Interestingly, the film's sentimental devices represent a throwback to an earlier, less cynical genre featuring honest-to-goodness legends drawn from life, films that could portray, without shame, the hero's magnificent powers, real and perceived. The quintessential example is, not surprisingly, *The Babe Ruth Story*, the 1948 film starring William Bendix. In addition to portraying the Babe's wondrous feats on the baseball field and the healing potency of his mere presence, there is a scene in that movie that betokens a distinctly American value system and that again connects the Ruth and Sinatra public personae very nicely. On a rainy night, Ruth goes to a nightclub for a typical night of carousing when he encounters a group of ragged-looking boys selling newspapers. Having known hardship in his days growing up in an orphanage, the expansive Ruth buys all of their newspapers and then invites them to join him inside the fancy club, much to the consternation of the club's snooty management and patrons. Eventually, he wins everyone over with lavish tips, gregarious good humor, fabulous fame, and the contagious force of his charisma. By his very presence, he thus joins together momentarily the high- and the low-brow, elite and mass culture, the social haves and have-nots. Babe Ruth is probably the first American media celebrity who lived the American Dream in all of its glory, rising from humble beginnings to acquire, through his own native talent and hard work, fabulous wealth, influence, and worldwide fame, but never losing touch entirely with those who still occupy the lower socioeconomic rungs.

This democratic spirit is a keynote of American popular culture that sets it apart from European hierarchical culture and that is so appealing today as America exports its popular arts and artifacts to the world. Those who begin with the advantages of money and influence do not, as a rule, become heroes, because the climb for them is not very high. Popular heroes are basically *common* men and women who rise to heights of prominence through their own abilities but who also never forget where they came from and what it feels like to be on the bottom of the heap. "American heroes are not aristocrats, King Arthurs or demigods we can only stand back and admire," Nachbar and Lause assert. "American heroes demonstrate *modesty*, arise from *commonplace* origins, and engage in *everyday activities* and events" (315).

More recently, not only class but race and ethnicity have entered the picture, with many pop heroes belonging to racial minorities or, even when they can dissolve in the white melting pot, openly ethnic. As noted in a *Time* magazine cover story in 1986, "a major pop phenomenon is com-

forting to Americans because it is spectacular evidence of consensus, a palpable national agreement that has nothing to do with quarrelsome issues
of race or religion or class. . . . Moreover, pop serves as a perfectly apolitical politics. . . . Pop is easy listening, easy watching, easy thinking. Yet it
is also authentically democratic. . . . [N]o other Western cultural genus has
been as inclusive as modern pop, so truly classless" (Andersen 69).

Even more than Babe Ruth perhaps, Sinatra represented the American
Dream to many people of his generation, notably those who regarded themselves as oppressed racially, ethnically, and politically. Owing perhaps
to his working-class background and his unabashedly ethnic self-
identification, Sinatra projected a sense of himself as the intermediary between cultural groupings. He was known and respected by heads of state,
royalty, business leaders, and show-business personalities, but his demeanor, acquaintances, and behavior also didn't do much to hide his roots.
If anyone annoyed him, he lashed out, and, at least vicariously, the people
who admired him lashed out, too. He represented, in the words of the same
Time article, "a flashy kind of Yankee individualism—spontaneous, self-
reliant and acquisitive." In this regard, he became a traditional American
middle-class hero who openly projected democratic values in his way of
life and in his art. Such values, particularly his early political stance on
racial and ethnic equality, were not without cost to him personally and
professionally. Nevertheless, he advanced a multicultural agenda long before it became fashionable to do so, and the black community at least has
noticed his pioneering efforts. In 1986, for instance, the black magazine *Jet*
did a story on Sinatra's relationships with blacks in response to Kitty Kelley's character assassination of the singer in her unauthorized biography.
It has not been widely reported, the magazine noted, that Sinatra had written a piece for *Ebony* magazine in 1958 entitled "The Way I Look at
Race," an article that *Jet* calls "the most significant stand taken by a famous
White person since Mrs. Eleanor Roosevelt . . . gave support to the cause
of racial justice and equality." Nor has it been noted—including by Kelley,
his purported "biographer"—that Sinatra earned an honorary doctorate
from a black college, Wilberforce University, in 1960 ("Relationships of
Sinatra with Blacks" 57–59). While some labeled him a turncoat as he
moved from openly liberal politics in his support of FDR and JFK to being
a close friend and supporter of the right-wing Nixon and Reagan admin-
istrations, his support of the social underdog did not waver a bit. But then
again, civil rights did not become fashionable and respectable in Washington until much later, prompting the argument that Washington changed
more than he did.

More dramatic and important to the creation of his mystique was his
musical art, whose conventional themes were intimately concerned with
abiding American myths. One commentator has noted that, while Sinatra
himself was an outspoken populist, his "music usually avoided political

matters" (Cocks 73). On the surface, that statement is true. The classic Tin Pan Alley song for which Sinatra is famous is indeed apolitical, concerned as it is with more lighthearted and everyday fare like love and marriage, love and loss, love and life. But on a subtle and ultimately more important level, the myths projected in this music lie at the very heart of the American psyche, and, at this level, they are nothing if not political.

The myth of romantic love is a distinctly American theme. From the nation's inception, hand in hand with the rejection of a European aristo-cratic caste system went a rejection of many aristocratic values, one of them being arranged marriages. Americans embraced instead the notion that the heart was the only guide in matters romantic, and that love was itself a greater good than lineage and attendant deep pockets. A perfect partner for all people exists somewhere, and only the heart can discover this special person. How many romantic comedies have been based on this very prem-ise? But, whereas a Shakespearean romantic comedy, say, would have the social underling "discover" his or her aristocratic roots in the end in order to make union possible, American versions would subordinate class to love. A good example is Disney's *Aladdin*, in which the Sultan clears the way for a commoner to marry a princess because the commoner has shown his mettle and, just as important, because they love each other! Although it is set in the Middle East, the theme of the story is clearly American in outlook and values.

It is, I believe, no coincidence that the apex of Sinatra's early rise as a romantic singer occurred while a world war raged whose aggressors were Germany and Japan. Many commentators have argued that his appeal to young women in the forties was due to the wartime dearth of young men. However, Sinatra's appeal extended to many young men, both here and "over there." "The theory that he was merely a surrogate for the absent servicemen," writes Gene Lees, "overlooks his popularity with a good many of those self-same servicemen" (103). Even the youngsters' parents liked Sinatra—so long as they didn't have to watch the silly swoonings of their bobbysoxed daughters. The romantic crooner was an ethnically de-fined, middle-class phenomenon, who lived the economic version of the American Dream and sang the mythic one, which involved love and sweet-ness, innocence and commitment—in marked contrast to the fiendishly rigid Germans and Japanese who occupied the popular imagination.

Along with this American predilection for freedom, individuality, and even iconoclasm in matters of the heart went another cultural ideal that ran counter to the perceived lockstep conformity of the Axis powers. Re-garding these rules-oriented cultures as coldly intellectual in their approach to human behavior, Americans saw themselves as "natural citizens" who are intelligent in practical and sentimental ways. "Intellectuals are mind-over-body types who fail to recognize that true human identity resides in the heart and not in the brain," write Nachbar and Lause (87), and Sinatra's life and art illustrated this distinction well. And, if you missed the subtly presented lesson on American values projected in his music, Sinatra had even provided overt, didactic commentaries on this theme. In the spoken introduction to one of his greatest romantic ballads, "Night and Day," on the retrospective album *Sinatra: A Man and His Music* (1965), for instance, he talked of American "substance." Contrasting conventional definitions of "greatness" as reflected in such highly visible leaders as presidents, scientists, and tycoons, he offered an alternative definition of greatness, one that his audiences could well appreciate: "Giovanni is a good husband, a good father, a good loyal friend." Not only does the patently ethnic identification bring the protagonist down to human proportions, especially to those in the heavily ethnic enclaves where Sinatra found his most loyal fans; it defined greatness in terms of sentiment rather than intellect—the stock in trade of those to whom Giovanni is contrasted. Now, one would imagine that Sinatra the man had a lot more to do on a day-to-day basis with the conventionally defined great rather than the Giovannis of the country, but that is immaterial. His enduring success as a performer had to do with his understanding and use of the myths that common people live by.

Finally, perhaps the most pervasive of American beliefs is the view of America itself as a special nation with a special destiny—the world's beacon of liberty, the protector of the underdog, the ideal toward which all other nations should strive. "America is the greatest country in the world" is an unexamined yet unquestionable national mantra, and Sinatra pop art advanced this concept from the outset of his remarkable career. Illustrations of this projection in his art and life are manifold. He won a special Oscar in 1946 for the film short *The House I Live In*, and he rendered emotional readings of the song on stages across the world for fifty years. There are special renditions of the song on two recorded concert films—*The Main Event* (1974) and *The Concert for the Americas* (1982)—and it is even included in his last album, *Duets II*, accompanied, not coincidentally, by Neil Diamond, whose *Jazz Singer* score (1980) featured the song "America." In each decade of his fame, this theme continually comes up. His live repertoire in the sixties featured "My Kind of Town" (Chicago) as a signature song, and, after 1980, he signed off with "New York, New York." His last solo album, *L.A. Is My Lady*, sought, without as much success, to glorify still another American city. Sinatra may have had an Italian surname, but his values were American through and through. Is it any wonder that he was awarded the Medal of Freedom, and, post-humously, the Congressional Gold medal, the nation's highest civilian honor? As befits the conventional citizen-hero, he defended through his art the culture that allowed him to prosper.

CITIZEN ROGUE

By the same token, American heroes also often embody conflicting values, and, as the Apollonian demands of civil and cultural conservatism tug them in one direction, the Dionysian urge to freedom pulls in the other. From colonial times, the mindset of Americans has been different from that of polite Europe, less civilized and refined, more individualistic and violent, more vulgar and rough. The schizophrenic nature of American civilization is clear at every turn in our history, affecting not only government but other institutions as well. The conservative arm of the Roman Catholic Church, for instance, bitterly complains about the individualistic American will, using the phrase "cafeteria Catholics" to describe those who would pick and choose which church doctrines (notably in terms of birth control) to follow, as opposed to their more "obedient" followers in Europe and the Third World. Popular leaders often feel themselves torn by this schizophrenic push toward civilization and pull toward the self, and, when this tug o' war occurs, they often find themselves bucking mass values and asserting other (sometimes higher) principles than those generally subscribed to by the status quo (which includes, ironically enough, the media).

Such figures are known as *rebel* or *rogue heroes*. This type of hero, who knowingly violates social norms and even laws, appeals to a cultural minority who feel oppressed by and alienated from the dominant culture, a minority group that takes pleasure in and a sense of vicarious freedom from the rogue's spontaneity and lack of restraint. Such heroes represent another, more extreme view of the American Dream not acknowledged in the conservative version: "absolute personal freedom in a land of infinite frontiers, endless roads, and limits set only by what the human body can withstand before collapsing" (Nachbar and Lause 320). Eventually, if these heroes survive the struggle to break free, their values often enter the mainstream, and so one era's rebel thus becomes a later era's citizen-hero when the values of the dominant culture change—often because people like the rebel hero.

Sinatra found himself in this tug o' war often enough in these six decades, and his agon won him both powerful foes and intensely loyal admirers. As noted earlier, for example, although civil rights is now a mainstream issue, his championing of it and other so-called left-wing causes in the forties cost him a considerable amount professionally and financially. In addition, he was accused of all manner of unrestraint, from running with the kingpins of the American mafia to uncivilized behavior toward people great and small. The interesting thing about all of these reports of his lack of conventional social control is that they were newsworthy enough to have kept him in the headlines for many years, that he rarely took the time to defend himself against the charges leveled against him, and, most interesting from a cultural perspective, that the perception of his bad behavior won him as many fans as detractors.

Indeed, his antics magnified his heroic proportions among his fans, and, when he sang boastfully about having done it "my way," everyone knew what he meant, whether you approved or not. "Crazy like a fox," Sinatra biographer John Rockwell has said concerning Sinatra's bad press. "All that stuff bolsters his image as a feisty guy who won't take crap from anybody" ("Looking Back over 50 Years" 81–82). Rockwell is not alone among Sinatra biographers in this view. Arnold Shaw wrote, "Courage is an elusive quality in our time. . . . If he lost his temper and let go with a fist or a million-dollar lawsuit, the admiration he drew from a timid world more than compensated for the beating he sometimes took in the public prints" (3). No less a personage than composer Irving Berlin advised biographer Earl Wilson, "Write about his *guts*! He may have been wrong many times, but he had the guts to stand up for his position, whether it was the government, or a country, or whoever the hell it was!" (Wilson xiv). Wilson, though less admiring perhaps than Berlin, did say this: "The gossip, the spread of the Sinatra mythology and the Sinatra mystique about his lush lifestyle and his ungovernable habits make him a more fascinating subject for study than most of the world's leaders" (xvii). Indeed, the bibliography on him alone may be longer than those on most of the world's leaders!

In my earlier book on Sinatra, I wrote about Sinatra's "art and heart," the idea that both his prodigious talent and his feisty behavior made him the most extraordinary entertainment figure of the century. Part of that "heart" was his overt defense of the underdog; part was, as we have seen, the mythology of love that his art advanced and that he came to represent; and part was his doing whatever he damn well pleased, a code of behavior that offended some and delighted others, notably those who feel put upon by societal strictures. In a sense, he represented to conservative adults the same kind of appealing rebel figure that youngsters found in James Dean and in Elvis Presley and the myriad rockers who followed him. Sinatra was the working man's and woman's rebel (with or without a cause), a punk performer in a tuxedo. Ironically, for all of his expressed distaste in the fifties and sixties for rock music and its practitioners, he was in many ways their prototype. When a rock group behaves badly in public, their fans cheer them on, and conservative cultural elements excuse both the rockers and their fans on the grounds that they are young, disaffected, and outside the mainstream anyway, whatever the mainstream is anymore. Those of Sinatra's generation, on the other hand, lived by a different, more conservative, code of social etiquette, at least on the surface of things. Take dress, for example. Sinatra would always perform in a jacket and tie, and typically in a tuxedo, the most formal version of that uniform. His fans approved, and many would wrinkle noses in distaste over the performance costume of, say, Mick Jagger or Axel Rose. Why, then, was Sinatra the tough-talking brawler a hero to so many of them? Why indeed!

In a *New York Times* piece on Frank Sinatra, Jr., John Marchese makes a sweeping observation about his subject's enduring father: "The fact is, every singer in the last half-century who has stepped in front of a big band has been measured in some way against Frank Sinatra" (49). Superficially, the statement is far too extravagant. After all, by its commercial nature, the marketers of popular culture are continually in search of new players to tickle consumers' fancies. Pop phenomena come and go, often with blinding brevity, and no one (Sinatra included) leaves a hole so large that it can't be filled by the next bankable act. On the other hand, the statement is also quite true. Sinatra *did* set the musical standard for those who have stepped in front of big bands, his own contemporaries (e.g., Dick Haymes), the next generation of singers (e.g., Tony Bennett), and those few "anach-ronistic" pop performers in the fifties who crossed over from rock to Sinatra-style pop (e.g., Bobby Darin).

However, more important, and more interesting, is the fact that he also influenced those who would step in front of little bands as well—rock and roll bands—not so much artistically as attitudinally. As John Rockwell notes in his biography, Sinatra became, in the words of *The Rolling Stone Encyclopedia of Rock and Roll*, "the model and envy of rockers from the beginning" because he was the first of the mass-media youth idols and because he built a career on "a feisty, nose-thumbing defiance of society's sillier conventions" (21). Indeed, he set the attitudinal standard that rock and roll front men and women would come to assume—continual defiance of "authority" (notably critics and journalists), deliberate violation of social norms and conventions, and ego-gratifying off-stage behavior carried back onto the concert stage to the delight of "rebellious" audiences. No one has analyzed the matter better for his own generation than rocker Bono of U2 when he said of Sinatra at the 1994 Grammy Awards, "Rock and roll people love Frank Sinatra because Frank Sinatra's got what we want: swag-ger and attitude. He's big on attitude—serious attitude, bad attitude. Frank's Chairman of the Bad. Rock and roll plays at being tough, but this guy . . . well . . . he's the boss. The Boss of Bosses. The Man. The Big Bang of Pop. I'm not gonna mess with him. Are you?"

The fact is that, while many live by conventional codes, they feel trapped by these codes as well, which include laws and social customs. The outlaw, the willing violator of society's rules, is applauded everywhere in American pop culture, so long as this outlaw figure has such redeeming qualities as prodigious talent and, most of all, a heart. "A man's gotta do what a man's gotta do" is not the motto of modern rebellious youth but of the frontier hero carried into urban America. Sinatra's anthemic "My Way" is simply a variant of that motto.

In the chapters that follow, a variety of distinguished writers and scholars consider the elements that went into the construction of this iconic American hero, the prototype of many superstars to come. The book is divided into three parts.

Part I, titled "Celebrity, American Culture, and Frank Sinatra," is concerned generally with Sinatra's fame, the ways in which his image and persona were formed, and the effect that that image has had on American popular culture. This part begins with a chapter by Sinatra himself. Written in 1945, it addresses the issue of civil rights, a cause that the singer championed throughout his long career. Following this excellent piece are four chapters by distinguished scholars assessing Sinatra's fame and its influence over our culture. T. H. Adamowski considers the conflicts and tensions produced by the fact that the singer's fans are multi-generational. Then, Roger Gilbert takes up the issue of the fifties Sinatra—the brash and swinging image of the performer by which many fans think of him even today—and how our concept of masculinity was shaped by this image. (Incidentally, much of the current interest in the so-called Rat Pack is centered around this very persona. Among other Sinatra projects currently in the works, HBO is shooting a movie about this period in Sinatra's life, with Ray Liotta cast in the main role.) Next, James F. Smith compares Sinatra's early fame with that of the next great teen idol to emerge, Elvis Presley. And Gil Gigliotti assesses the ways in which album liner notes, in particular those written by Grammy Award-winning writer Stan Cornyn, have helped to shape the Sinatra image. In the next chapter, Ken Hutchins, a computer expert and frequent contributor to Internet sites devoted to Frank Sinatra, looks at how Sinatra's fans have gathered over the years to express their admiration for the singer, including, most recently, through the many Internet websites and discussion groups that have sprung up. Finally, Dr. Lloyd Spencer, a practicing psychiatrist, considers the beneficial effects of Sinatra's music from both the personal and professional perspectives.

Part II, "The Troubadour as Modern Hero," addresses the area on which Sinatra's fame principally rests and in which his greatest artistic accomplishments lie—the music. It begins with a 1989 poem by Gerald Early, "Listening to Frank Sinatra," a fictional description of the emotional effects that Sinatra's music has on some unusual people. Following this poem are essays by four respected music critics. Dan Okrent, the editor of New Media at Time, Inc., and the former managing editor of *Life* magazine, looks at how Sinatra's early work influenced the shape of American music to come, his own and that of many others. Next, Chuck Granata, the archivist for Sony Music's Legacy Records series, looks at the unprecedented longevity of Sinatra the recording artist. Curiously, the only theatrical endeavor in which Frank Sinatra has never participated is starring in a Broadway play. And yet, more than any other single performer, he helped to keep the classic American show tune alive and well through his many recordings. Philip Furia, a university professor of English and distinguished author of *The Poets of Tin Pan Alley*, analyzes this unique achievement. Another musical irony lies in the fact that, although Sinatra never considered himself a jazz singer, most jazz musicians polled over the years have regarded him as among the greatest jazz singers ever. In a piece that includes interview quotes with a number of well-known jazz musicians, Sinatra-biographer Will Friedwald looks at this reluctant jazz singer. Next, Richard Iaconelli considers the distinctly American nature of Sinatra's musical style. Finally, Edmund Santurri, a university professor of religion, uses Sinatra's music as a "meditation" on the theme of love in the postlapsarian world.

Moving from cultural to personal experience, Part III contains individual reminiscences of the singer by people who have known him. The four voices in this section are well-known personalities associated with Sinatra over the years—Stan Cornyn, former Warner Bros. vice president and author extraordinaire of liner notes for many of Sinatra's albums over the years; Sinatraphile and collector Rick Apt; Emmy Award-winning television personality and Sinatra interviewer Bill Boggs; and longtime radio personality and close friend of the singer Sid Mark. Collectively, they provide a unique, up-close glimpse of the man and the musician.

It is my hope that the nineteen voices in this volume will provide new material for the ever-growing dialogue about Frank Sinatra's place in and influence over American popular culture in our time.

WORKS CITED

Andersen, Kurt. "Pop Goes the Culture." *Time*, 16 June 1986, 68–74.

Cocks, Jay. "The Chairman and the Boss." *Time*, 16 June 1986, 72–73.

DeLeon, Clark. "Please, Mister, Please; Play Fifty-Two-Oh-Nine." *The Philadelphia Inquirer*, 24 October 1993, B2.

Fernandez, Sandy. "The Iconography of Elvis and Marilyn." *The Chronicle of Higher Education*, 4 May 1992, A10.

Hamill, Pete. "An American Legend: Sinatra at 69." *50 Plus*, April 1985, 26–29, 64–66.

Hayes, Janice. "Bouncing Back from Adversity." *Arthritis Today*, November/December 1994, 42–44.

Kempton, Murray. "Sinatra: The Lion in Winter." *New York Newsday*, 17 November 1993, 7, 112.

Lees, Gene. "The Sinatra Effect." In *Singers and the Song*. New York: Oxford University Press, 1987, 101–15.

Lloyd, F. R. "The Home-Run King." In *The Popular Culture Reader*. Third Edition. Ed. Christopher D. Geist and Jack Nachbar. Bowling Green, OH: Bowling Green State University Popular Press, 1983, 212–28.

"Looking Back over 50 Years of Popular Music, a Critic Has Two Words for Sinatra: 'The Best.' " *People*, 28 January 1985, 81–82.

Marchese, John. "Owning the Name but Not the Fame." *New York Times*, 30
April 1995, 45, 49.

McClintick, David. "Sinatra's Double Play." *Vanity Fair*, December 1993, 50–52,
62–70.

Mustazza, Leonard. "Sinatra's Enduring Appeal: Art and Heart." In *The Frank
Sinatra Reader*. Eds. Steven Petkov and Leonard Mustazza. New York: Oxford University Press, 1995, 3–9.

Nachbar, Jack, and Kevin Lause. *Popular Culture: An Introductory Text*. Bowling
Green, OH: Bowling Green State University Popular Press, 1992.

Okrent, Daniel. "Saint Francis of Hoboken." *Esquire*, December 1987, 211–16.

"Relationships of Sinatra with Blacks That Book About Him Does Not Highlight."
Jet, 13 October 1986, 57–59, 62.

Rockwell, John. *Sinatra: An American Classic*. New York: Random House/Rolling
Stone, 1984.

Sciacca, Tony. *Sinatra*. New York: Pinnacle, 1976.

Shaw, Arnold. *Sinatra: Twentieth-Century Romantic*. 1968; rpt. New York: Pocket,
1969.

Wilson, Earl. *Sinatra: An Unauthorized Biography*. 1976; rpt. New York: New
American Library, 1977.

PART I

Celebrity, American Culture, and Frank Sinatra

What's This About Races?

FRANK SINATRA

A lot of what I want to say to you might perhaps be better said to us parents—and I don't have any trouble qualifying as a parent. But, after all, you are the parents of tomorrow. You'll be around here longest. So it's most important to you that some things which aren't quite the way they should be now get going right—and stay right.

Of course, there's another reason why I'd rather talk to you than to your parents. I guess maybe I can talk to you better, because I haven't forgotten anything that happened to me in school and on the way to school—and *after* school. I've noticed kids are smarter than they used to be. Anyway, they're smarter than *I* used to be. And that's a pretty big admission, hey! When I was going to school I didn't think anybody could be any smarter than me. Don't we all?

But what a lot I *didn't* know about. Things were going on I never even suspected. But I know now. Yes, sir, now I know why, when I was going to school over in Jersey, a bunch of guys threw rocks at me and called me a little Dago. I know a lot of things now. *I* know now why they used to call the Jewish kids in the neighborhood "Kikes" and "Sheenies" and the colored kids "Niggers."

Let's take it right from the top. Ever hear that corny old saying, "Sticks and stones will break my bones, but names will never hurt me?" That's not only corny—it's wrong. Names *can* hurt you. Show you what I mean.

Once there was a little guy named Dick who was ten years old . . . and lived all ten of his years in a neighborhood where there weren't any Negroes.

Then one evening his dad came home tired, hot, upset and kind of irritated and told his mother about how he had some trouble downtown with a "dirty Nigger." Now, Dick's dad sounded kind of sore, so naturally Dick gets the impression a "dirty Nigger" is something to get sore about.

Of course, Dick loves his dad, and anything his dad's against, *he's* against!—whether it's right or wrong! So, quick like a flash, he's against colored people. He's got a new phrase and a new dislike for a whole race of people he's never even seen.

But it may not always be "dirty Nigger." *Sometimes* a kid hears his father running down a "bid dumb Mick," or a "greasy Wop," or a "stingy Jew."

Let's take the Nazis. They were brought up to hate everybody—they even hate one another. They have killed millions of people in cold cruelty. First, they picked on the Jews—the Jews who are a cultured and wonderful people, peace-loving, home-loving and industrious. But the Nazis just don't want that kind of people around. So they picked on the Jews, took away their property and blamed them for everything that was wrong in Germany—*even after they killed them off!*

And while they were brazenly blaming the Jews, they were secretly blaming the same things on the Catholics, setting neighbor against neighbor. That's how the Nazis used racial and religious prejudice to weaken the people they wanted to defeat and enslave.

To excuse these atrocities in their own minds, the Nazis called themselves the master race and wanted to rule the world. The trouble is, though, that German people aren't a race. All their talk about a pure Aryan race is just pure Aryan applesauce.

The word "Aryan" is the name of one of the more obscure languages spoken in India. There is no Aryan race. No scientist in the world can examine blood and tell from which race of man it came. Take a brain from any man's head and no one can tell you positively from what race that brain came. Because every race produces men with big brains and men with small brains. Men with big, strong muscles, and men like me. Every race produces geniuses, smart men, and fools. The lungs, the liver, the intestines and other parts of all human beings are exactly alike. The only difference between a Chinese and an Englishman is the color of his skin.

It would be a fine thing if people chose their associates by the color of their skin! Brothers wouldn't be talking to brothers, and in some families the father and mother wouldn't even talk to each other. Imagine a guy with dark hair like me not talking to blondes. The more you think about all this, the more you realize how important Abraham Lincoln was talking when he said: "Our fathers brought forth on this continent a new nation conceived in liberty and dedicated to the proposition that all men are created equal." Get that—all men are *created* equal.

Look! The next time you hear anyone say there's no room in this country for foreigners, tell him *everybody* in the United States is a foreigner.

Now this is our job . . . your job and my job and the job of the generations growing up . . . to stamp out prejudices that are separating one group of United States citizens from another.

It's up to all of us to lay aside our *unfounded* prejudices and make the most of this wonderful country—this country that's been built by many people, many creeds, nationalities and races in such a way that it can never be divided, but will always remain the United States—one nation, indivisible, with liberty and justice for all.

Love in the Western World: Sinatra and the Conflict of Generations

T. H. ADAMOWSKI

It has been a long time since he was *not* a "celebrity." Hitler and Stalin were in power then, eyeing each other suspiciously, and FDR was completing his second term. The record for longest hitting streak in baseball history was *not* held by Joe Dimaggio, and the last man to hit .400 was *not* Ted Williams. In the universities, the New Criticism wasn't even *new* yet. In Paris, Jean-Paul Sartre and Simone de Beauvoir were known mostly to their friends; and Freud, dying in London, was a man in his early eighties, about the same age as Sinatra is now. By 1944, of course, Sinatra had become one of the most celebrated men in America. A decade later he would be one of the most celebrated in the world. Indeed, based on the numbers of his CDs that one finds in major record outlets, the sales of *Duets I* and *II*, the releases of commemorative boxed sets of his recordings, and the extent to which his eightieth birthday was discussed (not to mention his recent illnesses), he remains immensely celebrated still, with all that this comprises of love and hate maintained over six decades.

Sinatra managed this unparalleled feat in popular culture by generating audiences *beyond* the one that first made him famous. In the 1950s new listeners would swell that original audience, and more would appear through the mid-1960s. From that point, recruitment to his audience, although it would never cease, would remain relatively modest for twenty years. In recent years, however, there have been reports of renewed growth; and certainly my own observation of the age-profile of audiences at his performances in the 1980s and the early 1990s showed a steady increase in the number of people in their twenties and thirties.

Nevertheless, after *September of My Years* (1965), and despite some modest recruitment in that period arising from the success of "Strangers in the Night" and "My Way," Sinatra's audience had begun to stabilize. Not for nothing was this also the *real* beginning of the 1960s and the *apparent* beginning of what cultural historians of late-century America sometimes call "the youth movement," a phenomenon linked both to revolt in the universities and Beatlemania. In fact, it is arguable that the inception of the youth movement has been misdated and that either December 1942, when Sinatra opened at the Paramount Theatre, or the legendary "Columbus Day Riot" of 1944 should mark the birth of the twentieth century's youth archetype. To gauge the nature of that archetype, imagine a "back-morphing" of Michael Jackson's photograph that turns it into the face of Mick Jagger, then into the face of Elvis, and then, as it must, into the bony face of a twenty-eight-year-old Sinatra. However, an archetype's moment of origin tends to be forgotten, perhaps even *repressed*, by the success of its avatars. It is that repression I want to consider.

By the middle of the 1970s the celebrity currency that Sinatra still possessed for people born in the 1920s and 1930s had virtually disappeared for people born after about 1945. He very much possessed celebrity, but its currency—as a measure of his capacity for turning celebrity to *advantage* with new audiences, through recordings, films, and public performances—was diminishing.[1] For the great majority of the generation that came of age in the mid-1960s, he was descending into the kind of celebrity status that Al Jolson—an afterimage from another era—had owned for their parents. Moreover, his career moves to maintain currency were all of the wrong type.

Wisely, he knew he could never be a Mabel Mercer, for example, merely an archivist of a certain era's popular music.[2] But to maintain currency required that he confront the best material from rock that he might adapt to his own style. Foolishly, he and his advisers consistently chose some of the worst (e.g., "Downtown"), making clear for the first time that between Sinatra and a potential audience an irremediable "generation gap" had begun to yawn.[3] Wisely, he seemed to know that his reputation for political activism might be a career-aid in an age of renewed mass politics. Foolishly (at least, on a public-relations plane), he moved actively and visibly to the *right*, infuriating virtually everyone possessing opinion-making skills in the audience he hoped to win—and, indeed, infuriating many in the huge audience he still possessed.[4] In a do-your-own-thing era, he wisely maintained his reputation for being his own man; foolishly, however, he gave the impression that this meant flaying women reporters with obscenities, with nary a look to his political flanks.

Such misguided choices kept Sinatra celebrated, but, for this new and inheritor generation, celebrated for the wrong reasons. Around him had begun to form the dark aura of a *negative* celebrity that affects, still, the response of many of the "inheritors" to him.[5] And all the time demographics performed on his own audience its slow and merciless work. As it aged, Sinatra's audience bought fewer records, preferring instead to see their beloved "Frank" at the many public performances that ended his seclusion in the Las Vegas of the fifties and early sixties. As they gave up on record buying, millions of their children filled the gap, forming a demographically overpowering audience of record buyers that would relegate Sinatra's music to the nether reaches of retail outlets for the next three decades.

Worse, perhaps: Sinatra's age cohort began retiring from control of the levers of power in what he always called "the music business" and in Las Vegas. Inevitably, of course, new, young Pharaohs arrived on the scene, many of whom knew not Joseph in his greatness. A fifty-ish film producer from Los Angeles—who had actually met Sinatra a couple of times—told me recently that Sinatra "was a great star of the *1940s*." For this man's generation, popular music "stardom" really begins in the *mid-1950s*. Apart from rock, what existed in popular music in that decade was, by definition, anachronism. As this generation came to prominence in Vegas, in the 1980s, even Sinatra's music began to be pushed to the margins of many of the casinos. By 1995, in his Vegas performances, Frank Sinatra, Jr., was lamenting that his act included the only swing band performing "in the state of Nevada." By the 1980s, it had become common for admirers of Sinatra to hear from triumphalist members of the sixties generation such deeply misguided, and patronizing, remarks as "I thought 'Strangers in the Night' was really great." "Strangers in the Night"! *Not* a "Sinatra song." Just a Sinatra "hit" (what he called a song "for people who like lemon-flavored yogurt"). Taste in rock often seemed to be just that: taste in *rock*.

Certainly, there are many exceptions to the indifference to Sinatra that the inheritor generation displayed. The point is, however, to identify what had become an opinion so common that it will be recognizable to anyone who is an admirer of Sinatra. By the 1970s, he remained "hip" only to an older crowd. The icon of "older crowds," he would not stand a chance with their children.

My own favorite example of Sinatra's new silver-plated celebrity came from a student who was shocked to learn that I admired him. "He's a Republican!" she spluttered, under the impression that this was virtually an indictable offense. "He supported Reagan." When I saw that she refused to believe he had ever been the Warren Beatty of the 1950s and 1960s, I changed the subject. "So, tell me, what's your dissertation about?" "Oh, I'm working on the *Cantos* of Ezra Pound," she said, without a blush. "They're really quite marvelous." Well, whatever else we can say of him, at least Pound was no Republican!

But to point out such double standards was beside the point to the inheritors. For them "high culture" was increasingly sealed off from any popular culture *but their own*, and for their own the borders between "high" and "pop" had begun to blur. The Beatles would be compared to Bach. Bob Dylan would replace Dylan Thomas as the poet identified by a single, mythic name, and a friend tells me he is working to nominate Dylan for the Nobel Prize in literature. Sinatra? "He doesn't write his own songs" became the ritual reply, always delivered—in an era when "text" was valued more highly than "voice"—with what was thought to be terminating effect to the discussion.[6]

Is the Pound story merely anecdotal evidence or a representative instance? Like anyone who prefers novelists to sociologists, I lean towards the latter. What had occurred among the sixties generation was a kind of collective amnesia. Many of them must certainly have grown up hearing Sinatra, on their parents' high-fi's, singing not "Strangers in the Night" but "Angel Eyes," "I've Got You Under My Skin," or "Here's That Rainy Day." How on earth could they have forgotten *them*? The events of the 1960s that made Sinatra become, like others of his age, a kind of neo-conservative, dismayed by the break-up of the consensual American culture that had seemed to bring together many from his generation who had endured Depression and war (such events leading some left and others right) are merely *politics*, examples of what Saul Bellow has called modern "distractions," and of enduring interest only to future historians of displaced religions.[7]

But how to account for something *serious*? How to account for a tin ear? For that to have occurred, what was needed were changes in the *heart*.

Representative instance: a young white Canadian, doing his Ph.D. under my supervision, condescends, typically, to Sinatra. "He's OK. But I prefer jazz." "Oh, really," I reply. "And whom do you like?" "Miles Davis, Lester Young, Oscar Peterson, Ella Fitzgerald, Duke Ellington." I might have quoted T. H. Huxley's exuberant remark to an incautious bishop, "Oh Lord, thou hast delivered him into my hands." "And what did *they* think about Frank Sinatra?" I asked. Knowledgeable about the music of these great jazz performers, he could not believe they admired Sinatra.[8] Inextricably linked to black culture, jazz would be granted a generational reprieve by the politically sensitive inheritors (not that this meant they would buy much of it). Selective perception: otherwise called *repression*.

As for rock fans who, before *Duets*, thought no rock artist could have anything to do with Sinatra, they had selectively misperceived remarks of Marvin Gaye, Jim Morrison, or Billy Joel—as, later, they would dismiss the admiration of some of their children's heroes (Bono, for example) for Sinatra. If one called to the attention of rock fans the admiration that such rock performers had for Sinatra, the response could be unsettling. They would hear, but not *process*, the information: it may have entered their brains, but the effective signals from these data somehow became lost in their flesh and did no work. It was as if one put a quarter in a gum machine only to have no package come out.

After *Duets*, it became, "They did it for the money." Or, unaccountably, there were authenticity complaints about the use of electronic duets, as if double- or even triple-tracking had never occurred in the post-Beatles era. One of the notably unremarked moments in *Duets I* occurs when one hears Luther Vandross accompanying himself. Forget his accompaniment of Sinatra: how on earth did he accompany *himself*? In this case, selective perception could almost be forgiven, for such devices have been staples of rock producers for decades and are probably accepted by its listeners as a kind of "natural" phenomenon. What is interesting, however, is the assumption that by employing electronic techniques some astonishing breach of authenticity had occurred on Sinatra's part.

At its outer reaches, where, between 1944 and 1965, Sinatra walked alone, celebrity may come at great price, including, perhaps, such selectivity of perception. Through celebrity one may achieve what we call today "iconic" status, but, because it is cast in such high relief, celebrity may hold the icon hostage to the period in which the mantle of fame was placed on his or her shoulders. Beyond that period, all that may remain of celebrity are, in fact, the kitschy images that recall it—the photo of Fields in *David Copperfield*, Jolson on his knee in blackface, Marilyn (where is she now?) with her skirts lifted by a rush of subway-driven air.

Sinatra, too, perhaps: hat at a jaunty angle and a trenchcoat tossed over his shoulder? or reduced to one atypical "lyric" ("do be do be do")? Or will it be with his arms draped around members of the Gambino family? "Famous entertainer of the mid-century, thought to have been linked to organized crime figures." If it happens to Sinatra, take it to the bank, it will happen to others. Yoko and John in a Toronto bed, Mick Jagger with lips at full purse—all requiring captions, to explain to children who these people once were and what some reductive image of them connotes: "Bob Dylan: folk-rock performer of the 1960s whose contemptuous sneer and nasal whine signaled rejection of the older generation."

In Sinatra's case, such a destiny would mean that he had been reduced to the celebrity—emptied of all content—that once had been his. Humphrey Bogart is supposed to have said of him that for Sinatra heaven would be a place filled with "broads" and without reporters, not realizing that, where his career was concerned, it should be the other way round. The story is always told to Bogart's credit and against Sinatra's. In fact, however, Bogart could not have been more wrong. Such a heaven of reporters could have been appealing only to Sinatra the celebrity, not the singer. For the musical *career* to have been successful it needed to survive what the press loved: the women, the allegations of Mob connections, the punch-ups with reporters and random civilians who happened along at the wrong moment, the great wars with Australia, Mexico, Nevada, and New Jersey.

They were not what the career was about. They were merely the 1950s and 1960s as they passed through a sensibility possessed by a *daimon* with a life-span measured in more than decades, a *daimon* older than the Sinatra whose body it inhabited during our century.[9]

One sometimes hears that it is inappropriate to use highbrow words taken from foreign languages to discuss the phenomena of popular culture. By such a measure, *daimon* is a great offense. "It's Greek to me!" skeptics will say. During the celebration of his eightieth birthday, for example, offense was taken at the manner in which Sinatra's commentators occasionally compared him to classical artists who had bequeathed an "oeuvre." "Hey, that's French!" Sinatra shouts to Bing Crosby during their *High Society* duet. Other commentators who had blasphemously used Italian words like *rubato* or *appoggiatura* (Pleasants 181–197) to discuss his singing received stern scoldings (Ferguson). It would take us too far afield to engage this objection here, but one must at least notice what it betrays of *ressentiment* (hey, that's French!). Certainly, it recalls the various forms of haughtiness, earlier in this century, in the work of the Frankfurt School, of Martin Heidegger, or of F. R. Leavis toward "mass culture." Humanism this was not, for a true humanism does not turn its back on what appeals to *many*; and each humanistic generation knows that the last word on what has appealed *long* may not belong to it.

Essential to the celebrity, the *daimon* was essential also to what must, if the career was to have been a success, *survive* the celebrity. In short, the *daimon* was essential to the singer of songs. It has been said of T. S. Eliot that he possessed a supreme gift. He could take other men's lines and make them seem to have been his own. It takes just one example to chill the blood with the immensity of Eliot's achievement: "those are pearls that were his eyes." In the foothills of art, certainly not in its valleys, Sinatra did the same. The singer of songs identifies himself for us every time he commandeers Johnny Mercer's old lyric from "One for My Baby," opens himself to the *daimon*, and asserts that he's a kind of "poet."

How can such a poet survive a celebrity that must inevitably suffer when there are changes in the heart?

Changes in the heart. I mean, of course, that, when the moment of his era flickered, that of which Sinatra sang seemed, suddenly, to have become *passé*. Of what did he sing?

Of romantic love, as grand passion. Of course, too, there was always its sexual cutting edge, never more powerful than in the buoyancy of the unforgettably uptempo Riddle arrangements, with Sinatra turning on his heel and away from the thousand-year myth of the One Grand Passion toward those other great Western ideals, Don Juan or Lothario. So many changes he rang on these: performing on record "Here's That Rainy Day" or the nihilistic "Where Do You Go?"; from the 1980s, on television, doing the Kurt Weill/Maxwell Anderson "Lost in the Stars," so much in keeping with his pop-existentialist persona; from the mid-1960s, Sinatra, archetypally, in front of a huge orchestra, doing "Luck Be a Lady," virtually on fire, laughing, hurling imaginary dice, pointing exuberantly to the sky as the trumpets behind him, like his *daimon* within, soared.

The *daimon* made him that way, and it made him *celebrated*. If it came, unsummoned by the imagination, at a restaurant, he might explode at a friend or the poor waiter. Having a *daimon* does not excuse a man for such failings. It kept him awake until the wee small hours. It fueled his charisma, made him *Sinatra*, Chairman of the Board—and all that. But flesh is grass, and *that* is over now.

Indeed, for the inheritor generation it was over thirty years ago when, stripped of its enchantment, the One Grand Passion ran out. Love in the Western World now became as routinized as it had been, seventy years ago, for the typist, coming home at tea time, in Eliot's *The Waste Land*. Or it became the nightmare death-in-life of the middle classes, unforgettably represented by the lovers in Lawrence's *Women in Love* who drown in a pond when one tries to rescue the other. Something went out of the myth on which Sinatra had rung so many changes: "the moviemakers had *done* love, the songwriters had done it, what was left were jagged images, one after another, mocking, slicing in MTV like sharks' mouths in a feeding frenzy" (Updike 411–412). Perhaps its sources in adultery, diminished now into "the sexual revolution," had returned to the center of the myth and banished both the marriage ideal that had been superimposed on the old myth along with any notion of *One* Grand Passion. If we had attended more closely we might have seen it coming in Sinatra's very "celebrity" itself, for it had always been at odds with that of which he sang.

Yes, in the life, there was a Grand Passion for Ava Gardner, but there were also passions for other women, too numerous to count. One regularly hears of how close Sinatra has remained to his first wife, and this, too, curiously recalls certain features of the myth of love inherited from the Middle Ages, with its strange mixture of married love and adulterous grand passion. However, once all avenues were declared open to sexual self-expression, such myths could have little hold on the 1960s heart. Some of those avenues had been paved by Sinatra the Swinger, of whom we will certainly hear much more after his death (a dangerous time for anyone who hopes to survive celebrity). The great Hollywood entertainers had been doing this for two decades, projecting into the realm of popular culture new constructions of eroticism that had been elaborated in the novels of the Jazz Age and in the more reclusive lives of that era's social elites. By his flamboyant personal example, during the immensely stodgy 1950s, Sinatra projected those representations on the plane of popular culture, thereby teaching the rock stars who would follow him how to *be* Rock Stars. This was the Sinatra who did not have to *say* he was "bad" because we all *knew* he was! This was, finally, the Sinatra who lay hidden behind the boy-next-door persona constructed for him by the studios in the 1940s, an image under which the oversexed firebrand must have chaffed miserably. A widespread sentimentality insists that we should see the authentic Sinatra in the distant 1940s ephebe—a view that arises from the inheritor generation's dislike of 1950s masculinity and from the nostalgia of Sinatra's first audience—but that image began to unravel when the "troubles" started in the late forties. It would be abandoned, without a backward glance, once he again went straight to the top.

The quest for the authentic Sinatra is hopeless. As far as the singer was concerned, the boy next door matured into the man whose commerce with the *daimon* made him more poignantly wistful, more intensely passionate, and more deeply brokenhearted than the ephebe. What the ephebe never even gestured at was the kind of despair Sinatra would attain in the magnificent song of his old age, "A Long Night." When not summoned by Sinatra's voice, however, the *daimon* left us only with the prototype of the rock star, the swinger, beyond romantic love. Perhaps it is merely this Sinatra who arouses what I am told is the interest in him of Generation X "alternative groups" or of devotees of what is now called "lounge." If any Sinatra is to survive celebrity at all, this must *not* be the one. On the other hand, as I will try to indicate in a moment, that these newcomers to the dialectic of the generations are intrigued by Sinatra the man is not without relevance to the future of Sinatra the singer.

Yes, in the 1960s another generation came along, with different choices in clothing (no tuxedos) and preferring acid (at least for a while) to Jack Daniels. Eventually, it would not permit itself to be seen with a cigarette in hand. And it had undergone a change in the heart so profound that even to say "in the heart" may pose a problem for this generation, my generation, the one that, thirty years ago, broke ranks with its parents and that now takes its children to see not Sinatra but their own generational icon, Mick Jagger (older now than the Sinatra who recorded *September of My Years*: tick, tock, tick, tock). Most had no use for the celebration of Frank's eightieth birthday: old clothes, upon old sticks, to scare these middle-aged birds—who are growing older. (As I said earlier, if the work of demographics is slow, it is also *merciless*.) It may not be possible for him to touch their hearts as he did the hearts of their parents.[10] For this post-romance generation, Sinatra is *only* his celebrity, as Mick Jagger is not . . . yet.

For Sinatra to survive, then, his celebrity must be *forgotten*. That is, we must forget the forgetting of his music, and a new generation will have to rediscover it, as a preceding generation once lost it. But this assumes, of course, that the recent change in the heart is not permanent, and that love in the Western world, even as it was popularly celebrated, will not be forgotten. Any rediscovery among the inheritor generation of what had been repressed—Sinatra's music—must now await *either* the lifting of repression that may occur when inheritor generations age and rediscover virtues they had once dismissed *or* the appearance of new generations that have no interest in quarrels among aged and aging predecessors while being young enough to respond anew to the old stories that the "poet" Sinatra tells of love in the Western world.

This is to ask whether the "cunning of demography" will resurrect in an aging inheritor generation sympathy for the values "celebrated" in Sinatra's musical achievements. Can a generation's heart change *twice*? Or has it— in the span of a *mere* generation—altered irremediably?

It seems quite unlikely that the generation that turned its back on Sinatra will rediscover him. Over the next twenty-five years it is more likely that we will witness a replaying of ceremonies—the celebration of other birthdays, for other icons—that we have witnessed as Sinatra himself aged these past twenty-five years. Various fiftieths were recently noted (David Bowie's in January 1997, for example). In a few years, preparations will be underway for sixty-fifths. Along the way, we will notice that allowances seem to have been made for men who wear hairpieces. Then, with appropriate tears and nostalgia, seventy-fifths and eightieths will be celebrated (on television!). Last in line will be the obituary notices, and (to avoid a bad sixties joke) no one will remark that flesh is grass.

There are several reasons why this generation will not forgive Sinatra's celebrity and attend to the music they heard in their parents' living-rooms. My own suspicion is that this generation may never be able to take seriously the lyrics of the Grand Passion, even if many of them have known it. Remember, with Sinatra, those lyrics are in the spotlight and cannot be ignored. Nor can Sinatra, like Billie Holiday, be granted a general amnesty, on racial grounds, for having taken them so seriously. Schooled in toughmindedness, in college, by their New Critic teachers and by the modernist writers they made them misread, many opinion-makers of the sixties generation learned to view all expressions of unironized feeling, especially what they considered to be *middle-class* feeling, as being at risk of sentimentality. They will view their continued distaste for Sinatra as evidence of their long pursuit of truth—even as their elders, or as their generational enemies within, will view it as obstinate refusal of the truth.

However, the Grand Passion is very old, and this is merely one generation. People do have changes of heart, and what struck them as sentimental when they were twenty-five may touch their fifty-something hearts. So, for the sake of argument, assume that the sexual revolution and terminally ironic sensibilities don't survive baby-boom menopause. There remains another reason to doubt that this will materially help Frank Sinatra: *interest*. As when we say, "I have an *interest* in this issue." Interest need not represent a financial investment, after all. If I have invested twenty years in a certain view of things, committed myself, my personal being, to some position, I virtually *am* that position. My interest in matters of the spirit may be even more intense than my interest in matters of the material. To back away from that position—even if, after midnight, I suspect I may have been wrong—could open in my soul a deep narcissistic wound. Only the higher types of any generation can pull back from such lifetime investments of interest. The interest in this case would not be so much a certain view, pro or con, of a popular singer of the mid-century. Rather, it would be the various commitments—in social, political, erotic, and religious (or irreligious) attitudes—that comprise what I am calling a "change in the heart." A rejection of Sinatra and his hyper-individual, hyper-romantic music would be merely one of many rejections.

The likeliest route for his recovery is that other one. The inheritors of the inheritor generation never knew Sinatra's celebrity as something they had to reject in order to breathe. They knew it only insofar as it *had been rejected*. So astonishing was the musical career that sustained that celebrity that it is arguable that no other popular singer is so widely represented in major record outlets today as Frank Sinatra. Sheer availability of "product" is no minor asset. What is open to question is whether this newest generation can ignore parental rivalries and find its way to this music, hidden in the nether reaches of most retail outlets, under the unspeakably wrong rubric, "Easy Listening." After all, for anyone who looks, there is ample evidence of Sinatra's achievement: those records on the shelves, the critical appreciations, and the tributes by his musical peers. It should be no more difficult to rediscover a great popular singer than to rediscover any great novelist or poet who has suffered neglect at the hands of an inheritor generation. Pope, Dickens, Browning—they *all* came back, even when the attitudes that had made them suffer had become the norm, even when their eras were long since over.[11] It is not the children who matter but the grandchildren. If Sinatra is to have one more comeback, taking him this time *beyond* celebrity, we will know it by the puzzled looks on the faces of this future generation as they try to figure out what their elders were arguing about—before abandoning the effort and turning on the next "Sinatra song."

NOTES

1. By the 1970s Sinatra's film career was virtually over, and compared to the pace of release of the 1950s and 1960s, he would release very few albums from this point on.

2. In writing of Sinatra's decline in the early 1950s, William Ruhlmann shrewdly notes that, like Orson Welles, it was impossible to cast Sinatra in a minor role: "His art seems to require by its nature a mass audience. And, too, for a popular artist, a large following helps to guarantee that he will have an impact on the contemporary direction of his art. Like a politician who, however good, can only get so much done on a local level, an artist such as Sinatra performs best at a pinnacle of popularity, when he is reaching the largest number of people" (10–11).

3. By the time he had learned what to record—for example, George Harrison's

"Something" and Billy Joel's "Just the Way You Are"—it was too late. Neverthe-less, for those who know both the original performances and Sinatra's (from *Trilogy*), the latter have become "Sinatra songs."

4. It helped not at all that in the late 1960s millions of young people, lying outside the pale of "advanced consciousness," might have sympathized with his new politics. The problem was that they didn't sympathize with his *music*. For that to have happened he would have needed to show them that his style was not restricted to the dissemination of the best popular music of their *parents'* era.

5. See James's supercilious review of a recently discovered 1965 tape of a "Rat Pack" performance. Whatever her own birthdate, she views it entirely from the perspective of the inheritor generation. She also has no sense of the Rat Pack's history and seems to think that in 1965 it was still in its glory days. By that point, it had become a "nostalgia act" even to its members. It depended for its vitality on what Gore Vidal has called "the great national nap" of the 1950s—at times Frank and "the Clan" seemed the only people awake after 10:00 P.M. The 1950s only ended in the *mid*-1960s—thus the lack of success at the time of its release of *The Manchurian Candidate* (1962). By 1965, with the whole country wide awake and staring, the Rat Pack was no longer needed.

6. To this mindless dismissal of a performing art, the response is, of course, that neither did Maria Callas "write her own songs." Bob Dylan is the only popular entertainer since World War II whose voice approached Sinatra's in authority (which is not to say "in skill"). One can recognize the immense power that the Dylan "whine" of the 1960s had for his generation and be—as I am—an unyielding admirer of Dylan, without conceding that he is either in Sinatra's company as a *singer* or in Dylan Thomas's company as a poet. His vocal abilities make one feel sad for Hoagy Carmichael, born too early to profit from the latitude another gen-eration would grant amateur singers.

7. Of course, it was never so "consensual" as the nostalgic maintain. Never-theless, it is arguable that there was more consensus among Americans of that generation, who had endured economic depression and war together, than among Americans born in the 1940s. Sinatra's turn to the right is less surprising when seen by reference to the shift rightward of such intellectuals of his generation as Saul Bellow, Norman Podhoretz, and others. To set him in that context requires no suggestion that he was led by base motives that his cultural detractors never feel. That he—like some neo-conservative intellectuals—profited by his new politics is undeniable, but this tells us nothing about his—or their—motives.

8. For a discussion of Sinatra as jazz singer see Friedwald. This is an old source of argument among both Sinatra fans and jazz academicians, and it owes much to the extraordinary respect Sinatra's art obtained from jazz musicians of his era.

9. This is not to say that there was no connection between the often demonic man, Sinatra, and the singer. It is difficult to imagine how this particular singer could be divorced from his song. He was quite correct to call a television special in the 1960s *A Man and His Music*. This complex issue of the relationship between Sinatra as "subject," as we say now, and his art can only be touched upon here.

10. For a smirking account of calcified resistance to Sinatra, see Jacobson.

11. An analogy might be the fate in France of another "icon" whose star rose in the 1940s. The intellectual celebrity of Jean-Paul Sartre was every bit as hege-

monic as Sinatra's pop cultural celebrity. Like Sinatra's, Sartre's intellectual status would one day be compromised by his political choices and, once a new intellectual generation appeared on the scene, by the lifting from his shoulders of the mantle of "cool." To vary Elizabeth Taylor's remark on Richard Burton's relation to Shakespeare, we could call Sartre "the Sinatra of philosophy." The dominant figure of French intellectual life for three decades, he is known to the French Generation X only across an older generation's dismissal of him.

WORKS CITED

Ferguson, Andrew. "Sinatra at 80: Ring-a-Ding-Don't." *The Weekly Standard*, 11 December 1995: 32–36.

Friedwald, Will. "Sinatra: The Jazz Singer." *Down Beat*, March 1996: 16–21.

Jacobson, Mark. "Frank Talk." *Esquire*, February 1996: 31.

James, Caryn. "Time Capsule of the Pre-Legend Rat Pack." *New York Times*, 10 April 1997, national ed.: B6.

Pleasants, Henry. *The Great American Popular Singers*. New York: Simon and Schuster, 1974.

Ruhlmann, William. "Frank Sinatra." *Goldmine*, 17:9 (1991): 10–39, 116.

Updike, John. *In the Beauty of the Lilies*. New York: Alfred A. Knopf, 1996.

The Swinger and the Loser: Sinatra, Masculinity, and Fifties Culture

ROGER GILBERT

Even before his death, Frank Sinatra was cool again. His name, face, and voice are everywhere these days, from Don DeLillo novels to *New Yorker* covers to Nissan commercials. Given the restless cycles of obsolescence and revival in our fin de siècle culture, we should probably not be surprised by the current surge of interest in the Rat Pack and its accessories: the dry martini, the fedora, big band jazz, the language of "cats" and "broads." Now that most of its original members have passed from the scene, it may seem safe to recall and celebrate the high spirits they once embodied, purged of the seamier matters that went along with those spirits—alcoholism, misogyny, and organized crime, to name a few. And perhaps it helps that we no longer have to witness the aging bodies of those aggressively youthful men. In the long run, however, the current vogue for Rat Packery may do more harm than good to our appreciation of Sinatra's legacy. Lumped together with genial entertainers like Dean Martin, Sammy Davis, Jr., and Joey Bishop, Sinatra can easily seem like just one of the guys, offering little more than Vegas-style hipness and machismo to a generation starved for images of self-assurance. But for those of us who regard Sinatra as an artist, perhaps the greatest interpreter of song in this century, the Rat Pack is merely a colorful distraction. Dean Martin is no more Sinatra's peer than John Fletcher was Shakespeare's or Salieri, Mozart's. Full recognition of the nature of Sinatra's art requires that he be placed in a rather different sort of company.

In that spirit I'd like to consider the emergence of Sinatra the iconic "swinger" during the 1950s in the light of broader cultural tendencies of the period, manifested in such diverse areas as Method acting, Beat writing, Confessional poetry, Action painting, and Hard Bop jazz. All these aesthetics are explicitly fueled by anxiety—anxiety contained, withheld, struggled against, yet repeatedly manifested in volatile negotiations between exterior and interior, foreign and domestic, public and private space. Sinatra might seem an unlikely figure to approach in these weighty terms, yet I want to claim that his best work in the fifties (in the view of many, the best work of his career) is centrally concerned with the anxieties regarding authority, masculinity, and control played out in other aspects of both the high and popular culture of the decade.

Admittedly it takes a certain amount of estrangement to view the fifties as a culturally significant period, given the caricatures of it that flood our own pop culture with its endless capacity for "retro" irony. Our received image of the decade as a bastion of stodgy bourgeois kitsch and smug suburban morality is based on the most banal of its artifacts—deMille epics, Mantovani records, "I Like Ike" buttons, and so on. But it's worth asking what kinds of cultural products best represent a period, its generic mediocrities or its works of genius. (The distinction applies even to popular media like TV comedy: for every *Father Knows Best* and *Ozzie and Harriet*, insipid sitcoms enshrining paternal wisdom, there was a Sid Caesar, whose brilliant work tapped the maelstrom of male angst with the same intensity Brando brought to film acting.) When comparing the best works of the decade with those immediately abutting it, one is most struck by an absence of clear lines of moral authority. Neither the stark global antinomies of World War II and the patriotic fervor it fostered, nor the equally stark internal divisions produced by the sixties counterculture obtain; the best artists in the fifties seem driven not by utopian or didactic impulses, but by a need to dramatize ambivalences and anxieties that find no ready catharsis in the public sphere. Despite its domination of the decade's political rhetoric, the Cold War and the arms race it spawned remained too distant and theoretical to provide a solid focus for the culture's unease, simply reinforcing a vague sense that the primary threats to America's well-being couldn't be localized, that they lay both outside and inside at once.

In a recent essay on Method acting and fifties culture, Leo Braudy notes that much drama of the period "focused on the character vulnerable to contradiction and irresolution rather than either the stock types of earlier social realism, or the archetypal figures of romance or agitprop" (196). Braudy goes on to claim that fifties artists in many genres created "a layered self" that pitted conventionality against rebellion, public action against private feeling. Citing Tennessee Williams, Jack Kerouac, and Robert Lowell as examples, Braudy argues that "It was the interplay, the tension between these seeming opposites, that energized their works and gave them a permeability and an inconclusiveness that characterized Method acting as well" (197). Braudy doesn't mention Sinatra, but as I hope to show, many of his terms can also be applied to the singer's work in the fifties—in particular, permeability, inconclusiveness, and the notion of a layered self.

Masculinity became a site particularly fraught with tension during the fifties (arguably more so than in the sixties, when the long hair and unisex fashions of the youth culture masked some fairly traditional notions of gender). The period's most representative male artists—Sinatra, Brando, Lowell, Hank Williams, Jackson Pollock—and its most enduring artifacts—*Kind of Blue, Vertigo, Catcher in the Rye*—all manifest a nearly pathological melancholia, often disguised by exaggerated sexual drive and willed nonchalance, that points to a genuine crisis of male identity. Admittedly, male identity has never been the most stable of cultural constructs, but seldom have uncertainties about the value of aggression and the cost of vulnerability shown themselves so nakedly in the works of a single period. My central claim is that Sinatra became the classic embodiment of fifties culture not because he represented its idealized male image—Rock Hudson was there for that—but because as a great artist he fully articulated its contradictions, anxieties, and ambivalences.

Before taking a closer look at Sinatra's image and, most importantly, his music in the fifties, let me wax a bit anecdotal and suggest that his presence in the exalted company I've named isn't quite as incongruous as it sounds. Sinatra worked with Brando (or as he called him, "Mumbles") in the film version of *Guys and Dolls*, but their rivalry had begun several years earlier when Sinatra was passed over for the role of Terry Malloy in *On the Waterfront* and continued up through the seventies, when he lobbied Francis Ford Coppola for the part of Don Corleone. While eschewing the rigors of the Method, Sinatra was at times a serious and ambitious actor; more to the point, his singing employed devices such as slurring and sudden shifts of dynamics that resemble Brando's technique as an actor. Miles Davis and Sinatra openly admired each other's musicianship, and Davis often credited Sinatra with being a key influence on his own phrasing. (Sinatra tried to recruit Miles to play with him, but Davis wasn't about to back up any vocalist.) Sinatra also seems to have studied the Abstract Expressionists, to judge from his own paintings, which were published in book form a few years ago and include, along with the obligatory clowns, some surprisingly competent imitations of Kline, Gottlieb, and Rothko. Kerouac's *The Dharma Bums*, ostensibly a novel about spiritual awakening in Marin County and the Sierras, is littered with references to Sinatra, who's treated as a kind of Beat muse. As for Robert Lowell, there's no evidence that the two met or expressed any interest in one another, but some of the parallels between their art, careers, and private lives are quite striking. A poem like Lowell's "The Drinker," from his 1964 volume *For the Union Dead*, could easily fit on one of Sinatra's darker albums, like *Only the Lonely* or *No One Cares*. (If only Sinatra had hooked up with Lowell instead of Rod McKuen, with whom he made a maudlin album in the late sixties.) In short, despite appearances, Sinatra inhabited the same world as these artists and in at least some cases was aware of and responsive to their work.

To place Sinatra in the context of fifties art might seem perverse, since he first attained superstar status in the early forties as a young singer with the Tommy Dorsey band. But while Sinatra's forties work with Dorsey and later with the arranger Axel Stordahl is often very appealing, it shows little of the depth, darkness, and complexity he achieved in his fifties recordings. Decades may well be arbitrary markers, but in Sinatra's case the transition from the forties to the fifties was both harrowing and transformative. By the end of the forties his popularity was in freefall, his private life a shambles, and his voice a wreck. Sinatra's comeback in the early fifties, after being considered "washed up" by the press and Hollywood, is the stuff of show biz legend, and I won't rehearse the familiar facts in any detail (divorces Nancy, marries Ava; record sales decline; fired by MGM; voice fails, throat hemorrhages; divorces Ava; attempts suicide; plays Maggio in *From Here to Eternity*, wins Oscar; moves from Columbia to Capitol Records; teams up with Nelson Riddle, etc.). What remains most remarkable about this episode in Sinatra's career is the completeness with which he reinvented himself in the fifties. Like many great American artists, Sinatra had a real genius for self-revision; much of his fascination as a cultural icon lies in the restless way he kept redefining himself for new audiences and new zeitgeists. Surely the most spectacular transformation came in the fifties, when the fragile, wispy, boyish crooner who caused countless bobby-soxers to dampen the seats of the Paramount Theater gave way to the tough, worldly, swinging lover with hat cocked, cigarette dangling, and coat thrown over his shoulder.

It would be a mistake to imagine that this revision involved a simple act of substitution, with the fifties swinger cancelling out and replacing the forties crooner. The complexity and richness of Sinatra's work in the fifties is in part a function of the way that earlier image persists within the later image and serves as a crucial point of reference for it. Indeed one of the most striking things about the evolution of Sinatra's image over time is the way it built up in layers like a palimpsest, each new phase added onto rather than simply supplanting the one before. (Even his physical appearance reinforces this impression; over the years his face has gradually accrued layers of flesh that tease us with the thought of the boy singer's sharp cheekbones still lurking somewhere underneath.) Sinatra's appeal in the forties lay not only in the sweetness of his voice but the vulnerability it conveyed. With his notoriously thin frame, his floppy bowtie, and drooping curls, he seemed exposed and helpless in the face of powerful feelings—his own and those of his voracious fans. His songs of the period—"Time After Time," "I Fall in Love Too Easily," "If You Are But a Dream"—express adolescent longing, dreams of romantic love untempered by experience. Yet if the swinger of the fifties seemed infinitely more jaded and knowing, invoking his inamorata not as "darling" but as "baby" and singing of love not as a romantic dream but as "The Tender Trap," Sinatra found subtle ways to keep the essential vulnerability of his younger persona in view.

We can perhaps better appreciate the complexity of Sinatra's image in the fifties by setting him alongside flamboyant female stars of the period like Bette Davis, Judy Garland, and Maria Callas. For divas like these, femininity is explicitly an act or performance, a kind of theater whose artifice they both celebrate and ironize; hence the devoted gay following such female stars often enjoy. I would argue that Sinatra's masculine bravado is as much a theatrical projection as the exaggerated vulnerability of a star like Garland, and that he's just as interested in showing his audience what it conceals. (Of course, by this analogy Sinatra should have an avid lesbian following, which as far as I know he doesn't—yet.) In short Sinatra doesn't simply embody certain clichés of maleness, he parodies them, and he does so precisely in order to allow a contrasting sense of the self's interior spaces to emerge. His most memorable film roles of the fifties reveal this tension quite clearly. Characters like Maggio in *From Here to Eternity* and Frankie Machine in *The Man with the Golden Arm*, who start out as cocky, street-smart toughs, are eventually emasculated and made to undergo unspeakable torments. These roles display the startling capacity for showing pain that also lies at the heart of Sinatra's singing, despite his macho, finger-snapping swagger. Audiences in the fifties may have better appreciated than we can the extraordinary degree to which he allowed weakness, fear, and self-pity to inform his work. As much as Brando, Sinatra was willing to strip away the protective covering of poise and charm that had always characterized the star in order to expose the wounded ego beneath. Even that ever-present cocked hat, which seemed to epitomize his devil-may-care nonchalance, really served as an oblique sign of insecurity—surely everyone knew that its main purpose was to hide the singer's encroaching baldness.

It's important to recognize that Sinatra was not simply better than other popular singers of the fifties; he was fundamentally different from them, in ways that sometimes hurt his career. His main rivals, Bing Crosby, Perry Como, Dean Martin, and Nat Cole, all projected an easy, relaxed warmth that made them ideally suited to the casual intimacy of radio and television. Sinatra's first attempt at hosting a TV variety show flopped badly, and, while he eventually made some successful specials, the medium never took to him as it did to Martin and Como. What he lacked was the kind of stable, identifiable stage personality that allows an audience to feel at ease in one's presence. Sinatra's persona was too edgy, splintered, and ambiguous to translate well to the small screen. Even in film, where he was quite prolific, he never developed a true star image. With a few exceptions his movie performances were throwaways that lacked the scale and presence achieved by the great Hollywood stars. His true medium, of course, was the phonograph record, especially the LP album, a form he virtually created in the fifties. The LP proved ideal for Sinatra because, while he generally tried to give each of his albums a distinct mood, the inherent disjunctiveness of the form allowed him to explore a range of emotional tones, unfettered by the need to present a consistent persona; song followed song without the artificial glue of plot or patter. Treating each song as a discrete dramatic text, Sinatra gave himself to it with the same intensity and commitment a great actor brings to a role.

The slippery, metamorphic quality of Sinatra's performing self can be quickly gauged by glancing at the covers of his albums from the fifties and early sixties, all of which feature paintings or photographs of the singer. It's hard not to be struck by how wildly these cover portraits differ, so much so that an uninformed viewer might have trouble recognizing them as images of a single person. (Interestingly on some covers Sinatra looks more like other well-known movie stars than himself; on *All the Way*, for example, he resembles Henry Fonda, and on *Point of No Return* he's a dead ringer for Bogart.) The more upbeat albums feature images of a be-hatted and grinning Sinatra, often beckoning directly to the viewer, full of swagger and confidence, while the slower, more melancholy albums tend to show him with eyes closed or cast down, looking shrunken and oblivious to the presence of others. These contradictory poses suggest how much his work of the period pivots on a dialectic of aggressively projected masculin-ity and nearly autistic vulnerability. It's not clear whether Sinatra suffered from what we now call bipolar illness (though he once described himself as a "fifteen-carat manic-depressive"), but whatever his clinical status his art clearly feeds on a polarization of moods and affects so extreme that it tears the self into irreconcilable images.

It's in their musical content that these albums bring substance and inten-sity to the contrasting poses limned by their covers. When considering Si-natra's studio recordings of the fifties, we must distinguish between the contributions of three brilliant arrangers: Nelson Riddle, Billy May, and Gordon Jenkins. Each man orchestrated and conducted several albums with Sinatra at Capitol Records, and their very different approaches provide another clear index to the disjunctive nature of Sinatra's singing persona. Billy May tended to write driving, brassy big-band arrangements, usually without strings, full of humor and extroverted energy. He's best known for the trilogy *Come Fly with Me*, *Come Dance with Me*, and *Come Swing with Me*, whose very titles suggest an open, gregarious stance toward their audience. Gordon Jenkins wrote lush, brooding string arrangements for two crucial ballad albums of the fifties, *Where Are You?* and *No One*

Cares, records that plumb the depths of introversion and erotic suffering. Sinatra once said that Jenkins's arrangements made him feel he was "back in the womb," and, while the phrase suggests warmth and protection, it also implies a narcissistic withdrawal from a world of painful stimuli. (With their Wagnerian echoes, Jenkins's arrangements show a kinship with Bernard Herrmann's score for Hitchcock's *Vertigo*, arguably the greatest film of the fifties and a work that explores much the same region of obsessive eros and loss mapped by Sinatra's ballad albums.)

If May and Jenkins gave orchestral form to Sinatra's outer and inner personae, the swinger and the loser, Nelson Riddle developed a style that could bridge the two, allowing the singer to move between them convincingly in the course of an album and even within individual songs. Sinatra did his finest work with Riddle precisely because Riddle's arrangements helped him to articulate the relationship between inside and outside so fully. Where May worked only on swing albums and Jenkins on ballad albums, Riddle did both, including the two masterpieces of Sinatra's Capitol period, *Songs for Swingin' Lovers* and *Only the Lonely*. More to the point, Riddle learned to integrate the two modes and to play them against one another on a very fine level. An extremely versatile orchestrator with a special admiration for Ravel, Stravinsky, and Ellington, Riddle used both brass and strings to weave a complex antiphonal texture that blended elements of jazz and classical styles. Under Sinatra's guidance he created what's come to be called the "swing ballad" idiom, fusing operatic expressiveness and rhythmic drive. With its inner tensions and clashing colors, this style proved the perfect vehicle for Sinatra's exploration of the more slippery areas of his vocal self.

More crucial even than arrangements, of course, were the songs themselves in setting the expressive parameters for Sinatra's work in the fifties. To speak of an interpretive performer like Sinatra as a creative artist, an author or *auteur*, may seem problematic, especially in the era of the singer-songwriter. We're accustomed to thinking of Dylan, Springsteen, or even Madonna in such terms, but, while Sinatra did collaborate on a handful of lyrics, he almost always relied on the words and music of others. Yet I want to suggest that Sinatra's repertoire of the fifties can itself be thought of as a kind of meta-text, quite distinct in its characteristic imagery and thematics from the repertoires of other popular singers (Crosby, Martin, Cole, etc.). Sinatra performed and recorded literally hundreds of songs in this period, but a much smaller number of these came to assume special prominence in his repertoire, either because he recorded them several times or performed them regularly on stage and television. Just as certain songs became indelibly associated with Billie Holiday, to the point where they seemed almost as much her creation as those of their composers and lyricists, so Sinatra was able to transform particular songs he recorded into texts of his own making. Purists have often criticized him over the years for changing lyrics, interpolating favorite words and catchphrases, freely reworking melodies, and in general Sinatrafying the songs he sings, but his "authorship" runs considerably deeper as well.

When we look closely at Sinatra's core repertoire of the fifties, certain themes emerge with obsessive frequency. Among these are the fragility of elation: songs like "I've Got the World on a String," "Wrap Your Troubles in Dreams," and "Get Happy" all express high spirits while glancing nervously over their shoulders. Another recurring theme is the violence of love: in "All of Me" the singer methodically dismembers himself, inviting the lover to take his arms and lips, while in "I Get a Kick Out of You" he associates the sight of his beloved with a sharp blow to the posterior. A striking number of Sinatra's songs of this period are based on distinctions between age and youth: "Last Night When We Were Young," "You Make Me Feel So Young," "Young at Heart," "When the World Was Young." In all these lyrics, age is a function of psychology more than chronology, and we're reminded again of Sinatra's existential shiftiness, his propensity for slipping from one state of being to another. Entering his forties in the mid-1950s, he no longer embodied callow youth but hadn't yet earned the authority of age, and so his relation to those categories seemed to waver with his self-image from song to song.

It's also worth noting that many of the songs Sinatra recorded in the fifties were originally written for female singers; examples include "The Gal That Got Away," first sung by Judy Garland in *A Star Is Born*, and "Someone to Watch Over Me." This penchant for songs that treat desire, love, and loss from an androgynous perspective is in keeping with the sharp ambivalence regarding male sexuality that Sinatra's work in the fifties displays. At the heart of his repertoire in this period is a group of songs that depict sexual desire as an invasive force, infiltrating body and mind and subjecting both to an insidious power often linked with rhythmic repetition. "Night and Day," "Day In, Day Out," "Old Devil Moon," "The Song Is You," "That Old Black Magic," and "Witchcraft" all ring variations on this motif, but the masterpiece of the group is undoubtedly Cole Porter's "I've Got You Under My Skin," widely considered to be Sinatra's single greatest recording.

As arranged by Nelson Riddle, with pulsing ostinato figures in the horns, ascending cushions of strings, and a wild, polyrhythmic instrumental bridge, the song paints a brilliant portrait of romantic obsession, of a self permeated or invaded by otherness. It would probably be too glib to suggest that the record is a covert anthem for McCarthyism, yet the anxious sense of infiltration it projects is surely consonant with the paranoid vision of fifties films like *Invasion of the Body Snatchers*. Originally written by Porter as a frothy, elegant rhumba, Sinatra's performance brings an emotional chiaroscuro to the song that mingles ecstasy with panic; by the time he reaches the climactic chorus, after a *Bolero*-like crescendo in the brass, the pitched battle of internal and external forces has grown nearly demonic.

As usual, Sinatra takes some liberties with the original lyric, interpolating phrases that bring a more vernacular emphasis to the song's key moments. He treats Porter's melody in the same spirit, incorporating dissonant or "blue" notes, shifting phrases from their rhythmic moorings, and adding new melodic ideas that support the song's dramatic movement, like a descending scale on "Makes me stop just before I begin." Though seldom regarded as a jazz singer in the strict sense, Sinatra took a distinctly improvisational approach to his recordings, which are much closer to live performances than the elaborately canned, slickly produced, multi-tracked products of contemporary pop music. The sense of spontaneous invention and discovery that energizes Sinatra's finest records is another quality that allies his work with aspects of Method acting, Beat writing, and Action painting, all of which emphasize the artist's freedom to create and revise on the fly.

With its trope of a divided, permeable self and its violent drama of eros versus lucidity, "I've Got You Under My Skin" is a major expression of the embattled consciousness of fifties America. The record's amazing power stems above all from Sinatra's ability to articulate contrasting registers of desire and fear, outward bravado and inner doubt, through subtle variations in vocal color and phrasing (a dialogic approach crudely parodied by the 1994 duet version with U2's Bono, whose heavy breathing and moaning in the role of Sinatra's inner voice turns the erotic turmoil of the original to kitsch). As the closing diminuendo and final unresolved ninth chord suggest, the conflicts staged in the record subside without achieving any clear resolution. The track exemplifies the inconclusiveness Leo Braudy attributes to fifties art in general, with its preference for dramatic over didactic or ideological energies.

Before considering Sinatra's vocal technique more closely, it may be worth touching on a strictly visual aspect of his performance style that nonetheless has important implications for the music. From the very beginning of his career Sinatra made a habit of closing his eyes as he sang, and, while this mannerism was certainly not unprecedented, it was unusual enough to be incorporated in a number of early caricatures of the singer. By now it's become a cliché of popular singing, but initially I suspect that closing one's eyes onstage was a daring thing for any performer to do. The gesture seems to deny the presence of others, to establish a space so private that it risks alienating one's audience. In practice, of course, it had the opposite effect, contributing to the powerful illusion of intimacy that surely lay at the heart of Sinatra's appeal in his early years. (One of Sinatra's most intimate albums, appropriately titled *Close to You*, bears a photograph of the singer performing with eyes shut.) By the fifties he had learned to use this device for dramatic effect with great skill, and indeed it became one of his principal means for articulating the relation between his outward and inward personae. At moments of extroversion he tended to hold his famously magnetic blue eyes wide open, seizing the audience in his gaze; moments later as his confidence crumbled the eyes would close, drawing a curtain over the self that left it more exposed than before. In this regard, too, we can contrast Sinatra with singers like Crosby and Martin, not to mention Martin's secret disciple Elvis, who tended to sing with their eyelids drooping drowsily. If their half-closed eyes seem to blur the boundary between inner and outer selves, creating a relaxed, seductive space at once intimate and accessible, Sinatra's restlessly opening and closing eyes suggest that for him there is no safe intermediate zone, only anxious shuttling between public and private space, aggressive encounter and protective withdrawal.

Inveterate Sinatraphiles may come to feel they can actually hear the singer's eyes closing on his records, but, even in the absence of such real or imagined visual cues, Sinatra manages to convey transitions in persona purely through the power of his voice. Here, indeed, I think we approach the heart of his greatness as a musical actor or dramatic singer. Among the popular singers of the past half-century Sinatra did not possess the strongest instrument, the largest range, or even the truest pitch. What he did have was a palette of vocal colors that surpassed any other singer's in richness and variety, along with the ability to use all of them for maximum interpretive effect. Sinatra knew how to vary the weight and timbre of his voice in much the way a great draftsman modifies the thickness and texture of a line. While he achieves many subtle modulations, his singing voice has two primary sounds or colors that correspond quite closely to his two basic personae. Starting in the fifties Sinatra developed a brassy, belting, hard-edged tone that seemed to reach out aggressively to the audience; this was the voice of the swinger, the cocky, confident man-of-the-world. But alongside this bright tone could be heard a softer, more muted, slightly husky sound that suggested intimate self-communion. The contrast of tones is a bit like the difference between Miles Davis playing open and muted horn, but where Davis could only switch from one sound to another between numbers, or at most once or twice in the course of a tune, Sinatra learned to change his tone at will, often in the middle of a phrase. Again it's illuminating to compare Sinatra's highly articulated vocal sound with that of singers like Bing Crosby and Perry Como, whose creamy homogeneity reflects a much more stable sense of self and cultural value. Like everything else about him, Sinatra's voice is layered, mutable, possessed of an outside and an inside, and a key part of his artistry lies in the way he constantly adjusts its timbre to bring out the finest nuances of a lyric.

No recording Sinatra made in the fifties illustrates his mastery of vocal color better than the closing track from *Only the Lonely*, Harold Arlen and Johnny Mercer's "One for My Baby." If "I've Got You Under My Skin" is the greatest of his upbeat, "swing" tracks, "One for My Baby" is the undisputed masterpiece among the slower ballads, the ultimate instance of the genre Sinatra called the "saloon song." The album version features the moody piano of Sinatra's longtime accompanist Bill Miller, with strings and winds providing discrete patches of color. But an even starker version done in rehearsal with only Miller's piano and included on the recent three-disc compilation *The Capitol Years* (C2-94777) allows Sinatra's vocal technique to stand out more clearly. Mercer's wonderful lyric is so idiomatic that it needs none of the vernacular embellishment Sinatra brought to Cole Porter, while Arlen's bluesy setting is little more than a sustained vamp that allows the singer to come as close to the natural rhythms and pitches of speech as possible without losing the melody's essential line. With its total command of dynamics, pace, and phrasing, Sinatra's performance of this song is an intricate vocal dance of defensive bluster and wounded retreat. A lone bartender makes the ideal auditor for Sinatra because his presence is so vestigial to begin with, allowing the singer to move between forced chumminess and lonely self-absorption without breaking the song's narrative frame.

The continual shifting of tone and persona that structures the performance is audible even within individual phrases. In the piano-only version, an especially fine example occurs at the end of the second "A" section, with the repetition of the phrase "And one more for the road." Rather than following Arlen's original melody, which has an airiness that derives from its use of upper chord tones, Sinatra sings a much starker line: a repeated low B on the first five words rising to E on the last, or harmonically the roots of the dominant and tonic chords, about as basic and unadorned a sequence as possible. This reduction of the song to its bare bones beautifully evokes the collapse of the speaker's melodic impulses as he wearily contemplates the road ahead. But even more powerful is the way Sinatra divides the phrase into two distinct halves: the words "and one more" are almost barked or snarled, with a slight downward slur at the end, then after a long caesura, the rest of the line comes out in a low, breathy voice that seems on the verge of cracking. (The phrasing on the version with strings is similar, but the contrast in vocal color is much less pronounced.) In the space of a single bar—both kinds—Sinatra transforms himself from tough guy to broken man. The use of pause, hesitation, delay, to create a kind of musical enjambment is part of the secret here. If Sinatra's first impulse as a young singer was to master breath control so that he could produce long, continuous, legato lines free from artificial pauses, his second impulse was to learn where to put the pauses so that they could speak as forcefully as the words. But it's the way the very grain of his voice reveals precisely how and where his contradictory selves are joined, shows us the seam or scar that connects and divides swinger and loser, that makes this record such a monumental work of expressive art.

The track also affords us another clear example of the inconclusiveness Braudy claims for fifties culture in general. By refusing to pronounce the song's final word, Sinatra gives the record a hauntingly elliptical ending without resorting to the purely technological expedient of a fadeout. We might surmise that the speaker of "One for My Baby" is a man so wounded by endings that he can't bring himself to put a period to his own sentence. Interestingly in the version of the song he recorded for the 1994 *Duets* album—which while raspy and marred by Kenny G's saccharine soprano sax accompaniment showed that Sinatra could still put more nuance into a lyric than any singer alive—he finally pronounces that last "road," for the first time in any performance of the song by him I've heard. The change can be taken as evidence that Sinatra had at last come to terms with the necessity of endings. A year later he had retired from performing for good.

For all their differences of mood and style, "I've Got You Under My Skin" and "One for My Baby," along with many other superb tracks from the fifties, powerfully dramatize the edginess and uncertainty, the anxiety over boundaries between self and other, inside and outside, masculine and feminine, and the unsettled, inconclusive wavering of image and energy that characterize fifties culture at large. Sinatra's finest work of the period goes far beyond the bland optimism we've come to associate with the Eisenhower years. In its dark-edged ambivalence and self-division it shows him to be an artist who belongs in the company of Marlon Brando, Jackson Pollock, Robert Lowell, and Miles Davis as a delver into the decade's collective male psyche.

WORK CITED

Braudy, Leo. " 'No Body's Perfect': Method Acting and 50s Culture," *Michigan Quarterly Review*, 35 (Winter 1996): 191–215.

Bobby Sox and Blue Suede Shoes: Frank Sinatra and Elvis Presley as Teen Idols

JAMES F. SMITH

I celebrate myself, and sing myself,
And what I assume you shall assume,
For every atom belonging to me as good belongs to you.
                                        —Walt Whitman, "Song of Myself"

Writing in 1944, scarcely two years after Frank Sinatra's emergence as a solo performer, Bruce Bliven attempts to place the singer's unprecedented adulation by young fans into perspective. While he notes that American affluence, even during wartime, was the envy of the world, he nevertheless concludes that the teenagers of the era were not satisfied: "we have left them with a hunger still unfulfilled: a hunger for heroes, for ideal things that do not appear, or at least not in adequate quantities, in a civilization that is so busy making things and selling things as ours" (p. 593). Bliven's observation that passion is more important than prosperity, at least for the young, holds true a decade later when the comfortable formulas of the popular music world were again turned upside down by the coming of Elvis Presley and rock and roll. It can be argued that the popular success of performers is a commercial commodity to be made and sold after all, but the importance of Frank Sinatra and Elvis Presley transcends the millions of dollars they earned. In each case, a single artist came to be symbolic for the youth of an era, an idol representing not only contemporary taste but, perhaps, a generation's desire for recognition in the present and their collective hopes for achieving the American dream in the future. Each performer carried his original cohort of fans and added new acolytes as his music moved through time and evolved stylistically. Both transcended the realm of recording artist through live performance and through motion pictures. Coming from backgrounds that were simultaneously similar and different, they symbolized movements in mass culture touched by specific time and place, and, as they broke from traditional standards and boundaries, they appealed to the emerging self-awareness of youth in mid-century America. Through their contributions to American popular culture, Sinatra and Presley came to be identified with their eras—not only at their genesis as pop icons but throughout their careers.

Daniel Boorstin asserts that a celebrity is fundamentally a person who is known for being well known (p. 57).[1] In the same vein, James Monaco recalls the 1930s film *The Gilded Lily* in which a newspaper reporter, played by Fred MacMurray, defines a celebrity as "One of those peculiar people made strangely important by ordinary newspaper print" (p. 5). Both Boorstin and Monaco see a celebrity as a twentieth-century popular culture descendant of a traditional hero—a human icon of veneration, to be sure—but someone we think we know "well" thanks to what McLuhan has defined as the "global village" created by mass media. The media create the celebrity, while the hero is self-created, and, whereas a traditional hero is known for great deeds, the celebrity is known primarily for widespread fame. Such definitions can lead to the easy dismissal of celebrities as ephemeral and disposable cultural commodities of comparatively little value.

But in many respects, celebrities have assumed a conspicuous and more significant role in American culture during the past half-century. For one thing, Americans have become increasingly skeptical of the traditional hero, with the harsh glare of media attention revealing that great people may not always be as noble as their public image. Needing replacements for the visible role models and the cultural glue that hold a civilization together, we have seized upon contemporary examples of well-known people who reflect the values and aspirations of our changing cultural environment. And as social structures become more diverse and fragmented, certain public figures may come to represent the values and aspirations of a cultural subset more than those of the mainstream. A more careful examination of our celebrities reveals that they fall into two basic categories: "citizen" celebrities, whose adulation is in the mainstream, reinforce mass cultural values; rebel or "rogue" celebrities, whose fame rests on the admiration of a cultural subgroup, embody the particular tastes and values of their admirers, often in opposition to mass cultural values. In either case, the celebrity can assume the role of popular hero, making the adulating group feel good about itself and offering both a model to imitate and a vision of success toward which to strive.

During this same half-century, media-dominated America has also witnessed the growing cultural significance of its young people. The teenager as social and cultural force, and important economic market segment, is a fairly recent phenomenon. Loosed by the mobility and the relaxed restrictions on behavior of the homefront during World War II, teenagers often assumed roles earlier generations had reserved for adults. With many adults absent due to military service or extended and irregular work schedules in defense industries, young people had more freedom and responsibility. At the same time, they remained . . . well, *young*. As adolescents, their interests centered on finding and asserting their own identity in a rapidly changing world, and their growing affluence in the context of a booming wartime economy and available jobs or increased allowances enabled them to display that identity as a well-defined style.[2] In a way similar to the dawn of the nuclear age, once unleashed in the 1940s, the genie of youth culture could not be put back in its bottle after the war. With scarcely a hitch, the postwar economy continued to grow in satisfying the pent-up demand for consumer goods in a society characterized by middle-class aspirations and the procreation ethic. With a single-mindedness reminiscent of wartime patriotism, family life and affluence became cultural touchstones at least through the early 1960s, and once again young people were afforded the luxury of self-definition and self-indulgence. Buttressed by the growing baby-boom population, youth culture seemed here to stay, and so became a focus for cultural commentators and for shrewd market executives. As cohorts of teenagers sought to define and assert their collective identity, they naturally chose *personae* to admire who embodied their collective tastes and aspirations. So-called "teen idols" were most likely to be found in the media, and a medium that beat close to teen hearts was popular music. Both live and recorded performances were widely available; the music was portable and pervasive, an accessible and repeatable reinforcement of their style. Through their devotion to their music and their idols, teens were no longer "disconnected individuals" but shared a common interest (Jones, p. 72). The popularity of Frank Sinatra and Elvis Presley was not an accident, but a logical product of the intersection of mass media with an audience yearning for something to claim as its own. In each case, we find an expression of the values of a cultural subset whose importance is now taken for granted. And in each teen idol, we find a celebrity who embodies characteristics of both the citizen and the rogue.

The paths that led young Frankie Sinatra from Hoboken to New York and young Elvis Presley from Tupelo to Memphis may be hundreds of miles apart, but they follow a well-known route. The life stories of Sinatra and Presley leading up to their success strike a common and familiar chord, a rags-to-riches progress that begets a *persona* who appears to change singlehandedly the course of popular music and whose celebrity takes on a life of its own—first for the fans, later for the public at large. No matter how distinctive their styles and important their contributions to the history of American music, these two performers became popular because they gave their audiences exactly what they wanted. No matter how singular their personalities, they mirror, at least in their origins, classic American self-made men. Both Frank Sinatra and Elvis Presley gained notoriety by virtue of their appeal to the youthful audiences of their respective eras. Denounced by adult cultural arbiters at first, Frankie and Elvis endeared themselves to cadres of loyal fans as they helped to redefine both the boundaries and the course of popular music through their own performances and the reactions of their fans. Both Sinatra and Elvis represented something with which their teen fans could identify, and their success would come to represent a twentieth-century version of Horatio Alger's mythology of hard work and ambition and steadfast dedication leading to material success and public recognition.

Alger stories of deserving poor boys making good are classic tropes, descending from both traditional myth-narratives and the American religious and secular preaching of the work ethic. In the scores of tales he wrote, Horatio Alger created an archetypal American hero in the composite of his young protagonists. The Alger hero is a young man forced by circumstances to assume adult responsibilities at an early age. Most often an only child, if he has any family at all, it is likely to be his mother; his father is usually deceased or absent. Alger's mothers are seen both as dependent on the hero and as pivotal in encouraging him to succeed. Most often, the hero makes his way through a "modern" (usually urban) environment, encountering frustrations, setbacks, and personal or circumstantial antagonists; whatever his gifts, success does not come easily. What sustains the Alger hero, above all, is his ambition and desire to succeed. Focusing his hard work, conspicuous moral character, deferential respect and concern for others, and adventurous spirit, this ambition enables the hero to take advantage of the lucky breaks that come his way, to merit the confidence of his mentors, and to emerge triumphant. And when success is finally his, the Alger hero appropriately does not forget his humble origins, for he is scrupulous about repaying debts, sharing his rewards with those less fortunate, and caring lavishly for those who depend upon him. While real life rarely imitates the art of fiction in every detail, to a great extent, the early Sinatra and Presley *personae* depend on exactly this archetypal character.

Both the Sinatras and the Presleys were no strangers to hard times and personal struggle, and, although the urban ethnic enclaves of Hoboken stand in sharp contrast to the rural hard scrabble of Tupelo and the segregated southern gumbo of Memphis, the two families shared many common experiences.[3] Above all, Marty and Natalie ("Dolly") Sinatra shared with Vernon and Gladys Presley a desire for respectability and for the chance to carve at least a small piece of the American pie for themselves. Marty scratched out a living as a prize fighter, dock worker, saloon keeper, and for many years a Hoboken fireman; Dolly, too, was committed to bettering their position, working as a candy maker and midwife, and ultimately becoming a local political figure. Moving from the cold-water tenement where Frankie was born, the Sinatras settled into working-class respectability first in an apartment on Hoboken's Park Avenue, and later in a three-story single home on Garden Street. Less obviously ambitious than Marty Sinatra, Vernon Presley began married life with Gladys in a two-room shotgun house he built, having neither running water nor electricity, and it was there that Elvis was born. Gladys stopped working at a garment plant in the last stages of her pregnancy, and Vernon worked a variety of odd jobs through the depression, barely making ends meet. Later they moved from one rented house to another, and from relative to relative, until the promise of war work brought the Presleys to Memphis. Their chance for respectable stability came after the war when Vernon found steady work at a paint company, and the family moved from a boarding house to Lauderdale Courts, a subsidized housing project. Ironically, both families found their path to respectability clouded by brushes with the law: Dolly was alleged to have performed abortions during her career as a midwife; Vernon spent eight months on a work farm for forging a check. Nevertheless, the Sinatras and the Presleys tried their best to provide a solid foundation for their sons, articulating their goal that the boys should finish their formal education, the conventional way to ensure their status. In this respect, the Presleys were more satisfied than the Sinatras: Elvis graduated from Humes High in Memphis while Frank dropped out of A. J. Demarest in his senior year.

Another parallel in the backgrounds of Frank and Elvis is the fact that they were both only children; moreover, each can be seen to have survived a traumatic birth experience. Delivering a baby weighing thirteen pounds was true labor for Dolly Sinatra, who was less than five feet tall herself, and the doctor's forceps scarred Frank badly. Held under running cold water by an aunt until he finally gasped for breath, Frank overcame the obstacle of being born. Daughter Nancy reflects on his birth this way: "The struggle of the infant would shape the character of the boy and remain a motivating force in the man. Perhaps in those few moments lie some of the forces behind the impatience, the steamroller ambition, his exhausting pace, his extravagant style" (p. 16). Gladys Presley delivered her first child, a stillborn son named Jesse, followed a half-hour later by his twin, Elvis. Legend and family memory celebrate the "relationship" between the brothers, and Elvis's own appraisal follows his mother's belief that "when one twin died, the one that lived got all the strength of both" (Guralnick, p. 13). Neither Dolly nor Gladys would bear another child. Indeed, both birth narratives portend the arrival of someone special, though at the time the proud and grateful parents could not begin to imagine the magnitude of the omen.

Perhaps because of the circumstances surrounding their births, both Frank and Elvis developed a particular closeness to their mothers. Furthermore, the dynamics of the Sinatra and Presley family relationships made the mother-son connection significant. In each case, their doting and devoted mothers were seen as dominant personalities. Both Dolly and Gladys were outgoing and determined women, and both defied convention in order to find happiness with the men they loved. Dolly eloped with Marty in 1913 because her parents opposed her romance with a man seen by her family to come from a lower class; twenty-one-year-old Gladys subtracted two years from her age (while Vernon, only seventeen, added five to his) on their marriage license when they ran off to another town in 1933. Each woman was seen as the lively partner, a self-reliant spark in the relationship. Conversely, Marty and Vernon are described as quiet, even taciturn, in their devotion to their families. Wanting the best for their sons and willing to tend American dreamer Jay Gatsby's green light of an "orgiastic future," both mothers would prove to be inspirational devotees to the emerging celebrities, feeding their ambition and building their confidence. At the same time, both boys occasionally seemed to take on the recessive traits of their fathers. Though he ran with the other kids in Hoboken, Frankie was described by friends as "soft," generous, and quiet, like his father. Elvis, too, seemed shy as a boy, not really a loner or outsider, as some have contended, but someone easily passed over in a crowd.

The relationship between the fathers and sons is a bit more difficult to characterize. Not really "absent" as in the Alger stories, these fathers seemed to portray an earnest but anonymous way of life that their ambitious sons would want to transcend; at the same time, all accounts support the idea that the two men were singularly devoted to their wives and sons. In turn, Frank and Elvis loved their dads. Sinatra reflects, "My father was a darling man, a quiet man. . . . [H]e never touched me if I got in a jam. . . . He used to stare at me once in a while and I knew what was behind that stare. . . . I adored him. In some ways, he was the greatest man I ever knew in my life" (Sinatra, p. 20). As a youngster, Elvis seemed especially concerned with his father's safety. Vernon recalls, "When we went swimming, Elvis would have fits if he saw me dive. He was so afraid something would happen to me" (Guralnick, p. 13). Later, Elvis would tell those around him, "My daddy may seem hard, but you don't know what he's been through" (p. 14), and Vernon would remain an important part of the Presley entourage for his son's entire career, even if his direct influence on Elvis was overshadowed by Gladys and manager Tom Parker. Even so, neither father was enthusiastic over his son's desire to be a performer. Marty wanted Frank to avoid the music business after leaving school, saying, "Do you want to get a regular job? Or do you wanna be a bum?" (Sinatra, p. 21). When young Elvis declared that one day he would clear family debts and buy his parents a fine house and *two* Cadillacs, Vernon, too, was skeptical, saying, "I didn't want him to have to steal one" (Guralnick, p. 16), and adding that he had never known a guitar player to amount to much. In each case, the uncertainty of a performer's career, while accepted by Dolly and Gladys, was a too-risky proposition to pass unchallenged by Marty and Vernon.

While still in their teens, both Frank and Elvis tried the "regular jobs" that their fathers understood, giving the traditional path to respectability a try, but neither was satisfied with the rewards of the working class. Frank toiled first at the docks in New Jersey, later in New York hauling crates, and finally as a plasterer for his future father-in-law, but neither his talent nor his patience allowed him to succeed. During his high school years, Elvis ushered at Memphis movie theaters, and, after graduation, he worked in a machine shop and later as a driver for Crown Electric. In some respects, Elvis adjusted to the workaday world better than Frank. For one thing, Elvis saw himself as contributing to his family's welfare, particularly in light of his parents' uncertain income, while Frank, who had tried living "on his own" for a brief period in 1932, seemed intent on developing a singing career, since his family, though not prosperous, really did not depend on his income. In a sense, though, both boys—still in their teens—had assumed "adult" responsibilities: Frank, in his interest to support himself and to win the confidence of Nancy Barbato, whom he had met in 1934; Elvis, in his desire to provide security to his parents.

Both Frank and Elvis consciously nurtured their interest in music through their struggling years. At first, their ambition focused on the conventional singing styles which surrounded them. Frank admired Bing Crosby, the reigning crooner of the mid-1930s, and, after seeing a performance at Loew's Journal Square in Jersey City, he declared to his future wife, "Someday, that's gonna be me up there" (Sinatra, p. 25). Elvis preferred the gospel quartet harmony of the Statesmen and Blackwood Brothers to the sound of the Grand Ole Opry, but most of the people acquainted with him in Memphis remember his singing conventional ballads, including "My Happiness," the song he recorded for his mother's birthday, and the future hit, "That's When Your Heartaches Begin," which he sang for Sam Phillips in an early audition. At the same time they tried to enter the popular mainstream, both boys recognized that they were somehow set apart. Frank recalls that, although he regarded Crosby as an idol, he never wanted to sing like him: "My voice was up higher, and I said, 'That's not for me. I want to be a different kind of singer'" (Sinatra, p. 24). Similarly, when asked by Marion Keisker, the secretary at Sam Phillips's Memphis Recording Service, "Who do you sound like?" Elvis replied, "I don't sound like nobody" (Guralnick, p. 63). Frank would have considerable success in conventional settings, beginning with the Hoboken Four on the Major Bowes' radio program (and subsequent tour) and later with the Harry James and Tommy Dorsey bands until the time of his solo debut, while Elvis went virtually unnoticed by anyone other than his family and friends until his "discovery" in July 1954. Nevertheless, each saw his "difference" as a key to his future success, in spite of the fact that neither Frank nor Elvis deliberately set out to change the parameters of popular music. For each, the world of musical performance was a way to express individuality, to transcend the ordinary, and to achieve the fame and material success he craved.

Frank and Elvis learned "the music business" from mentors who recognized their talent and gave the boys their first big breaks. As in the case of the Alger hero, if it were not for their "pluck"—hard work and determination—they never would have taken advantage of the "luck" that came their way in the form of valuable professional and personal associations. Their talent needed crafting and a platform for its display, and people such as Harry James, Tommy Dorsey, Sam Phillips, Scotty Moore, and Bill Black made both possible.

Sinatra's career as a band singer, following his stint as a singing waiter at the Rustic Cabin, gave him his first real taste of success. When Harry James left Benny Goodman and needed a singer for his new band, he signed Frank to a two-year deal at $75 per week.[4] A relentless road of one-nighters followed, but Sinatra received the exposure he craved. After all, a job with a popular big band was the "end of the rainbow" for a vocalist, or so it seemed in 1939. His association with Harry James allowed him to record his first hit, "All or Nothing at All," and receive favorable mention in George Simon's *Metronome* review of the band's performance at Roseland in New York City (Sinatra, p. 35). But as the popularity of the James band began to falter, Frank consciously planned his next move. Tommy Dorsey, who had the number-one band in the country, was to visit the Rustic Cabin, and Frank arranged an "audition" by singing with Bob Chester's band that night. When Dorsey's featured male vocalist, Jack Leonard, left for a chance at a solo career, Dorsey offered Frank a contract, and the twenty-four-year-old singer thought that he had finally made it.[5] And so he had. The Dorsey band was featured in the best venues around the country, often for weeks at a time, drawing large audiences and favorable press. They also were booked on both local and national radio programs and were featured in the motion picture *Las Vegas Nights*. "I'll Never Smile Again" became the first Dorsey/Sinatra recording to reach the top of the popularity chart in 1940. Just as important as this exposure, though, was the education in technique Frank learned from the trombonist while being allowed to develop his own style. Copying Dorsey's breathing technique, Sinatra recalled, "I was able to sing six bars . . . without taking an audible breath. That gave the melody a flowing, unbroken quality, and that's what made me sound different. When I started singing that way, people began taking notice" (Sinatra, p. 44). Songwriter Sammy Cahn agreed: "I'd never heard a popular singer with such fluidity and style" (Sinatra, p. 44). More important, however, was the fact that by 1941 Sinatra had become the top male vocalist of the year in *Billboard* magazine and a favorite of the teenage audience. As Dorsey told a reporter: "You could almost feel the excitement coming up out of the crowds when that kid stood up to sing. . . . I used to stand there so amazed that I'd almost forget to take my own solos" (quoted in Sinatra, pp. 47–48). When Frank decided to break from the Dorsey band in 1942, the move heralded a new direction not only for him but for the male vocalist as a performer. No longer content to be just another "instrument" in the band, Frank felt that he should be the center of the attention that already seemed to be directed his way, and a few months after his final performance with Dorsey, he would come to witness the magnitude of that attention.

The apprenticeship of Elvis Presley was not quite so formal, and his discovery not quite so calculated. Whatever his raw talent and his dogged determination to be a popular singer, Elvis would benefit from the instincts and talents of people from outside the pop music tradition. Sam Phillips, Scotty Moore, and Bill Black would form the unlikely trinity that would make Elvis a phenomenon. Phillips, who owned the Memphis Recording Service, had made a name for himself by recording the black musicians and vocal performers that no one else would. Like the Memphis radio personality Dewey Phillips (no relation) who would debut Elvis Presley's first commercial record, Sam was fascinated with the rhythms and the sounds of black music, from spirituals to the blues, and knew that in there was a market for his records in the South, not only among blacks but also among a growing number of white teenagers. Sam's studio was where Elvis recorded his first acetate in the summer of 1953, a present for his mother's birthday, at the cost of $3.98, even though he could have made a record more cheaply at W. T. Grant's. Elvis wanted to record for Sam, as well as for himself, and so he was disappointed when Phillips did not emerge from the control booth to socialize, though he said politely that Elvis was an "interesting" singer and that "We might give you a call sometime." Presley chatted up Marion Keisker, however, and she made a note of his name with the comment "Good ballad singer. Hold" (Guralnick, p. 64).

Elvis made other attempts at recording and often stopped by the studio to ask Miss Keisker if there were any opportunities for him to sing with a group. But nothing happened for nearly a year, and the disappointment of his unsuccessful visits began to make itself evident, particularly to the sympathetic Marion Keisker. Finally, she urged Sam to put Elvis in touch with Scotty Moore, a young guitarist from a country group, the Starlite Wranglers, to see if they could work out some new ballad material that Sam had brought back from Nashville. Teaming with Scotty and bassist Bill Black in the studio, Elvis attempted to impress Sam with "Harbor Lights" and "I Love You Because"—unsuccessfully. And then, as the story goes, during a break in the frustrating session, the boys started "kidding around" with Arthur Crudup's "That's All Right [Mama]," and made rock and roll history. The combination of Elvis, Scotty, and Bill was magic to Sam Phillips, although as Scotty recalls:

> It sounded sort of raw and ragged. We thought it was exciting, but what was it? It was just so completely different. But it really flipped Sam—he felt it really had something. We just sort of shook our heads and said, "Well, that's fine, but good God, they'll run us out of town!" (Guralnick, p. 96)

This trio (D. J. Fontana's drums would be added later) created the sound that would be the Elvis phenomenon on Sun Records and in performances throughout the South; later, following Sam's deal with RCA and Tom Parker's becoming Presley's manager, the sound would invade households around the country through their appearances on the Dorsey brothers, Milton Berle, Steve Allen, and, finally, Ed Sullivan television programs and through their records that routinely reached the top of the charts.

Since most of the time they did the driving themselves, the days and nights on the road were even more exhausting for Elvis and the boys than for the big bands and Sinatra who had the "luxury" of bus transportation. Nevertheless, Elvis learned valuable lessons as they moved from roadhouse to fairground to school auditorium, virtually any venue that would have them. Naturally "wired" and impatient, full of nervous energy, Elvis benefited from Scotty's phlegmatic calm and technical skill. Bill, always the clown and a favorite with audiences, helped Elvis, who was shy and awkward during the "patter" between songs, learn how to "work" the crowd. And from Sam's instinct for the right "sound," they all learned that the energy, spontaneity, and abandon that could get them "run out of town" were the keys to their success.

Neither Frank Sinatra nor Elvis Presley set out to be teen idols; they wanted to be successful as *popular* singers. But for each, early success and distinction would be the result of hysterical fan reaction among teen audiences. Interestingly enough, both singers recall being frightened by the spontaneous chaos among teenaged fans at their first featured public performances. At Sinatra's appearance on December 30, 1942, at the Paramount, the reaction of the teen audience was dubbed the "proclamation of a new era."[6] Sinatra himself described his reaction to the pandemonium: "The sound that greeted me was absolutely deafening. It was a tremendous roar. . . . I was scared stiff. . . . I couldn't move a muscle" (Shaw, pp. 19–20). This is an unexpected reaction from a twenty-seven-year-old veteran band singer who had been working in front of live audiences and recording professionally for three years. Not surprisingly, nineteen-year-old Elvis, who had nowhere near the experience performing in public that Frank did, recalls a similar reaction on July 30, 1954, at Overton Park in Memphis: "I was scared stiff. It was my first big appearance in front of an audience, and I came out . . . and everybody was hollering and I didn't know what they were hollering at" (Guralnick, p. 110). The parallels are dramatic: performers who were "scared stiff" and masses of teenagers who seemed to lose all control.

What provoked these outbursts of hysteria? In contrast to the later appearances of Elvis Presley and the Beatles, Arnold Shaw comments on the style of Sinatra's early stage *persona*:

> He just stood at the microphone, clutching it as if he were too frail to remain standing without it. But the mike mannerism, the limp curl, the caved-in cheeks, the lean, hungry look, "the frightened smile," as one reporter put it—all emphasized a *boyishness* that belied a wife and child and brought him as close as the boy next door. (p. 21)

Conventionally dressed with a jacket and bow tie, singing mainstream popular songs in his flowing baritone, Frank seemed more vulnerable than threatening,[7] although a *Down Beat* reviewer would accurately observe that "his spell is not as artless as it looks. He knows his feminine audience and fires romance—moonlight moods—at them with deadly aim" (quoted in Shaw, p. 23). In his Overton Park appearance, fiddling with the mike and twisting the stand so hard his knuckles turned white, Elvis, too, appeared "artless" when he performed "That's All Right," as Scotty Moore recalls:

> [Instead] of just standing flat-footed and tapping his foot, well, he was kind of jiggling. That was just his way of tapping his foot. Plus I think with those old loose britches that we wore—they weren't pegged, they had lots of material and pleated fronts—you shook your leg, and it made it look like all hell was going on under there. During the instrumental parts he would back off from the mike and be playing and shaking and the crowd would just go wild, but he thought they were actually making fun of him. (Quoted in Guralnick, p. 110.)

But Elvis was a quick study. Buoyed by Sam Phillips's confidence and then-manager Bob Neal's observation that the audience was hollering because he was wiggling his legs, Elvis caught on at once: "I went back out for an encore, and I did a little more [leg wiggling], and the more I did, the wilder they went" (Guralnick, p. 110).

Standing at the mike, caressing it with his voice and at the same time making every female in the audience believe that he was singing to *her*, Sinatra made love to his audience. Gyrating on the balls of his feet, yanking the mike to his sneering lips or flailing at his guitar, Elvis created a very different stage *persona*. But whether couched in vulnerability or abandon, the magic spell cast upon the audience was one of sex. An element of the

Alger hero so far undiscussed is his "conspicuous moral character." To some extent, both Frank and Elvis could be said to illustrate the importance of this trait, but in very different ways. Sinatra's "morality" could be seen in his appearance, devotion to his family, and conventional stage and public behavior; in fact, when he first strayed from the image during his affair with Ava Gardner, his popularity suffered. On the other hand, Presley's public image on stage belied a comparatively straightlaced private life (at least for a popular rock and roll performer) that was often cited by his defenders. But in the reaction of the growing ranks of teenaged fans, mainstream critics found cause to fear the influence that Frank and Elvis were having on their respective generations of America's youth. In each case, perhaps, the young audiences saw and heard exactly what they wanted in their pop idols.[8]

In the crucible of wartime uncertainty, it was comforting to admire a young man, once described by Tommy Dorsey as "a skinny kid with big ears," whose performance was fundamentally "nice" and conventional.[9] In many ways he seemed just as young and as ordinary as his audience, even if his appearance was famous enough to be caricatured in cartoons and mocked by adults; and he was careful to identify with his audience in his public utterances, saying "we" instead of "you." Thus, he not only represented their collective hopes and dreams in his fame and material success, but he affirmed their own sense of personal worth. In the words of one fan, "He's made us feel like we're something" (Shaw, p. 26). As a teen idol, Sinatra was the boy next door and then some—a rogue celebrity in citizen disguise, whose "danger" was made apparent only in the reactions of his fans. Shaw cites Harold Hobson, writing in the London *Sunday Times*, to explain the Sinatra magic: "The shy deprecating smile with the quiver at the corner of the mouth makes the young ladies in the gallery swoon in ecstasy and the maturer patrons in the dress circle gurgle with delight" (p. 27). His surface vulnerability masked the obvious sex appeal, at least until later in his career.

The mid-1950s present a different picture. In an era characterized in its own time and in popular memory as one of middle-class conformity, Elvis appeared on the scene as the antithesis of everything for which Mom and Dad and Ike stood. Rather than reassurance, the new teens wanted change, and Elvis would oblige in a variety of ways. His origins were different from the masses of teenagers who would come to embrace him. His music was not conventional at all, but a blending of two "outlaw" traditions—hillbilly and rhythm and blues—along with a touch of gospel fervor, which would combine to be the new musical idiom of postwar America. His slicked hair (he used three different ointments to get his look just right), his long sideburns (in imitation of long-haul truck drivers), and his Beal Street attire (from Lansky's, which catered to blacks) contrasted sharply with the popular crewcuts and pressed chinos of his peers, although the "Elvis look" would become a badge of teenage male-rebel self-definition. His stage *persona* was more blatantly sexual and accented by the audience reaction to his every move: if his "jiggling" legs appeared first by accident or stage fright, they immediately became the trademark of Elvis "The Pelvis." The boy whose off-stage demeanor was shy and excruciatingly polite was transformed into another person when he was "on." A "citizen" in rogue-celebrity disguise, Elvis flaunted his sexuality. If Frank caressed the microphone, Elvis manhandled it—after all, mikes were for mainstream idols. His slung guitar was his prop (assuring its image as rock and roll icon), and he beat time and strummed rhythm vigorously enough to routinely break strings. With every pelvic thrust, ducktail toss, and sneering grin, the stage-Elvis provoked audience hysteria. His aggressive and obviously sexually charged performance masked his personal vulnerability, his need for acceptance, and his devotion to his parents.

Two particular performances by these teen idols, each roughly two years into their early careers, highlight their impact on their fans and upon culture as a whole, and they crystallize the criticism from the arbiters of mainstream tastes.

In mid-October 1944, Frank Sinatra was again booked at the Paramount in New York, the scene of his first solo performances. When Frank arrived for an early-morning rehearsal on October 11, nearly a thousand girls were on line, some having arrived the previous afternoon, defying the mayor's 9:00 P.M. curfew on juveniles. When the doors opened at 8:30 A.M., the theater's 3400 seats were filled as the line continued to grow outside. Once admitted, patrons stayed in their seats for hours through at least two or three shows, to the chagrin of waiting fans. By Columbus Day, a legal holiday in New York, more than 10,000 fans lined up outside the Paramount, a larger audience than Mayor LaGuardia drew to his holiday speech, and an estimated 20,000 more clogged Times Square. Frustrated by their inability to enter the theater, the throng smashed shop windows and destroyed the Paramount ticket booth; more than 400 police reserves, 200 detectives, and 20 squad cars could not prevent what would come to be known as "The Columbus Day Riot."[10] The problem, of course, was not Frank Sinatra himself or the style of his performance, but the *effect* that Sinatra had on the bobby-soxers. Many not caught up in the hysteria must have secretly applauded the sailors who threw overripe tomatoes at the Sinatra cutouts on the Paramount marquee late at night, while the guardians of polite society lamented the degeneracy of youth.

A series of Elvis performances in Florida during the summer of 1956 saw a similar wave of hysteria, and, when the singer arrived in Jacksonville on August 10, a local preacher offered prayers at a Baptist church after declaring that Elvis had "achieved a new low in spiritual degeneracy" even as the faithful lined up before dawn to attend the shows. Judge Marion Gooding, who remembered the frenzy provoked at Presley's performance in town the previous year, prepared warrants charging the singer with impairing the morals of minors, which he would serve if Elvis performed in a way that, in his opinion, "put obscenity and vulgarity in front of our children." The judge attended the first performance at 3:30 P.M. and met with Presley to press his order that the shows be toned down.[11] For his part, Elvis maintained that "I can't figure out what I'm doing wrong. I know my mother approves of what I'm doing." But he did subdue his stage performance, substituting "lascivious" wiggling of his finger for his trademark gyrations. There was no riot, at least on the scale of Sinatra's Columbus Day debacle, but the *effect* of Elvis Presley's stage *persona* was undiminished, even if it was triggered by a twitch of his little finger.

Todd Gitlin explains the tension between the adult mainstream's fear and loathing and the teenagers' generational defiance in this way:

[Earlier] generations of parents had also been disturbed to see their children writhing with abandon, treating their bodies like erotic instruments, screaming at idols like Frank Sinatra. Popular music often serves to insulate young people against the authority of previous generations, and the commercial search for The Latest makes generational tension over music virtually automatic. But in rock's heyday there was a special intensity on both sides. When teenagers screamed themselves hoarse at Frank Sinatra in the Forties, whatever quality it was that teens celebrated and editorialists deplored was the possession of a single skinny singer. Now both sides agreed that rock was all of a piece, love it or leave it. (p. 43)

By the 1950s, the mainstream found cause for alarm not only in the antics of the young but in the music itself, and Elvis was only its most notorious example. The "noise" that parents deplored became magnetic to youth because their parents could not comprehend or appreciate it. However, in the case of both Frank Sinatra and Elvis Presley, age and the passing of time succeeded in doing what the parents, press, and preachers could not do. Failing to suppress the menace in its heyday, the mainstream eventually absorbed both performers.

Mainstream acceptability for Frank Sinatra came at a price: he had to die, at least in one *persona*, in order to re-create himself. The "boy next door" had become a song-and-dance movie star, then an outspoken advocate for racial and ethnic tolerance, and then a singer-on-the-skids who had seen his audience drift away to the new idols who followed him while he made few truly satisfying recordings and even fewer "hits." His personal life was the subject of scandal sheets, and in April of 1950 his throat hemorrhaged. But within three years, he was back on top again with a Best Supporting Actor Oscar, a contract with Capitol Records, and a new image to go with his new sophisticated "older" sound. From the 1950s onward,

Frank would be the swinger instead of a heartthrob, a dangerous but likable rogue who ran with the hipsters of the "rat pack" and who appealed to women and men alike. As always, his music was squarely in the popular mainstream, but it now would never be really *square*. Instead, he and his sound seemed to define the "cool" of the adult postwar world as dry martinis became the drink of choice in the cities and suburbs of modern America. Both Frankie, now more worldly-wise than boyish, and the bobby-soxers had grown up.

Elvis, too, was re-created in the late 1950s, though perhaps less by his own hand than by the skillful manipulation of the Colonel and the timely intervention of Uncle Sam. In March of 1958, Elvis was inducted into the Army, and in August his beloved mother died. Although he was only twenty-three, the trauma of losing Gladys and the ordeal of becoming a soldier at the height of his fame caused Elvis to do a great deal of growing up. But his uncomplaining acceptance of military service (as well as the identifiable grief at his loss) warmed the public to the rock and roller. Todd Gitlin confirms that the rebel had indeed become a citizen in the public eye: "That sneering, vibrating kid denounced by preachers and teachers and politicians turned out to be a good American boy after all. Mainstream culture sighed in relief" (p. 44). In hindsight, it is amusing to discover the very real fear that Elvis, and many of those close to him, felt about the effect his absence would have on his career. But thanks both to Tom Parker's strategy of releasing stockpiled records every few months to keep Presley hits on the charts and to the endurance of rock and roll itself, Elvis need not have worried. When he was discharged on March 5, 1960, he was reborn as a civilian and as a performer. As a singer, his repertoire began to include more of the pop tunes he had tried to record in Sam Phillips's studio.[12] But his career took another turn: he made three movies in a matter of months and completed three extensive recording sessions between his discharge and the end of the year. Elvis might have been back, but in many respects he was a different Elvis; in fact, except for two charity performances in Memphis during early 1961, he would not perform again on stage until the summer of 1969 and the triumphant Las Vegas concert appearances which heralded the last phase of his career. His appearance had changed; "sharkskin" Elvis had a sleek pompadour with moderated sideburns, and the sneer was now a smile. The rock and roll energy could still be detected in a record or two, but his style was shackled in the more than thirty formula movies (far cries from Oscar vehicles) and soundtracks he made. The rogue was mainstreamed, and while teenagers looked elsewhere for heroes, the rest of America embraced Elvis as an icon.

A symbolic juxtaposition of the two idols occurred when Frank welcomed Elvis on a Timex television special in May of 1960 to celebrate his return from the army. Though he was just beginning to define his 1960s movie *persona*, the subdued Elvis was evident from the start. And for his part, Frank, who had no taste for rock and roll and who represented the mainstream popular music establishment, seemed to enjoy clowning and singing with Presley. The welcome home appearance with Sinatra clearly presented the "good boy" Elvis image to the mainstream, even as it caricatured elements of his early appeal. Once during an appearance on the *Steve Allen Show* in the 1950s, Elvis was forced to dress in formal attire and sing to a basset hound in order to tone down his performance and soothe the critics. On the Timex show, Elvis again appears in a tuxedo, but he no longer needs toning down. He "imitates" Sinatra mannerisms in his rendition of his newly recorded song "Fame and Fortune," as well as in his "Love Me Tender/Witchcraft" duet with Sinatra. The music and the man were tamed and glossed for a mainstream audience, and the appearance of the two *former* teen idols together heralded the culmination of RCA's and Tom Parker's mass-marketing of a teen phenomenon into a mainstream star.

Within the first decade of their careers, both Frank and Elvis transcended the teenage market. The teen idols became pop stars through media exposure, film careers, public acceptance by the mainstream of their personal images and of their chosen musical forms, and probably the aging of their original fans. Teens continued to seek The Latest musical forms to distinguish themselves from adult tastes and sensibilities.[13] In their later careers, there is a kind of anachronistic quality attached to the success of the two idols. Sinatra became the "hip" organization man for the generation cashing in on postwar prosperity; always the consummate "swinger" and epitome, he stood in sharp relief against the musical and cultural pyrotechnics of the 1960s, the shallow preening of disco and the sensitivity of male singer-songwriters in the 1970s, though it could be argued that his vulnerability, most seen in saloon songs, was always a part of his appeal to both sexes. Presley, the flamboyant rebel of post-materialistic rejection of the mainstream and an exaggeration of the excesses of "style" and appetites in later years, seemed to be even more out of tune with changing times as he moved through the movies (with greater appeal to mothers than to teen women and less than ever to males). If Sinatra could be seen as a "model" for a particular kind of male identity or lifestyle, celebrated even now in the "cocktail culture" of the 1990s, Presley became a kind of burlesque or caricature of the 1970s excess in his grooming, sequined clothes, elaborate staging and orchestration, and drug abuse and slaking of other appetites. If anything, Frank always remained a "hip" figure, even as he aged. Elvis was the wild "hillbilly cat" in his youth but was tamed beyond the wildest dreams of his critics in the 1960s, and, when he re-emerged as a live performer in the 1970s, the polished showman was no longer dangerous, at least in public.

The debate over which image of Elvis would appear on his commemorative postage stamp is significant. The young, rebellious Elvis won hands down over the older, bloated pop star, suggesting that his greatest influence and most memorable significance was as a teen idol. It might be much harder to fix an iconic image of Sinatra, since representations from each stage of his career—"Bones" with his bow tie, the cocky hipster of *Pal Joey*, the suave leader of the Rat Pack, the Reaganite solid-citizen, and the tuxedoed master of the pop music form—say something worthy of memory to the American audience. Elvis had his greatest musical significance as the harbinger of a new music form, the key to his enduring popularity. Sinatra, however, evolved as a performer and cultivated a personal image that seemed to relate more consistently to changing times and expanding audiences.[14]

Neither Frank Sinatra nor Elvis Presley set out to exploit teen hysteria, but both found that their popularity among teens was a useful vehicle to propel them to stardom and give them the clout they needed to succeed. At the same time, in each artist's journey to stardom and in their respective musical articulation, the teenagers found ways to express their identities as well as their hopes for the future. And while Elvis Presley's contribution is most associated with a particular era and Frank Sinatra's music and style are timeless, both singers lived and sang stories fundamental to the human spirit and the American dream. The teens may have outgrown their idols, just as Frank and Elvis outgrew the teens, but their relationship has had a lasting impact on American cultural history and on the course of our musical heritage.

NOTES

1. Technically, as Boorstin points out, the word *celebrity* describes a state or condition, derived from the Latin *celebritas*, meaning "fame."

2. The popular press began to pay considerable attention to the young during the war years. The cover story of *Life* magazine's 23 August 1943 issue is a good example. Focusing on the swing dance form of jitterbug, or the Lindy Hop, a pictorial documents the steps of youthful dancers acting out "American impatience with the restrictions of conventional forms" (p. 95). Similar pieces in other issues looked at hairstyles, clothing fashions, and make-up as youngsters created a subculture. Accordingly, George Frazier's "Frank Sinatra" in *Life* (3 May 1943), pp. 54–62, places the singer in this context.

3. Biographical details are indebted to Nancy Sinatra's account of her father's youth in *Frank Sinatra: An American Legend* (pp. 15–22), and to Peter Guralnick's *Last Train to Memphis: The Rise of Elvis Presley* (pp. 3–16).

4. James knew Sinatra from publicity photos given to him when he left Goodman and from the local radio broadcasts of Rustic Cabin shows. At first, he suggested that Frank use the name "Frankie Satin," but Sinatra, who had briefly used the monicker "Frankie Trent" during the Rustic Cabin stint, refused.

5. The stories surrounding the Dorsey contract contribute to the Sinatra legend. In contrast to Harry James, who let Frank out of his own contract with grace and good wishes, Dorsey was tight-fisted. The $100 per week and association with a

top band came at the price of Frank's loyalty. When Sinatra wanted to leave Dorsey for his own solo career, the bandleader demanded 43 percent of his professional income for life.

6. Arnold Shaw's "Sinatrauma: The Proclamation of a New Era," reprinted in Petkov and Mustazza, *The Frank Sinatra Reader*, pp. 18–30, provides considerable insight into Sinatra's early success with teenage fans.

7. Bruce Bliven, who witnessed one of the October 1944 performances, comments that Sinatra's baritone is "untrained," "light," and "weak"—he would be all the more vulnerable without his microphone. Yet Bliven, too, comments on Sinatra's sense of confident showmanship disguised behind his apparent bashfulness (pp. 592–93).

8. It is also interesting to note that in explaining the reactions of fans to both Frank and Elvis, the term "Holy Roller" appears both in critical articles and in sermons from the pulpit. Confronted by the phenomenon of fans lost in ecstasy, observers find the analogy of a religious conversion or hysterical trance a convenient—if somewhat scary—explanation of the teens' behavior.

9. Shaw lists several contemporary "explanations" of the Sinatra attraction to bobby-soxers (which Frank ridiculed on stage during his patter between numbers), among them: "mass psychology built up by his press agent," "wartime degeneracy," and "the maternal urge" (p. 27).

10. See Arnold Shaw (pp. 23–25), Bruce Bliven (pp. 592–93), and Nancy Sinatra (pp. 64–65) for more discussion of this performance.

11. Guralnick (p. 322) also notes that a representative of the American Guild of Variety Artists told Elvis that he would have to post bond and join the Guild (which represented exotic dancers, among others) because of his "suggestive movements." Colonel Parker, who now led the Presley entourage as his manager, took care of this nuisance.

12. In his liner notes for *Elvis: From Nashville to Memphis: The Essential 60's Masters I*, Peter Guralnick notes that Elvis's first recording session following his Army stint included "Fever" (made popular by Peggy Lee), "It's Now or Never" (patterned after "O Solo Mio" and a 1949 Tony Martin song), and "Are You Lonesome Tonight?" (a favorite of the Colonel's wife and a hit in 1927 by Gene Austin). The latter two sides had success as pop-rock singles, both reaching #1 on the charts during the summer and fall of 1960.

13. At the height of their fame in the 1960s, the Beatles paid homage to Elvis during a visit to Graceland even though the teens of the era had pretty much abandoned him.

14. Presley died before his appeal was exhausted; Sinatra fades into peaceful fulfillment away from the public eye. Both did it their way, but Sinatra finished the song. There is still speculation on what Elvis would have been had he lived. There always will be Sinatra music in our popular imagination, much as Presley's, but will there be a Sinatra equivalent to Graceland as a destination for faithful pilgrims on important anniversaries?

WORKS CITED

Bliven, Bruce. "The Voice and the Kids." *The New Republic*, 6 November 1944, 592–93.

Boorstin, Daniel. *The Image: A Guide to Pseudo-Events in America*. New York: Atheneum, 1972.

Gitlin, Todd. *The Sixties: Years of Hope, Days of Rage*. New York: Bantam, 1987.

Guralnick, Peter. *Last Train to Memphis: The Rise of Elvis Presley*. Boston: Little, Brown, 1994.

————. "Elvis Presley" [liner notes for] *Elvis: From Nashville to Memphis: The Essential 60's Masters I*. RCA 66160-2/4, 1993.

Jones, Landon. *Great Expectations: America and the Baby Boom Generation*. New York: Ballantine Books, 1980.

Monaco, James. *Celebrity: The Media as Image Makers*. New York: Delta, 1978.

Petkov, Steven, and Leonard Mustazza (eds). *The Frank Sinatra Reader*. New York: Oxford University Press, 1995.

Shaw, Arnold. "Sinatrauma: The Proclamation of a New Era." In Steven Petkov and Leonard Mustazza, eds. *The Frank Sinatra Reader*. New York: Oxford University Press, 1995, pp. 18–30.

Sinatra, Nancy. *Frank Sinatra: An American Legend*. Santa Monica, CA: General Publishing Group, 1995.

The Composition of Celebrity: Sinatra as Text in the Liner Notes of Stan Cornyn

GILBERT L. GIGLIOTTI

In late 1995, when Reprise Records released its limited-edition twenty-CD boxed set *Frank Sinatra: The Complete Reprise Studio Recordings*, it was decidedly appropriate that the producers devoted approximately a quarter of the 96-page hardcover book included in the set to "Eye Witness," an essay by Stan Cornyn (see Cornyn's "Eye Witness" in Part III of this book). Since 1964, Stan Cornyn has been, in a very tangible—if somewhat paradoxical—way, the voice of Frank Sinatra. For it is his distinctive voice in the liner notes[1] that sets the stage and mood of sixteen Sinatra albums[2] even before the first note is heard, the first lyric sung.[3] Pregnant with dramatic images, hep-cat language, and tortured syntax, Cornyn's lyricism would be elemental in both capturing and promulgating the Sinatra image at the very peak of his celebrity: entertainer and artist, cynic and romantic, survivor and star.

Twice winner of the Grammy Award for "Album Notes (Annotator's Award)" and nominated five times in all (Kaplan 325, 329, 334, 336, 354), Cornyn celebrates Sinatra's preeminent status as "The Chairman of the Board"[4] by wrapping him in images and cadences so distinctive and individual that they become integral to Sinatra's albums and almost inseparable from the recordings themselves.[5] Cornyn's annotation for the 1967 LP *Frank Sinatra: The World We Knew* is found, after all, on the *front* cover and, by 1969, Cornyn only needed to initial his *My Way* notes.[6]

In the end, Cornyn's mix of "New Journalistic" detail and bardic intonation would play a major role in the creation of the iconic Sinatra: the man who lives our life, the artist who gives us voice.

Cornyn's annotation of Sinatra albums began rather modestly on *It Might as Well Be Swing* (1964), the second collaboration between Sinatra and Count Basie, with a back cover interview of the album's arranger/conductor Quincy Jones. Such interviews would comprise three of the first five liner notes Cornyn would write for the artist. The "conversation" with Jones—as would the subsequent interviews of producers Jimmy Bowen and Sonny Burke for *Sinatra '65* (1965) and *My Kind of Broadway* (1965), respectively—covers a variety of topics but focuses primarily upon the process of preparing and recording the albums: song selection, chart writing, and, most significantly, the working relationship of the musicians, conductors, and singer during the sessions themselves. What becomes clear in all three interviews is that Sinatra is not merely a great popular singer but a great musician as well:

> *Jones*: And Basie's drummer, Sonny Payne, remarked at the time what a pleasure it was to work with so musical a singer and to work, moreover, with a man who, in a sense, was able to swing *him*.

> *Bowen*: [The musicians] are honored to be there. Hal Blaine, my drummer, fourteen years he waited to play on a Frank Sinatra session. I never forget [*sic*] when I first called him on the phone and I said "Frank Sinatra date" he didn't say nothing for three minutes. I think he fainted.

> *Burke*: The guys he works with are pros, and he's a pro's pro.

Cornyn's focus on the artistic process of Sinatra's recording would predominate even more on *Softly, As I Leave You* (1964). But instead of simply reporting the reflections of participants in the recording session, Cornyn takes his readers there:

> He walks into a recording session about a half an hour after the orchestra has begun running down the songs. He looks smart, what your mother used to call "natty." His wide-banded hat is tipped back, one inch off straight flat. He doesn't come in with a fanfare. He's there though. He strolls through the studio obstacle course, the mike booms, the cable spaghetti, the music stands. Softly and with a grin he greets the musicians who've been working his sessions for years. "Hi ya, Sweets." "Evenin', Sunshine."

Here the annotator clearly has begun to co-opt the methods and techniques of the "New Journalism," which newspaper and magazine writers such as

Gay Talese, Jimmy Breslin, and Tom Wolfe were only beginning to develop in the early sixties (Wolfe 34–37).[7]

The "New Journalism" essentially applied the techniques of fiction writing to reporting. First and foremost, according to Wolfe in his seminal 1972 *New York* magazine essay, the new approach demanded a level of detail only to be gleaned by the reporter's "arriving on the scene before the main event in order to gather the off-camera material, the by-play in the make-up room, that would enable him to create character" (38). These details, however, were communicated through the strategies traditionally associated with the novelist: the distinctive narrative voice of "someone who was actually on the scene and involved in it" (38), chameleon-like switches in points of view (43), and the "lavish" use of any number of more literary "mannerisms," such as interjection, pleonasm, and the historical present (45). As Wolfe writes, "The idea was to give the full objective description plus something that readers had always had to go to novels and short stories for: the subjective or emotional life of the characters" (45).

In his *Softly, As I Leave You* liner notes, Cornyn for the first time takes his readers to the recording session to see, hear, and, to some extent, be the artist at work. Cornyn also begins to develop a basic paradigm of anticipation, entrance, performance, and appreciation[8] by which he attempts to capture everyone present in the studio, a pattern to which he consistently would return for *September of My Years* (1965), *Sinatra at the Sands* (1966), *Francis Albert Sinatra & Antonio Carlos Jobim* (1967), *Francis A. & Edward K.* (1968), *Ol' Blue Eyes Is Back* (1973), and *L.A. Is My Lady* (1984). In *Softly, As I Leave You*, for example, the point of view continually shifts from various spectators (the " 'in' crowd of semi-invited guests sit[ting] against the wall," or "the girl" who, when she hears Sinatra's singing, finally "forgets to wonder if he's noticed her"), to the musician, with the mute tucked guardedly between his knees, because he knows "a dropped mute means a blown take. A possible explosion." Ultimately, Cornyn shifts to Sinatra himself. Through Cornyn's words, the audience inhabits, as it were, the singer—as he readies himself:

His hands stuff into his pockets. His knees bend half an inch, like a tennis pro waiting for his opponent's best serve. He studies the microphone—friend or enemy? He fiddles with it, moving it maybe a quarter of an inch closer. He balances on the balls of his feet, his eyes feeling their way through the already memorized poetry before him.

As he sings:

The action is up at the solo mike. He leans into the words with deceptively casual grace. Like a high jumper when he's loping down the gravel path to the point of no return.

And when he finishes:

> He looks over the top of the music stand. For the first time he has a
> Lucky going. He leans into the mike with the boyish pride of a kid
> who's just made his first bike ride around the whole block no hands.

Through Cornyn's notes, the reader thus intimately experiences the action
in a way most pre-MTV record buyers could only dream of: not merely in
the studio or from the orchestra but from behind the microphone as well.

Besides shifting points of view, the Reprise annotations display what
would become distinctive literary mannerisms of the Stan Cornyn style: the
"lavish" use of similes, motifs, repetition, and allusions. The similes, which
on later albums will develop almost their own patois,[9] seem to be Cornyn's
first attempts at developing a Wolfian narrative voice. With the aforementioned tennis player, the high jumper, and the boy on his bike, gone is
"that pale beige tone" traditionally expected of an objective observer
(Wolfe 38). In its place is a voice which tries to reflect the oxymoronic
nature of Sinatra: the hard work and raw talent, the experience and innocence, the toughness and tenderness, that the singer will come to epitomize in the American popular imagination.

Within the individual annotations, Cornyn's motifs frequently unify the
texts. For example, in the *L.A. Is My Lady* (1984) note, entitled "The
anchovy tonight is an endangered species," food images predominate. From
the smell of pizza in the elevator and the musicians' buffet of "chicken
wings, greens, slaw, shrimp, and macaroons" to the professional jargon of
"clams" and "anchovies," Cornyn details how Sinatra, Quincy Jones, and
an all-star band have whipped up "the newest Frank Sinatra Cook Book"
("Anchovy").

On *That's Life* (1966), war provides a powerful vehicle for the controlling simile.[10] "Like wars," Sinatra LP's are "best remembered not by the
issues, not by the countries, but by the havoc they create and the ingenuity
of their arms makers. Havoc with brand new arms came again with 'That's
Life.' " Throughout the annotation, the title track remains "the latest war,"
and, when describing Sinatra's performance of the song as a concert finale
in Las Vegas, Cornyn concludes that it is "a reasonable size war. Other
than that not much else is happening." The bravado (and even flippancy)
of such a statement cannot be overstated considering that by December of
1966 some 385,000 U.S. military personnel were already in Vietnam (Kutler 555). Sinatra recordings now apparently rank as historic events.[11]

Consistent with the "New Journalism," a variety of traditional rhetorical
patterns of repetition also marks the Cornyn style. In characterizing his
record of "That's Life," the "ONE SONG" Sinatra went into the studio
to record—despite the fact that "nobody in his right puttees goes in to
record ONE SONG"—Cornyn employs alliteration, consonance, and ho-

moioteleuton in the alternately plosive and sibilant phrase: "A totally persuasive, percussive, permissive, unpassive thing." For *My Way* (1969), Cornyn's anaphoric organization can lead to only one man:[12]

> If a man moves through life . . .
> If a man grows in harmony . . .
> If you pass a man whose face looks . . .
> And if you hear a man who will only do it his way . . .
> And if you can find a man who can remember and walk and grow
>   and look in all these ways—that man is worth the listening.

And "that man," naturally, could only be Frank Sinatra.

Cornyn also packs his texts with allusions to both the current release[13] (e.g., "Softly and with a grin he greets the musicians . . .") and previous Sinatra landmarks, such as the Capitol LP *Point of No Return* (1961). In this way the reader is faced simultaneously with Sinatra's impressive past and still-potent present.[14] The characteristically loud drumming at the *Softly, As I Leave You* sessions, for example, is a "hangover from the dance band days a couple a [*sic*] decades back." Who else is there, Cornyn's texts repeatedly ask, who still does or, for that matter, ever did it as well as Sinatra?

This appreciation for both the man and his history is captured best on *September of My Years* (1965). Here Cornyn's tone and approach, while explicitly stating the album's theme—a man's reflecting upon his past— also aim to cultivate an air of solemnity toward the stature and artistry that Sinatra's hard-fought and fully-lived life has merited:

> Tonight will not swing. Tonight is for serious.
>   Inside, the musicians, led by coatless, posture-free Gordon Jenkins rehearse their voice-empty arrangements. Waiting for his arrival.
>   Outside, in the hall, the uniformed guards wait and wonder what to do with their hands.
>   Unruly fiddle players, who love recording like they love traffic jams, tonight they bring along the wives, who wait to one side in black beaded sweaters.
>   And these wives and these fiddle players and all of these are different tonight. For in a few minutes a poet will begin to speak of years ago.

This reverent anticipation of Sinatra's advent, uttered in almost hushed tones, is dispelled temporarily by the singer's casual entrance and easygoing conversation. The audience's high regard for him must not, after all, blind them to his humanity:

He arrives. Tie-loosened, collar loosened. The guards at the studio door edge out of the way.

"Good morning, sir," he says. "Who's got the game on?"

Thirty orchestra wives wish they had the late scores memorized. Four men look around for a transistor radio.

"Hello, Sidney, how are ya. What's happenin' in the music business?"

However, once the music commences, his joking[15] with arranger-conductor Gordon Jenkins and the musicians abruptly ends (and the duly reverent tone of the text thus returns). Jenkins is "not leading the orchestra" but "*being*" it. From the podium, he "beams down attentively, his face that of a father after his son's first no-hitter." "The wives in their black beaded sweaters muffle their charm bracelets." A heightened, antiquated diction and a syntactically challenged sentence structure govern the remainder of the text as "this archetype of the good life . . . graces his memory with a poet's vision":

He sings of the penny days. Of the roselipt girls and candy apple times. Of green winds, of a first lass who had perfumed hair. April thoughts.

He has lived enough for two lives, and can sing now of September. Of the bruising days. Of the rouged lips and bourbon times. Of chill winds, of forgotten ladies in limousines.

September can be an attitude or an age or a wistful reality. For this man, it is a time of love. A time to sing.

Besides alluding to any number of songs on the album ("It Was a Very Good Year," "When the Wind Was Green," and the title track, for example), the note concludes with what amounts to Cornyn's lapidary appraisal of the timelessness of Sinatra's art: "A thousand days hath September." More than a singer, more than an artist, Sinatra becomes in Cornyn's language an icon to be revered.

The liner notes in which Cornyn does not follow the anticipation-entrance-performance-appreciation pattern are even more poetic ventures into fashioning a legendary Sinatra. The myth-making language of epic, for example, fills the five columns on the inside of the gatefold cover of *Frank Sinatra: A Man and His Music*, the two-record anthology narrated by the singer in celebration of his fiftieth birthday in 1965. What begins simply with "This is the story of a lean man and his music" concludes, "Sinatra is fifty. But when he walks into a room—or into a world—there is no doubting where the focus is. It is on that singular man. On that man who stands straight on earth, sure in a universe filled with doubt. On that man, no taller than most, who came and saw and conquered." The writer, it seems, has elevated Sinatra to the apex not simply in the world of musical entertainment but on a more epochal (and even metaphysical) plane. No longer relegated to a former generation or even to the present, Sinatra now is for the ages.

Appropriately enough, in "On Sinatra or How to Be Timeless Tonight" for *Strangers in the Night* (1966), Cornyn returns to the site of one of the singer's earliest triumphs in order to juxtapose the ephemera of contemporary rock culture with the permanence of Sinatra:

> Back in New York, where he started, where twenty thousand bobby-soxers once pressed themselves against the doors of the Paramount Theatre to see him, things are different. The brilliant bronze doors are green with neglect. On one side wall, the chalk legend: "The Animals Are Loved Only by Girls Named Josephine." Animals may come, and they sure do go, but Sinatra stayeth. He stays to sing. Whatever it says at the top of your calendar, that's what Sinatra sings like: 66, 67, 99. . . . He isn't *with* the times. More than any other he *is* the times.

There's no need for Sinatra to adapt to the changing times; for if, at any point, he perhaps may seem out of touch, it is only because his "honesty" renders him natural and his naturalness universal and atemporal.

On *Moonlight Sinatra* (1966), even any thought of his obsolescence is illusory; he is our life's blood:

> To sing of the Moon, and not of missiles, of romance and not of fudge, of love and not lollipops, is old-fashioned. Something out of Grandma's day. Out of date, like the stars. Non-chic, like Valentines. Corny, like your own heart's beat.

For *Frank Sinatra: The World We Knew* (1967), Sinatra is a force of nature:[16]

> The sun had plunged into the Pacific, somewhere southwest of BelAir. In Studio One, Sinatra, like the Pacific, makes his own waves.

And, by *My Way* (1969), the solar system has become all but Sinatracentric:[17]

> If a man moves through life, walking as if he knows the planets are watching him, and might be amused by the presumption—that man is Frank Sinatra.

Vigorous but vulnerable, everyman yet individual, he is no mere "saloon singer."[18] For in his liner notes Cornyn, over the course of several years, steadily removed Sinatra not only from the domain of the commonplace but also from the glamorized realm of Hollywood. In its place, he created for the entertainer a cosmos of his own.

The bardic lyricism of Stan Cornyn, the employee of Reprise Records,[19] was intended, of course, to sell records. He aimed at creating a marketable image for Sinatra the Franchise.[20] Nevertheless, as literary critic Robert Scholes suggests in his delineation of a "rhetoric of textual economy" in *Protocols of Reading*, advertising and poetry are far from mutually exclusive endeavors (108). Scholes invokes the categorization by semiotician Charles Morris of poetic language as "appraisive-valuative discourse" to illustrate poetry's capacity to sell an idea by making it attractively convincing (Morris 125). As Scholes writes, "Poetry exists . . . to make the bird birdy and the whale whaley, or even, as in the case of Archibald MacLeish, to make the poem poemy. . . . Or as a more recent semiotic critic like Umberto Eco might put it, poems and ads exploit the same metaphoric and metonymic pathways within the network of unlimited semiosis to achieve their similar ends" (Scholes 116).

Poets, in other words, sell readers on their visions of the world by making readers see the world, even if but for a moment, just as the poets wish. This "exchange of pleasure and power" occurs at what T. S. Eliot called the "bewildering minute" when readers succumb to the authority of the writer's vision/image/sales pitch (Scholes 108). Stan Cornyn's liner notes, in the end, were successful at selling the franchise because of his ability to evoke Eliot's "bewildering minute" so consistently, to achieve again and again "the greatest single virtue of art," according to Scholes, a "change from the normal, a defense against the ever-present threat of boredom" (121). Each Sinatra album that Cornyn annotated offers a startlingly fresh view of the singer's world—from the description of the well-traveled arrangements of Count Basie and his orchestra performing live with Sinatra at the Sands in Las Vegas in 1965:

> Ask for "One O'Clock Jump" and they'll bring out a sheet of music that looks like a hunk of Kleenex after a flu epidemic.

to the recording sessions for *L.A. Is My Lady* (1984):

> One of the elevators doesn't work. Everything else does.

And, for good or ill, work these liner notes did. Indeed, it might be argued that the textual Sinatra as written by Cornyn became so compelling that it began to eclipse both the man and his music as well as to encourage, at least partially, the criticism of the new, more conservative Sinatra who arose in the seventies (Rockwell 202–211). Ralph Gleason's 1974 essay,

"Frank: Then and Now," for example, sadly depicts a Sinatra larger than life and, consequently, divorced from it:

> The voice is good today. Those warm tones are there and the phrasing. He can really do it like a true professional. But I don't believe, anymore, that he is one of us. He's one of *them* now, singing from the other side of the street and I guess he doesn't even have a whiff of how power-mad and totalitarian it all seems, those bodyguards and the Rat Pack and all that egocentric trivia that has nothing at all to do with the music. (227)

No longer the voice of his audience, Frank seemingly had become someone, even something, else. Sinatra, according to critics like Gleason, had destroyed his relationship with the public by getting lost in the trappings of Cornynesque celebrity instead of remaining true to his heart, true to his art. Of course, whether Sinatra, either the man or the artist, in fact, had changed significantly is immaterial. The "Sinatra" genie that ad-man Cornyn helped to fashion already had been let out of its commercial bottle, and, with its "aggregate, cumulative . . . [and] almost, one might say, immanent" power, there was simply no recapturing it (Wicke 175). This dynamic is not unlike the evolution of advertising as described in Jennifer Wicke's 1988 *Advertising Fictions: Literature, Advertisement, and Social Reading*. While advertising owed its origins to literature, "the institution of advertising" quickly developed to the point that it no longer needed and even surpassed (or, at the very least, bypassed) literature: "Advertising once announced fictions—that was its job, to accompany them into the world of discourse as a mediating shield and a triumphal herald. Advertisement was the hieroglyph of fiction, until its own fictions became the book of the modern world" (Wicke 175). The relationship between Cornyn's annotations and Sinatra's albums closely parallels this description of the historical development of advertising. Originally meant only to trumpet the new Sinatra product, Cornyn's composition of a Sinatra icon soon took on a life of its own.

In the final analysis, despite—and, perhaps, even due to—the excesses inherent in both the compositional strategies and rhetorical language of his annotations, Stan Cornyn contributed immeasurably to the complex iconography of Frank Sinatra. Cornyn, after all, provided the audience with precisely the confident, if somewhat prickly, image we always had desired for understanding ourselves and our place in *The World We Knew*:

> Decades spent in living, in recording, and in singing small but poignant truths about loving. This ambiguous man with clear, touching insights. Sinatra at a microphone, nurturing a bouquet of emotions,

then plucking them in full flower, without first checking for possible thorns.

APPENDIX

The following is a chronological listing of Frank Sinatra's Reprise albums for which Stan Cornyn wrote the liner notes:

1964

It Might as Well Be Swing

Softly, As I Leave You

1965

Sinatra '65

September of My Years* #

My Kind of Broadway

Sinatra: A Man and His Music

1966

Strangers in the Night

Moonlight Sinatra

Sinatra at the Sands* #

That's Life

1967

Francis Albert Sinatra & Antonio Carlos Jobim*

Frank Sinatra: The World We Knew

1968

Francis A. & Edward K.*

1969

My Way

1973

Ol' Blue Eyes Is Back*

1984

L.A. Is My Lady

1995

Frank Sinatra: The Complete Reprise Studio Recordings

Notes:
*Grammy nomination for Best Album Notes (Annotator's Award).
Grammy winner for Best Album Notes (Annotator's Award).

NOTES

The author would like to thank colleagues Stuart Barnett, Mary Anne Nunn, and Tony Cannella from the Central Connecticut State University Department of English for their suggestions and critiques in the writing of this essay. He also would like to thank Stan Cornyn for his generosity and inspiration.

1. Liner notes have held a significant place on Sinatra releases at least since songwriters Sammy Cahn and Jimmy Van Heusen offered their thoughts on the back of the Capitol LP *Only the Lonely* (1958) and Ralph Gleason wrote an essay for the Capitol LP *No One Cares* (1959).

2. The self-deprecatingly comic introduction to "Eye Witness" only mentions "a dozen or more liner notes for Frank Sinatra" (55). His 16, however, comprised the majority of the 25 Sinatra LPs (excluding compilations, soundtracks, "The Reprise Repertory Theatre" albums, or other projects for which the singer only appears on some tracks) Reprise would release during the period 1964–1995. See the Appendix in this chapter.

3. The equating of Sinatra's and Cornyn's voices is made more manifest in the rather ambiguous final sentence of the introduction to "Eye Witness": "Stan Cornyn has tried his level best, re-creating a composite of those many nights, many sessions, many albums with many cast changes, but with one voice constant" (55). In so many ways that constant voice was the annotator's as much as the singer's.

4. In 1963, by selling his controlling interest in Reprise, Sinatra "had at last achieved what he had originally set out to do at Capitol in 1959: run his own subsidiary label where he could call the shots and yet let someone else sign the checks. And that's without taking into consideration the millions that went into his own pockets" (Friedwald 415–416).

5. Cornyn would annotate albums for other Reprise artists and members of the Rat Pack (e.g., Dean Martin's 1965 *Houston* and Sammy Davis Jr.'s 1966 *Sammy Davis Jr. Sings, Laurindo Almeida Plays*) but never with the same frequency or consistency as those he did for Sinatra.

6. Note the indebtedness to the Cornyn style of both Gene Lees's 1967 essay on the Sinatra-Jobim sessions, "The Performance and the Pain" (130–132) and Paul "Bono" Hewson's introduction of Sinatra at the 1994 Grammy Awards (213–214).

7. Gay Talese, during the mid-1960s, would publish two pieces of "New Journalism" on Sinatra. For *The New York Times*, in July 1965, he would write "Sinatra Means a Jumping Jilly's and a Lot Less Sleep for Another Cat at His Favorite Bar" and, for the April 1966 issue of *Esquire*, the now-classic "Frank Sinatra Has a Cold."

8. The appreciation may be Cornyn's, the collaborators', or, as in the case of

Frank Sinatra: The World We Knew, the singer's. Underneath a candid photograph of Sinatra, in suit and tie, sitting on a trunk and smiling somewhat bashfully: "And then, after a time, he moves to one side. He sits down on raw wood. Listens back to his voice. And, reacts like any man."

9. Consider, for example, "It has begun like the World Soft Championships. The songs, mostly by Antonio Carlos Jobim. Tender melodies. Tender like a two-day, lobster-red Rio sunburn, so tender they'd scream agony if handled rough. Slap one of his fragile songs on the back with a couple of trumpets? Like washing crystal in a cement mixer" (Cornyn, "At Last").

10. Interestingly, it is the absence of war in the *Moonlight Sinatra* liner notes of the very same year that, in Cornyn's view, distinguishes the timeless Sinatra from the fleeting folk singers: "To sing of the Moon, and not of missiles . . . is old-fashioned."

11. See "At 7 PM the orchestra, assembled here with much the same care that went into assembling the Invasion of Normandy, is ready" (Cornyn, "Anchovy").

12. Cornyn would use anaphora for *Ol' Blue Eyes Is Back* (1973), as well: "He is maybe a bit tanner. He sings with his hands on top of the music stand. . . . He sings and it's the voice. . . . He is still, no contest, the best this world knows."

13. Cornyn also alludes to or incorporates the title of the album into his notes for *September of My Years* (1965), *Strangers in the Night* (1966), *My Way* (1969), and *Ol' Blue Eyes Is Back* (1973).

14. This is a theme that Cornyn will return to again and again in liner notes. Note the past-meets-present theme of "After All These Years" on the back of *Francis A. & Edward K.* (1968).

15. Sinatra's joking at recording sessions is stressed repeatedly by Cornyn (e.g., "That was an *old* Chesterfield that just came up on me. Around 1947, it felt like" [1967]; "Let's play some dirty songs" [1968]; "I just figured I'd do some work. No fun trying to hit a golf ball at eight at night" [1973]; "Anybody got any oxygen?" [1984]). The lameness of the humor only leads Cornyn to another conclusion about the man's power. As he writes in "On Sinatra or How to Be Timeless Tonight," "And if he tosses off a tired joke about his tired tonsils . . . If he smiles about hoping one of his kids comes along soon so he can retire . . . If he clears his throat with a line about having just swallowed a shot glass, the people all laugh. If they didn't, he'd know he was in trouble. When they stop laughing, then you're in trouble. But Frank ain't in no trouble."

16. On *Francis A. & Edward K.* (1968), his singing even eclipses the beauty of roses given to Duke Ellington for his birthday; on *L.A. Is My Lady* (1984), Sinatra in the studio resembles a rite of spring.

17. On *Ol' Blue Eyes Is Back* (1973), Cornyn seems to satirize his own hyperbole by quoting the "record executive" who "whispers in anticipation . . . how he wants to 'go on the road with this album and compare him . . . to Lincoln.' " It might be argued that due to the critical distance made possible by Sinatra's two-year retirement, the writer rethought some of the immoderation of earlier notes.

18. Sinatra, on the Capitol CD *Sinatra 80th: Live in Concert* (1995), addresses his categorization as a "saloon singer" in his introduction to "Angel Eyes," recorded 24 October 1987 at the Reunion Arena in Dallas, Texas.

19. Cornyn would become Executive Vice President of Warner Brothers Records ("Eye Witness" 55).

20. Michael Schudson describes advertising as "capitalist realism," which tries to "picture reality as it should be—life and lives worth emulating" (85). Cornyn's depiction of Sinatra, with its mix of grandeur and humanity, certainly presents the singer as an exemplum to which the audience might aspire.

WORKS CITED

Cahn, Sammy, and James Van Heusen. "Notes." *Only the Lonely*. W-1053. Capitol Records, 1958.

Cornyn, Stan. "After All These Years." *Francis A. & Edward K*. FS-1024. Reprise Records, 1968.

———. " 'The Anchovy Tonight Is an Endangered Species.' " *L.A. Is My Lady*. QWest 25145. QWest Records, 1984.

———. "At Last." *Francis Albert Sinatra & Antonio Carlos Jobim*. FS-1021. Reprise Records, 1967.

———. "A Conversation with Mr. Jones." *It Might As Well Be Swing*. FS-1012. Reprise Records, 1964.

———. "Eye Witness." *FAS: Frank Sinatra—The Complete Reprise Studio Recordings*. 46013–2. Reprise Records, 1995: pp. 55–74.

———. "Francis Albert Sinatra (b. 12 December 1915, Hoboken, NJ)." *Sinatra: A Man and His Music*. 2FS-1016. Reprise Records, 1965.

———. "Frank Sinatra Sings All There Is to Know About Love." *Softly, As I Leave You*. FS-1013. Reprise Records, 1964.

———. "Frank Sinatra Sings of Days and Loves Ago." *September of My Years*. FS-1014. Reprise Records, 1965.

———. "Frank Sinatra Sings the Greatest Songs from Musical Comedy: An Interview with Sonny Burke." *My Kind of Broadway*. FS-1015. Reprise Records, 1965.

———. "My, My." *That's Life*. FS-1020. Reprise Records, 1966.

———. "On Sinatra or How to Be Timeless Tonight." *Strangers in the Night*. FS-1017. Reprise Records, 1966.

———. "Sinatra at the Sands." *Sinatra at the Sands with Count Basie and the Orchestra*. 2FS-1019. Reprise Records, 1966.

———. "The Singer Today: An Interview with Jimmy Bowen." *Sinatra '65*. RS-6167. Reprise Records, 1965.

———. Untitled. *Frank Sinatra: The World We Knew*. FS-1022. Reprise Records, 1967.

———. Untitled. *Moonlight Sinatra*. FS-1018. Reprise Records, 1966.

———. Untitled. *My Way*. FS-1029. Reprise Records, 1969.

———. Untitled. *Ol' Blue Eyes Is Back*. FS-2155. Reprise Records, 1973.

Friedwald, Will. Sinatra! *The Song Is You: A Singer's Art*. New York: Scribner's, 1995.

Gleason, Ralph J. "Frank: Then and Now." *The Frank Sinatra Reader*. Ed. Steven Petkov and Leonard Mustazza. New York: Oxford University Press, 1995: pp. 225–227.

———. "Notes by Ralph J. Gleason." *No One Cares*. W-1221. Capitol Records, 1959.

Hewson, Paul "Bono." "Introduction: Lifetime Achievement Award." *Legend: Frank Sinatra and the American Dream*. Ed. Ethlie Ann Vare. New York: Boulevard Books, 1995: pp. 213–214.

Kaplan, Mike, ed. *Variety Presents the Complete Book of Major U.S. Show Business Awards*. New York: Garland, 1985.

Kutler, Stanley I., ed. *The Encyclopedia of the Vietnam War*. New York: Scribner's, 1996.

Lanham, Richard A. *A Handlist of Rhetorical Terms*. 2nd ed. Berkeley: University of California Press, 1991.

Lees, Gene. "The Performance and the Pain." *Sinatra: The Man and His Music— The Recording Artistry of Francis Albert Sinatra, 1939–1992*. Eds. Ed O'Brien and Scott P. Sayers, Jr. Austin, TX: TSD Press, 1992: pp. 130–132.

Morris, Charles. *Signs, Language, and Behavior*. New York: Prentice-Hall, 1946.

Rockwell, John. *Sinatra: An American Classic*. New York: Random House/Rolling Stone Press, 1984.

Scholes, Robert. *Protocols of Reading*. New Haven: Yale University Press, 1989.

Schudson, Michael. *Advertising: The Uneasy Persuasion*. New York: Basic Books, 1984.

Talese, Gay. "Frank Sinatra Has a Cold." *The Frank Sinatra Reader*. Ed. Steven Petkov and Leonard Mustazza. New York: Oxford University Press, 1995: pp. 99–129.

———. "Sinatra Means a Jumping Jilly's and a Lot Less Sleep for Another Cat at His Favorite Bar." *Legend: Frank Sinatra and the American Dream*. Ed. Ethlie Ann Vare. New York: Boulevard Books, 1995: pp. 91–92.

Wicke, Jennifer. *Advertising Fictions: Literature, Advertisement, and Social Reading*. New York: Columbia University Press, 1988.

Wolfe, Tom. "The Birth of 'The New Journalism': Eyewitness Report by Tom Wolfe." *New York*, 14 February 1972: Cover, 30–38, 43–45.

Sinatra's Fans: Discussions in Three Tenses—The Past, the Present, and the Future

KEN HUTCHINS

Frank Sinatra's musical career has spanned seven decades, and, from his first public appearances in 1935 with Major Bowes to his last public performance at the Frank Sinatra Celebrity Invitational Golf Tournament in February of 1995, he has significantly influenced the course of American popular culture. As the consummate interpreter of the Great American Songbook, Sinatra's influence has touched those familiar with his recordings, concerts, radio and television appearances, movies, and even "rock videos" with Bono of U2 fame. It seems that almost all of the songs that Sinatra sang *are* the American popular standards. Prior to his death in May 1998, while living the life a retired troubadour, Sinatra continued to influence his fans worldwide—fans from all age groups. Indeed, in a manner that mimics the three sections of Sinatra's biggest album release, *Trilogy* (Reprise 1980), his career and his fans' enthusiastic responses to it can be seen in three distinct cycles: the past (1940s), the present (1950s–1990s), and the future.

THE PAST

Frank Sinatra's earliest singing can be traced to many small clubs, union halls, and bars in the northern New Jersey and New York City area in the early to mid-1930s. Perhaps the earliest documented performance is from WAAT, Jersey City, featuring Frank Sinatra broadcasting from 5:15 to 5:30 on April 16, 1935. It is possible that Sinatra appeared on the station as early as 1932, occasionally backed by guitarist Tony Mottola. While these performances provided a valuable "education" for the young singer, they certainly did not cause the pandemonium and rioting that occurred at later performances at New York's Paramount Theatre. It would be hard to identify any fans of Sinatra who could actually trace the source of their devotion to Sinatra to these earliest performances.

Frank Sinatra's first documented vocal performances are two songs that exist from the *Major Bowes' Original Amateur Hour*, on which he appeared as a member of the Hoboken Four. Recordings of these two songs, "Shine" and "The Curse of an Aching Heart," have been in the hands of collectors for many years. "The Curse of an Aching Heart" is from an aircheck transcribed on September 4, 1935, while "Shine" survives from an aircheck of a September 8, 1935, performance at New York's Capitol Theatre. These performances by a singing group contrived by Major Bowes himself (Sinatra was to appear as a soloist, while a trio from Hoboken was also scheduled for the program) produced enough reaction to Murray Hill 8-9933 and the on-stage audiometer to secure a place for the group with the Bowes traveling show. Traveling with the *Major Bowes Amateur Show* would lead to a steady income of $50 per week, a movie short featuring "Shine" (which does not appear to have survived), and ultimately a trip to the West Coast, where Sinatra left the tour and the group to return to New Jersey. While many people liked the performances of the Hoboken Four, it was difficult to determine Sinatra's influence. In fact, Sinatra sang "Shine" in a boo-boo-booing style that was closer to Bing Crosby's than the one that Sinatra would later cultivate as a big-band singer.

After Sinatra's appearances with Major Bowes, he returned to the sustaining broadcasts on WAAT and to singing at various club dates throughout northern New Jersey. An outgrowth of one such event survives with Sinatra appearing on Fred Allen's May 12, 1937, show, as conductor (!) of The Four Sharps. While these appearances excited the girls in the Newark area, there still was not enough substance to have a concentrated group of people become interested in the music of Frank Sinatra. The singer's two main venues in the late 1930s were the Rustic Cabin (on scenic Route 9W in Englewood Cliffs, New Jersey) with its important "wire" that was used to broadcast over New York's WNEW radio station, and radio broadcasts for carfare from New York radio stations WOR and WNEW. One of the less memorable events from these performances occurred when Sinatra attempted to sing "Night and Day" to Cole Porter at the Rustic Cabin. As luck would have it, Sinatra forgot the words!

However, the Rustic Cabin did provide Sinatra with his next opportunity. In the summer of 1939, Harry James was looking for a "boy" singer. James, who was in New York at the time, heard the broadcast from the Cabin over WNEW and liked what he heard. The next night, James went over to the Rustic Cabin to see the boy singer. After singing a few songs for James that night, Sinatra auditioned at the famed Paramount Theatre the next day. Sinatra now had his first major break. His first appearance with the Harry James Orchestra occurred on June 30, 1939, at Baltimore's Hippodrome Theatre. Sinatraphiles are in disagreement over whether any airchecks survive from this date. Two songs that were on the program for that first appearance, "My Love for You" and "Wishing (Will Make It So)," do survive from later remote broadcasts.

Sinatra and the James band returned to New York for an engagement at the famed Roseland Ballroom as early as July 8, 1939. Aircheck recordings exist for several broadcasts from that engagement (which have been issued on Columbia's *Harry James and His Orchestra Featuring Frank Sinatra: The Complete Recordings*). The first Harry James–Sinatra recording session dates from July 13, 1939, when "From the Bottom of My Heart" and "Melancholy Mood" were recorded. Collectors have paid over $500 for a copy of the original 78-rpm record of "From the Bottom of My Heart." Airchecks also exist for performances from Atlantic City's famed Marine Ballroom on the Steel Pier (late July and early August 1939), the Roseland Ballroom (July and August 1939), the 1939 World's Fair in Flushing, New York (August 31 and September 14, 1939), and Victor Hugo's in Hollywood, California (November 9, 1939). During the last of these engagements, Sinatra even suffered the abuse of a drunken fan who shoved the microphone in Sinatra's face.

One telling aspect of the popularity of Frank Sinatra can be seen in what is thought by many to be Sinatra's first hit song, "All or Nothing at All." The record sold all of 8000 copies when first issued by Columbia in 1939, about half of what a good hit would have sold at that time. Still, the recording, which would sell many more copies when Columbia reissued it during the peak of Sinatra's popularity, reveals many of the classic stylistic mannerisms that would define his style for years to come. And for the skinny kid from Hoboken, it was The Voice that eventually thrilled millions and that would capture the hearts and minds of millions of bobby-soxers during the World War II era.

Frank Sinatra joined the Tommy Dorsey Orchestra in January of 1940. His first recording with Dorsey, "The Sky Fell Down," was made shortly after joining the orchestra. The first major hit for Sinatra with the Dorsey orchestra was "I'll Never Smile Again." This was the first of twenty songs that made *Billboard*'s top ten list between 1940 and 1942. In addition to recordings with the Dorsey orchestra, there were two feature films that showcased the band and its boy singer: *Las Vegas Nights* and *Ship Ahoy*. Dorsey's orchestra was also featured on many big-band remotes, and Sinatra's prominent place in the orchestra enabled him to be voted top band singer during his tenure with Dorsey. Sinatra's growing popularity enabled him to record four solo recordings, with arrangements by Axel Stordahl, in January of 1942. Two of these songs, "The Song Is You" and "Night and Day," would be long associated with Sinatra's recording career. Eventually, the singer decided he wanted to try a solo career, and Sinatra's last recording with Dorsey occurred in July of 1942. In fact, Sinatra's last few performances amounted to an extended farewell tour.

After leaving the Tommy Dorsey Orchestra, Sinatra initially lost the wherewithal to keep his image in the eyes of the public. Although several sustaining radio shows and an appearance in the film *Reveille with Beverly* singing "Night and Day" would help to keep Sinatra's presence felt, the next defining moment for Sinatra was his appearance at the Paramount Theatre, as an "added attraction" to the Benny Goodman Orchestra. With this late December 1942 appearance, Sinatra became an immediate media star. The bobby-soxers screamed and swooned, something they would continue to do for the next five years.

Sinatra's fame was accompanied by a growing number of fan clubs, composed mostly of young girls who met to read and discuss the exploits of their hero, Frankie. According to E. J. Kahn, Jr., author of the first book on Sinatra, *The Voice: The Story of an American Phenomenon* (1947), there were 2000 fans clubs by 1947, each consisting of about 200 members. These fan clubs were typically comprised of people who lived within the local neighborhood of the club. In some cases, membership cards were produced. Mostly the groups gathered together to listen and swoon to Sinatra's music. The fans followed his every movement, camped out near his New Jersey home, mobbed and screamed at his concerts and radio performances and couldn't wait until his new recordings were released. Through it all, they loved Sinatra. Some of the names of those early fan clubs were The Singing Society of Sinatra Swooners, Slaves of Sinatra, Girls Who Would Lay Down Their Lives and Die for Frank Sinatra, Frank Sinatra Fan and Mah-Jong Club, and The Sinatrettes. One of the names of the clubs associated with Sinatra was Moonlight Sinatra, foreshadowing the name of the last great album Sinatra would record with Nelson Riddle. One such club even published a newsletter called "Swoon Time News."

Then, almost as soon as it began, Sinatra's popularity began to diminish. By 1949, the sale of his records diminished sharply, and some of his movie performances were being panned. (Portraying a priest may have helped Bing Crosby's career, but *The Miracle of the Bells* did not do wonders for Sinatra's.) Moreover, the press, previously friendly to the rising performer, turned against Sinatra at this time, mostly because of his failing relationship with his first wife, Nancy. By 1952, his recording contract at Columbia was cancelled, and his movie career appeared finished, too. Although he remained on the radio and he still sang in public, it was apparent to many that Sinatra's star had faded. Yes, there were still fans who were loyal to Frankie, but those numbers were greatly reduced. Eventually, most of the Swoonatra clubs disbanded, just a faded memory of days gone by.

THE PRESENT

Fans began to rediscover Frank Sinatra with his early recordings at Capitol Records and his Academy Award-winning performance as Maggio in *From Here to Eternity*. At Capitol, Sinatra met and began his long collaboration with arranger Nelson Riddle, whose excellent arrangements, matched with Sinatra's mature singing and new image as a "swinger," rekindled a career that almost everyone had considered over. The most interesting aspect of Sinatra's rebirth lay in the fact that he no longer appealed mainly to women. At this point in his career, many of Sinatra's fans were men, drawn initially as much to Sinatra's style as the music. The 1950s also saw the re-establishment of Sinatra fan clubs, only now their membership was word-wide rather than merely local, as was the case in the 1940s.

In the United Kingdom, The Sinatra Music Society (SMS) was established in 1955 and continues until this day, over forty years later. This club issues a publication called *Perfectly Frank*, which for many years has been the standard for all other Sinatra fan-club publications. The Sinatra Music Society encourages local gatherings throughout England or wherever a group of fans can congregate to discuss Sinatra and related performers.

In Australia, the International Sinatra Society was created to provide a locally supported publication and fan club for fans from "down under," where Sinatra has been a major presence since 1955, when he first performed there. By the 1980s, the United States became home of the International Sinatra Society under the leadership of the late Gary Doctor, who published the bimonthly *International Sinatra Society Magazine*.

Focusing on a key "hotbed" of Sinatra fans, The Sinatra Social Society caters to members in the Philadelphia area. While its newsletter often reprints newspaper articles, there are also original articles written by its members, and, in keeping with its social nature, the fans get together twice a year for a summertime swim-club meeting and for the annual Frank Sinatra Birthday Dinner.

Sid Mark, the host of the nationally syndicated radio show called *The Sounds of Sinatra*, is the head of The Sidnatra Club. This club produces a periodic newsletter that features press releases, interviews, and updates on many topics related to Sinatra. Orange Productions, which syndicates the radio show, also distributes the complete line of Reprise videos and other merchandise.

Other societies include the Sinatra societies of Japan, Holland, Belgium, and Sweden—all producing newsletters with features similar to those described above. The one common feature of all of the Sinatra societies is the one-way distribution of information. While subscribers may contribute articles and photographs for submission, these publications are really prepared by the editor for distribution to subscribers. This form of communication allows for information to be disseminated, but does not encourage or enable continuous and ongoing dialogues, nor do the publications offer a forum for asking and replying to questions.

THE FUTURE

As we come to the 1990s, the impact of the Internet is everywhere. Today, we cannot read the newspaper, watch television, see a movie, or even listen to the radio without noticing some reference to the Internet generally and the World Wide Web specifically. Even if you do not know much about the web, you can't help but notice its addresses (e.g., WWW.MY_SLOGAN.COM) appearing on television commercials and newspaper ads. When it comes to discussing Frank Sinatra, it turns out that the Internet is now one of the easiest ways for fans to engage in the worldwide exchange of information. Early on, however, there were major problems with this medium, notably with where to find such information and how to determine its quality.

The major on-line services have all offered discussion areas that featured topics related to the music of Frank Sinatra, but none of them was entirely satisfactory to the real Sinatra fan. For example, Prodigy had a musical-interest area that featured an area to support Frank Sinatra discussions. CompuServe had a jazz-oriented music area in which people would talk about Sinatra. America OnLine had an area sponsored by Warner Brothers/Reprise. Although these areas served a certain segment of the Sinatra fan population, the closed approach to information led them to lapse into fairly routine postings. The Prodigy discussions, for instance, focused mostly on individuals' favorite recordings—a limited and limiting discussion, at best.

One of the most hyped features of the Internet is the fact that it contains a wealth of information. The pundits usually follow that often-accurate comment with this caveat: "if you can find it!" That was one of the many limiting factors of trying to establish a broadly supported Sinatra discussion group at an on-line service. Even though more and more people were being connected to the Internet in the early 1990s, there was really no central discussion group that everyone could join and where they could take part in the serious exchange of information. In addition, one of the challenges to discussion-oriented groups themselves was that the messages tended to be lost after the conversations ended. This led to the question of where to find reference information that could help supplement the on-line discussion groups.

Several initial attempts were made to start a place on the Internet to talk about Sinatra. My own first experiences came in late 1993, when I was a subscriber to Prodigy. Located within one of the musical facilities was a small discussion group that focused on Sinatra. At the time, however, Prodigy was plagued with a poor user interface and a screen that was almost half consumed with advertisements. There were two other limiting factors that hurt Prodigy as a place to house a permanent discussion group on Sinatra. First and foremost, Prodigy suffered mostly from a lack of subscribers. It was third, in 1993, in the number of on-line subscribers. Second, the level of discussion tended to be far too personal. While there were a few people discussing Sinatra, most of the postings seemed to exchange personal information about the subscribers rather than actually discussing the subject. Beyond the exchange of opinions on the top records recorded by Sinatra, there wasn't much of real interest or use being exchanged.

Next on the scene was America OnLine (AOL). Here was an opportunity to have a fully graphical user interface, with all its benefits, along with a growing number of subscribers. While it was not the largest in 1993, it would soon grow to become just that. Nevertheless, even on AOL, information on Sinatra was isolated in small interest areas. As near as I could tell, the only place to discuss Sinatra was in the Warner Brothers/Reprise sponsored area—a discussion group designed to exchange information about the many artists who recorded for those labels, one of those artists being Frank Sinatra. In this discussion area, many questions were asked, some opinions were expressed, but very few answers were forthcoming. The site's sponsor, moreover, would not comment on releases of Sinatra recordings other than those issued on Reprise, and many of the people were like the typical Prodigy users, focusing on only a few songs and offering very little analytical depth. After I'd spent a few months at AOL, it became apparent that, while AOL is a fine service for many people, it was not the likely home of a major Internet service devoted to discussions of Frank Sinatra by serious fans. Although AOL's chat rooms provide one way for a limited group of people to have a dialogue for a period of time, these transient chat rooms come and go like April snow. Nothing lasting or easily accessible could exist at this service.

I also tried CompuServe, at the time (1994) the leading provider of on-line services and one of the oldest, dating back to the late 1960s. CompuServe has usually been described as a "computer jockey" support service. While that service was of some interest, my most pressing requirement was where to discuss Frank Sinatra. I quickly found that, here too, there was no single discussion area focused solely on Frank Sinatra. However, there was an interesting jazz/big-band-oriented discussion group in a musical forum. After separating the jazz and big-band postings, I did see some Sinatra-related postings. One of the member names actually looked familiar—a guy who went by the name Uncle Wilsci and who was exchanging some serious questions and answers about Sinatra. I sent an e-mail to this CompuServe i.d., and, to my delight and surprise, Uncle Wilsci turned out to be Will Friedwald, author of many pieces on music, including the book *Jazz Singing*, a variety of compact-disc liner notes, and a forthcoming musical biography of Frank Sinatra. Remember, this was early 1994, and *Sinatra! The Song Is You* was still over a year from publication. At the time, Will Friedwald needed some information on people who had worked with Sinatra, and I was able to supply some of that information. From that brief exchange, a friendship began.

Several other people were in those CompuServe discussion groups as well. One such person was Doug Mataconis, who had followed Sinatra Internet discussions for many years. After identifying a couple of devoted Frankenmavens, we started to converse privately about the possibility of creating either a newsgroup or mailing list. Back in the summer of 1994, there was no such group. However, we did discover that a student in the Midwest was trying to start a newsgroup and that a guy up north, in Canada, was talking about a Sinatra web page. Wow, there actually *was* interest in Sinatra on the Internet!

In late summer 1994, Canadian Bill Denton started both a Sinatra web page and a mailing list devoted to Frank Sinatra. Among the initial list subscribers were Doug, Wilsci, myself, and a few others, and, at last, we really started to have some interesting dialogues. Some of the information exchanged even appeared on Bill's web page. Unfortunately, though, it did not last. Just as we were ready to talk about *Duets II*, Bill had to kill the mailing list. As Bill describes the environment, the mailing list server "imploded," most likely because of the small volume of hits. By October of 1994, the number of Sinatra fans who found this site numbered fewer than fifty, and there were only a few handfuls of Sinatra e-mail a day. A new home had to be found so that the growing number of networked Sinatra fans could get together and exchange information.

It was obvious to us that we had the capabilities, we had some interest, and now all we needed was the girl. For that, Eleanor Cicinsky appeared and volunteered to house the Frank Sinatra Internet Mailing List at Temple University. As an existing list owner, Eleanor was capable of running a mailing list and could work with the kind systems support staff at Temple (many thanks to Temple's list master, Stan Horwitz). With these items falling into place, the new mailing list was created during the Thanksgiving Day weekend of 1994. The Internet once again had a place to discuss Frank Sinatra!

The number of subscribers grew from fifty to over one hundred people within a few months, and, unlike the earlier on-line discussion forums, here there were many topics discussed, from concerts and recordings to radio and movie performances. As we talked about Sinatra, we also talked about ourselves, although not always directly. In one of those unique occurrences of shared memory and experiences, we had become a family, with new people finding the mailing list every day. Eventually, it grew to well over 400 subscribers from a variety of countries, including Australia, Brazil, Norway, Holland, England, Germany, and the Philippines.

Most interestingly perhaps, just as Sinatra did not perform in a vacuum, so the Sinatra list does not exist without discussing the people who were influenced by Sinatra, and people who influenced Sinatra himself—professors, administrators, teachers, writers, singers (Jon Secada was a list member for a few months), computer people, and just people devoted to Frank Sinatra. We also had a link to the bobby-soxers. People like Janet Cohen, who was one of the original bobby-soxers, discovered the list and was able to convey what it was like to be a fan of Sinatra back in the 1940s.

As with all social gatherings, however, the Sinatra mailing list is subject to the kinds of tensions that cause disagreement among various groups and individuals, and some uncivil behavior even invaded the list. To many long-time subscribers, the list appeared to be crumbling and falling apart. Given this state of affairs, Eleanor decided to send a note to the membership indicating that the list would be closing. The outcry matched the cries of England at the turn of the century when Conan Doyle decided he had had enough of Sherlock Holmes! The outpouring of e-mails, questioning why the list was closing, was overwhelming. These e-mails revealed a hidden interest in the mailing list that was virtually unknown to the active participants. With several impassioned pleas to keep the list going and some protective measures to help the list to survive the periodic bursts of destructive behavior, Eleanor agreed to carry on, and the list should continue to thrive for many years into the future. (To subscribe to the Sinatra Internet mailing list, send an electronic message to LISTSERV@VM.TEMPLE.EDU with the body of the message consisting of the words SUBSCRIBE SINATRA. After you have subscribed, you can send your comments and messages to a group of about 300 devoted fans of Sinatra by sending electronic mail messages to SINATRA@VM.TEMPLE.EDU.)

Complementing the discussions on the Frank Sinatra Internet mailing list are the various Frank Sinatra web sites that exist to provide information on Sinatra. There are two official sites. First, Nancy Sinatra runs a site (http://www.sinatrafamily.com) containing updates and comments on Frank Sinatra and the entire family. Each member of the family has his or her own page including photographs and commentary. Nancy Sinatra responds to e-mail via links that exist on the web page. Next, Barbara Sinatra is involved with the Barbara Sinatra Children's Center. The Center has recently started a web site (http://www.sinatracenter.com) that includes information on many of the things related to the BSCC, including their fundraising activities, the annual Frank Sinatra Celebrity Invitational Golf Tournament, and the *Frank Sinatra Celebrity Cookbook.*

The oldest and best web site devoted to all aspects of Frank Sinatra is Bill Denton's site (http://www.vex.net/~buff/sinatra), a labor of love started in the summer of 1994. Over the years, it has grown with many sections and links including a searchable Frankspeak index, a discography, and a song-lyric project.

The Frank Sinatra Internet mailing list has had for several years an associated web page. Joe Berg's Sinatra mailing list home page (http://www.sinatralist.com) has been the repository for information that has been distributed through the Sinatra Internet mailing list. Included at this site are an extensive listing of Sinatra's recordings by month (thanks to Tom Rednour) and reviews and analysis of many of Sinatra's compact-disc releases. In addition, a link to Sandy Singer's *Date with Sinatra* site is one way to listen to Sinatra through the Internet.

Several collectors also have web pages. One of the leading collectors and dealers of Sinatra memorabilia is Rick Apt's Collectibles (http://www.blue -eyes.com). Rick's site includes many rare items that are available through his mail-order business. The International Sinatra Society, run by Dustin Doctor, also has a site on the Internet (http://www.sinatraclub.com). The site features an electronic commerce-based system to order safely through the Internet various Sinatra compact discs and other items. One last site is very interesting. It is called Frank-E-Mail (http://www.pscentral.com/frank). This site translates your e-mail messages into the words of "Old Blue Eyes" (sic).

The easiest way to find any of the information on the Internet is to use the popular search engines, such as Yahoo! or InfoSeek. Just enter the word "Sinatra" and click on the search button to open a fascinating window on the life and music of Frank Sinatra! Since Internet sites change frequently, it is always advisable to use one of the many search engines in case any of the listed Internet sites changes its location or address.

CONCLUSION

Three distinct eras can be identified with Sinatra, and three different ways that fans receive and exchange information about their icon. In a sense, with on-line dialogues through mechanisms like chat rooms and mailing lists, fans of Frank Sinatra have utilized the technology of the Internet and computers to return to a style of communication evocative of the 1940s. However, with advancements in technology, those locally based conversations can extend to a worldwide audience. With the World Wide Web, information known only to a handful of people just a few years ago can be accessible to any fan of Sinatra. Even with tools like mailing lists and web browsers, paper-based "fanzines" will continue to have a place for many years to come. People still look forward to receiving their mail, which they can savor and enjoy. However, the essential elements that combine to produce a periodic fan-club publication are increasingly becoming available on the Internet. It will be just a matter of time before an entire Internet-based Sinatra fanzine will be produced by some dedicated fan. Through the correct formatting and active links, we will soon see Sinatra fan-oriented publications directly viewable on the web. As we move to the end of the twentieth century, we see Sinatra's continuing presence, transcending global wars, cold wars, the tearing down of the Berlin Wall, and now the Internet. Not bad for a simple saloon singer.

Sinatra: Psychiatric Musings

LLOYD L. SPENCER

As a board-certified psychiatrist with thirty-seven years of medical practice under my belt, I have sometimes been asked to venture an explanation of the elements of Sinatra's character and psyche that underlie his unparalleled power to move, motivate, and exhilarate through the medium of popular song. I've come up with a few observations, but, without prodding, I'm not much inclined to analyze anyone. Besides, it would be unethical to offer a psychiatric opinion without a personal evaluation, permission, and, preferably, lots of information from close friends and relatives. When the invitation to contribute to this book came along, however, I couldn't help myself. I would analyze Sinatra—but purely from a personal perspective. And so, what you are reading is less scientific analysis and more the musings of a mad medicine man (a popular media portrayal of the psychiatrist).

Before setting finger to key I sat back, closed my eyes, and mused, drifting back forty-four years to an icy subzero January day in Joliet, Illinois. I was a freshman at "the first public junior college" and making some money on the side delivering the gym towels to the large Joliet Township High School and Junior College. My "van" was a black, four-door, 1941 Chevy sedan, from which I'd removed all the seats, front and rear, and bolted in a Model A bucket seat from Lockhart's Salvage. One dark 6 A.M. on the icy road, out of nowhere (well, out of my Motorola, at any rate), came these words:

Fairy tales can come true.
It can happen to you,
If you're young at heart.

What's that? The road melted away as I was riveted by each word and phrase. "Come on, tell me the rest of the story," I urged.

You can go to extremes with impossible schemes.
You can laugh when your dreams fall apart at the seams.
And life gets more exciting with each passing day.
And love is either in your heart, or on its way.

When it was over (too soon!), I wondered who the singer was. The DJ must have heard me: "That was Frank Sinatra, and I predict he's going to make a comeback." Wow! I'd thought he was dead. The twig who'd entranced the bobby-soxers, who'd proclaimed he could sing better than Bing, who'd not suited up for World War II (though we now know he did his best to enlist). These were cardinal sins to us boys in the forties. But when he smote my young heart that winter morning, I forgave him instantly.

Over the ensuing months, I reveled in my "discovery," and, as it turned out, I wasn't alone. Sinatra was a household word again. But the skinny Swooner had become the suave Swinger, and the sky was the limit. I began listening to a lot of Sinatra, and songs I had heard a hundred times before took on fresh meaning, blossoming to maturity. The tunes of Irving Berlin, Cole Porter, Jerome Kern, George and Ira Gershwin, Richard Rodgers and Lorenz Hart, Sammy Cahn, and many others came fully alive for the first time, now conveying the depth and excitement, the nuance and poignancy, that these gifted men had intended but had heard only in their wildest dreams.

By 1956, the world was my oyster. I was settled into the University of Illinois College of Medicine's class of 1960 and doing well academically and socially. I was about to be engaged to the loveliest, most loving, and most beautiful girl I'd ever known (now my wife of thirty-nine years). Then, with little warning, I was plunged to the bottom of a dark, dank pit with sides so slippery I didn't stand a chance. It was years before I knew the name of that hell—depression. Although it didn't occur every minute of every day, I was paralyzed much of the time, curled mute in bed when I should have been in class. It got worse. And after about a year there were times when I made only one or two lectures a term (usually the first and last), if that. When I went to my counselor for help, I was advised, "Get to your classes and study more."

I tried. I cried. I almost died.

I tried Student Health. Nothing. I tried the career counseling center at the University of Chicago, believing medicine was the wrong field for me.

I paid $100 out of my pocket (a king's ransom then) and after a series of tests I met with the director, a Ph.D. psychologist, who was so impressed that I was in medical school and doing well (academically) that he told me I didn't need help and should celebrate my good fortune. I crawled back to bed. One Chief Resident in surgery whom I seldom saw sneered "Speaking of the devil" to my classmates when I showed up on the ward one day. Later that day he told me in private, "Spencer, if you ever graduate from medical school, you'll be a purulent pimple on the face of medicine." Married by then, I tried to hide all this from my wife, who would be crushed. She was nineteen, living in a strange big city, and pregnant. I didn't think she knew that I was home in bed or wandering around Chicago while she was working in the blood bank at the university.

One morning I lay in a fitful sleep, broken by crazy tortured dreams, when BAM! A bolt of song blasted a boogeyman.

> I've got the world on a string, sittin' on a rainbow,
> Got the string around my finger,
> What a world, what a life, I'm in love!

Betty had put on Sinatra as she left for work that morning. Slowly my corpuscles began to stir, carrying little buckets of oxygen to my brain and muscles. "I've got a song that I sing. I can make the rain go. . . ." A twitch, an eye opened, I dug myself out of bed. "What a world. Man, this is the life. . . ." I actually dressed, and through some miracle made it to class that morning. "Hey, now! I'm so in lovvvvvve. . . ." Thank you, Sweetheart. My one and only love. Sinatra became my daily wake-up call, and I started making a lot of classes. And in that pre-Walkman era, I waltzed through the wards with "Lucky me, can't you see, I'm in love!" swingin' in my head with the crystal clarity of a gold CD and a $10,000 stereo.

When our son, Darren, was born in 1960, I took a day off from school and went to Marshall Field's in the Loop to get an anniversary gift for my brother and his wife. While browsing, I found a new Sinatra album, *Nice 'n' Easy*. I debated a good hour (including more browsing) over the stereo versus the monaural version. In the end I picked the monaural and saved a buck. Less music, more baby food. I got home, put it on, and kicked back. Before long:

> She may be waiting,
> just anticipating
> things she may never possess.
> While she's without them,
> try a little tenderness.

Neon images from the past! Betty's green quilted dress, not shabby, but worn . . . Cardboard in her shoes . . . Only Christmas gift a white scarf for the cold five-mile walk home from school . . . No plumbing . . . Dreaming over the pages of *Modern Screen*. . . . Hot tears tumbled down my cheeks and neck. I ran to the hospital and held her, murmuring, kissing, caressing, vowing to cradle her forever.

Fast forward two years: Dori with the Laughing Face is born on the fifth of July, the first day of my residency at the University of Iowa. The World War II barracks is an oven. Sinatra coos "Try a little tenderness" from our hybrid stereo, and I melt down again. Roses, a trip to Sears for an automatic washer (pre-Pampers). I hook it up. Then scrub, vacuum, and dust 'til I drop. The cost of tenderness in dollars and sweat has gone up.

The years whip by. How many records, songs, tears, and kisses? How much hooting and dancing, tenderness and loving? How little depression? How few pills?

December 1988: For two years, they said it was nothing. Although those lumps in Betty's neck haven't grown, they just don't belong there. It's cancer of the thyroid. And it's all through her neck and down into her chest. We get the news on the twentieth. Nice Christmas present. A white scarf would have been lovely. I'm in the car heading into town for groceries, stomach in a knot. I push in the tape, and it's Sinatra singing the slow Reprise version:

> Have yourself a merry little Christmas.
> Let your heart be light.
> Next year all our troubles will be out of sight.

Streaming tears of joy! When FS says it'll be all right next year, you'd better believe it. This man doesn't bullshit. When I got home I had Betty listen, and she knew it, too. Thank you again, Mr. Sinatra, for that Yuletide gift. Imagine the miles of pain you have erased. The acres of joy to millions. Thank you!

Where is all of this leading? Well, I'm a psychiatrist fighting Demon Depression to the death. The pills work much of the time, but without proper diagnosis and skillful medication management, you end up using a file to drive a nail, or a dull file to smooth a psychic burr. Proper diagnosis and management take time. Psychotherapy also works, but takes even more time. And in today's climate of HMOs and other managed cares, the premium is upon quick and affordable. We need more tools, more weapons, to root out and stamp out depression. Do we have alternatives? Yes. Try running regularly. Try lots of brisk walking. Try meditation. Try listening to the boy singer, Sinatra!

I have given many tapes to patients. Always hand-picked songs and custom introductions (not always Sinatra). And my patients get better. But how do you separate the gift from the giver, the "thought" from the gift, the songs from the pills? I haven't tried. Too much depression. Too little time. But we will have to answer these questions soon. Fortunately we now have sophisticated brain imaging techniques at our disposal. When we look at the brains of depressed persons, we find they can be distinguished from those of non-depressed "controls." There are several chemical and meta-bolic differences (like the rates of sugar and oxygen consumption in very discrete brain structures) that show return to normal following treatment with potent medications. We find, moreover, that these same changes can often be wrought through non-chemical interventions, such as psychother-apy—and, perhaps, songs by Sinatra! It takes little imagination to envision a time, not too far distant, when selective music therapy for depression will be commonplace, and not just Sinatra, of course. The great classics will doubtless prove to be potent antidepressants. That is one reason they have survived.

Another is that they can be forever re-created from the original compo-sitions by new musicians and are not dependent on sound recording for their immortality. Until this century, vocal performances died with their echoes and were buried with their artists. And the vocal artistry of Caruso, Jolson, and Crosby, though not gone, remains boxed in by the limitations of their archaic recordings. Thankfully, Sinatra has not suffered that fate. Although true "high fidelity" was not possible until roughly 1950, much of Sinatra's work from about 1943 to 1950 was surprisingly well recorded and preserved. Recent re-masterings have further enhanced these recordings to the point that his emotional force and nuance emerge intact. And from 1950 to the present the fidelity of his recordings to the live performance has leaped exponentially.

I'm always astonished at the power and purity of his early Capitol re-cordings—easily capable of moving the listener at every level as much as his later works, even without stereophonic sound. But what shoots Sinatra over the top of this century and into the new millennium in company with Bach, Beethoven, Mozart, and Tchaikovsky is the advent of digital tech-nology. No longer is a singer confined to his own era. Vinyl and tape deteriorate with time, and each successive copy is less faithful to the orig-inal. But digital recordings remain forever faithful. Now Sinatra of the fifties will continue as immediate, intimate, pristine, and pure into the next century as the day he stepped into the studio or onto the concert stage. (How ironic that something so cold as binary numbers can preserve some-thing so warm and vital.) This technology will enable Sinatra to soothe a disquieted soul as much in the year 2098 as he does in 1998, or rouse a depressed student in 2159 as well as he did in 1959.

With sophisticated brain probes, close clinical observations, and scientific patience, we will soon be able to determine which music most effectively normalizes (or elevates) which moods and emotions in which persons. Clinical application will be about as simple as supplying the ailing person with appropriate music and instructions to bring about maximal healing. This will be no simplistic cure-all, but a valuable adjunct to other measures in speeding recovery. Though no one can predict which music will prove most mollifying, healing, or energizing, I believe that among vocal musicians Sinatra will stand at the top of the heap. For who other than Sinatra has moved so many millions so deeply? Many entertain, but none has the power to so deftly jolt our synapses and perk our brain chemicals as does Sinatra.

Whatever he does, it is very elemental, very visceral, and entirely universal. Our intuition tells us he is a man of great emotional range and substance who has lived the gamut of human passions. But still, how on earth is he able to penetrate so deeply into our souls and then so delicately soft, as dew kissing a leaf, pluck *I love you* on our heart strings? No one will ever know. At other times he slams us with the sizzling truth of a Joe Louis uppercut, rocking our heads and hearts to the core. No other singer has achieved such force and intimacy in rendering a lyric, each phrase sustaining the awe and wonder of a soaring Babe Ruth home run. None ever will. And, amazingly, he can hurl his ardent message from a vinyl groove with the same authority as he can from a concert stage. How in heaven?

Perhaps the simplest and most straightforward explanation comes from Sinatra, himself. I recall reading his interview in *Playboy* magazine in the early 1960s, while I was still in residency training. He was asked how he was able to communicate such feeling and intensity in his singing. (Think about that a moment. To what other singer would anyone pose that question?) He replied, "I think I get an audience involved personally in a song— because I'm involved. It's not something I do deliberately. I can't help myself. If the song is a lament at the loss of love, I get an ache in my gut. I feel the loss myself, and I cry out the loneliness, the hurt, and the pain. . . . Being an eighteen-karat manic-depressive and having lived a life of violent emotional contradictions, I have an overly acute capacity for sadness as well as elation" (quoted in Nancy Sinatra's *Frank Sinatra: My Father*, p. 209).

As a musing psychiatrist I'm inclined to put a lot of stock in that statement, especially since reading Nancy Sinatra's two excellent biographies of her father, in which she gives numerous first- and second-hand observations that flesh out Sinatra's brief sketch. At one point she writes, "Dad was an only child and often came home to an empty house. Not long after my oldest daughter, A. J., was born, he said, 'I hope you'll consider having another baby. It was lonely for me. Very lonely' " (*My Father*, p. 42). Elsewhere in the same book, she quotes a close companion: "They fly in his plane, eat his food, drink his whiskey, get fantastic gifts, are entertained internationally; and with all the friends, *he has always been a complete loner*" (p. 193, italics mine). Sinatra is not one to bare his feelings to others or talk about emotional issues with his friends. Dean Martin once said, "I don't discuss his girl with Frank, or who he's going to marry. All I discuss are movies, TV, golf and drinking" ("Sinatra: Where the Action Is," p. 94). Close friend Rosalind Russell believed the quality that best defined Sinatra was compassion. But she further observed, "one he may not like my discussing: Sinatra the loner, the constant observer, a profoundly sensitive man. . . . There have been some troublesome times, painful times, which he has harbored within himself and *shared with no one*" (Russell, p. 149, italics mine). In his famous magazine piece for *Esquire*, "Frank Sinatra Has a Cold," Gay Talese told of Sinatra singing "Nancy" in a TV studio: "the private side was in this song about the girl who, it is said, understands him better than anybody else, and is the only person in front of whom he can be unashamedly himself" (Talese, p. 6). Yet, somewhere I have read or heard that Nancy says even she cannot get her father to really open up, reveal his deeper feelings. So in whom does he confide?

One Sunday afternoon not long ago, my wife Betty and I were out for a ride, twisting through the Ozark foothills. In preparation for this article, I had been wrestling with an explanation for Sinatra's uncanny and unequaled ability to convey the scale of emotions with such force and conviction. Though always fascinated by the enormous potential of rhyme and rhythm to enhance a vocal performance dramatically, I explained to Betty that we are too rarely awed by a Laurence Olivier Shakespearean performance, that a merely "adequate" attempt ruins the message and embarrasses the actor. Now, I reasoned, as tough as Shakespeare is, just imagine adding music to it. You'd blow away most of the aspiring performers and have an art form begging for an artist.

But just such a marriage of words and music was being arranged by men like Berlin and Porter in New York City soon after the turn of the century. Tin Pan Alley, named for the cheap pianos that could be heard plinking out of music production houses up and down 28th Street, was turning out flocks of increasingly delightful songs with rich and sophisticated lyrics. But the singers weren't up to the task, especially as they strayed too far from the comedic to the dramatic. And while Bing Crosby spun the lighter songs (many of which had been written for him) with beguiling credibility, he lacked the emotional range and punch needed for more demanding works.

Then came Sinatra, setting the world of pop music on its head as he fully tamed the high-spirited Melody for the first time. Molding her into his unique ally, he breathed new life into poetry set to music, further personalizing a lyric and stamping it indelibly into our hearts and brains. I assured Betty that it wasn't all witchcraft, that he employed many proven techniques of the great composers and best musicians, but so subtly as to render these techniques nearly invisible. Above all, he had honed and crafted his art through endless toil and repetition, through decades of dynamic inter-action with his audience. Yet, I mused, his ability to transcend the lyric, transforming the very art itself and carrying us to lofty emotional pinnacles on the wings of song, remained for me one of the great mysteries of our age.

As I was rambling on like this, and looking for affirmation, I became aware of Betty's voice, a little distant: "and his feelings are probably so strong and private he's afraid to bare them directly to another person. It's safer for him to pour them out to us in song." And before I could (auto-matically) object: "That's probably why he won't write his autobiography." My mouth just hung in mid-sentence, great psychiatric mind struggling to digest this double whammy. Thoughts and images tumbled into place: Si-natra's dark loneliness and isolation. His fierce pride and sensitivity. His mercurial temper and impatience. His difficulty expressing deep emotions to those closest to him. Nancy Sinatra's words: "His passions are greater and so is his pain. . . . He suffers as violently as he loves" (*My Father*, p. 289). Sinatra's anxiety before each performance, hands trembling, know-ing at some level the force of feelings he is about to share, reveal . . . un-leash!

And write an autobiography? He has etched his life in vinyl for sixty years, articulated with such honesty and intensity that the words spin and spiral free of their grooves, silken tendrils reaching, caressing, ensnaring, and finally drawing us captive to his inner world. . . . Yes, we are his con-fidants.

Meanwhile, back at the clinic . . .

I am an excellent, even extraordinary, physician and psychiatrist. I've been hearing this for years from patients, co-workers, supervisors; even from pharmacists—and from the results of a poll of Arkansas physicians a couple of years ago. It embarrasses me to say this, but it is necessary to illustrate a point. For a man, I am above average in empathy, but only average in caring, compassion, and nurturance. I am also impatient and a little selfish. So it doesn't add up.

When I was five years old I jumped off our back porch and slipped on the ice as I turned to go up the steps for another leap, tearing a hole in my cheek on a large splinter. Blood, tears, and fear—lots of fear. My grand-father took me to the doctor. He deadened my cheek, and, as I felt the mending tug of silk through skin, Dr. Lofdahl's reassuring words calmed my fears. I floated out on a feather, pausing only while my Grandpa picked up a pack of Life Savers in the drugstore. From that day I knew I would become a doctor and combat fear. The pain was nothing. It was the fear. And except for the slight derailment I confided earlier, I've been pretty much on course the whole time.

But about twenty years ago I became a little restless. I'd always had a gnawing notion that I should go into administration or politics to make a better world, or that I should write the Great American Novel, one that would educate through drama and suspense and help eradicate the stigma of mental illness. But one memorable evening I vowed, instead, to be my very best each time a patient stepped into my office. I would be better prepared and more knowledgeable by keeping abreast of the mountains of literature. I would be well rested and more alert, no more three or four hours of sleep before a working day. I would be more intent, more curious, and more tenacious. I would be warmer, more empathetic, and more cheerful. I've been faithful to that vow ever since. I know who I am and why I'm here. I train like an athlete for my work, and sweat the details. Dedication and attention to detail moved ordinary to extraordinary and, moreover, led me to understand better the subject of this chapter, a man of *exceptional* talent, compassion, and sensitivity.

It is vital that we not overlook the enormous importance of grueling hard work to the perfection of any art. It's perhaps a little ironic that it was Thomas Edison, the father of sound recording, who observed that genius is only 1 percent inspiration and 99 percent perspiration. Sinatra has worked incredibly hard throughout his career. The endless hours of running and underwater swimming (during which he would silently sing lyrics) as one means of perfecting his legendary breath control, is one example. (I have been running for thirty years, and, fifteen or twenty years ago when I was competing in marathons and training fifty miles a week, I was able to swim underwater for over two minutes. But when trying to sing along with Sinatra in the living room or car, taking a breath only when he did, I was left far behind, gasping.) This is only one facet of Sinatra's tremendous devotion to his art. And fortunately for us, while he has often been a nonchalant one-taker on TV and in films, he has put his greatest efforts into his studio recordings. Ric Ross, Sinatra sleuth extraordinaire, once told me that Sinatra strove through thirty takes of "Last Night When We Were Young" before he was satisfied. Speaking himself of the care he puts into his recordings, Sinatra has said, "Somewhere in my subconscious there's the constant alarm that rings, telling me what we're putting on that tape might be around for a lotta, lotta years. Maybe long after we're dead and gone somebody'll put a record on and say 'Jeez, he could've done better than that' " ("Sinatra: Where the Action Is," p. 96).

Yes, he sweats the details in blood. And grades far above a "C" in caring and compassion, though the lid has been kept pretty tight on this until recently. In 1943 a twelve-year-old girl lay terrified, facing possible death from a serious throat infection that had spread from her tonsils and invaded the surrounding tissues. Although she needed surgery, her temperature had run up dangerously high and stayed there, and the doctors could do nothing. This was pre-penicillin, when germs were deadly killers. Her father, Freeman Gosden (Amos of the popular *Amos 'n' Andy* radio show), knew how much Virginia admired Sinatra. Though Gosden did not know Sinatra personally, he contacted him through a friend and explained the situation, asking if the singer would see his daughter. Gosden was shocked by Sinatra's reply: "I'll be there in twenty minutes" (Nancy Sinatra, *My Father*, p. 79). He was, and he sat on the side of Virginia's bed for another forty-five, answering her questions, telling her how he started in show business, what his favorite songs were, and many other things. Gosden says she brightened before his eyes. Sinatra kissed her cheek before leaving and promised that he would think of her every day. Four hours later a messenger arrived at the hospital with a package. Sinatra had gone to a studio and recorded a very personal get-well message for Virginia, the song "Sunday, Monday, or Always." Her fever soon broke and, after successful surgery, she went on to recover.

In 1974 Sinatra was having dinner with a longtime friend, Honolulu newspaperman Buck Buchwach. Sinatra had heard his friend was having trouble with his heart, but Buchwach made light of it. Sinatra told him to clean up his desk immediately and hop a plane for Houston to see Dr. Michael DeBakey, the famous heart surgeon. A couple of days later DeBakey peformed a double bypass. Buchwach later told daughter Nancy, "Every single day I was recuperating in Portland I received a phone call in the early afternoon from Frank, wherever he was, inquiring about my condition, kidding me, boosting my spirits, massaging my ego and transmitting as much encouragement as anyone ever got over a phone line. I was scared. I thought I was going to die. Those calls were life-sustaining doses, *far more effective than any prescription*. I never had a friend who asked so little and gave so much of himself" (Nancy Sinatra, *Frank Sinatra: An American Legend*, p. 238, italics mine).

Those of us who have followed Sinatra for decades have been aware of some of these quiet and covert acts of compassion. But when Variety Clubs International, a large charitable organization, hosted a televised "All-Star Party" for Sinatra in 1983, I was unprepared for the impact of Richard Burton's acknowledgement of Sinatra's altruism over the years. Burton's address, written by Paul Keyes, was entitled "Mr. Anonymous." Said Burton:

I have never sung a song with Frank Sinatra. Never acted with him, shared his stage nor been a member of an orchestra under his baton. We are, however, old friends of some thirty years and I have risen to my feet to applaud his blazing artistry at numerous charity performances raising countless millions for the victims of the world. . . . Frank is a giant. Among the givers of the world, he stands tallest. He has more than paid rent for the space he occupies on this planet, forged as he is from legendary loyalty and compassion carefully hidden . . . hidden because he has ordered it. Mr. Anonymous you have asked to be; Mr. Anonymous you shall be called. At risk of further offending you, I appear as the herald of grateful multitudes who have opened those unexpected envelopes . . . special delivery answers to their prayers . . . those awakened by late-night phone calls which remedied their problems only on condition they share your covenant of secrecy . . . those who were surprised by signed checks with amounts not filled in . . . those performers down on their luck, who suddenly landed that role they never expected and still don't know whom to thank . . . and for untold beneficiaries of the caring and kindness of this splendid man who truly is his brother's keeper. And they are legion . . . those whose lives took a turn for the better because of this man. (Nancy Sinatra, *Frank Sinatra: An American Legend*, pp. 285–86)

The point is obvious. This remarkable man through word and deed has benefited millions.

And Sinatra in song has benefited untold millions more. Through art and magic he has distilled his essence into song. The wonder would be if Sinatra's work *did not* heal and inspire. When I suffered depression and survived, I determined I would do something to relieve that pain in others. I cannot imagine Mr. Sinatra having vowed any less. When he endured and overcame hardship and heartache, you can be sure it wasn't just Sinatra who was the better for it. He certainly filed the experience away, to use it later in his art. But it also enlarged his heart. And we are all beneficiaries.

William Menninger, co-founder of the world-famous Menninger Clinic in Topeka, Kansas, asserted that the most important medicine any physician can administer is his personality. Sinatra does much more than administer his personality. Using his songs as keys and conduits, he unlocks the floodgates of his soul, freeing his seraphs and demons, and completely *immerses* us in torrents of the love, passion, anguish, and pain that boil and brew there, sharing his most ecstatic joys and deepest sorrows. We are his awed and grateful confidants, recipients and repositories of his most precious and prodigious gift—his exquisite heart laid bare through art.

WORKS CITED

Russell, Rosalind. "Sinatra: An American Classic." In *The Frank Sinatra Reader*. Ed. Steven Petkov and Leonard Mustazza. New York: Oxford University Press, 1995: pp. 147–50.

Sinatra, Nancy. *Frank Sinatra: An American Legend*. Santa Monica: General Publishing Company, 1995.

———. *Frank Sinatra: My Father*. Garden City: Doubleday, 1985.

"Sinatra: Where the Action Is." In *The Frank Sinatra Reader*. Ed. Steven Petkov and Leonard Mustazza. New York: Oxford University Press, 1995: pp. 90–98.

Talese, Gay. "Frank Sinatra Has a Cold." In *The Frank Sinatra Reader*. Ed. Steven Petkov and Leonard Mustazza. New York: Oxford University Press, 1995: pp. 99–129.

PART II

The Troubadour as Modern Hero

Listening to Frank Sinatra

GERALD EARLY

As a boy, when you entered the tent,
Darkened and wet, like your childhood,
You kept straining to see, around or
Through the adults who were there;

You thought it smelled worse than any
Place you'd been before, and so you strained
Not to smell and you strained to see as
They paraded out, a sorry lot they were, too:

A grossly fat woman, a man with scaly skin,
Someone with a body like a tube, someone
With an appetite for glass and nails, and,
Last, a man with a bag over his head, a

Plain, brown, ordinary bag that everyone,
Waiting in hope, thought concealed behind
The horror of horrors, the most grotesque
Of the grotesque: he was your star that day.

With one sharp intake of breath, the shudder
Of utter joy that you were not, at last, this
Junk heap, we saw his fare and wondered, *this*?!
And as he told his story, someone asked, jokingly,

What do you do all day? and he said, smiling,
Why, listen to Frank Sinatra, as if *that* was,
As if everyone should or would do what was the
Naturalest thing in the whole wide natural world,

Reclining somewhere after work to listen
To "At Long Last Love," or "You Make Me Feel
So Young," or something else that helps
Get you through another day of just living.

And then you thought later, what could he know
Of Frank Sinatra, of sitting with a girl in
A darkened room, kissing wet kisses; driving
Along a dark, wet road, with the hum of the radio.

But when you left the filthy tent that day
It was all you could remember, all you thought
Of, even after you forgot the face of horrors:
Listening to Frank Sinatra gets you through a day.

Ahhhh, such a story I like to tell my children
When we go out to tents and shows and sideshows
And I keep straining to hear Frank Sinatra off
Somewhere on a PA or someone's radio and they,

My children, always staring, wondering why
Their father is the crazy one who wants to
Hear Frank Sinatra where there is no Frank Sinatra,
Where no one else wants to hear Frank Sinatra at all.

To which looks I reply that if Frank Sinatra could
Do so much for the man who was the horror of horrors,
To sing such that he could make it through a day
Just think what such listening can do for me.

At the Heart of American Music

DANIEL OKRENT

You know the voice from the very first notes, but it took a while to get there. Columbia Records had signed a 27-year-old band singer to his first contract in 1942, nine months before the first song was recorded. Six months had passed even since he had initiated an American pop culture ritual—i.e., a riot of teenage girls—at the Paramount Theatre. Now, in front of a purring, twelve-member chorus (the American Federation of Musicians had gone on strike, and its members would not record), Frank Sinatra opened his mouth, his throat, his heart. He sang "Close to You" and began what would become the longest lasting, most influential, and most consistent solo career in American musical history. Half a century later, the voice is as familiar as if it had been recorded yesterday. It is, unmistakably, Sinatra.

In some ways, though, the Sinatra of his first great period (the Columbia years, 1943–1952) seems hardly related to the figure we'd come to know in the Capitol era and after. How can we reconcile the finger-snapping, ring-a-ding-dinging Chairman of the Board with the vulnerable, boyish crooner of "I Should Care"? How do you match the edgy auteur of concept albums like 1958's *Only the Lonely* with the sentimentalist who, in 1945, could commit the schmaltz of "Full Moon and Empty Arms"? How marry the Palm Springs tycoon who loved to visit Nancy Reagan in the White House with the crusader who not only sang the paean to racial equality, "The House I Live In," but made an Academy Award-winning short built around it, and carried its message to high schools, civic groups, and virtually any audience he could find?

As powerful as the contradictions are, they tend to diminish when placed into their historical context. The soft balladeer is a perfectly sensible precursor to the mature swinger if you remember that Sinatra went solo not even a full year into World War II. He had already demonstrated his uncanny ability to swing with Harry James and Tommy Dorsey, and by the time of his very first solo session in front of an orchestra late in '44, closed the argument with "Saturday Night (Is the Loneliest Night of the Week)." But the war had left millions of female hearts bereft of the men they loved, and all arguments were on the side of ballads—rapturous ballads like "These Foolish Things," vulnerable ballads like "I Fall in Love Too Easily," overdone ballads like "You'll Never Walk Alone." Listen to how he sighs the title phrase of "People Will Say We're in Love," or to how he slowly draws his legato across the lyrics of "Dream." Now, imagine a young mother listening to him, and thinking of her husband on a ship in the vast Pacific: you'd stick with ballads, too, the more heartachey the better.

"Full Moon and Empty Arms" as precursor to *Only the Lonely*? Hard as it may be to imagine from today's perspective, there was a time when Sinatra, even at his '40's peak was, yes, something more than your average singer, but still only a . . . singer. Just as Hollywood studios dominated the careers of actors back in the days of long-term, multi-picture contracts, so did the recording companies exert comparably powerful influence over the talent that was legally yoked to them. Much has been made of the schlock that Sinatra was "forced" to record when Mitch Miller took over A&R at Columbia in 1950. ("Mama Will Bark" is the most frequently cited excrescence, followed closely by "Feet of Clay.") But even before Miller and "Mama" came into Sinatra's life, he was recording equally unlikely, inappropriate, or just plain bad material. There are only two possible explanations for why Sinatra recorded "The Dum-Dot Song" or "Chattanoogie Shoeshine Boy": Either his taste was bad, or he sang what he was asked to sing. I think we can guess which was the likelier reason.

It's also worth remembering that as big a star as he was, Columbia-era Sinatra wasn't nearly the dominant figure memory or legend may make him out to be. In this entire collection [*Frank Sinatra: The Best of the Columbia Years, 1943–1952*], spanning his best work over a nine-year period, there are only three songs that made it to the very top of the pop charts. (Pretty unlikely ones, too—1945's "Oh, What It Seemed to Be," 1946's "Five Minutes More" and, a year later, the egregious "Mam'selle." That these three numbers soared beyond such brilliant records as "She's Funny That Way" or "Guess I'll Hang My Tears Out to Dry"—neither of which made the charts at all—may be proof of critic/songwriter Gene Lees's dictum that the 1930's, and definitely not the '40's, was the last decade in which "popular music was good and good music was popular.")

Explaining the path that led Sinatra from "The House I Live In" to the Reagan White House may be an issue best settled in a different venue. But if you wish to find a musico-historical etiology for this political transmigration, it's right there in our concert halls and on our radio stations: the America that embraced Sinatra was a united country waging, winning, and finally celebrating the victory of a war that engaged the entire nation. The America that, at least in the sense of pop charts, air play, and audience attendance, turned its back on Sinatra two and three decades later eschewed his style for a music of rebellion, outsiderness, and social as well as musical dissonance. Such a situation might make you turn to Nancy Reagan, too.

Just as there are clues to the essential Sinatra in his early music, they are present as well in his choice of collaborators. Certainly he knew how to find out who was writing the good songs of the day; among Jule Styne, Sammy Cahn, and Jimmy Van Heusen, not one had yet made a reputation of any size before hooking up with Sinatra. Scan the orchestra lists from the Columbia sessions and you find such fine jazz soloists as Ziggy Elman, Barney Kessel, Billy Butterfield and, most notably (and notable here on "I've Got a Crush on You" and "Body and Soul"), Bobby Hackett. (I omit, because of the impromptu circumstances, the tight handful of Metronome All-Stars with whom he recorded "Sweet Lorraine" in 1946, including Coleman Hawkins, Johnny Hodges, and Buddy Rich.) Dig deeper, into the orchestras, and there among the violins is Felix Slatkin, on the way to his conducting career; Bernard Greenhouse with the cellos, prepping for his distinguished tenure with the Beaux Arts Trio; Gunther Schuller on horn, years before his own rise to eminence as a musical polymath. And then there are my own favorite unlikelies: Van Heusen's collaborator on "Nancy," Phil Silvers, about a decade before he became Sergeant Bilko; and lyricist Abel Meeropol (the pseudonymous "Lewis Allen"), who contributed "The House I Live In" to the Sinatra canon half a decade after he wrote "Strange Fruit" with Billie Holiday, and about eight years before he adopted and raised as his own the two young sons of the executed atomic spies Julius and Ethel Rosenberg.

But Sinatra's signal collaborator in the Columbia years—and, given how the partnership set him on his future course, perhaps the most important collaborator he would ever have—was arranger/conductor Axel Stordahl.

By all accounts, Stordahl was a lovely man. His arrangements, gentle as feathers, certainly don't contradict this impression. Tinkling celestas, cascading strings, a river of woodwinds combine in most of them to form a warm wash of sound, cushiony support for The Voice. Stordahl's ballad settings made room for the young Sinatra—a more revolutionary concept than it first might appear, coming as it did in the wake of the Big Band

Era. Even those big band arrangers who worked for the astute Tommy Dorsey, who knew Sinatra was nothing if not a meal ticket, by and large considered the singer another instrument that had to be accommodated with a solo chorus or two. And even during a big band singer's 32 bars up front, the chart rarely had the band laying back, out of the way, while the canaries chirped. But Stordahl, like all the best conductors, directors, basketball coaches, or others who exist to help shape the work of others, knew when to get out of the way.

In the process, he also accelerated the development of Sinatra's most distinctive strength, the one attribute that served him not only in the mooning Columbia years, but also during the swinging-and-soulful Capitol era and the ring-a-ding-dinging Reprise epoch, an attribute that never deserted him even during his last concerts in the '90's: his phrasing. As much as the orchestral instrumentation, or the languid tempos, or the neat little intros and outros that mark Stordahl's work, his characteristic Sinatra arrangements (ballads all) are distinguished by something that's nearly missing, namely a noticeable rhythm. With occasional exceptions, Stordahl kept the pulse so vague, so distant, that the listener leans to find it in the singer. With the beat a mere whisper in the orchestra, Sinatra was freed to sing his lyrics—to make his statements—in a pattern that so nearly approximated heartfelt speech it could hardly surprise anyone that women wept or screamed or swooned when he addressed them. Listen to how he phrases the bridge of "You Go to My Head" or the entire chorus of "A Ghost of a Chance." This isn't mere singing; it's confession.

We can't possibly know whether, in crafting his particular self-effacing style, Stordahl (who died in 1963) was simply doing what Sinatra asked for, or whether he was putting the singer in a place where Sinatra would be compelled to draw on his known resources. But I come down on the side of the latter. For it is sensible to believe that Stordahl knew what he had in the young Sinatra—an audacious young man who had his eye trained not on the base rewards of greatness, but on its very substance.

Early in his baseball career, Sinatra's contemporary Ted Williams said that all he ever wanted out of life was to be known as the best hitter who ever lived. I don't know whether Sinatra ever said anything comparable but, having listened and listened to the [Columbia] recordings, I'd be surprised if he didn't think it. Young he may have been, but the audacity that would later become part of his public persona in the Rat Pack years was with him from the beginning. Consider the artists whose signature songs he dared to cover. Bing Crosby and "White Christmas," Fred Astaire and "Night and Day," Lena Horne's "Stormy Weather," Walter Huston's "September Song" (in the process slowing it nearly by half and establishing the tempo at which it would ever after be performed), Nat Cole's "Sweet Lorraine," even Charlie Parker's "Now's the Time" (uncredited, unroyaltied, and repackaged as "The Hucklebuck"). Consider the range of material: he sang "Home on the Range," he sang "Begin the Beguine," he sang "Guess I'll Hang My Tears Out to Dry." He sang great songs and he sang lousy ones, and not once was he intimidated by the former nor did he take ironic distance from the latter. He sang and sang and sang over the length of a decade that would do nothing less than establish forever his huge, enduring place at the very heart of American music.

Frank Sinatra and the Art of Recording

CHARLES L. GRANATA

When I was a youngster, maybe ten or eleven years old, I found myself rummaging through a stack of old records at a neighborhood yard sale. Suddenly, I stumbled upon a whole slew of the great Capitol and Reprise albums that Frank Sinatra made with Nelson Riddle and Billy May. They caught my attention, as I was somewhat familiar with Sinatra because of my Mom's collection of his earlier Columbia LP's. But these albums seemed different from the ones we had at home, which depicted the singer in his youthful, "crooner" phase. Instead, these albums, with their gorgeous, full-color covers, looked much more contemporary and exciting than any Sinatra album I had ever seen; so neat, I'm sure I thought of them as being downright "hip!"

With eager anticipation, I scooped them up and, after spending the afternoon listening, quickly recognized that these newfound records were quite different from anything I had ever heard before—the singing remarkably mellifluous, oozing with confidence. They immediately became a cherished part of my expanding record collection. Being a frustrated drummer, I was totally awed by the deceptively simple rhythmic patterns that were the foundation of those tremendous swing charts. Of course, names like Alvin Stoller and Irv Cottler (two of the rock-steady percussionists who were the cornerstones of the Sinatra rhythm section) were unknown to me then, but the spark and vigor of the amazing music emanating from those discs was not lost on my young ear. During the many hours I spent studying those incredible records, I would eventually memorize every detail of the arrangements, right down to the very last drum fill and afterbeat.

What supplanted my musical interest, though, were the albums' jackets, which were some of the simplest and most classy record covers that I had ever encountered—twelve-inch, one-dimensional inanimate objects that superbly evoked the fabulous era in which they were made. Obviously designed with great care, they visually captured the essence of the singer's musical message, and effectively communicated the carefree, swinging style that his work in the 1950s and 1960s personified. From the smug swagger of *Swing Easy* and the rapturous joy of *Songs for Swingin' Lovers*, to the desolate feel of *Wee Small Hours* and the devastating melancholy of *Only the Lonely*, each album offered an aesthetically balanced cover portrait that beautifully underscored each individual mood.

The covers I liked best were the ones that sported off-the-cuff shots of Frank in the recording studio: fingers snapping, tie jauntily loosened, wide-band Cavanaugh hat tipped perfectly on his head. My eyes and mind absorbed all of the peripheral elements of those cover photos: the microphones, the instruments, the layout of the orchestra. The minutest details (like the color of the sweater that the percussionist and trombonists were wearing on the cover of *Sinatra's Swingin' Session!!!*—bright red) captured my attention and became an integral part of the listening experience. The colorful artwork piqued my interest and added an extra dimension to my enjoyment of the music.

I'd listen to the singer belting out "I've Got the World on a String" or "Lonesome Road" or "My Blue Heaven" and imagine what it must have been like to be there—watching Frank Sinatra, the very essence of "cool," standing front-and-center amid the swirl of activity, that big band blaring right behind him, alternately pushing him, then backing off at just the right moment. These were records made to express love and passion and energy, and everything about them, from cover to lead-out groove, brimmed over with an exuberance that was new to me and special enough to strike a chord that would have a profound effect on my lifelong appreciation of all music. I remember thinking, "What is it about Sinatra? How did he get there? What forces conspired to translate the sounds he was hearing in his head to his collaborators and, as an end result, to the grooves of a phonograph record?" Although I didn't realize it at the time, these images, both real and imagined, were the beginning of my fascination with the mystery and the excitement of how these records came to be made. I wanted to be there, or, at the very least, to learn about exactly what happened at a recording session. A Sinatra session. Wouldn't that be, after all, a music buff's greatest thrill? To actually have been there, smack-dab in the middle of it all, at Capitol Records, circa 1956?

Only a fortunate few have had the opportunity to observe a master craftsman on the level of Frank Sinatra work in the arena where he has made his most indelible musical impressions. For those who haven't, I invite you to step through the hitherto closed doors of the world of the recording studio, for a revealing look at what made one master's musical mind tick.

IN THE BEGINNING

On July 13, 1939, twenty-three-year-old Frank Sinatra, a relatively unknown "boy singer" with the Harry James Orchestra, entered a New York recording studio to wax his first commercial recording. Even Sinatra couldn't have been farsighted enough to see the incredible musical and technological advances that would define and ultimately *redefine* his art. How could he, as he stood on the edge of fame on that hot summer day, have imagined the decades of dramatic change that would help shape him into the most visible and enduring vocal artist of the twentieth century?

Certainly, nothing has had more of a profound effect on Frank Sinatra or our perception of his talent than the new and exciting ways in which sound was being recorded and reproduced. This recording process made it possible to document one of the most fertile periods in American culture, the age of the popular song—perhaps America's most meaningful contribution to musical history. That very process, in fact, gave voice to *The Voice*, providing Sinatra with a path that led directly to our ears and, ultimately, our hearts. "I adore making records," Sinatra once said. "I'd rather do that than almost anything else" (Douglas-Home 36). And make records he did! From that first Brunswick session in 1939 to the dubious *Duets* of the mid-1990s, he recorded well over a thousand songs, almost all intended for (and released as) commercial records. It was through his recordings that Frank Sinatra uttered his most powerful musical statements.

By the time of his first full-fledged solo recording as a Columbia Records artist in June of 1943, all of the personal creative tools that the singer needed to carve his niche as one of the first true multimedia superstars of the modern age were already in place. As he relaxed between sets at Hollywood's Palladium Ballroom one evening in the early forties, Sinatra remarked to his friend, songwriter Sammy Cahn, "I am going to be the world's greatest singer!" Cahn's response, as he later related it to me: "I looked at him, and said, 'Without a doubt!' He was pleased, and made me repeat what I said. He seemed so intense, that there was no way I could dispute what he had said." Later, Cahn ran into Tommy Dorsey, who was gigging at the same venue with Sinatra's replacement, Dick Haymes. "He's doing the same songs, the same arrangements—but it's not nearly the same," Dorsey remarked. From early on, the singer simply had the confidence and assertiveness to be able to almost will himself to astounding, even ethereal success.

What Sinatra did, in the years to follow, was embrace the rapidly advancing art and science of sound recording, utilizing the burgeoning technology to his best advantage, devising and mastering techniques that would serve him well as he progressed through each successive phase of his spectacular career. More importantly, he vigorously immersed himself in every last detail pertaining to his work—a determining factor in guaranteeing the success of the conscious, deliberate steps he took to position himself as not only a creative musical artist, but a commercial one as well.

Prior to his first solo decade, Sinatra gained valuable insight during his tenure as the band vocalist with both James (1939) and Dorsey (1940–1942). It was during these gigs that he befriended many of the talented musicians who would weave their way into the very fabric of his musical existence: the aforementioned Sammy Cahn, arranger Axel Stordahl, and musician Skitch Henderson among them. Then, too, came the first inkling of his discriminating taste for top-quality songs, and his knack for selecting only those tunes that he instinctively knew fit his style like a fine leather glove. Much of the singer's musical wisdom stems from the day-in, day-out trials and tribulations he experienced as a rising band singer. As far back as the early 1940s, Sinatra credited Tommy Dorsey with providing the rudimentary elements that he would adapt to fit his vocal styling, carefully refining his approach to develop a distinct method of phrasing that would become unmistakably his own.

The single most important benefit of the vocalist's big-band experience was undoubtedly his discovery of the tool that would become his own personal, secret weapon: the microphone—a device that came of age concurrently with Sinatra's initial rise to vocal power. Building on the foundation laid by his original inspiration, Bing Crosby, Sinatra brought the use of the microphone to its fullest and most creative potential, as a logical extension of his incredible vocal talent. "One thing that was tremendously important was learning the use of the microphone," he said. "Many singers never learned to use one. They never understood, and still don't, that a microphone is their instrument" (Sinatra 87).

He likely drew this conclusion in part from the reaction of the largely female audiences to his early stage appearances, in which he would grasp the tall microphone stand (seemingly for support!), and lean into not only the mike itself, but the note as well, physically communicating the figurative *and* literal dynamic that he desired. The simple stage maneuver perfectly accentuated his unique vocal styling, prompting him to observe that if he bent or looped the note, the audience would wail. His response to their enthusiasm was to incorporate subtle hand gestures and microphone caresses into the performance, giving us the first glimpse of his understanding of the relationship between stage acting and the sexual subtext of his vocal art. Although other performers of the day followed suit and used the modern microphone to their advantage, none handled it more fluidly or effortlessly than Frank. To some singers it was a barrier between performer and audience; to Sinatra it was a tool that strengthened the bond of intimacy between himself and his listeners—a stage prop used to perfect effect during concert and nightclub appearances.

Of his technique, the singer has observed, "It's difficult to explain, but I think the first rule is to use it with great economy. You don't crowd it— you must never jar an audience with it. I think you must keep it as subtle as possible." More importantly, the microphone served as a natural dynamic range expander during a recording session. "You must know when to move away from the mike, and when to move back into it. To me, there's no worse sound than when a singer breathes in sharply, and you hear the gasp over the microphone. The whole secret is getting the air in the corner of the mouth, and using the microphone properly" (Sinatra 87, 99).

A quick listen to a handful of recordings from any one of his four major periods will immediately bear out the soundness of Sinatra's theory. It was this level of artistic intuition, combined with his careful attention to every last detail, that helped set Frank Sinatra apart from every other vocalist and make his recordings stand out as quintessential models, worthy of emulation. To understand the significance of these performances, and how they fit into the overall scheme of what Sinatra, from early on, intended for his future, we must first consider the circumstances under which he created them; they were carefully planned and executed by an artisan who devoted a lifetime to perfecting his musical style, as well as to refining the craft of recording it for posterity.

Sinatra left little to chance, especially when, for him, singing meant exposing his soul in such a deeply personal way. Like Duke Ellington before him, Sinatra was a perfectionist who understood that a record was forever. He once said, "You can never do anything in life quite on your own, you don't live on your own little island. I suppose you might be able to write a poem or paint a picture entirely on your own, but I doubt it. I don't think you can even sing a song that way, either. Making a record is as near as you can get to it—although, of course, the arranger and the orchestra play an enormous part. But once you're on a record singing, it's you and you alone. With a record, you're IT" (Douglas-Home 36).

The three years or so that Sinatra spent traveling with the James and Dorsey orchestras were simply the prelude to the years of prolific recording activity that would follow. The process, however, of making band records was vastly different from the methods that the singer would discover worked best for his own solo recording sessions. "Every moment was absolutely real," Sinatra has said of the hectic pace of the early years. "Driving five hundred miles through the night to the next one-night stand, and having forty minutes to get out of the bus and into the hotel; turn on the shower and the steam, hang up the dinner jacket to allow the wrinkles to come out of it, grab a sandwich, show up on the bandstand, and then . . . the greeting from the audience was the greatest reward in the world!"

Dorsey alumnus Jo Stafford further recalls that "in those days, we were so busy doing one-nighters, that we really didn't have time to rehearse, and hash out arrangements for recording sessions, *per se*. We'd try out new songs and arrangements on the road, and if they went well, we'd get into the studio in New York (or, on occasion, Chicago or Hollywood), and just record the songs that we were doing on our one-nighters. We really didn't *need* to rehearse!"

During the late 1930s and early 1940s, recording methods were still fairly crude, although they were infinitely better than the acoustic or early "electrical" waxings of just two decades before. Commonly, only one or two microphones would be placed among the orchestra, and the vocalist or vocal group would, of course, have their own dedicated mike. Popular microphones used for both recording and stage performances from the mid-1930s to the early 1940s were Western Electric models 630-A (moving coil) and 639 (ribbon), as well as the classic RCA 44 (ribbon) microphone.

Until late 1942, most records were made by etching the recording grooves onto a soft, waxy disc, then creating a metal plated master from this soft impression, which resulted in a sturdy (but, compared to vinyl, rough-surfaced) master disc. It was this metal "part," as it is called in the industry, that would create the stampers from which thick, brittle 78-rpm "shellac" discs could be struck, for commercial sale. Since the original wax masters were irreparably altered during the plating process, the metal parts struck from them remain the truest original recording sources for these early big-band recordings and are the primary choice (over the 78-rpm discs made from them) as the sound source for modern digital restoration.

While Sinatra's band vocal recordings evoke a very nostalgic warmth and charm, it wasn't until he signed with Columbia records in 1943 that he gained almost complete control over his sessions and focused on the elements that would aid him in realizing the perfection he sought. The Columbia years (1943–1952), in fact, find the singer experimenting with a wide variety of musical settings, laying a solid foundation for what (ten years later) would be his greatest period, with Nelson Riddle, Billy May, and Gordon Jenkins. It was here that Sinatra became intimately acquainted with the most personal of creative processes and learned the value of keeping a watchful eye on the proceedings. Undoubtedly, a determining factor in the beauty of the recordings beginning around this time was the direct supervision of the singer himself. From the Columbia era on, Sinatra simply choreographed his own recording sessions, a task that most other artists, whether through feelings of supremacy or inadequacy, ignorance or apathy, left to those around them. Although staff producers (usually Morty Palitz, Mitchell Ayers, and on occasion, Sinatra friend and label executive Manie Sachs) were customarily assigned to work with the singer, he assumed responsibility for and oversaw nearly every facet of his record dates, from start to finish. This attitude quickly turned his recording sessions into occasions that those who participated in them remember as genuine "events," in every sense of the word.

"Quite frankly, I was intimidated," recalls Columbia Records producer George Avakian, who worked on several Sinatra sessions in the forties. "Frank would come off the elevator with his bodyguards. Two guards would come off the elevator, they'd look right and left. Then Frank would step out, and two other guys would step out, and *they'd* look right and left. They looked like five diamonds walking up the hall!" Once inside the recording studio, the atmosphere relaxed, though, and from all accounts, Sinatra became just another guy in the band or in the booth. Any air of superiority was left at the door, and for good reason. Sinatra simply knew that what went down in the studio was a permanent record and a reflection of his aesthetic values. Certainly, he realized that his existence as a popular singer depended on the cooperation of many people, not the least of which were the musicians who helped make his songs "sing" and the technicians entrusted to faithfully preserve them.

"He had a great respect for musicians, all of them," recalls violinist Dave Frisina, who was the concertmaster on numerous Sinatra dates at Columbia and would continue to be a first-call player on the singer's sessions well into the 1980s. "He knew everybody in the orchestra—I suppose he just made it his business to know everyone. He could hear—he was enough of a musician himself to understand when people were playing, if they were really capable musicians." George Roberts, a veteran of the Stan Kenton band and a musician who would play a key role in shaping the direction of the singer's next musical plateau, recollects, "The days I spent working with Frank are, to me, the epitome of everything I had ever dreamed of . . . to be doing those things in association with Frank, you know, was unreal. He has a charisma, or whatever it is about him, that no one else has," Roberts emphasizes. This sentiment has been echoed by dozens of sidemen and technicians who have spent years working with the singer.

Everything hinged on the fundamental basis for his work—the song. Beginning with the right tune was always of primary importance, an essential ingredient in Frank Sinatra's recipe for success. "They usually say that an artist is as good as his material, and I think that in nine out of ten cases that holds true," he explained in a 1949 radio interview with New York disc jockey Jack Ellsworth. When, in the mid-1980s, Sinatra felt that he had exhausted the ubiquitous supply of "standard" songs (he hadn't—there were still scores of great, old pop songs that he hadn't addressed, either on the concert stage or commercial record), he implored young songwriters to write better music. "There's nobody writing good songs anymore," he often lamented. "I wish some new cat would come along, and write something decent for me."

Although he cherished top-quality songs, he wasn't necessarily effusive with praise and could be difficult for songwriters to read—unless they were able to get close enough to him to communicate their efforts in person. "I stand in front of him when I sing him a new song," Sammy Cahn once told me. "Sinatra just stands there, his thumb on his lower lip. When I finish, he just nods—that's all." "But," adds Cahn, wryly, "I wouldn't be standing in front of him unless he nodded." The singer's chosen method of publicly endorsing a particular song came during his many personal appearances, where in addition to performing the tune (instantly focusing attention on it), he religiously credited each individual songwriter and arranger from either the stage or from behind the radio microphone. While this became a Sinatra trademark during the concert-arena period of his latter years, it was, in fact, a practice that he maintained from his earliest personal appearances.

The singer's most admiring acknowledgement of a particular tune, however, would be his decision to record it—and, if it was extra-special, re-record it through the years, each time approaching the tempo and setting from a completely different perspective. The Sinatra standard "Night and Day" is an example of his constant need to keep a favored song fresh. Between 1942 (when he chose the song for his first solo recording session) and 1977 (his last official recording of the song), he performed it in at least six remarkably different musical settings. During his career, Sinatra has officially released five unique recordings of the song, including ballad, swing, and disco arrangements. (He didn't stop there. At least two completely different arrangements were used—jazz and solo guitar—for live performances.)

When recording, and considering tunes that would become part of an album, Sinatra himself would sit down and make the selections, then work out the order of the program, carefully controlling the pacing and flow of what he envisioned for the final record:

First, I decide on the mood for an album, and perhaps pick a title. Or sometimes it might be that I had the title, and then picked the mood to fit it. But it's most important that there should be a strong creative idea for the whole package. Like *Only the Lonely* or *No One Cares*, for instance. Then, I get a short list of maybe sixty possible songs, and out of these, I pick twelve to record. Next comes the pacing of the album, which is vitally important. I put the titles of the songs on twelve bits of paper, and juggle them around like a jigsaw puzzle until the album is telling a complete story, lyric-wise. For example, the album is in the mood of "No One Cares"—track one. Why does no one care? Because there's "A Cottage for Sale"—track two. And so on, until the last track . . . the end of the episode. (Douglas-Home 36)

Once the songs slated for recording are chosen, the task of orchestrating them (creating aesthetic backdrops to enhance his vocal lines) must be accomplished. For this, the singer has always had the finest arrangers in the world at his ready disposal. Sinatra describes the genesis of an arrangement.

> Once we choose the songs that will be in a particular album, I'll sit with Bill Miller, my pianist, and find the proper key. Then, I will meet with the orchestrator, and give him my thoughts on what I feel the background should be, from either eight measures to eight measures, or four measures to four measures. Should we use woodwinds, or brass, or strings behind the vocal? We discuss it, then I'll ask, "How wrong am I?" More than likely, he'll say, "You're about sixty-percent all right . . . but let me explain how I think it should be done." Usually, we wind up doing it the way the arranger feels it should be done, because he understands more than I do about it. (Douglas-Home 36)

Clearly, if not for talented musicians interpreting fine arrangements of superior songs, there would be no Frank Sinatra. His instinctive selection, on a song-by-song basis, of the orchestrator who would custom tailor the musical settings to communicate sympathetically the exact measure of emotion that he desired was the pivot on which Sinatra's genius is predicated. It was also his insistence on having his orchestrators receive prominent credit on record labels and album jackets that resulted in the modern pop "arranger" being brought to the forefront, where their efforts could be highlighted, and truly appreciated by the listening public.

While he would work with dozens of talented individuals throughout the sixty-year span of his career, he remained loyal to a relatively small group of arrangers who used his boundless musical energy and insight as a springboard for creating not only his orchestrations (which were usually far superior to any they wrote for other singers), but as the inspiration for their own personal work as well. "A good arranger is vital, because in a sense, he's a recording secretary," Sinatra told British author Robin Douglas-Home in a rare candid 1961 interview. "I must admit something," he says. "I'd never argue with someone like Nelson [Riddle] on a record date. You respect the arranger. It's his date—he's the leader" (36).

Mutual respect and understanding brought Frank Sinatra and Axel Stordahl together in the early forties to develop their working relationship into one of the first true musical partnerships of the pop-music era. From the first four solo sides that he made for Victor's Bluebird label in January of 1942 to the first Capitol Records session in April of 1953, it was Stordahl who faithfully served as Sinatra's musical "director," creating hundreds of orchestrations and musical cues for his seemingly endless flow of commercial recording sessions, radio programs, personal appearances, Hollywood films, and television shows. "In those days, Axel was writing things that were beautiful. Nobody wrote ballads as pretty as he did until many years later, when Nelson came along. Axel Stordahl really was the 'Daddy' that people began to learn from in the sense of writing orchestrations—he really was the most prolific [arranger] of his time," Sinatra once said in a interview with radio legend Sid Mark. Stordahl's sumptuous string arrangements for Sinatra became synonymous with the suave, romantic image that enveloped him as the premiere "crooner" of the 1940s. Simplicity is the key to their beauty and understated sonority. Their presence on the landscape of popular music creates a vista from which to view a modern romantic era that, save for the efforts of a handful of film buffs and cultural historians, may well be in danger of extinction.

"Axel was a very good string writer, and he also wrote with a very good harmonic sense," remembered colleague Paul Weston. "He used to have what we called an 'Axel Ending' on the end of some of the ballads, where he would use a complicated tag where he would change key a couple of times in the last four bars. Also, Ax and I would write counter-melodies for the strings, to be played against the vocal. Most arrangers simply used the strings as 'pads'—few wrote counter-melodies against the vocalist." Much of Stordahl's inspiration came from his love of classical music, and strains of Rachmaninoff, Debussy, Ravel, and Tchaikovsky ring clear in the lush swell of his most lovely arrangements. "Axel's sound was the French school of writing, more impressionistic; using the harp, and the suspension, and the major seconds and semi-tones," according to musician/bandleader Skitch Henderson.

Unfortunately, little has been documented about the details of the pair's working procedures and how they outlined their ideas. Stordahl's untimely death in 1963 and a rumored dispute between the pair precluded in-depth interviews regarding their collaborations, leaving researchers with just the millions of notes that remain a part of the permanent "record." One can surmise, though, that because the two spent such an inordinate amount of time in close musical proximity, it was relatively easy for Stordahl to comprehend what Sinatra desired and effectively create the backgrounds with ease.

We are able to study and fully appreciate the historic significance of the Sinatra-Stordahl recordings of the early years, as they were beautifully recorded and preserved with previously unrealized clarity, owing to the ideal conditions under which they were made, as well as dramatic improvements in the direct-to-disc recording methods of the early 1940s. While earlier recordings had their grooves cut onto heavy, coarse metal plates, Sinatra's master recordings from 1943 onward were cut at 33 ⅓ rpm on smooth glass or aluminum discs that offered a much quieter recording and playback surface. These sixteen-inch platters, coated with a soft plastic "lacquer," revolutionized the sonic quality of both recording studio and radio recordings and were the forerunner to the modern "Long Play" (LP) record. While the end result of a session committed to the newer master discs in the early

1940s was the comparatively noisy shellac 78-rpm disc of the time, the fidelity of the original session lacquers always remained and is what has allowed the recent spate of superior CD restorations that reflect the remarkable quality and depth of the original recording sessions, the crucial moments during which the artistic and technical worlds met to preserve the performance permanently.

Sessions typically lasted for three hours, during which time three or four tunes were completely recorded and mastered. About an hour or so before the start of the session (usually 8:00 p.m. for Sinatra dates—he felt his voice was sufficiently loosened by this time of evening, and it also accommodated his busy daytime film schedule), the musicians would arrive at the studio to lay out their instruments and peruse the evening's orchestrations. Milt Bernhart, an extraordinary trombonist who came to the Hollywood film and recording studios in the early fifties following a successful stint with the Stan Kenton band, was a keen observer of the complex behind-the-scenes forces that drove the studio music world in its heyday. As a first-call player for Frank Sinatra's record, film, and TV sessions for over twenty-five years, Bernhart offers invaluable insights. "We never saw the charts prior to the session," explains Bernhart. "But I might show up at the studio early, to see what was there. I wanted to get nervous, I suppose. Most people would say, 'Don't look at it until it's time to start playing,' but I really had to look at the charts, to start thinking about what I was going to do."

Naturally, when Sinatra arrived (usually precisely on time, if not earlier), the assembled cast would begin with a short rehearsal, so the engineers could properly balance the sound. Until the stereo "tape" era (1957), the direct-to-disc recording method necessitated a perfect mix of all the orchestral elements (strings, horns, woodwinds, percussion), plus the vocalist and occasionally a choral group. Bear in mind that these were monophonic (one-track) recordings, being balanced and mixed "on the fly," with no chance to go back and fix technical (recording) or performance mistakes after the fact. After multi-track tape entered the studios, and stereo recording became the accepted standard, individual elements (such as the singer's vocal) would have separate "tracks" or space on the tape, isolated from the orchestra. This isolation would facilitate editing or manipulation once the session was over, and engineers could easily re-balance or enhance the sound originally captured at the live recording session.

Monophonic recording setups of the 1940s and early 1950s, however, were extremely simple. Limited by a lack of sophisticated mixers and multi-track recorders, the engineers achieved remarkably well-balanced sound with a minimum of fancy gear. "In those days, CBS made their own equipment," says Frank Laico, a retired Columbia engineer who began working sessions in the mid-1940s. "The mixing console had only six positions! So if you had a large orchestra, you had to be careful about how you balanced it. For pop recordings, you had rhythm that had to be heard, so you'd use an RCA 44B microphone (the old diamond-shaped, box-style mike, two-sided) with the bass player on one side, and the guitarist on the other. Over the drum kit, we might use a single RCA 77D, because you couldn't mike individual elements of the drum set up. You'd use one or two mikes to pick up the brass and woodwinds, and one for the strings. And, of course, your vocalist would have his or her own mike. If we had a vocal group, they couldn't be put on a separate mike, so we'd put them behind the string section, and microphone them together, from high up."

The preferred mike for Sinatra's vocals during the Columbia years was the standard of the industry, the RCA 44B ribbon microphone. Noted for its smooth, warm sound and superior reproduction of high frequencies, it was a natural for both close instrumental and vocal recording. Not surprisingly, it is this "old-fashioned" microphone design that is commonly used to depict the familiar "crooner" image that is closely associated with the Sinatra of the 1940s.

Once the balance was deemed satisfactory, the orchestra would run down (play through) the song, *sans* vocal, so that the singer and the musicians could acquaint themselves with the orchestration. This was also the point where the arrangement could be modified, and errant notes transcribed by the copyist could be corrected. Everything at the session was real time: these were live, in-studio performances that offered a freshness and spontaneity that dwindled with the advent of sound-on-sound and multi-track overdub recording in the years to follow. Basically, the musicians were expected to perform these charts, which they were reading for the first time, as though they'd been playing them together for years! But then again, these were the very finest musicians in Hollywood and New York—many from the motion-picture studios and the Philharmonic orchestra—or, better still, from the ranks of Benny Goodman, Glenn Miller, or Tommy Dorsey aggregations, or later, Stan Kenton's band. If anyone did make a mistake, it was back to square one for all involved.

Most of the time, Sinatra's sessions were relaxed, as everyone knew what his or her role was. While the musicians and crew had their fun and enjoyed their work immensely, the atmosphere in the studio was never less than professional. Some of the greatest laughs came after flubbed takes, especially when Sinatra was poking fun at himself. On one memorable Columbia date (August 27, 1945), Sinatra was recording "Silent Night." The arrangement set the tone for Sinatra's performance, which was appropriately reverential. The orchestra captured superbly the joyous sound of the Christmas season. Suddenly, two-thirds of the way through a *beautiful* take, Sinatra blew a line. Realizing his error, he smashed the solemnity of the moment. "Son of a bitch!" he fumed. "I sang the wrong God-damned words!" Faced with this incongruity, the musicians responded with spontaneous laughter, which, of course, egged the singer on. After some good-natured ribbing, the session resumed, a perfect take was made, and everyone went home happy. There were many such occurrences over the years, each one serving to strengthen the bond between the vocalist and the musicians who respected and admired him.

At Columbia, Sinatra's recording activity was split between New York and Hollywood, depending upon his schedule and availability. The famed "Columbia sound" was achieved through the employment of the very best engineers, custom-designed equipment, and the finest recording facilities—all skillfully coordinated under the watchful eye of label chief Goddard Lieberson. Just as legendary concert halls have important bearing on the resultant signature sounds of the renowned symphony orchestras that play in them, the careful selection of specific recording studios once played a huge role in creating identifiable acoustic characteristics that became an integral part of the highly individual sound of the recordings created by the major record labels. "Columbia's sound became famous largely through Harry James' trumpet recordings at Liederkranz Hall, which had a great echo sound," George Avakian explains. "Liederkranz was a large studio in a beautiful building, located at 115 East 58th Street, and was actually run by the Liederkranz Society. It had very natural sonic properties, because it was large and had a lot of old wood." (Early in 1948, CBS-TV took over half of the facility and created two television studios. From all accounts, this completely altered the characteristic sound of the original studio, which alteration essentially lost the ambience that had made it a favorite with producers and engineers.) Columbia used Liederkranz extensively, along with its own penthouse studio facilities, located at 799 Seventh Avenue. It was at these two locations that Frank Sinatra did the bulk of his New York recording during the early Columbia period, from 1943 to 1949. "There were four studios at 799 Seventh Avenue, Studios A, B, C and D. They recorded Sinatra up there, in Studio B," remembers retired Columbia engineer Bill Savory. Once Columbia acquired its famed 30th Street studio, most of the East Coast pop recording activity for the label emanated from that facility, and many of Sinatra's recordings from 1949 to 1952 originated from 30th Street.

Compared to today, sound engineers in the 1940s had far fewer technical accoutrements at their disposal, and, when dealing with such issues as reverb, they would need to devise their own unique methods of dealing with the problem. Their solution was very simple and very effective. For a time, the men's room became the natural echo chamber at Liederkranz Hall! "Bob Fine had done that with me at Mercury," remembers Mitch Miller, then Columbia's A&R director. "He was a fabulous engineer. I said, 'Bob, we've got to put a halo around the voice. It sounds like they're singing into a hunk of wool.' So he came up with it in a second. He put a speaker in the bathroom—at Reeves Studio in New York, this was—with a mike hanging there. They sent the signal in there, then took the little bit of the sound that came out of the bathroom speaker, and added it to the original mix," describes Miller. While technically sound, this method was not without its drawbacks, however. "There were many stories of recordings being spoiled by someone going to the bathroom," recalls Avakian. "But it always seemed to happen on other people's dates—I don't believe it ever actually happened, but I heard stories like that." The engineers at the 799 Seventh Avenue studios handled the situation in a similar yet somewhat more refined manner. With the studio situated on the top (seventh) floor, the engineers had a back stairwell with seven stories of natural echo at their disposal. Bud Graham, whose primary responsibility was classical recording, explains, "We tried some other things, a narrow room with highly polished surfaces, but it wasn't nearly as good as the stairwell. You see, in the stairwell, frequencies changed—they dissipated, and weren't the same all the time. It just had a character that I don't think any of the electronic or digital echoes could ever have," he points out.

Sometime in 1948, with Liederkranz Hall all but destroyed for the purposes of audio recording, Columbia located and purchased its crown jewel—a huge Greek Orthodox church located at 30th Street and Third Avenue in Manhattan. This is the studio that would become the legendary facility known simply as "30th Street." As the primary Columbia recording facility, the 30th Street studio went on to earn a reputation that outlived its sale (and ultimate demise) in the mid-1980s. That success could be directly attributed to the studio's magnificent sonics and the thousands of famous recordings that were made there. Ironically, the 30th Street location was initially avoided by most Columbia staff producers and engineers. Bill Savory, involved in opening the studio, recalls its tenuous birth: "Everybody that came in and listened to it said that it was too live. So finally, we did something there with Goddard, one of those early Broadway cast albums [*South Pacific*], and he said 'This is just what I want! This is the most flexible place on Earth! You can make it sound like Broadway, or whatever you want.' After that, it became popular, and they dropped Liederkranz."

Engineer Frank Laico recalls that Mitch Miller, relentless in his pursuit of a slick, unique "pop" sound, also fell in love with the studio. "It was a great acoustic room, about 100 feet by 100 feet, and almost 100 feet high. We all got down there to look at it, and loved the sound. Mitch walked in and told all the brass in our division, 'There will be nothing done to this room, as long as I'm here. We are going to use it as is.' There were drapes hanging crazily, dust everywhere. It was nothing to be proud of, physically. He wouldn't let them touch the floors, because the first thing they would do is come in and sand the floors!" The acoustics at 30th Street were outstanding—much better than nearly any other studio, anywhere. "The sound on those records is something that everyone in the world was trying to duplicate, especially for the strings," says Laico. "The room itself was so *beautifully* resonant. And yes, we did use echo, too, mostly for vocals, and sometimes on the strings. We found a room down the basement that wasn't being used, and used it as an acoustic echo chamber. It was a very smooth, elongated echo—it was sensational! We would have engineers come from England that used to come in and say 'God! Tell us how you get that sound, that echo!' and, of course, I wouldn't tell them."

Thankfully, the producers and technicians entrusted with carefully preserving the fruits of Sinatra's labor approached the task with the utmost respect, and their contributions to the ultimate success of the vocalist as a recording artist cannot be praised enough. Their ability to adapt themselves to Sinatra's style of recording, and function as largely uncredited yet dependable supporting players, was a primary factor in the ultimate quality of the final recordings. During the Columbia years, Fred Plaut and Harold Chapman were two of the label's engineers largely responsible for transcribing Sinatra's sessions. Their peers, as well as engineers who came to Columbia years after them, attribute much of the company's reputation for superior sonics directly to their efforts. "Chappie's work was unique in the field," believes Sony Music Studios engineer Larry Keyes, himself with Columbia since the 1960s. "When you listen to the recordings that Chappie and Fred Plaut did, you hear every instrument; nothing is blocked out. They had wonderful ears—they were superb engineers."

Columbia's technical team was also on the cutting edge of research and development, which might explain their early, successful attempts at overdubbing—adding a vocal track to a previously recorded instrumental to create a composite master. While extremely rare for the time (the dubs were made disc-to-disc), the earliest Sinatra overdubs were done in March 1948, the singer dubbing vocals to orchestra tracks recorded the previous December ("It Only Happens When I Dance with You" and "Fella with an Umbrella"). The decision to use this technique on this first date, as well as another in December 1948 in which the orchestra was recorded in New York and the vocal in Hollywood ("Once in Love with Amy"), was probably made because of scheduling problems.

Sinatra's first major recording to depend on the evolving technical process of overdubbing was his first full-length ten-inch Columbia LP, *Sing and Dance with Frank Sinatra*, recorded in April 1950. This time, though, the process was not chosen to accommodate busy schedules. It was borne of necessity, because at the time the singer was experiencing many vocal problems. "When we came to do those records, Frank's voice was in terrible shape," recalls Mitch Miller, the producer of the sessions. "Frank's voice was very fragile. It was great, but it was fragile. He would be in the booth, and he'd sing a beautiful phrase, and then on the next phrase, his voice would go. But you couldn't edit! There were a lot of musicians involved, so to save the session, I just shut off his microphone and got good background (orchestra) tracks. Didn't even tell him! Then, after it was over,

I got him. I said, 'When your voice is back . . . ' We'd come in crazy hours, midnight, whatever—the doors were locked so no union representative could come in," Miller continues. "You see, I could have been kicked out of the Musicians' Union because tracking was not allowed. And that whole album is tracked!"

The tracking process is one technical advance that Sinatra chose not to embrace. Instead, he opted to achieve balanced, natural sound through perseverance and the arduous task of performing multiple takes, singing along with the band. A rare look at a Sinatra recording date from the singer's transitional phase, documented on safety copies of a complete Columbia session, allows us to peek inside the studio—and leaves little doubt as to exactly who was calling the shots.

It's July 10, 1949, and the location is Columbia's 30th Street studio. Sinatra and conductor Hugo Winterhalter are auditioning a second run-through of George Siravo's arrangement of "It All Depends on You." Listening to a passage by the brass section, Frank feels that something is amiss. Even before the session got underway, there had been problems. For whatever reason (it might have been set in the wrong key), the chart needed some revision, and, because Siravo was on the West Coast, Winterhalter and Sinatra had asked Sid Cooper (an amazing lead alto player and a gifted writer) to re-score both "It All Depends on You" and "Bye Bye, Baby."

Now on the actual date, the band has run down the chart, and Sinatra has joined in the second time for a vocal run-through. He has already had Winterhalter make some further adjustments in the arrangement, but he still senses a deficiency, somewhere in the trumpets or trombones. "I'd like to hear the introduction, with the muted brass," he asks the conductor. After hearing the passage, Sinatra carefully instructs both the musicians and the engineers: "I'd like to get that as tight as we can. Trombones, you may have to turn around and face the microphone or something. I'd like to hear the six of you, as a unit," he says. The engineer brings down a microphone with two sides, to help capture the precise tonal quality that Sinatra desires. With the offending section played through again, the singer continues. "Just once more, Hugo, and would you use less volume in the reeds, with the clarinet lead? And would you play it lightly, trumpets and trombones, if you don't mind? I mean, *softly*."

The trombone problem rectified, Sinatra, now in the booth, turns his attention to the rhythm section. He inquires of drummer Terry Snyder: "You got enough pad on the bass drum? It booms a little bit." Then, without hesitation, to the studio prop men: "Would you put in a small piece of carpet, enough to cover the entire bottom of the drum?" Once satisfied, he turns to the pianist. "Say, Johnny Guarnieri, would you play something, a figure or something, and have the rhythm fall in? We'd like to get a small balance on it." Guarnieri begins an impromptu riff on the melody, as bassist Herman "Trigger" Alpert, drummer Snyder, and guitarist Al Caiola join in. After a few moments, Sinatra's directions continue. "Bass and guitar: Trig, can you move in about a foot or so, or you can pull the mike out if you wish. And the guitar, also move in a little closer. Just a shade—uh, uh, uh—that's enough." After another recorded test, the producer (probably the ever-present Mort Palitz) affirms the changes that Sinatra has made, agreeing: "That's much better."

For Sinatra and company, this scenario has been played out session after session, decade after decade. After all, the changes that Sinatra insists on, the perfection he seeks, all make sense in the final analysis. Pianist Stan Freeman recently commented on Sinatra's approach in the studio: "I only remember him being very aware of what he wanted, and getting it! If he thought a flute or oboe part should be left out of one section, he would say so. He didn't have to take charge, but nominally he was in charge—and everybody knew that. He was always very pleasant, never any tantrums or anything."

Some biographies have reported that the Sinatra of the late Columbia period (1951–1952) was so bitter and so difficult to deal with that engineers at his sessions purposely tampered with the controls in the studio in order to damage the sound deliberately, thereby discrediting him. This is patently untrue. First, the engineers at Columbia were professionals and would not have jeopardized the high esteem in which they were held, by many artists other than Sinatra. Second, no aural evidence exists to support this assertion: all of the vocalist's Columbia recordings are of uniformly high quality, the proof of which is the proliferation of fine digital restorations made from the master session discs and tapes.

It was true, however, that late fall of 1952 found Sinatra at the lowest point in his life. The public's tastes were changing, and there was little interest in booming, postwar America for his sweet, pensive vocals, which served as reminders of the turmoil of the last decade. Intense personal problems forced the singer's emotional hand, and he eventually found himself devoid of all that he held dear: his beautiful wife (Ava Gardner), familial stability, and, on the professional side, a movie or television deal.

At Columbia Records, Sinatra found himself floundering to gain solid ground against Mitch Miller's controversial approach, which would, depending upon your perspective, revolutionize or bastardize pop music. Almost ignored at the time, both his brash, gritty recording of "The Birth of the Blues" and nearly painful rendition of "I'm a Fool to Want You" from the 1951–52 period are the finest indicators of the real strength of his voice (sharply dispelling the myth that he had lost his vocal edge) and, moreover, pointed up the direction he envisioned for his future. Clearly, he knew *exactly* where he wanted to go, and *exactly* how to get there. Miller and the powers at Columbia didn't share his vision, though, and before long, he would be unceremoniously dropped from the label. (After the master take of his final recording for the label, ironically titled "Why Try to

Change Me Now?" Miller is heard over the booth's speaker saying, wearily, "That's it, Frank.")

As the recordings amply illustrate, the Columbia years were merely the prelude to the truest expression of this singer's great art, for if at Columbia Sinatra had engaged in musical foreplay, his new association with Capitol would enable him to convincingly consummate his act.

HOLLYWOOD AND THE PEAK OF PERFECTION

Musically, the transition from Columbia to Capitol, between June of 1952 and April of 1953, involved a complex series of creative and personal changes for Sinatra and culminated in a complete revitalization. After shedding some personal baggage and shifting his base of operation entirely to the West Coast, the singer emerged with a completely new look, attitude, and sound. Gone were the floppy bow ties and slicked hair of yesteryear; in were stylish cravats of the finest silk and pattern and a jaunty felt hat, a style that communicated sophistication and wit. Not intended to be fancy props, these tasteful touches breathed freshness into his fading image and, consequently, into his work. A brand new Sinatra had emerged, and every inch of this transformation is reflected in the enthusiastic approach to the two main crafts he concentrated on: acting and singing. With an Academy Award for Best Supporting Actor in *From Here to Eternity* under his belt, he was now free to concentrate on revamping his image and re-establishing his position as the world's premiere pop vocalist.

Not surprisingly, many paths in Frank Sinatra's career neatly coincide with important technical developments in his chosen field, and this critical juncture probably had the most profound and lasting effect on the singer's work. Early in 1949, Columbia Records had introduced a new playing medium: the lightweight, vinyl "Long Playing" record (LP). Whereas previous platters were made of a fragile shellac compound (a comparatively rough surface) and spun at a dizzying seventy-eight revolutions per minute (allowing a typical ten-inch pop disc to contain no more than three-and-a-half minutes or so of program material), the new LP was a ten-inch disc with a smoother, quieter plastic surface, traveling at a much slower 33 ⅓ rpm. In addition to the incredible improvement in sonic capacity, the new discs also allowed for far greater playing time. Within just a few short years, the ten-inch disc (the standard of the pop music industry from 1949 to 1954) would give way to a twelve-inch platter, which offered nearly forty minutes of playing time per side.

Crucial as well was the introduction of recording tape into the studios, for this advancement, as well as refinements in microphone and recorder technology, allowed studio engineers to capture performances with such astounding fidelity that it was as close to "live" as being there. The use of high-fidelity tape, coupled with the superior reproduction system of the vinyl LP, brought Sinatra's razor-sharp diction and fabled phrasing front-and-center, for anyone and everyone to hear. The greater playing time and crystalline sound quality of the new LP also allowed the singer finally to realize his vision for the full-blown, thematic concept album.

Sinatra, and his essential vehicle, had arrived.

"I announced that we [Capitol] had signed Sinatra at our national convention in Colorado," remembers former Capitol Records President Alan Livingston. "There must have been a couple of hundred guys there . . . and the whole room went, 'Unnhhoooo.' My answer to them was 'I only know talent, and Frank is the best singer in the world. There's nobody that can touch him.'" Thus, within a very short time, Sinatra found himself three thousand miles and a cultural world away from Manhattan, comfortably ensconced in the Capitol recording studios—then operating from the old KHJ Radio studios, neatly tucked away at the very end of Melrose Avenue in Los Angeles, just a few yards from the entrance to the famed Paramount movie lot. From April 2, 1953, until February 22, 1956, KHJ studios would be the locale for all of Sinatra's commercial recordings and, as such, would play a pivotal role in enabling him to stage one of the greatest comebacks in entertainment history. It would be here that Frank Sinatra would make some of the most appealing and recognizable recordings of his career.

"KHJ was a wonderful studio," retired Capitol engineer John Paladino has said. "Studio A was on the upper story and was the original radio theater, with audience and stage facilities. Downstairs, there were two smaller studios and the control room. For a long time, Studio C was the key studio and was perfect for smaller groups. I distinctly remember recording some of Sinatra's albums like *Wee Small Hours* and *Close to You* in Studio C. The dance band recordings, with Nelson and Billy May, were done in Studio A, which was better suited for larger orchestras." Fronting the building that housed KHJ was Nickodell's bar (a favorite among the world's best classical and jazz musicians who continually made their daily rounds through the studio doors); across the street was Lucy's restaurant, where, on occasion, Sinatra would visit after wrapping up a session.

While there is no doubt the singer held the musicians who performed so dependably for him in high esteem, he rarely socialized with them, outside of the studio setting. "Once in a while, he did invite the musicians over to the Villa Capri restaurant after a record date. Even there he almost never made the rounds of the room, staying at his table in the back. We would approach him and say 'thanks,' and he'd beam, and that was that," remembers Milt Bernhart. On occasion, after a special session, Sinatra might throw an "in-studio" party for the technicians and the members of the orchestra. "After he finished *A Jolly Christmas from Frank Sinatra* in July of 1957, he threw a huge Christmas party for everyone," recalls Sinatra pal Frank Military. "It was incredible—catered food, drinks, everything. It was really something to see. Everyone appreciated it," he says.

Milt Bernhart also recollects a gathering that took place in the mid-1950s at Sinatra's home, off Coldwater Canyon:

Sitting in the entry area were Lauren Bacall, Adolph Green, Bill and Edie Goetz—all Hollywood people. In the main living room were some musicians; me, Murray McEachern, and a bunch of other guys. I felt a bit funny because Frank spent several hours with us, completely ignoring his other guests! And they were terribly aware of it, because one by one, they left. But this was his day with us—only Sinatra would do that. At one point during the visit, I thought I was going to make a hit with him. He brought some pizza to me and my wife, and I thought, "Now I'm going to say something that will really go over with him." His recording of "The Night We Called It a Day" from 1942 had always riveted me. I was a fan from the day I bought it, back in my band days. So I told Frank that, and I expected him to brighten up a little. Instead, his face darkened. I'll never forget it. He said, "Well, have you heard the record I made with Gordon Jenkins?" I hadn't, so Frank said, "Well, you've got to hear that." We went over to his big hi-fi setup, and he played it for me. Stood there while I listened! And I must tell you, it bore no resemblance to the original at all. It was lemonade—it was nothing to me, compared to the Stordahl version. I don't know what I said, but I didn't make the hit I had planned. That's when I knew, and I knew it right away. Something was up between him and Axel. Years later, I was on the sessions for the last album they did together at Capitol, *Point of No Return*. I remember that Sinatra was all business. He was having some difficulties with the record company then, but the strain between them showed in the studio. He just walked right up to the microphone and said, "What's up?" On most of the tunes, he did only one, maybe two takes. At one point, Dave Cavanaugh [the producer] asked him for another take on a song, and Sinatra refused. The lead sheet was already on the floor. He just said, "Nope. Next tune."

While few outsiders had penetrated the sanctity of Sinatra's Columbia recording sessions, the atmosphere was markedly relaxed after his move to Hollywood and Capitol Records. "There was always a crowd at those Sinatra sessions on Melrose," says Bernhart. "They should have charged admission! Because KHJ had been a radio theater, it had a big auditorium. And the place was packed to the back! You weren't just playing a record date; you were playing a *performance*. They took a great chance on the people applauding, because they could get caught up in the thing and ruin a take . . . but believe me, they were sitting on the edge. And it was an 'in' crowd: movie stars, disc jockeys. It was big, big. It was hard to get in; you had to be invited. But they'd fill the damned place!"

Barely a year removed from the tumult and near-fatal disaster of his darkest hour, Sinatra thrust himself into the Capitol era with remarkable, unbridled energy. He used each newfound opportunity to his best advantage, eagerly coming to the game prepared to play, knowing it had to be hard and fast. That the decidedly downcast singer and the rapidly advancing technology collided and landed him into the Hollywood studios of the relatively young Capitol Records was undoubtedly a fortunate occurrence. With all these worlds crashing together, it was almost certain that the fallout would be spectacular. As with all things Sinatra, it turned out to be downright electrifying—half the current, in this case, supplied by a young, talented arranger named Nelson Riddle.

Of all the arrangers the singer worked with, Riddle complemented Sinatra's talents better than anyone else. Whereas Sinatra could rely on Stordahl and Gordon Jenkins to pen wistful orchestrations that spoke tenderly of love and youth and spring, and Billy May to sound all the whistles and bells with his full-steam-ahead tempo charts, it was Nelson Riddle and his unflappable temperament who provided an even keel. From their first studio session on April 30, 1953, the duo carefully crafted and perfected such an extraordinary signature sound that Riddle became sought after by dozens of other famous vocalists wishing to duplicate the immensely successful Sinatra-Riddle style for their own recordings. With the first song they tackled on that momentous occasion, the dynamic, explosive "I've Got the World on a String," the tone was set. It was obvious that the pair were of one musical mind and that their perspectives had quickly melded into a totally cohesive, effective mass to produce, from the very start, some incredibly tight and polished performances.

While Riddle mainly stuck to string-oriented arrangements for his earliest work with Nat Cole (primarily scoring his ballad sessions), he began to feature his own favored instrument, trombone, prominently in his charts for Sinatra. Bass trombonist George Roberts recalls the birth of Riddle's unique instrumentation. "I was over his house an awful lot, and we would talk about a lot of things. He said he needed 'identification.' I told him I thought he should use flute, Harmon mute trumpet [tastefully provided by Harry "Sweets" Edison], bass trombone, and strings, and do something with that combination, which he did. And that was where his 'identification' came from! I always said that I felt bass trombone was as melodic a horn as any horn there is, and it should be written as a melodic horn. Nelson said to me, 'You must have the heart of an elephant,' but then, he wound up writing bass trombone melodically, and I'll be damned if it didn't work for him. He was the only one doing that at the time." As samples, Roberts's very melodic solos on "Makin' Whoopee" (*Songs for Swingin' Lovers*, 1956) and "How Deep Is the Ocean" (*Nice 'n' Easy*, 1960) clearly demonstrate the beauty and progressiveness of their thinking.

Comfortable with nearly any tempo or style, Nelson had a knack for painting backdrops that were richly layered in texture and tone, cushioned and sparse enough to allow plenty of room for Sinatra to toy with the tempo and timing of the lyric. At the same time, his orchestrations were complex, infused with fine gradations of color and unique instrumentation. Even after hundreds of repeated listenings, there are still surprise figures and counter melodies and musical phrases that will pop out from within the arrangement, as if they hadn't been buried in there for the past forty years or so! Nelson Riddle provided the musical support that enabled Sinatra to stand behind the microphone and make powerful proclamations and potent statements with a renewed sense of passion and urgency. In this sense, the style that Riddle developed and perfected for Frank Sinatra went far beyond the arrangements he was doing for Nat Cole and Judy Garland, which were very special in their own right. "Frank undoubtedly brought out my best work," Riddle told Robin Douglas-Home. "He's stimulating to work with. You have to be right on mettle all the time. The man himself somehow draws everything out of you" (Douglas-Home 33).

Of interest is the fact that Sinatra seemed to spend more time discussing ideas and planning for recording sessions with Riddle than with anyone else, their uniquely detailed working methods being a critical link to their widely acclaimed studio collaborations. To appreciate fully why they were so effective in bringing their tremendous forces together in the studio, we must first assess the underlying foundation of their musical partnership and how intense pre-studio planning had, in the end, just as much of a hand in the outcome as the actual sessions themselves. An in-depth look at the Sinatra-Riddle "marriage" serves to illustrate the optimal relationship between all vocalists and arrangers and the often inexplicable factors that combine to produce music of uncommon beauty.

"Nelson is the greatest arranger in the world," Sinatra told Douglas-Home. "A very clever musician. He's like a tranquilizer—calm, slightly aloof. There's a great depth somehow to the music he creates. And he's got a sort of stenographer's brain. If I say to him at a planning meeting, 'Make the eighth bar sound like Brahms,' he'll make a cryptic little note on the side of some scrappy music sheet, and, sure enough, when we come to the session, the eighth bar will be Brahms. If I say, 'Make like Puccini,' Nelson will make exactly the same little note, and that eighth bar will be Puccini all right, and the roof will lift off!" (Douglas-Home 35).

"Frank and I both have, I think, the same musical aim," Riddle contended. "We know what we're each doing with a song—what we want the song to say. Frank would have very definite ideas about the general treatment, particularly about the pace of the record. . . . He'd sketch out something brief, like 'Start with a bass figure, build up second time through and then fade out at the end.' That's possibly all he would say. Sometimes, he'd follow this up with a phone call at three in the morning with some other extra little idea. But after that, he wouldn't hear my arrangements until the recording session" (Douglas-Home 33). The planning, though, could become tedious. Shortly before his death, Riddle spoke at great length about the planning meetings with Sinatra. "In those days, twelve or more songs comprised an album. Frank would start with the most agonizingly specific comments on the first few tunes, often referring to classical compositions for examples of what he expected to hear in the orchestration. This hot, precise, demanding pace would continue for an hour or two, perhaps through the first four or five songs. Then, as if he too were beginning to feel the strain, he would start to slack off. The comments would grow less specific, and perhaps a tune or so later, he would say, simply, 'Do what you think is best.' My headache would start to subside, my pulse return to normal, and another Sinatra-Riddle album would be launched" (Riddle 170).

Riddle further described his systematic approach to scoring a Sinatra record. "In working out arrangements for Frank, I suppose I stuck to two main rules. First, find the peak of the song and build the whole arrangement to that peak, pacing it as he paces himself vocally. Second, when he's moving, get the hell out of the way. When he's doing nothing, move in fast and establish something. After all, what arranger in the world would try to fight *against* Sinatra's voice?" "Most of our best numbers were in what I call the tempo of the heartbeat," Riddle further explained. "That's the tempo that strikes people easiest because, without their knowing it, they are moving to that pace all their waking hours. Music to me is sex—it's all tied up somehow, and the rhythm of sex is the heartbeat. . . . I usually try to avoid scoring a song with a climax at the end. Better to build about two-thirds of the way through, and then fade to a surprise ending. More subtle. I don't really like to finish by blowing and beating in top gear. . . . Though Frank never really learned how to read music, much less play an instrument, he is a man attracted to all the arts, especially classical music. When writing arrangements for him, I could often indulge myself in flights of neo-classical imagery, especially in introductions and endings. . . . If he feels I have caught the right mood in the introduction I have written, he is quick to acknowledge it" (Douglas-Home 34).

The creation of inventive musical fills, floating buoyantly atop a soft bed of feathery-light sustained strings, deftly arranged to contrast against Sinatra's vocal lines, is a technique that Riddle is the master of. The road traveled to arrive at the perfection of that technique was not without incident, however. Milt Bernhart once recounted a situation that arose on a record date, shortly after Sinatra and Riddle began working together:

> They were going to do an album, so we came into Capitol, and I remember clearly that the first arrangement was for "Wrap Your Troubles in Dreams." Sinatra was at his lead sheet—I don't think we'd even made a take yet. He was running the song over, and suddenly stopped—cold. And the band stopped. And Frank said to Nel-

son, "Give them a break." And he crooked his finger at Nelson, and they walked out of the studio. I don't know why, but I followed them and watched them in a smaller studio, from the hallway. Nelson was standing frozen, and Frank was doing all the talking. His hands were moving, but he was not angry. . . . He seemed to be telling him something of great importance. When we came back, the date was over. And I was positive that I knew what Frank was telling him—it was about the arrangement! I could tell it was very busy. *Too* busy. At that point, Nelson had a lot of technique as an arranger, but he had to be told to take it easy when writing for a singer. And he was told!

Like many highly creative individuals, Frank Sinatra could, at times, be extremely demanding. In all probability, this stemmed from his continuous search for perfection. While it was rare for him to display this side of his temperament to his colleagues, the pressure was on, and it manifested itself in subtle ways. Nelson Riddle once confided his feelings to George Roberts. "There's only one person in this world I'm afraid of. Not physically, but afraid of. [It's] Frank, because you can't tell what he's going to do. One minute he'll be fine, but he can change very fast." Roberts vividly recalls their conversation: "Nelson told me the reason he was so paranoid when we went to do a Sinatra date was because he [Nelson] wanted a performance the first time. He said, 'I want it right—*now*.' He didn't want to give Frank the chance to say, 'I don't like the chart.' Nelson really did feel a lot of pressure."

Publicly, Riddle offered these observations:

At a Sinatra session, the air was usually loaded with electricity. The thoughts that raced through my head were hardly ones to calm the nerves. On the contrary, questions such as "Will he like the arrangements?" and "Is the tempo comfortable for him?" were soon answered. If he didn't make any reference to the arrangement, chances are it was acceptable. And as far as the tempo was concerned, he often set that with a crisp snap of his fingers, or a characteristic hunching of the shoulders. . . . Frank contributed a lot to the orchestral part of his own records, just by leveling a hostile stare at the musicians, with those magnetic blue eyes! The point of this action was to make me, or any other conductor, feel at that exact moment as if he had two left feet, three ears and one eye. But it was a positive factor that found its way into the record. And that, I ruefully admit, is what counts. (Riddle 171)

With Billy May, Sinatra rarely involved himself with pre-session particulars. "He's easy to work with, as far as I'm concerned," May told me. "All we did was figure out the tunes. We might get to a session, and he'd say 'Let's try this a little differently,' and then we'd try it at a completely different tempo, and usually, it worked very well." In his extensive interview with Robin Douglas-Home, Sinatra spoke of his fondness for May's work.

> Recording with Billy May is like having a cold shower, or a cold bucket of water thrown in your face. Nelson will come to the session with all the arrangements carefully and neatly worked out beforehand. But with Billy, you sometimes don't get the copies of the *next* number until you've finished the one before—he'll have been scribbling away in some office in the studio right up until the start of the session! Billy works best under pressure. . . . [He] also handles the band quite differently from Nelson or Gordon. . . . With Billy, there he'll be in his old pants and a sweatshirt, and he'll stop them and he'll say, "Hey cats, this bar sixteen. You gotta oompa-de-da-da-ch-Ow. OK? Let's go then." And the band will GO! Billy is *driving*. (Douglas-Home 37)

When discussing the pure fun that most of the participants recall about their sessions with him and Sinatra, May recently said, "I figured, 'What the hell?' If you're going to go in and do it, what the hell is the use of doing anything unless you're having fun with it? I try to make it that way. I feel we're lucky to be able to be musicians and be professional about it." May's comment to me at the end of one casual conversation probably sums up his feeling best: "I feel privileged and fortunate to have worked with two of the greatest musicians in the world, people I truly admire—Glenn Miller, and Frank Sinatra."

Sinatra found a devastatingly sad sound in the arrangements of Gordon Jenkins, whose style, like the compositions and orchestrations of the legendary film composer Bernard Herrmann, relied heavily on sheets of sound created almost solely from the string section of the orchestra. To this monochromatic panorama of strings, Jenkins added the barest whisper of minor key woodwinds, horns, and soft (mallet) percussion, lending the songs a back-alley, late-night color that hauntingly portrays the very essence of Lonely Street. "With Gordon Jenkins, it's all so beautifully simple that, to me, it's like being back in the womb," Sinatra observed (Douglas-Home 37). In an interview with Sid Mark, Sinatra went on: "Gordon was a man who was always open to suggestions, but he was one man that I felt I could almost leave alone—just let him work by himself. I think he was probably the most sensitive man about orchestrations. . . . You can hear it in his music. . . . I used to call him 'Lefty' because he had a very good left-handed [golf] swing. But also, it was confusing to me when I first started to work with him, because when you're used to looking at a conductor in front of you on a podium, waving his *right* hand, and suddenly, you're looking for the beat and he's on the other hand . . . it was confusing for the first couple of dates, but it worked out in the end."

Arguably, this chapter in Sinatra's career (1953–1962) is his very finest, the singer reaching the absolute peak of vocal perfection in early 1955, as evidenced by the incredibly supple intonation and vocal shading he achieved on the classic album *In the Wee Small Hours*. In addition to his voice maturing to a naturally darker tone, it was around this time that he began to take more noticeable liberties with the timing and meter of his vocal lines, within the context of the musical orchestration. In a radio interview, Sinatra elaborated:

> I've always believed that the written word is first, always first. Not belittling the music behind me, it's really only a curtain. . . . You must look at the lyric, and understand it. Find out where you want to accent something, where you want to use a soft tone. The word actually dictates to you in a song—it really tells you what it needs. I figure speech is the same way. Syncopation in music is important, of course, particularly if it's a rhythm song. It can't be "one-two-three-four/one-two-three-four," because it becomes stodgy. So syncopation enters the scene, and it's "one-two," then maybe a little delay, and then "three," and then another longer delay, and *then* "four." It all has to do with *delivery*.

The "heartbeat" meter previously described by Riddle, in combination with Sinatra's just-ahead-of or just-behind-the-beat syncopation, is the crux of the total effectiveness of their work and probably the singer's most characteristic vocal technique. An audition of such classic recordings as the 1956 versions of "Night and Day," "Oh! Look at Me Now," and "From This Moment On" (among dozens of other fine examples) reveals awesomely powerful, subliminally sexual overtones, stunningly achieved through the mounting tension and release of the musical arrangement and Sinatra's beat-teasing vocal lines.

A fine recording that succinctly defines Riddle's genius as an arranger is "River, Stay 'Way from My Door," from April of 1960. The chart begins with a loose, laid back tempo. From chorus to chorus, though, the song builds in intensity as the brass section gradually soars, climaxing to so fierce a level that on the last chorus, your mind is conjuring up images of the drummer, who sounds as if he might just be standing on the balls of his feet, emphatically battering the skins of his kit, punctuating every beat in exact 4/4 time, with deliberate, pounding force. By the song's end, Sinatra, sparring with the band, sounds as though he's lunging at the microphone, as if to shout in admonishment, "Yeaahhh. . . . THERE! Take THAT!" (In fact, the energy is so great that it is one of the few times that Sinatra's vocal power pushed the capability of his microphone to its very limit, the strain on the instrument clearly audible. The singer was obviously pushing himself to the "max" as well, which is apparent in his final emphasis of the word "heart," just before the out-chorus.) While on the surface it appears as though the entire song has modulated from a medium-slow to fast tempo, it doesn't waver at all from the prescribed "heartbeat" meter. Not only does Riddle cleverly weave musical dynamics into the arrangement, but he crafts them so adroitly that the *illusion* of a change in tempo becomes an integral part of the performance and its cumulative emotional effect! Listen for the dramatic impact of the ending, when Riddle suddenly drops the orchestra way down and then, in concert with Sinatra's vocal, executes a gradual, controlled crescendo—the orchestra quickly returning to full volume, which it sustains to the finish line.

One would assume that a technique resulting in such driving force could only be applied to snappy, up-tempo song treatments, but a similar effect was achieved on more subdued ballad recordings as well. The 1963 Reprise album *The Concert Sinatra* is replete with orchestral dynamics that utilize tremendously swirling and sweeping strings, pretty woodwind counter-melodies, and repetitive harp glissandi that raise the goosebump factor to stratospheric heights. "I Have Dreamed," "You'll Never Walk Alone," "Ol' Man River," and "This Nearly Was Mine"—all songs on the album—are a testament to Riddle's sensitivity and ability to stir the soul in a deeply meaningful way. The superb orchestrations offered here are surpassed only by Sinatra's carefully controlled phrasing and razor-sharp diction.

The arranger, in his textbook *Arranged by Nelson Riddle*, describes the importance of building dynamics into the orchestration.

> Dynamic shadings are a vital part of presenting music effectively. Some of the most effective crescendos I ever incorporated into my arrangements were not achieved by writing dynamic markings or exhorting an orchestra to observe my flailing arm motions. They were accomplished by gradually adding orchestral weight until the desired peak was reached. The same can be said for diminuendos, in which case the orchestra is progressively thinned out until a *ppp* (*very piano*, or *softly*) is accomplished. True dynamics [changes in loudness] in an orchestra are achieved beautifully and naturally by a combination of orchestral textures and lines. When "peaks and valleys" occur under these conditions, they sound so logical and effortless as to appear perfectly natural, which they are. Nothing makes an orchestration as attractive as the contrasts achieved by close attention to sensible dynamics. (171)

"Frank accentuated my awareness of dynamics by exhibiting his own sensitivity in that direction," Riddle comments. "It's one thing to indicate by dynamic markings (*p*, *mp*, *mf*, etc.) how you want to have the orchestra play your music. It's quite another to induce a group of blasé, battle-scarred musicians to observe those markings and play accordingly. I would try, by word and gesture, to get them to play correctly, but if, after a few times through the orchestra still had not observed the proper dynamics, Frank would suddenly turn and draw from them the most exquisite shadings, using the most effective means yet discovered: sheer intimidation!" (Riddle 171).

While Sinatra had gained a reputation for refusing to do repeated takes on a movie set (he felt it robbed the scene of freshness and believability), he didn't subscribe to the same theory when in the recording studio, where, dogged by a relentless pursuit of perfection, he would spend whatever time was necessary to arrive at what he felt was his finest effort. "With Sinatra, it was unusual that he would have to go past four or five takes," says Milt Bernhart. "But I remember he was being careful, *very* careful, at that time. This man had instinct. He knew what was going to be important." It took twenty-two takes to reach a level of perfection that satisfied the singer for Cole Porter's "I've Got You Under My Skin," the impeccable reading confidently affirming the validity of his artistic rebirth, forever etching Sinatra, vintage 1956, into the American consciousness. Sublimely erotic and seductive, this recording is surely the turning point in the Sinatra-Riddle period, the pivot on which all future Sinatra efforts would hinge. Ironically, it almost never came to pass, as the song had been added to the list of tunes for the *Songs for Swingin' Lovers* album on the night before the session at which it was recorded. In the forty-plus years since its waxing, the recording has justifiably become one of the most studied and admired Sinatra performances of all time. "When we ran the arrangement down the first time, the band played it like they had played it many times before, and when they were through, they applauded Nelson, probably because somebody knew that he wrote it in a hurry," recalls pianist Bill Miller.

To breathe new life into the tune, Riddle enlisted bass trombonist George Roberts to help him devise an intriguing musical passage that would lead up to the song's "bridge," the instrumental middle of a song to which all the tension builds before releasing. "Nelson called me up, and said, 'Frank wants a long crescendo for the middle of "Skin." Do you know any Afro-Cuban rhythmical patterns?' And I said, 'Well, why don't you steal the rhythmic pattern out of Stan Kenton's '23 Degrees North, 82 Degrees West'? He said, 'How does it go?' And I gave him the beginning trombone lines, the Afro-Cuban sounding thing, which he developed into the 'BOP-*BOP*/BOM-BOM/BOM-*BOM*-BOM-BA-DOP' crescendo that led up to the trombone solo."

"I left the best stuff I played on the first five takes," believes Milt Bernhart, the man responsible for the blistering trombone solo that absolutely blew the top off the record. "It was a spontaneous solo. As with many of Nelson's charts where there was room for a solo, there were chord symbols sketched out in the chart—but nothing was written out," he says. "Frank kept saying, 'Let's do another.' This was unusual for Sinatra! I was about ready to collapse—I was running out of gas! Then, toward the tenth take or so, someone in the booth said, 'We didn't get enough bass. Could we get the trombone nearer to a microphone?' I mean, what had they been doing? There was a mike there for the brass, up on a very high riser. 'Can you get up to that one?' they asked. And I said, 'Well, no—I'm not that tall.' So they went looking for a box, and I don't know where he found one, but none other than Frank Sinatra went and got a box, and brought it over for me to stand on!"

"After the session, I was packing up, and Frank came over and said, 'Why don't you come in the booth and listen to it.' *That* was special!" Bernhart says. "You know, it never really went past that. If you weren't able to play like that, then why would they have called you? You knew that you were there—we *all* were there—at Frank's behest. Rarely, if ever, would he directly point something out in the studio." On one session, Bernhart recalls, French horn player Vince DeRosa executed an extremely difficult musical passage. "We came in to do a date on the next night, and Frank said something to the band like 'I wish you guys could have heard Vince DeRosa last night,' and then, typically Sinatra, he added, 'I could have hit him in the mouth!' We all knew what he meant—he had loved it! And believe me, he reserved comments like that only for special occasions. You see, it was very hard for him to say, 'It was the greatest thing I ever heard.' But that's Sinatra. He could sing with the grace of a poet, but when he's talking to you, it's *Jersey*!"

Always critical of his own work, Sinatra said in a radio interview that it is difficult for him to listen to his recordings after the sessions are completed: "There were times that we might have rushed it a bit . . . maybe we should have done one more take, to get it right. When I listen, I hear where those problem areas are—where I might have hit a 'clam,' or there might have been a little something with the orchestra . . . and I cringe."

The vibrancy and richness of Frank Sinatra's priceless Capitol recordings remain unparalleled, because they were, from a technical standpoint, the finest recordings of his career. The sound that Capitol was able to produce, from the mono era through the early days of stereo, is nothing less than amazing. The clarity, warmth, and depth of the original tape masters vividly bring every vocal and instrumental nuance and texture to the very front of the sound stage. "We were the very first to go to tape," says Alan Livingston, speaking of the transition from disc to tape recording in the late 1940s. "On top of that, we prided ourselves on our sound and in our use of *pure* vinyl for our pressings. I believe Decca was using sand or some type of recycled material in the vinyl for their records, and they had the worst quality in the world," he maintains.

"The whole secret of Capitol's sound, and something that was given a great deal of attention, was the use of acoustic echo chambers," asserts

John Paladino. "We were very, very lucky to have people that spent the time and money to develop the chambers. In the early days of mixing, it was a 'hands off' style: you had only a few microphones, and you'd try to position the musicians in a room that was acoustically good, like Liederkranz Hall. But we wanted to have control over the sound in a physically limited situation, like a small studio. The only way we could do that was to concentrate on proper equalization, use of the best mikes, and developing the best echo chambers," he says. From the time that Capitol began recording at Radio Recorders, through the KHJ era, the chambers were placed on the roof of the building. In order to create a realistic sonic portrait, the engineers manipulated the reverb and controlled the amount that was used on each individual microphone.

"Capitol was known to be a progressive company, and the manufacturers knew this," says Paladino. "We'd get the newest and best microphones, speakers and tape machines, but the boards [mixing consoles] were really simple, basically one step up from a radio board! Capitol designed the consoles, which were twelve-position boards with rotary pots. There was basic EQ available on ten of the twelve channels, and I mean *basic*—two positions for high frequencies, two for low. At that point, at KHJ, we were using the Ampex 200 tape machine, running at 30 ips [inches per second: the speed of the tape passing through the machine. Faster speeds produce greater sonic accuracy].

"Everything was monophonic at Capitol until around 1958, when we began recording most things in stereo, although we were doing some experimental stereo recording early in the game, on Melrose," he recalls. The polyester-based tape stock, which has held up remarkably well in the intervening decades, was usually Scotch 100 or a similar formulation manufactured by Audiotape. So good was the setup and balance and the final tape recording that it is hard to believe the current CD re-masters (that feature sound of superb clarity and dynamic range) were made from session tapes that are more than forty years old. "The tape at that time was not a high-output type, so we were very careful about setting levels, and riding the gain, so that we didn't get too much noise. Those early tape machines could introduce a lot of noise, so we tried to get the best signal-to-noise ratio possible, to minimize it," Paladino explains.

One of the most outstanding characteristics of the early Capitol recordings, when compared with the Sinatra recordings on previous labels, is the enhanced fullness of the singer's voice. The preservation of the exact timbre and tone of Sinatra's voice was achieved through the use of a fairly new, ultra-sensitive condenser/tube microphone, the Neumann U47, which almost immediately became the state of the art. "The U47 was a good choice for a vocalist, because it had a fine cardioid pattern, and gave nice direction, for isolation," Paladino explains. "On Frank's vocals, I would cut him off at 8 or 10 Khz; otherwise, we'd have to deal with (high frequency) sibilance, which the tape machines didn't handle very well." Paladino details his studio setup for a typical Sinatra dance band session at the Melrose studio:

> At a session, every microphone would be placed to its best advantage; each mike had a certain characteristic, so we would utilize the proper mike to get the best sound. The RCA 44, with a bit of EQ, was a hard microphone to beat; for a typical mono session, I'd use a 44 split on reeds, placed low (around 18" off the floor) to get that nice, "fat" sax sound. Then, off the side of this mike, I'd use another 44, or a Neumann U47 for the trombones. Now, above the trombones were the trumpets, which were picked up by the trombone mike, but I'd still give them their own mike as well. The piano would be miked (I favored the 44 for piano); the drums would have one RCA 77 over the top of the kit, and for the acoustic bass, I'd either use a 639, or an Altec contact mike that could be strapped to the bass. The guitar got its own mike as well. Frank would be out in front of the band, always with a Neumann. Miking strings along with so much rhythm and brass could be a problem. Of course, we couldn't record them separately and cut them in later, so we just dealt with it.

At the time, it was the standard operating procedure to run one tape machine, although later, with the move to the new Capitol studios on Vine Street, at least one additional recorder would be run as a backup. Contrary to popular belief, it was unusual for the engineers to let the tape roll for the entire session: once the take was over, the machine was routinely stopped until the aggregation was prepared to start the next attempt. This didn't always happen, however, and extant tapes containing longer pieces of the chatter and rehearsals that occurred between takes are fascinating and have been critical tools for historians interested in studying the artist's working habits.

"Frank always preferred to be on the stage, with the band," says Paladino. "He wanted eye contact with everyone; he *charged* the musicians— that's what made his sessions so special. Usually, I kept him right there, with the band, but sometimes we'd use a small isolation screen. When we were recording the *Songs for Swingin' Lovers* album, we had so many musicians on the stage in Studio A at KHJ that I put Frank down below, on the floor, to get better isolation. And it worked out fine," he adds. "Some of the best recordings I remember making were Billy May's dance band records, which we recorded the same way. I think it was a matter of space, because that studio had the stage, and you could blow the band over the top, and the kickback wouldn't come until a bit later. That simple process produced great sound! It was much harder to accomplish when we went up to Vine Street, because without the open space on top, the sound would just slap right back at you," he says.

"The playbacks were very important to Frank," Paladino continues. "It gave him the chance to relax, and he got the admiration of everyone around him. He listened very intently. If we had some editing to do, we'd do it right then, after the playback, with him in the booth." After the playback, Frank and his producer would decide which take would be used, and it would be leadered (plastic tape inserted at beginning and end) and later extracted and spliced onto the master reel in the sequential order in which the songs would appear on the album. If the song was to be released as a single, it would be cut off the session reel and added to, in Capitol terminology, a "phonoreel," which was an amalgamation of every artist's singles, in sequential recording order.

Precious little film exists showing Sinatra in the working environs of the recording studio. Footage shot in 1965 for a *CBS Reports* documentary called *Sinatra* includes the Reprise session for Ervin Drakes's Sinatra classic "It Was a Very Good Year." The studio setting is much as you'd expect, with Gordon Jenkins conducting from a raised podium, and Sinatra, a few feet away on the floor, caressing and massaging the lyric with every fiber of his being; between choruses smoking a cigarette, proudly beaming at the orchestra. In a marked departure from "standard operating procedure," the singer's trademark hat rests not on his head but on the end of the boom microphone stand, lending a very relaxed touch to the studio's somewhat sterile atmosphere. What is most revealing about the scene is the pleasure that Frank Sinatra obviously derived from listening to the playback of a song he's just recorded. During the playback of "Very Good Year," Sinatra is seen listening intently, eyes closed, swaying to the gentle rhythm of the melody. When he hears a particularly sensitive passage, he cocks his head, leans in, and shrugs his shoulders. With a knowing smile, he nods appreciatively to Jenkins. One thing is clear: Sinatra invests as much of his soul in grooving on the playback as he does in the actual performance. It shows here in this a rare glimpse of Sinatra digging Sinatra!

"Working with Frank was different from other artists," Paladino warmly remembers. "He had the entire band under his control, and he was so completely professional about his approach and his use of microphones that it really amazed me! And Voyle Gilmore, who kind of inherited Frank when he came to Capitol, was a mild-mannered producer, although Frank dominated him. What could you do? If you said a take was good, and Frank said it was lousy, you knew what was going to happen, so you went along, and kept things flowing. Voyle was very good at that, but Frank made all the critical decisions," Paladino asserts.

The engineer also points out that the arranger, and his knowledge of the technical side of recording, helped things flow smoothly on a record date.

"Nelson understood recording, so if you told him, 'I can't control this,' he would know exactly how to correct it within the orchestration. Nelson had it down pat, so that by the time of the session, it was completely worked out. He would have already made arrangements that considered the technical pitfalls of recording," he says. While Paladino specifically cites Riddle's capabilities, both Billy May and Gordon Jenkins were equally skilled in this area.

In *Arranged by Nelson Riddle*, the arranger cautions students on the importance of understanding how various instruments will sound in different acoustic settings. "The violin has a tendency to 'thin out' as it climbs, which means that the upper notes, to be effective, must be reserved for the large string section. To write a 'C' above high 'C' for the violins of a six-violin section is quite foolish since the note, even if played in tune by all six, is thin and ineffective. Such heights should be reserved for sections including at least eight violins, more if possible. If you are writing an arrangement for a recording session, a skillful engineer can place the string mike in a position that will ensure a warm, intense 'C' above high 'C,' even though the violins may number as few as the eight I mentioned" (Riddle 14). The situation changes when the performance takes place in a less controlled environment, for example, a TV studio or outdoor concert venue. In these instances, adjustments to the orchestration must be made accordingly.

Frank Sinatra was once again the focus of recording history when, on February 22, 1956, he presided over the very first recording session in Capitol Records' new studio-office facility, the Capitol "Tower," strategically located at Hollywood and Vine Streets in Hollywood, just steps away from busy Sunset Boulevard and the famous "Walk of Fame." (This time, however, he traded his tonsils for a conductor's baton, leading a full symphony orchestra in a series of musical vignettes composed by the day's top composer-orchestrators for an album simply titled *Tone Poems of Color*.) Designed by architect Welton Beckett, the Capitol building's unique cylindrical shape replicates a stack of records, complete with a "needle" on top (the building's spire, which contains a red light that spells out "Hollywood" in Morse code). The structure remains one of the most recognizable and historically significant landmarks in Hollywood.

The transition from Melrose to Vine, and from mono to stereo, were not without incident. While the new Tower studios were designed to replicate the acoustics of the KHJ studios, they couldn't possibly be the same. "The sound at Melrose was so good it took us about a year to work things out so everyone was happy, including Sinatra," Paladino recalls. "The control rooms were initially set up for mono, but for a time we ran both stereo and mono recorders at the sessions. The big question was, how do you produce your stereo records? Do you make a separate mono recording, or mix to mono right off the stereo? What *is* stereo? There was always an argument between the purist approach to stereo and the practical approach. Stereo sound could simply be sound coming out of two speakers, or it could be a true duplication of the sound of the room, in which case you'd try for a fairly straightforward setup. It was up to the engineer to determine the most effective use of microphone placement, and balance."

As on Melrose Avenue, much of the sound quality at the Capitol Tower was related to reverberation. "On Hollywood and Vine, the echo chambers are buried about fifteen feet below the ground, under the parking lot," Paladino says. "They were carefully designed—very highly developed. There are four wedge-shaped chambers, made of hard cement, each eight to ten feet high. Humidity became a problem with the underground chambers, so different epoxy paints were tried until the sound was perfected. The microphones used underground are the very best; it was a bi-directional setup. Most of the time, we'd print the reverb directly to tape at the sessions: for mono, we'd use one chamber, for stereo it would be two chambers and two mikes," he explains. The natural chambers are still used at Capitol today and are especially helpful when the studio's engineers are re-mixing and restoring multi-track tapes made at the facility years before.

Three studios, re-dubbed A, B, and C after the move from Melrose Avenue, comprise the bulk of the Tower's ground floor. Studio A, the largest in the building, was host to a sterling cast of vocalists who, in addition to Sinatra, dominated the pop-music field throughout the 1950s and early 1960s: Nat Cole, Judy Garland, Dean Martin, and Peggy Lee were all signed to the label, and recorded most of their signature songs there. The impressive facility was also a prime jazz recording venue, with Benny Goodman, Harry James, and Duke Ellington embarking on updated "hi-fi" re-recordings in the studio, joining the undisputed "king" of Capitol jazz, Stan Kenton. As well, many of Norman Grantz's Verve recordings, including some classic Clifford Browne and Dinah Washington jam sessions, and the early Ella Fitzgerald *Songbooks* were made in the main studio.

Today, the history of the studio's past is unfurled with each visitor's step through the hallowed hallway leading into Studio A. That hallway is lined with oversized, framed photos of the giants who were the impetus for the most admired musical moments in history. For those who love the music and appreciate the finest nuances of its creation, these few yards (the same path that Sinatra took) that lead into the very room where such treasured sounds were made is almost spiritual—as if, by being there, you become somehow magically connected to the past.

In December of 1960, concurrent with his Capitol Records activities, Frank Sinatra quietly entered the studios of United Western Recording in Los Angeles and began taping an album that would be released not by Capitol, but his own newly formed label, Reprise Records. It was, for the time, a bold move, its boldness difficult to imagine now, at a time when it is common for artists to have their own label or imprint. Having made a mountain of spectacular successes for the folks at "The Tower," he was ready to move on to his next phase—with or without the consent of the folks at Capitol. From 1960 to 1962 he would record and release albums for both Capitol, to whom he was contractually obligated, and his own Reprise label. From 1962 to 1993, when he made a bizarre return to Capitol for the surreal *Duets* projects, all Sinatra recordings would be recorded and distributed by Reprise. While the new recording outlet enabled him to maintain more artistic control and freedom than he had ever enjoyed before, Sinatra seems, at this point, to have lost interest in personally supervising the technical details of the recording and mixing sessions that would result in records whose labels bore not only his name but his likeness as well.

Next to the astonishingly beautiful sound quality of the Capitol recordings, many of Sinatra's Reprise efforts pale by comparison. In fact, the biggest problem with the singer's recordings from this period are their uneven sound quality: one album might be marred by such anomalies as mild distortion, excess reverb, an abundance of tape hiss, uneven mixing and balance; the next could be an audio delight. The recent discovery of copies of master tapes, missing from the Reprise vaults for years, reveals some interesting clues regarding the less-than-perfect sonic merits of some of Sinatra's Reprise recordings.

Since its initial release in 1960, Sinatra's first Reprise album, *Ring-a-Ding-Ding*, has been plagued with a brittle, hissey, echoey sound that has robbed the listener of the full, dynamic experience that Johnny Mandel's percussive, swinging arrangements should undoubtedly offer. For many years, Sinatra aficionados believed that the original recordings were inferior, as these problems were noticeable in the first pressings of the album (both mono and stereo), as well as its most recent compact disc release. A study of the aforementioned session tapes, however, contradicts this theory. While the tape copies are mono and therefore preclude any evaluation of the details of the stereo mix, they are startlingly clear: essentially flat (no reverb), with very distinct separation noted among the instruments of the orchestra, indicating that all of the inferior sound of the album came during post-production, *after* the original recordings were made.

Being a new entity, Reprise didn't maintain its own studios as the major labels did. Instead, it utilized independent recording facilities. Sinatra's favorite studio was United Western Recording, on Sunset Boulevard, operated by Bill Putnam, the engineer he would come to trust implicitly. The singer was so sure of Putnam's abilities that, when extenuating circumstances forced him to relocate for a session, his discomfort was sure to be reflected in his attitude on the date. Arranger Marty Paich, who had occasion to record only two songs with Sinatra, recalls their meeting at the RCA Victor studios in Hollywood. "He really wouldn't do a session without Bill, until he had to do our record. There was no studio available over at United, so we brought him over to RCA Victor, and I got the feeling at the time that he was a little perturbed about it. Because Frank, at that time, pretty much got his own way, and it just felt to me that maybe he would rather have been over at United, with Bill Putnam," Paich observed, shortly before his death.

One of the exceptions to the hit-and-miss sonic rule, the *Sinatra & Strings* album, is a landmark recording that documented the first meeting of Sinatra and arranger Don Costa. For this master, the producer and mixing engineer wisely chose to enhance the flat session tapes with just the right shower of reverberation, resulting in an appealingly glossy, wet sound that perfectly underscores the plaintive feel of Sinatra classics like "Come Rain or Come Shine," "Yesterdays," "Prisoner of Love," and "That's All," each elegantly emphasizing the colors and textures that mark the arranger's finest hour. This combination of undistilled performance and thoughtfully crafted sound resulted in the rare capture of the late-night club ambience that honestly illustrates the essence of Frank Sinatra.

Conversely, an album that is absolutely exquisite from a performance standpoint, yet falls a bit short of the sonic mark, is the impressive *The Concert Sinatra*, recorded with Riddle in February of 1963. An ambitious undertaking, the project sought to present a program of carefully chosen, extended Sinatra performances, recorded in the richest, highest fidelity possible. Since virtually no other studio could accommodate the massive, seventy-three-piece symphony orchestra required for the sessions, the recordings were made on Stage Seven of the Samuel Goldwyn film studios in Hollywood, a hall noted for its naturally reverberant qualities. With the careful deployment of a battery of the finest microphones known to humanity, the proceedings were preserved via the highly touted Westrex 35mm recording system: a sprocket-type multi-head magnetic recorder, utilizing 35mm recording film for the highest possible signal-to-noise ratio. With such intense preparation and attention to detail, this recording should have been one of the most powerful, vibrant recordings in history. In fact, the audio community was so impressed with the project that in the album's liner notes Raymond V. Pepe, president of the Institute of High Fidelity, remarked, "Pages could be written about the technical details of the equipment employed and the techniques used in this recording. . . . It could well serve as a guide to all recording companies to achieve the ultimate in a disc recording."

Unfortunately, the anticipated superior fidelity of some of the most spectacular recordings of Sinatra's career was lost in the transcription of the 35mm tapes to the standard two-track, 1/4-inch master that would be used for production. Lee Herschberg, an assistant engineer at United Recording who would eventually supervise Sinatra's recording activities in the late sixties, describes the mix-down process. "I believe they had one eight-track,

35mm recorder running, and a whole bunch of separate 35mm tracks that could be synced together later, for a total of twenty-one tracks. Now, they were actually locking those twenty-one tracks together after the sessions at Goldwyn and mixing them down to three-track tape. I was back at United, mixing the three-track tapes down to a final, two-track master," he recalls. The degradation of what was undoubtedly a well-recorded album came, once again, after the original sessions. By the time the film-stock session masters were twice mixed to regular tape (two generations removed from the originals), then pressed on vinyl, they had lost almost all of the spatial ambience and sonic detail that made them unique. (Presently, the original 35mm session tracks are presumed lost. It is not known if they were retained after the tracks were mixed to the three-, then two-track tapes. The current CD issue, mastered from the two-track mixdown, finds the entire recording bathed in tape hiss.)

As sessions go, by the early sixties, Sinatra had it nailed down. He'd get in, do his job, and get out. Rarely were the performances dull, even in the unusual event that the singer wasn't on a vocal par, as was the case when in June of 1962 he arrived in England, weary from the rigors of a massive world-tour but determined to complete a scheduled recording date with admired British arranger Robert Farnon. Historic, in-depth interviews with Farnon and producer Alan Freeman, as well as the availability of unissued studio session outtakes, allow us to paint a realistic picture of the events that occurred in a British studio over three nights in June of 1962.

ANATOMY OF AN ALBUM: LONDON, 1962

The dates: June 12, 13, and 14, 1962. The location: the CTS Bayswater Studio in London. The event: three evening sessions for *Great Songs from Great Britain*, Frank Sinatra's very first album to be recorded outside of the United States.

The idea for the album was his entirely. Word had come from Sinatra's office in Los Angeles six months before that Frank would be wrapping up an extensive charity tour in June, and that he thought it might be nice to record an album in England. The specifications were simple: all the songs must be of British origin, with Robert Farnon creating the arrangements.

The six months prior to the first session had been hectic for Sinatra's British collaborators. Among their tasks was the imposing job of working with the singer to select dozens of appropriate tunes, which would eventually be narrowed down to the twelve that would be taped at the sessions. When word of the planned album hit the press, producer Alan Freeman found himself swamped with requests from numerous songwriters to include their songs on the album. "Eric Maschwitz, who wrote 'A Nightingale Sang in Berkeley Square,' called me up and drove me mad!" says Freeman. "He insisted that this would be the most important thing that could happen to his song and career. And I said, 'I think it would stand a great chance [of being included],' and I sent it along to Frank. Personally, I think that's the song that came out best on the album," Freeman admits. "Frank picked out 'We'll Meet Again,' 'I'll Follow My Secret Heart,' and 'Garden in the Rain,' I believe. He also adored 'London by Night,' which was written by Carroll Coates, an Englishman who was living in the States," Freeman remembers. One song chosen personally by the singer, the lovely "Now Is the Hour," almost wasn't included, because it was not a British song. "It's near enough British!" Sinatra had said, and the song remained.

"Don Costa, who was working closely with Sinatra, was a big champion of my work," remembers the record's orchestrator, Robert Farnon, whose sweeping style is reminiscent of Stordahl's. "Perhaps it was Don, more than anyone, that suggested I arrange the album," he speculates. "I was sent the songs and the keys by Frank's pianist, Bill Miller. And he just told me, 'Go ahead and write whatever you like,' which I did. They gave me *carte blanche*! It was a delight to work that way . . . to have that freedom," he says. "I met with Frank at the Savoy Hotel before the sessions, just to say hello, and check the keys. Bill Miller was there, to assist us as well," he adds.

A week before the sessions, Bill Putnam, Sinatra's trusted engineer from Los Angeles, made a surprise visit to the studio, which was a relief to Alan Freeman. "I knew Bill was in Paris, and he phoned me and said, 'I appreciate the state you've been in—I've been there!' I told Bill, 'It would be a Godsend if you could get over to the studio and do a once-over and give us some hints.' He came in, looked around, and said, 'This should be fine; he'll like this.' Knowing that Sinatra liked to stand near the rhythm section, Putnam advised Freeman on the singer's preferences. 'Get him a screen, and surround him with rhythm,' Putnam told me, and that's exactly what we did," he remembers.

Several hours before the first recording session, Freeman was visibly nervous. He'd been at the studio for hours, to allow himself some time to relax and get the feel of the place. He was concerned about whether he'd have the luxury of a few minutes alone to acquaint himself with Frank. Freeman's function over the next three nights was to run the technical business and make sure the singer was comfortable in this strange environment. Due to the special nature of this project, and the artist involved, he refrained from imposing or enforcing his ideas on the vocalist. Sinatra, he knew, produced for himself.

Frank, nearing the end of a grueling world tour, was exhausted. Having been in the audience for Sinatra's rousing midnight show at Royal Festival Hall, Freeman knew that the famed voice was under a tremendous amount of stress. It was, in fact, nearly worn out from overuse. In addition to the many benefit concerts the world tour demanded, he was doing nightly club dates at Mesmer Hall. The producer thought about this as the call came that Sinatra was en route from his suite at the Savoy Hotel. "I just wanted to be able to talk to him alone, to have two minutes to sell myself to him, before we actually got into the studio," says Freeman. "Twenty minutes after we got the call, he arrived, in the chocolate-brown Rolls he'd borrowed from Douglas Fairbanks, Jr. I was at the door, and I was really shaking . . . petrified! When he walked up, I was introduced to him, and he shook my hand and said, 'Hi, my boy, glad to know you.' And the way he said it, with a twinkle in his eye, led me to believe he knew the tremendous strain I was under. I said something like, 'Obviously, Frank, this is the greatest thrill that ever happened to me, as it would be any producer working with you,' to which he responded, 'Well, it's nice to be here.' As we entered the studio, all the musicians and guests started applauding, and I felt very proud walking in there with him," Freeman warmly recalls.

The first tune up that evening was a Sinatra favorite, "If I Had You," which he had recorded twice before, in 1947 (Stordahl) and 1956 (Riddle). Freeman started the proceedings from the booth. "Take One, 'If I Had You.' " Then, "Okay, Bob," as Farnon counted off, cueing the orchestra. "One, two, and three. . . ." With the downbeat came immediate understanding of why Sinatra admired the beautiful perspective of the arranger, Robert Farnon. After tentatively negotiating himself through a series of hoarse, raspy lines, at three minutes and fifty seconds into the first attempt, Sinatra aborted the take. "All right, hold it—cut it," he directed. The orchestra worked out a few minor bugs, then played a few sections to give Sinatra a better sense of the timing of the melodic line. "He had great difficulty figuring out where to come in at the beginning of the song, because it had such a long intro, and he had no idea what the intro was," recalls Farnon. This affected the pacing of the rest of his vocal, which Sinatra was approaching with a bit of trepidation. "Frank is only human. . . . This intro would have thrown any artist," the arranger insists.

Then, take two. This time, twenty-seven seconds in, another vocal scrape, this time on the word "glad." "One more, please," Frank requested. Takes three and four are broken down before the vocal began and remain incomplete "false starts." Take five is complete, but a bit rough vocally. Then, after a few more incomplete takes, a near calamity, as Alan Freeman relates: "The most disastrous thing happened in the middle of recording this number—the piano broke down! The action on the piano went, and this had never happened to me before, and it never happened to me again. And the guy had been nursing that concert grand all day—tuning and re-tuning it. Well, can you imagine this on a Sinatra session, the first night, the first title? None of us was particularly at ease then, and I don't suppose Frank was, either. He was in a strange studio; he had never recorded outside of the States before. He didn't know what the hell we were all about. So the piano breaks down, and he says, 'Have you got another piano?' We didn't, so I said, 'No, Frank,' and he said, 'Okay, we'll do it on celeste.' I thought,

'Oh, thank God. . . . You know, I thought we were going to have a tantrum there, first time out," he says. For the eleventh and twelfth takes, pianist Bill Miller plinked on the celeste, an unexpected twist that added immeasurably to the picturesque quality of the album.

Patience tested and tension broken, the session continued.

"After the second title, 'The Very Thought of You,' we had a break," remembers Freeman. I knew that Frank liked Jack Daniels, so I had three bottles of it waiting in the studio. As we broke, I asked, 'Would you like a drink, Frank?' He said, 'What have you got?' So I said, 'This,' slapping it on the table. And he looked at me right in the eyes, and said, 'You've been doing your homework, haven't you?' So Frank had a drink and asked me, 'Have you ever tried this stuff?' I said, 'No.' He said, 'Would you like one?' I responded, 'Love one.' 'Have you got a glass?' he asks. 'No, I haven't got one here.' Frank says, 'Alright, share mine.' And Harold Davison took me aside, and said, 'You must be in, if he shared a glass with you.' And from that moment on, I couldn't go wrong. I felt great!" exclaims Freeman.

"I was impressed with his musicality," says Farnon. "There was a bearded chap, a trombone player, that made one or two fluffs on one of the numbers. Sinatra, of course, caught it and walked over during the orchestral interlude, and whispered to him, 'I'm afraid you got a little bit of whisker in there, mate.' That broke the orchestra up, and we had to stop playing. It was so lovely, because he heard this note even though the orchestra was playing. And it wasn't the first trombonist; it was Ray Primo, the bass trombonist!" Farnon emphasizes. Sinatra, who couldn't read a note of music, had neatly demonstrated his unerring facility for detecting a "clam" (his term) from within the deepest recess of the orchestra.

Throughout the taping, Sinatra constantly coughs and attempts to clear his throat, and the frayed edges cropping up on the ends of many notes remind one of the fragility of his instrument. Sinatra always had a self-deprecating way of joking about his vocal shortcomings on a record date. "I think I swallowed a shotglass," or "I got a busted reed," or "That was a Chesterfield, from oh, about 1947" were all typical tension-breakers, following blown notes or flubbed lines. In London, it was, at first simply, "One more, please," or "Once more, Bob—for me." After feeling out the British contingency, he loosened up. Then, after a coughing spell, he wisecracked, "Man, we gotta sleep indoors," which elicited laughs from the assembly. Freeman recalled that during one problematic song, Sinatra stopped the orchestra, looked up at the ceiling, and pleaded, "Don't just stand there. Come down and help me!"

As in Hollywood, the sessions were an event, with the venue filled to capacity, much to the consternation of the British recording team. "There were so many people in the studio that had nothing to do with the recording," Farnon recollects. "There were people sitting on my podium, under the piano, on the piano, all around us—the studio was absolutely crammed with people: the press, musicians, and fans who were privileged to gain admission. Frank loved it—he didn't mind at all." Freeman, who claims to have been a bit frightened by the unusual number of onlookers, estimates that one hundred twenty people were jammed into the studio, "in addition to the orchestra! And thirty of those people were in the control room." Among the visitors was Nelson Riddle. "On one occasion, Frank went over to Nelson, and said, 'Listen to that woodwind writing. . . . That's what I like!' and of course, my tail started to wag, 'cause it was quite a nice compliment," says Farnon.

Technically, this may have been the best-covered Sinatra session ever, being recorded simultaneously on four different tape machines. At the time, Reprise in the United States was recording all masters at 30 ips, and the CTS Studios were set up to record at 15 ips. Since Reprise had specifically requested that the masters be run at the superior 30 ips, an additional two tape machines were brought in. One Ampex and one Philips machine transcribed the tapes at 15 ips; a second Ampex and a second Philips operated at the required 30 ips. This plethora of tapes may account for the numerous "alternate" takes that have shown up on various commercial releases of the album through the years. Originally available only in England, oddly enough, *Great Songs from Great Britain* was not released in the United States until nearly twenty-five years after its creation. The first British pressings are still among the most collectible Sinatra items on the market. (Today, the album is available domestically on compact disc.)

On the second night, everyone, including Sinatra, was more at ease. The orchestra had been pared down a bit (the four trumpets weren't needed), and everything ran smoothly. Then, during Sinatra's performance of "The Gypsy," Freeman detected something unusual and began to worry. "He was doing some funny things in the middle. And Nelson Riddle was in the control room, so I said, 'Nelson, what he's doing is rather funny, isn't it?' And he replied, 'Well, this is a song that he doesn't know all that well. The phrases aren't quite right.' 'Would you like to tell him?' I ask. Nelson said, 'No, you're the director of the session—you tell him.' 'Well, I can't tell him the phrase is wrong!' I reply. 'Yes, you can,' he said. So, during the playback, we came up to the troublesome part, and I comment, 'Sounds like something's wrong with the phrasing there, Frank.' He tells me, 'I'm trying to put a little syncopation in there.' 'I think it's wrong,' I say. And he said, 'Well, I like it.' He gave me one of those smiles, with a glint in his eye, and I replied, 'Okay! That's fair enough—you're the boss.' And that little section worries me to this day," Freeman insists.

While it was unusual for Sinatra to follow the accepted practice of editing multiple takes together to create a composite master (he remained insistent on performing each take live, as he always had, well into the tape era), he would occasionally allow an "intercut" to be made. If there were minor problems with a small section of a recording, the short passage would be re-recorded, and intercut (spliced) into the master take in the appropriate place.

"With 'A Nightingale Sang in Berkeley Square,' there were only two takes," recalls Freeman. "And that's the one we did an edit on, because Frank loved Harry Roche's trombone solo." The session tapes reveal Sinatra's explicit instructions for making the cuts. "Intercut, using bar fifty-two on out for me. . . . The trombone solo is excellent, so let's save that," he directed. "This was the first time in the two nights' work that Frank actually came into the control room during the session," Freeman says. "And he came in to tell the engineer to make the splice right there, on the spot . . . very frightening! And he stood over him while he did it. The guy was trembling, and I was having a thousand fits. What if the blade were to slip? The engineer making the cut was only nineteen years old, and I think this was his first multi-track session. Frank watched him do it, and it worked. We all breathed a sigh of relief!" says the producer.

The one true rarity to emerge from the London sessions was a song that Sinatra historian and critic Will Friedwald cites as his own personal favorite, the lovely "Roses of Picardy." Dropped from the final album, its obscurity became a topic of debate among Sinatra enthusiasts, and, while the intervening decades have finally seen its official release, Freeman's story behind its exclusion bears repeating. "On the last night, we were in the control room, having a drink and listening to all the playbacks. Frank said, 'Scrub "Roses of Picardy." I don't like it.' I told him I thought it was rather nice, and he insisted, "No, I didn't like it.' I tried to reason with him. I thought it was a beautiful Bob Farnon arrangement, and he put so much emotion into it, he sang it with tremendous feeling. I asked him, 'Is there anything we can do to get it right?' and he just said, 'No, no . . . just forget it; we'll go with eleven tracks.' He was quite definite about it," Freeman recollects. "He was putting a lot of wisecracks in, as if maybe he'd already made up his mind he didn't want it—as if he was going through the motions of recording it, but not taking it seriously." (On the session out-takes, Sinatra can be heard, after muffing a take, "I don't think I'm gonna make the rest of that mother, I'll tell ya right now!" Later, obviously tired, he says, "My old man warned me about nights like these . . . but he was a drinking man! What did he know?")

After the sessions were completed and playbacks run on the third and final night, Sinatra seemed happy with the album. "He was very happy with the musicians. He said, 'You know, I love the British strings—there's no strings in the world to touch them," Freeman remarks. Summing up the once-in-a-lifetime experience, he describes the atmosphere after Sinatra had vacated the premises. "I got my mother and father in on the last night, because they were dying to meet him, and I couldn't leave the studio when it was over. I just sat in that huge studio on my own, with my mother and father in the control room. I said, 'Just leave me alone,' and I sat and listened to the whole bloody lot of master takes. It must have been one o'clock in the morning before I left that studio. I didn't want to leave it, because it was all over. It was gone," he concludes.

FULL CIRCLE

Taking full advantage of the reason he parted ways with Capitol, Sinatra continued to pursue interesting, vital recording projects at Reprise throughout the 1960s, working with such diverse artists as Count Basie, Duke Ellington, and Antonio Carlos Jobim, as well as his reliable contingent of arrangers. In what proved to be a short-lived hiatus, he "retired" from recording and performing in 1971, only to return a year or so later to make some lackluster recordings and begin his newly devised career as a touring concert artist.

Although the early seventies on saw his recorded output diminish dramatically (consider that at his peak in the 1950s as many as three Sinatra albums a year were released), several of his post-retirement recordings are noteworthy—if not for content, then for their value as technical milestones.

The most ambitious Sinatra album ever, a multi-disc set entitled *Trilogy*, was produced in 1979, the last project to be created in collaboration with his longtime producer Sonny Burke. *The Past*, a collection of older songs that had either escaped the singer's attention or merited re-recording, was taped in Los Angeles in July, with Billy May handling the orchestrations. Sinatra wasn't happy with the results, and almost all of the songs were redone in September. *The Present*, featuring contemporary numbers (including his signature "New York, New York") arranged by Don Costa, saw the singer's return to New York, and the Columbia 30th Street studio, in August. (Some songs for this portion would be re-recorded in September and December, in Los Angeles.)

The original inspiration for the project, an extended Gordon Jenkins suite called *The Future*, was completed over two days in December. A complex work, subtitled *Reflections on the Future in Three Tenses, The Future* involved not only Frank Sinatra but the 154-member Los Angeles Philharmonic Symphony Orchestra and Mixed Chorus. So large was the ensemble that, in order to accommodate them for recording, the sessions were held at the Shrine Auditorium in Los Angeles. "That was the first digital recording we did with Sinatra," recalls engineer Lee Herschberg. "It was thirty-two track digital, but we ended up using the analog tapes for the album, because digital editing was so new, we couldn't possibly edit that number of tracks. They didn't have the digital editing machines we have today."

Another series of New York outings held between July and September of 1981 yielded *She Shot Me Down*, arguably the finest Sinatra album to emerge from the singer's "late" period. Again returning to his old haunt (30th Street), Sinatra planned this to be his quintessential torch album, his sage advice on living with the despair of the "gal that got away" reflected in the husky, deep-voiced musings of one who has trod a darkened path. Not since *Only the Lonely* or *Sinatra & Strings* has the somber, bittersweet atmosphere of a late-night saloon permeated a record as palpably as on *She Shot Me Down*. The sheer power of the mood and tone achieved are certainly a credit to engineer Frank Laico's careful hand in the studio and Gordon Jenkins's piercing orchestrations—some of his most outstanding efforts on behalf of the vocalist. "Frank was so easy to work with," Laico remembers. "I came out of the booth and adjusted the microphone for him. I told him that I didn't like to mike the vocalist too close—that it would sound better if he were just a bit further away. He was wonderful about it. He called me 'Cheech'—he knew I was Italian!"

Frank Sinatra would tape his very last "real" album (the slick *L.A. Is My Lady*, which would be his first full digital recording) in Manhattan in 1984. Videotaped documentation of the sessions show Sinatra to be in top form, working along with revered producer Phil Ramone, toiling diligently to record contemporary tunes as well as a cache of older tunes that he'd not yet recorded. The all-star band under the direction of Quincy Jones sparked the aging singer, who turned in some truly memorable performances. This time, the sessions were held at A&R Recording, which had been Columbia's old studio at 799 Seventh Avenue. The mood became nostalgic when Jones, who'd worked with Sinatra since the early sixties, brought out a photo of Sinatra and Mitch Miller at a 1952 Columbia session, standing in the same studio, in nearly the very same spot! The album would be the last ever recorded there, for shortly after these sessions, A&R sold the historic building, which was later razed.

Between 1984 and 1993, there would be only a handful of singles sessions, most remaining unissued until a recent twenty-CD compilation of Sinatra's complete Reprise recordings.

In a strange twist of fate, Capitol Records, the site of some of Frank Sinatra's greatest recording achievements, was also the site of his most-debated work among Sinatra buffs: the *Duets* and *Duets II* albums of the mid 1990s. Created from highly edited performances (both studio and live concert recordings), the singer's rough vocal tracks were electronically linked with those of contemporary performers representing an array of musical genres. The results, in light of the decades he spent fastidiously tending to every last detail of his sessions, were disappointing. Surprisingly, the recordings that became the most commercially successful efforts of his career are those suffering the most from a lack of artistic vision and attention to detail, devoid of the spontaneous energy that had long been a hallmark of his craft.

Despite this, flashes of the old Sinatra shine through, with a piano and vocal rendition of "One for My Baby" surviving as a profound reminder of the power contained in his simplest of interpretations. Other enjoyable performances include "For Once in My Life" (Gladys Knight and Stevie Wonder), "My Funny Valentine" (Lorrie Morgan), "Come Rain or Come Shine" (Gloria Estefan), and "New York, New York" (Tony Bennett). A rousing "My Kind of Town" is especially interesting, as it is the only commercial recording to pair Sinatra vocally with his talented son, Frank Jr. Regardless, in the final analysis, the *Duets* projects symbolize the complete antithesis of what Sinatra, as a recording artist, always stood for.

As of this writing, on the eve of his eighty-second birthday, Frank Sinatra holds the distinction of being the only performing artist in history to have recorded in each of the last seven decades, a remarkable feat and one that makes him a virtual living chronicle of the revolutionary technical advances that have occurred within this period as well. Essential, too, is the timely and relevant social commentary that is preserved within the exceptional body of work Sinatra has painstakingly crafted over the past fifty-plus years. This, more than anything, will certainly affect the way future historians view this creatively explosive period in American musical history.

Frank Sinatra has undoubtedly left an indelible impression on the face of American popular culture. His recorded legacy is part of a rich communal tapestry that, while an indispensable link to our past, simultaneously binds us to the next century and future generations. Unfettered by the ravages of time or space, these precious performances remain both musical and technological triumphs, a combination of ideals resulting in superior interpretations that have proven to be timeless. They are ours for the asking, readily accessible to be enjoyed again and again—now, and for the ages. In retrospect, we must be thankful for the meticulous manner in which Frank Sinatra approached his very special recording sessions, and for the commitment of the collaborators and technicians involved as they strove to realize his vision.

POSTSCRIPT

A recent afternoon found me out for a short drive with my six-year-old daughter Katie in tow. It was a gorgeous fall day, and Katie was upbeat, singing along with her all-time favorite Sinatra tune of the day, "Everybody Has the Right to Be Wrong." Suddenly, she turned to me, cocked her head, and asked, "Dad, were you there when Frank recorded this song?" There was a gleam in my eye as I smiled back at her. "No, Kate, I wasn't. But I sure wish that I had been." If only she knew!

I would like to gratefully acknowledge the many fine individuals who were willing to share with me their invaluable recollections of working with Frank Sinatra: George Avakian, Milt Bernhart, Sammy Cahn, Robert Farnon, Alan Freeman, Stan Freeman, Dave Frisina, Bud Graham, Skitch Henderson, Lee Herschberg, Larry Keyes, Frank Laico, Alan Livingston, Billy May, Frank Military, Bill Miller, Mitch Miller, Marty Paich, John Paladino, George Roberts, Bill Savory, Jo Stafford, and Paul Weston.

ACKNOWLEDGMENT

Special thanks to my friend Linda Corona for her editorial assistance.

WORKS CITED

Douglas-Home, Robin. *Sinatra*. New York: Grosset & Dunlap, 1962.
Riddle, Nelson. *Arranged by Nelson Riddle*. Secaucus, NJ: Warner Bros. Publications, 1985.
Sinatra, Frank. "Me and My Music." *Life*, 23 April 1965: 86–87, 99–104.

Sinatra on Broadway

PHILIP FURIA

Although he never performed in a Broadway musical, Frank Sinatra has done more than any other singer to transform songs from musicals into "standards"—songs that transcend their own era to become timeless evergreens, as fresh today as when they were first written. Sinatra was not the first performer to look beyond current hits to older songs written for the Broadway stage. In the 1930s, torch singer Lee Wiley took a bouncy duet, "I've Got a Crush on You," from a flop Gershwin show of 1928 called *Treasure Girl*, slowed the tempo, and turned a forgotten song into a hit—much to the pleasure of George and Ira Gershwin. Artie Shaw in the 1940s performed a similar alchemy on "Begin the Beguine," from Cole Porter's 1935 musical *Jubilee*, then went on to record other songs from older Broadway shows as an alternative to relying upon current *Hit Parade* favorites for his band's repertoire. As Will Friedwald points out, however, few other performers followed Shaw's lead:

> It took the coming of Sinatra to establish what became the Great American Songbook, not least because Sinatra's rise entailed the new supremacy of the singer as the dominant force of mass market music. The Voice announced to art-conscious vocalists that if they didn't take a serious look at the classic show tunes of the previous two generations, then they were stuck with whatever happened to be on the *Lucky Strike* show that week. (Friedwald 155)

Even though Sinatra had greater commercial success with new songs, he continued to perform and record the songs that Cole Porter, Rodgers and Hart, the Gershwins, and other composers and lyricists had written for the Broadway stage. His example, in turn, has inspired other singers, from Ella Fitzgerald and Linda Ronstadt to Willie Nelson and Harry Connick, Jr. Today, thanks in large part to Frank Sinatra, the great standards are alive and kicking—the closest thing America has to a classical repertory of song.

When sung by faithful preservationists like Joan Morris, these songs clearly sound like what jazz buffs sometimes derisively refer to as "show tunes"; when sung by a jazz stylist like Mel Tormé, on the other hand, their Broadway origins are barely discernible. Yet when Sinatra sings these classics, they come off not as show tunes or jazzy "takes," but something in between that he himself would probably call "saloon songs." This chapter attempts to describe one of the factors in that complex and remarkable transformation. While Sinatra's singing style, his arrangements, and other musical factors are crucial in turning a show tune into a saloon song, I want to focus solely on the lyrics of the songs he chose from Broadway musicals. Sinatra has said many times that it is the lyrics—and the often overlooked lyricist—that draw him to a song, and one of his great achievements as a singer is his uncanny ability to "read" a lyric. Reading a lyric not only entails giving each word its appropriate emotional nuance but also conveying the dramatic situation and assuming the character—the "persona"—conjured up by the words of a song. In the first part of this chapter, I describe the particular nature of theater song lyrics in the era Sinatra drew upon for most of his Broadway borrowings. Then I analyze how Sinatra adapted and even altered these lyrics to suit the dramatic character of his "saloon singer" persona.

The lyrics of Broadway musicals from the late 1920s to the early 1940s usually lacked the integration that has characterized songs from musical theater of the last fifty years. Ever since Rodgers and Hammerstein's success with *Oklahoma!* in 1943, Broadway songs have been closely integrated into the dramatic situations and characters of the "book" of a musical. Even if we hear such a song as "The Surrey with the Fringe on Top" performed apart from the show itself, it immediately evokes the scene where Curly paints his vision of a carriage to Laurey. While Broadway songs before *Oklahoma!* may have lacked integration, they had another quality, sometimes dubbed "particularity," that sets them apart from earlier theater songs. For example, "Someone to Watch Over Me," which George Gershwin wrote with his brother Ira for the 1926 musical *Oh, Kay!* defines a much more particularized character and situation than does a song like "Somebody Loves Me," which George wrote with lyricists Ballard Mac-Donald and Buddy DeSylva for *George White's Scandals of 1924.* "Somebody Loves Me" is a typically bone-simple expression of romantic longing that moves from the assurance of the title to the coy suggestion that perhaps it is "you." In "Someone to Watch Over Me," the singer is also yearning for an unnamed someone, but instead of innocence she exudes a world-weary sophistication. Although she hasn't yet found him, she says, with an air of hardened experience, that he is the only man she ever thinks of with regret. Similarly, while she portrays herself as a little lamb, she is aggressively seeking *him* and, with a distinctly unlamb-like insistence, she takes the lead and demands that he put on some speed and follow her.

Within the musical *Oh, Kay!* the song "Someone to Watch Over Me" had little relation to character or plot. In fact, it was so lacking in integration that the star, Gertrude Lawrence, sang it in the middle of Act II, long after she had met, kissed, and cavorted with the leading man. Audiences of the time, however, cared more for the song than the story. To showcase the song, Lawrence, instead of singing it directly to the audience from center stage, as was customary, stood off to the side and sang to a rag doll she cradled in her arms. With that introspective, dramatic delivery, "Someone to Watch Over Me," as one critic put it, "wrung the withers of even the most hard-hearted" and provided the audience "with an experience they would remember and relate for years" (quoted in Shirley). Those same words could describe the effect of a Sinatra performance on a nightclub audience, and it was to such particularized songs that Sinatra was drawn, songs where he could place himself, even without scenery, costume, or props, into the character and dramatic situation evoked by the lyrics.

Like many of the Broadway songs Sinatra adapted from this era, "Someone to Watch Over Me" was written for a female character. In the formulaic boy-meets-loses-then-regains-girl plots of the day, romantic ballads of longing or lament were assigned to female characters, on the conventional assumption that women were more given to wistful or melancholy effusions, while male characters were more often given songs of romantic importunity. In the Gershwins' *Girl Crazy* (1930), for example, Ginger Rogers sang the mournful "But Not for Me," while Alex Kearns had the more forthright plea of "Embraceable You." By singing both kinds of songs from Broadway shows of this era, Sinatra extended the emotional range of his singing persona, and, when he did an album of romantic laments such as *Only the Lonely*, the lyrics defined subtle emotional facets of that character.

In order to adapt songs written for female characters in Broadway musicals, however, Sinatra usually had to alter the lyrics, sometimes quite extensively. What is striking about his rendition of "Someone to Watch Over Me" is that he did not sing the "male" version of the lyric which Ira Gershwin, as lyricists typically did, wrote for male vocalists who wanted to perform or record the song apart from the musical as an independent number. In rewriting the lyric for a male singer, Gershwin eliminated his clever rhyme between *man some* and *handsome* and substituted such formal expressions as promising *hereby* for the colloquial phrases in the female version. Sinatra, however, chose to sing the female lyric, retaining its clever rhymes and vernacular idiom, and giving the gender reversal an additional twist by portraying himself as a lamb-like male seeking her protection and imploring her to be more aggressive in her pursuit of him.

In such adaptations, Sinatra only compounds the gender crossings already present in the original lyric, which, like many Broadway songs written for female performers, gets some of its particularity by having the woman sound like a man. When Ginger Rogers sang "But Not for Me," for example, Ira gave her a pugnacious opening line and gritty invectives like "bananas." By adapting already masculinized feminine lyrics, Sinatra used songs like "Someone to Watch Over Me" and "But Not for Me" to project, beyond his street-wise, tough-guy stage presence, a poignant, vulnerable, and "lost" persona. Perhaps that is why, as Will Friedwald observes, "bobby-soxers wanted to mother him as well as wrestle him in the back of a DeSoto" (Friedwald 151).

The era that produced such richly "particular" Broadway songs for him to draw upon might have been very short-lived. Already in 1927, Oscar Hammerstein and Jerome Kern moved beyond particularity toward integration when they wrote *Show Boat*. Hammerstein himself adapted Edna Ferber's novel into a libretto that closely wove songs like "Ol' Man River" and "Can't Help Lovin' Dat Man" into the story and its characters. Yet the age of the fully integrated musical was still some fifteen years away. While Hammerstein wanted to move further in the direction of integration, other songwriters, such as Porter, the Gershwins, and even Kern himself, still thought more in terms of the song than the story. More than anything else, however, it was the Crash of 1929 and the Depression that retarded the evolutionary development of the Broadway musical. Beginning with *The Little Revue* of 1929, "book" shows gave way to the loose format of "little revues" with their self-contained songs and sketches where the emphasis was upon wit and sophistication rather than huge casts and lavish sets. That emphasis increased the need for "particularity" in songs, where a lyric created its own sense of character and dramatic situation. When a producer was fortunate enough to get a beautiful set—even a second-hand set from another show—he wanted a song that would take full advantage of it. Thus, when the producer of the 1932 revue *Walk a Little Faster* inherited a Parisian set, he summoned his songwriters to create a number around it. The composer, a Russian emigré named Vernon Duke (formerly Vladimir Dukelsky), had lived in Paris and easily tossed off a sophisticated, haunting melody. However, the lyricist, E. Y. "Yip" Harburg, who had grown up wretchedly poor on New York's Lower East Side, had to go to Cook's travel agency, grab some brochures, and, seated at Lindy's restaurant in New York, wonder what Paris was like. It would have been easy for him to conjure up the hackneyed theme of Paris in the spring, where one thinks of a lost lover from youth. What Harburg came up with, however, was a clever twist to that cliché—a woman who has never been in love but, in an even greater tribute to the power of Paris, is so moved by the city that she wishes she *had* been in love so that now she *could* have such memories. Such particularity surfaces in every detail of the lyric for "April in Paris," from *chestnut* (not plural) in blossom to the urbanely grammatical use of *whom* to run to.

Because Harburg had designed his lyric to be sung by a female performer, Evelyn Hoey, Sinatra had to omit the verse for the song, as he had for "Someone to Watch Over Me." While not so explicitly feminine, Harburg's verse imagines April itself as a woman, wearing a gown, waltzing through the streets of Paris and getting tipsy on a mere *tang* of wine in the air. Verses were a holdover from the nineteenth century, when songs alternated between verse and chorus, but by 1920 the verse served merely to introduce the chorus (or, as it is sometimes called, the refrain). Pop singers frequently omitted the verses of songs, but Sinatra retained them when they suited his purpose (he even made a separate recording of the verse—and only the verse—from Mitchell Parish and Hoagy Carmichael's "Star Dust").

While verses were not important in pop performances of songs, they were a critical component of Broadway songs (and thus for Sinatra's adaptations of theater songs). The melody of a verse was usually less opulent than that of the chorus, and the lyric was closer to speech, so that a verse served to ease the transition from dialogue to singing as performers "talked" their way into the full-throated lyricism of the chorus. In romantic stage duets, there was often a "boy's" verse and a "girl's" verse, while the chorus, which the romantic leads usually sang together, was "unisex." That androgynous chorus, where a genderless "I" croons to an equally ambiguous "you," meant that a song could receive maximum exposure beyond the show by male and female singers through radio and recordings. In the case of "April in Paris," however, there was only a "girl's" verse, so that all Sinatra could do was omit it. However, he created the feel of a verse by taking a section from the chorus, the part usually called the *bridge* or *release* (since it differs musically from the other three sections of songs built on the common AABA formula) and making it introduce the song as well. Thus his version of "April in Paris" starts out with the bridge as a verse and then leads into the chorus.

Sinatra performed a similar restructuring of "Little Girl Blue" from Rodgers and Hart's 1935 production of *Jumbo*. Written for Gloria Grafton, the song had no verse but did have a "Trio Patter" section that served as a transition between the chorus and its reprise. Hart wrote the trio patter as the woman's memory of her youth, when the world seemed younger than she, and the sky was like a circus tent strung with stars. In the chorus, Hart has her address herself in the second person—at times as if she were her own naughty child (ordered to count fingers) or a chiding but sympathetic friend (an old girl). That second-person address made Hart's chorus appropriate for male as well as female vocalists, but Sinatra still chose to sing the "Trio Patter" section as well, even though by changing *I* to *you* he lost the rhyme with "sky." Sinatra's choice has the advantage of making his own persona seem more sympathetic toward the woman he addresses, empathizing with her childhood dreams but also offering brutally tender advice as he tells the old girl that she's through. Sinatra even changes Hart's lyric from cheer *a* to cheer *up*, a vernacular revision that defines his persona as a paternal friend who commiserates with, rather than chides, "Little Girl Blue."

By the mid-1930s "book" musicals like *Jumbo* had begun to return to Broadway, but songs remained "particular" rather than integral, providing Sinatra with more of the kind of self-contained lyrical drama he could adapt for his own performances. In addition to "Little Girl Blue," *Jumbo* gave him "The Most Beautiful Girl in the World" and "My Romance." He found an even richer store in Rodgers and Hart's 1937 musical *Babes in Arms*, which provided him with no fewer than four superb standards—"Where or When," "I Wish I Were in Love Again," "The Lady Is a Tramp," and "My Funny Valentine." The first two numbers were done as duets, so he could sing them with little or no alteration, and all he had to do with "Lady Is a Tramp," originally written as a solo for Mitzi Green, was change *I* to *She* in lines such as the first one, in which it is not the speaker who gets too hungry for dinner at eight, but the woman. Arguably, Sinatra's version is more effective as a man's defense of the unconventional woman he loves than the original, in which the woman herself pugnaciously flaunts her disdain for affectation.

A more profound change occurs when he sings "My Funny Valentine," which in the show was sung by Mitzi Green to Ray Heatherton (who played a character named Valentine). Like Shakespeare's sonnet, "My mistress' eyes are nothing like the sun," Hart's lyric overturns traditional romantic compliments and deals realistically and ironically with a lover lacking in any apparent charm. Instead of praising her beloved's features, the singer mocks them—his looks are laughable and unphotographable, and his less-than-Greek physique and his weak mind, matched by a weak mouth, elicits her rhetorical question about whether or not he's smart. Such imagery is conventionally more applicable to a male rather than a female character, as is the formula of a beautiful woman in love with a homely man. For Sinatra to sing such a lyric *to* a woman required a complete recasting of the tone of the song. Instead of singing it with coy, tongue-in-cheek mockery, Sinatra rendered "My Funny Valentine" with straightforward, almost solemn, sentiment.

To do so, he had to eliminate the verse, which was so critical in balancing the lyric's ironies in the Broadway production. For one thing the verse contains definite indications that the singer is female, such as her calling her lover a gent. But the verse was also laced with archaisms, such as *thou* and *hast*, which allowed the singer to temper her mockery while holding her real emotions at bay with romantic hyperbole. By omitting the flippant verse and starting in directly at the chorus, Sinatra brings out the song's understated sentiment. At the end of the chorus, when he finally implores her not to change a hair for him, the line comes off not as an affectionate afterthought but as a passionately climactic plea.

Sinatra performed a similar transformation on Cole Porter's "Just One of Those Things," which in *Jubilee* (1935) was sung as a duet by the romantic leads. Again, the verse, with its allusions to Dorothy Parker and Abelard and Heloise, made the lyrics too literate and sophisticated for Sinatra's taste. Moreover, when Porter has Juliet tell Romeo to face the hard cold fact that their romance was, as the title says, "Just One of Those Things," it makes the singers dismiss the break-up of their romance with coolly casual aplomb. By starting in at the chorus, Sinatra again makes the lyric more passionately remorseful at the passing of an affair that, if it were indeed a trip to the moon on gossamer wings, was hardly as trivial as the title phrase implies.

When a verse suited his persona, however, Sinatra retained it. For Porter's "I Get a Kick Out of You," from the 1934 *Anything Goes*, he sings the verse exactly as Porter had written it for Ethel Merman. Although it had touches of urbane elegance, such as the singer's lament that she is fighting *ennui*, the verse leads into the chorus with a vernacular punch as she suddenly sees her beloved's fabulous face. For the unmiked Merman, the line was an invitation to blare a perfectly enunciated compliment to the last row of the balcony; Sinatra, however, delivers the line more as speech than song, an understatedly spoken declaration of love at first sight that then launches him into the chorus.

It was there that the lyric underwent major surgery. Some of Sinatra's alterations, such as his insertion of the word *boot*, were probably his own improvisations. It may have been such liberties that supposedly prompted Porter to tell Sinatra that, if the singer didn't like the songs as Porter wrote them, then he shouldn't sing them (though, as Porter came to see how Sinatra's performances were transforming his old songs into standards, he warmed to the renditions). Nonetheless, the "boot" line is not far from a phrase in Porter's own first draft for the lyric. Coming where it does, it gives the lyric itself a slangy kick that offsets such arch phrases as *mere* alcohol.

More problematic are the lyrics that Sinatra frequently sang in place of Porter's own lines about a *sniff* of cocaine. Sinatra sometimes sang Porter's original lyric, as Merman did, with a deliciously ironic pause on "bove me ter-if——fic'ly too" to suggest that perhaps a sniff of cocaine might not be as "kickless" as the lyric asserts. In other versions, however, he sang lines Porter did not write, about a *whiff* of Spanish perfume and a *riff* from a bop refrain. The alterations probably were made to avoid problems with censors, but it is more interesting to speculate about who made them, as well as who made the many other changes in lyrics that Sinatra sang. Some have suspected that it was lyricist Sammy Cahn who refashioned lyrics for Sinatra. Cahn, who wrote many original songs for Sinatra, such as "I Should Care" and "My Kind of Town," claimed to have guided the singer toward the work of the generation of superb songwriters who had preceded him. "I take great pride in the fact that I introduced Frank to a lot of the great, great songs," Cahn said:

> That was our love, all of us. We loved the great standards. How are you not going to love them? Whenever we'd be around someplace, we'd always play the great songs. . . . I [would say] "Frank, there's a song. . . ." Because he's got a good sense of music, you can lay a song on him [and he'll say], "Oh, geez, that's good. Let me have that!" (Friedwald 156)

With his tremendous admiration for the artistry of lyricists like Hart, Gershwin, and Porter, Cahn must have taken a secret delight in revising their words to suit Sinatra's persona. In most cases the retouchings are so astute that they go unnoticed, though at times they mar the original, such as substituting "gal" for "guy" and losing Porter's intricate skein of rhymes on "Flying," "high," "guy," "sky," "my," and "idea." Perhaps Cahn was trying to make up for the loss when he wrote his own paean to aviation, "Come Fly with Me," with its quadruple rhyme of *there, where, air*, and *rarefied*.

If Sinatra did have Cahn's help, it might help explain why he was able to take some of the most intricate of Boadway songs from this period— songs that are sometimes called "catalog" songs—and transform even them into saloon songs. Derived from the "list" songs in Gilbert and Sullivan operettas, such as "I Am the Very Model of a Modern Major General," "catalog" songs like "You're the Top" bristle with witty imagery and literate allusions to everyone from Botticelli and Shelley to Dante and Jimmy Durante. In Broadway musicals of the 1930s, catalog songs were so beloved by audiences that lyricists had to supply chorus after chorus to satisfy audiences who wanted multiple encores. Ethel Merman once had to tell a wildly applauding audience that there simply were "no more lyrics" for such a show-stopper.

By the time Sinatra recorded these catalog songs, many of their allusions had lost their currency, but from their numerous choruses he—perhaps with Sammy Cahn's assistance—was able to select enough lines of enduring significance to turn them from period pieces into standards. The title song from Porter's 1934 *Anything Goes* listed many contemporary figures, from Sam Goldwyn and Anna Held to Whitneys and Vanderbilts, who had been impoverished by the Depression to illustrate the point of the title phrase.

"Anything Goes" also referred to the moral abandon of the era, and Porter had his singer, Ethel Merman, catalog the shocking goings-on in low bars and at nudist parties. She also asked her lover if he preferred Mae West or "me undressed," and an early version of the lyric even alluded to affairs with young bears.

Ignoring all of the contemporary allusions and the sophisticated flaunting of convention, Sinatra carved out lines from different parts of the catalog to create a persona who is not a frenetic participant in the mad revels of the age but a bemused observer of them. By adding a line not in any of Porter's versions of the song—"when most guys today that women prize today are just silly gigolos"—Sinatra further distances himself from the moral abandon. He concludes his version of "Anything Goes" with a marriage proposal, saying that while he knows he is no "great romancer," in a world where "anything goes," he is sure his beloved will accept this most traditional of propositions.

It was clearly with Sammy Cahn's assistance that Sinatra altered lyrics for Ira Gershwin's catalog song "I Can't Get Started" from *The Ziegfeld Follies of 1936*. Ira's original lyric created a comically egotistical character who, finding himself stymied for the first time in romance, tallies up all of his amazing feats, from flying over the North Pole to settling "revolutions in Spain." The lyric was so "particular" that Ira Gershwin, who never wrote the book for a musical, found he could write a comic sketch around the song for Bob Hope and Eve Arden. The sketch opens with Hope imploring Arden for a kiss, then, when she refuses, he sings "I Can't Get Started." Arden is so moved by his lament that she gives in, but once Hope kisses her, she is so overwhelmed that she gasps, "Heavens! You're wonderful!" "That's all I wanted to hear," Hope says and casually strolls off.

Ira Gershwin was called upon for chorus after chorus of lyrics for "I Can't Get Started" to satisfy Broadway audiences. Then radio stations wanted him to write a version without proper names so they could play the song without fear of libel suits from contemporary celebrities named in the original lyric. Next, female singers wanted a catalog that included such feats as being "Miss America twice." Twenty years after he had written his original version of "I Can't Get Started," Ira Gershwin was asked to update the lyric yet again for a duet by Bing Crosby and Rosemary Clooney. With Sammy Cahn's help, he wove in allusions from Elvis Presley to digging the Fourth Dimension and rhymed such sophisticated phrases as *non compos mentis* with the vernacular "what a gent is." Sinatra's rendition of "I Can't Get Started" uses lines from all of these different versions of the lyric, as well as others that Cahn may have written specifically for him. Rather than deliver the lines with Bob Hope's flippant insouciance, however, he brings out the song's emotional core of romantic frustration. In his hands, even the comic allusions sound mournful, such as one of the few original references from the 1930s that have remained current—comparing himself to the comic-book hero Superman who turns out to be a flash in the pan.

No catalog sung underwent a greater sea change at Sinatra's hands than "Bewitched" from Rodgers and Hart's 1940 production, *Pal Joey*. The show, which was based on a series of satirical stories by John O'Hara about a small-time gigolo, was attacked by critics for its gritty departure from the usual frothy formulas of musical comedy. "Bewitched," in particular, was singled out by critic Brooks Atkinson as a "scabrous" lyric (quoted in Hart 155). In the show, it was sung by Vivienne Segal in the role of a horny, hard-nosed, and well-heeled ex-stripper who finances a night club for Joey, played by a young Gene Kelly in his first starring role on Broadway. After a drunken romp, Segal wakes up to find her half-pint lover still out cold on the floor, and she sings "Bewitched" as a cynical commentary on their affair. The verse begins with her astonishment that she doesn't have the shakes even after drinking a quart of brandy. She attributes her lack of a hangover to Joey's sexual prowess that has filled her with school-girlish innocence and energy. Through a series of choruses she celebrates her new-found joy even though she realizes it is based purely on lust. She sees all of Joey's faults and knows he is just sleeping with her for her money, yet she admits he is at his best—horizontally speaking. She also mocks her own hot and bothered giddiness yet delights in it nonetheless. The catalog abounds in triple rhymes like "vexed"/"perplexed"/"over-sexed" and "chance"/"ants"/"pants." As originally written, "Bewitched" is one of the most un-sentimental—even anti-sentimental—songs Hart or any lyricist ever wrote, and its acerbity is heightened by the fact that it is sung by a female character who is far removed from the typical Broadway ingenue.

In Sinatra's hands, however, "Bewitched" becomes a tender ballad of romantic enthrallment. Selecting bits and pieces from its four choruses, Sinatra, presumably again with Sammy Cahn's expert help, pieced together a lyric that bears little resemblance to its original. Where Hart's character vowed to worship the trousers—and clearly what's in the trousers—that clung to Joey, Sinatra's persona idealistically longs to cling to *her*. The original line where Segal calls Joey a laugh then adds that the laugh is *on* her is a naughty pun on *on*, but in Sinatra's tender "male" version of the lyric the sexual innuendo disappears. "Bewitched" even loses its catalog character and becomes a stream-lined love song. Vivienne Segal's persona, who mocked her infatuation even as she reveled in it, is transformed into Sinatra's character of a gently self-deprecating but totally ardent lover.

Pal Joey was one of the last Broadway shows Sinatra was able to mine for "particular" songs, and "Bewitched" is so much a part of the story and characters of the show it actually anticipates the era of the "integrated" song. That era arrived in full force in 1943, when Richard Rodgers turned from Lorenz Hart to Oscar Hammerstein as his collaborator on *Oklahoma!*

After *Oklahoma!*, songs had to be integrated into the dramatic situation of a musical and be closely tied to the character who sang them. The role of the lyricist in a musical also changed after *Oklahoma!* Ira Gershwin, Lorenz Hart, and Cole Porter saw themselves as pure lyricists and never attempted to write the book of a musical, a task they invariably left to a playwright. Cole Porter, in fact, always puzzled over why anyone would want to "write a book," since the story of a musical was usually nothing more than a clothesline for hanging songs. For these lyricists, a good show was a show with a lot of good songs, and they measured a show's success by the number of songs from the score that went on to become independently popular through sheet-music and record sales.

In the era of integration, by contrast, Broadway marquees usually carried the phrase "Book and Lyrics by . . ." Oscar Hammerstein, Alan Jay Lerner, or Frank Loesser. Such lyricist-librettists adapted existing literary works—James Michener's *Tales of the South Pacific*, George Bernard Shaw's *Pygmalion*, Damon Runyon's *Guys and Dolls*—into a libretto where they could create the dramatic context for their songs. Despite their integral relation to the book of a musical, such songs frequently went on to become independently popular. *Oklahoma!* was one of the first musicals to produce an original cast recording—a boxed set of 78-rpm records—so that even people who had not seen the show could listen to the score. Consequently, some of the most integral songs from the show—"The Surrey with the Fringe on Top," "I'm Just a Girl Who Cain't Say 'No,' " "Kansas City"— became "hits." With the advent of the LP in the 1950s, the "cast album" could fit on a single disk. At the same time, Hollywood turned away from creating original film musicals, such as *Top Hat* and *Meet Me in St. Louis*, and instead merely made cinematic versions of Broadway shows, thus making the scores even more familiar. By the mid-1950s, such integral songs as "The Rain in Spain" from *My Fair Lady* and "Trouble" from *The Music Man* could be heard on radio's "Top Forty."

Significantly, however, Sinatra recorded relatively few songs from the era of the integrated Broadway musical. To be sure, he did "Almost Like Being in Love" from *Brigadoon*, "Luck Be a Lady" from *Guys and Dolls*, and "I Could Have Danced All Night" from *My Fair Lady*. But most integrated songs from this era, such as "Bali Hai" from *South Pacific* or "Maria" from *West Side Story*, are so recognizable as "show tunes" that it would have been difficult for him to transform them into saloon songs. Occasionally, as with "Send in the Clowns" from Stephen Sondheim's *A Little Night Music*, he found a song with the kind of particularity he sought, but after *Oklahoma!* the Broadway musical was no longer a treasure house of songs for him.

In going back to the musical theater of the 1920s and 1930s, Sinatra was actually turning to the lyricists who had preceded his own contemporary songwriters such as Johnny Mercer and Sammy Cahn. Those lyricists, who primarily wrote for Hollywood films, continued to create songs with particularity long after Broadway lyricists, such as Sheldon Harnick and Stephen Sondheim, had embraced the principle of integration. Mercer's "One for My Baby" and "Something's Gotta Give," Cahn's "I Guess I'll Hang My Tears Out to Dry" and "Call Me Irresponsible," are squarely in the lyrical idiom of Hart, Porter, and Gershwin. Neither Mercer nor Cahn had success on the Broadway stage, even though their collaborators, such as Harold Arlen and Jule Styne, went on to triumph with other lyricists on shows such as *House of Flowers* and *Gentlemen Prefer Blondes*. Along with such lyricists as Tom Adair ("Everything Happens to Me") and Carolyn Leigh ("Witchcraft"), Mercer and Cahn maintained the tradition of the particular song that evokes its own sense of drama and character.

By directing Sinatra to his own lyrical forebears, Sammy Cahn did a double service. Not only did he provide Sinatra with superb material; he helped songs from forgotten Broadway musicals of the 1920s and 1930s become standards. If it was indeed Sammy Cahn who artfully altered the lyrics of the great masters, his service was even more valuable. Had it not been for his revisions of a "female" line, Sinatra might never have recorded a gem like "It Never Entered My Mind," which Rodgers and Hart wrote for Shirley Ross in the 1938 musical *Higher and Higher*. Although Sinatra could not sing the lines about powdering his nose or putting mudpack on his face, he could salvage enough from the catalog of choruses to add yet another intricate and sophisticated dimension to his singing persona. He, in turn, did equal wonders for the songs he took from Broadway. If they supplied him with literate wit and urbane elegance, he rendered them with a sensuous, vernacular, emotional power that they often lacked in their original stage performances. To paraphrase Katharine Hepburn's famous remark about Fred Astaire and Ginger Rogers, if these Broadway songs gave Sinatra "class," he gave them "balls."

WORKS CITED

Friedwald, Will. *Sinatra! The Song Is You: A Singer's Art*. New York: Scribner's, 1995.

Hart, Dorothy, ed. *Thou Swell, Thou Witty*. New York: Harper and Row, 1976.

Shirley, Wayne. "Introduction." *Oh, Kay!* Smithsonian Collection Recording, LP R 0085.

Sinatra and Jazz

WILL FRIEDWALD

One night in September 1956, Lester Young was playing Birdland, and, between sets, happened to drift into the Colony record shop. Making his way to the LP section, Pres was recognized by the clerk, longtime fan Bob Sherrick, and asked him, "Let me hear something by my man, Frank." Sherrick took out a copy of *In the Wee Small Hours*, Sinatra's then most recent ballad album, and Young told him to pick out any tune from it.

Sherrick proceeded to put on "When Your Lover Has Gone" and noted Young's reaction. "He was very quiet, in his porkpie hat, with a reflective look on his face," Sherrick says. "I could see that he was totally immersed in what he was listening to. He didn't exactly cry, but his eyes were, like, a little watery." When the song was over, Sherrick asked Young if he wanted to hear something else, but clearly that sole tune was as much as Pres could handle. Young stood up and as he ambled towards the door, Sherrick could hear him muttering, primarily to himself, "Man! I gotta make that tune in the next set!"

Which only goes to show the high regard with which jazz musicians have held Frank Sinatra. Zoot Sims, one of Young's greatest disciples, once introduced this man who has never needed an introduction simply as "a great musician." Billie Holiday, one of Pres's closest musical allies and a major influence on Sinatra, paid him the compliment of including many Sinatra signature songs on her final albums, revealing that the master had learned a trick or two from her pupil. No singer or musician knows better what to do with a song than Sinatra; nobody fathoms either the musical or the dramatic possibilities anywhere near as profoundly.

In a recent *Time* magazine article, Jay Cocks postulated that Sinatra's greatest secret has always been his craft. Perhaps an even more closely guarded point is that Frank Sinatra has always been, fundamentally, a jazz musician. In researching my book, *Sinatra! The Song Is You* (Scribner), I asked the great swing arranger Billy May if he considered Sinatra a jazz singer. May, who has worked with Sinatra since the mid-1940s and conducted over half a dozen classic albums for him, began his answer by calling for a definition. "If your definition of a jazz singer is someone who can approach a song like an instrumentalist and get [the melody] across, but still have a feeling of improvisation, a freshness to it, and do it a little bit differently every time, then I would agree that Frank is."

No one would be surprised that Sinatra's swing-era colleagues, such as May, Red Norvo and Benny Goodman, would be so impressed with the singer's achievements. What many people may not realize is the extent to which so many contemporary players, who reached musical maturity long after Sinatra's heyday, cite the Chairman of the Board as one of the key influences in modern music. To instrumentalists as well as singers, Sinatra casts a shadow every bit as colossal as Miles Davis, who himself had grown up under the spell of The Voice.

GETTING TO THE ESSENCE

Saxophonist Bob Berg, best known for his work with Miles Davis, describes himself as a typical young (postmodern) musician who listened to Sinatra in his youth ("because I grew up in an Italian neighborhood in Brooklyn") but spent most of his early career eschewing such "conventionally" melodic music. "We were all into much wilder things for a while, but then, in the early eighties, I heard the record with Jobim [*Francis Albert Sinatra & Antonio Carlos Jobim*]. A light went off in my head: What have I been missing? Unlike my parents' generation, who grew up with Sinatra, I had to rediscover him. I was struck by how the purity of his voice really gets to the essence of the music. In a certain way, vocal music is usually simpler than instrumental because you don't have all those keys to press. But for Sinatra to be able to approach that music and come from such deep places was a real revelation to me. It really made me re-examine my whole approach."

Another contemporary saxophonist who, like Berg, is "wild about Frank," Ken Peplowski raises a relevant point. "Sinatra always talks about how much he learned from Tommy Dorsey, his breath control and phrasing and how to put forward a melody. Today, it's almost come full circle since a lot of instrumentalists are learning from him and Nat King Cole and the great singers." Peplowski, whose ten Concord Jazz CD's are peppered with his thoughtful, original interpretations of Sinatra-associated songs (particularly "It's a Lonesome Old Town," which takes its name from a song on Sinatra's *Only the Lonely* album), explains further:

> A lot of beginning singers want to improvise and scat sing, and in effect imitate instruments. To me, that's ironic, because all we [players] are trying to do is put forward the same amount of emotion in a song that a good singer does, but without using the words. The best compliment I could possibly receive would be for somebody to come up afterwards and say that they could feel what the song was about. As Lester Young always used to say, a soloist should think of the lyrics and the whole picture, and there's nobody you could learn from better than Frank Sinatra. More than anybody, if he sang a song he made it his: he sounded like he was making it up as he went along, like he was writing (or thinking of) the words extemporaneously. That's the ultimate step in music, to have that kind of intensity and immediacy of emotion, and to be able to convey that to the audience. Sinatra is really head and shoulders above any other singer, because he's recorded such a broad range of music, and has been influenced by and then himself influenced so many styles. He's outlasted just about everybody too—the amount of years that he's recorded and sung is truly amazing. And with the possible exception of the last couple of years, he sang great up to the end. Even with the instrument—his voice—going, he took all his other reserves, and sang with even more emotion and depth. He's really telling a story up there, and that's also the best thing you can hope for if you're improvising. You try to have a beginning, middle and end and you try to give a little part of yourself. I really tried to learn that from him.

ROMANCE AND RHYTHM

Not surprisingly, it's Sinatra's prodigious talent as a rhythmic virtuoso that most musicians respond to. Although some Sinatra albums have more of a jazz "feel" than others—particularly the three with Basie and five with Billy May (including one with May conducting Duke Ellington's band)—there's a jazz foundation to *everything* he does, particularly his ballads (even with such string-strewn backgrounds as those of Gordon Jenkins). Never content to remain within the parameters established by his predecessors, Sinatra took what was useful to him from such musical father figures as Dorsey, Bing Crosby, Louis Armstrong, and contemporaries Ella Fitzgerald and Billie Holiday, but went beyond them in terms of establishing his own rhythmic identity.

"Sinatra swings his ass off," says John Scofield, one of the leading guitar players on the scene today. "His phrasing is very musical. I think he's an incredible, natural musician who took the songs of the day and added a whole new artistic level to them."

According to bassist Dave Finck, best known for his work accompanying singers such as the great Mary Cleere Haran, "musicians used to joke around and call it 'the mafia feel,' or 'the tough guy beat.' " To Finck, "Sinatra creates a great sensation of powerful quarter notes," where most recent jazz is based on eighth notes. At times, as in the Jimmie Lunceford-influenced rhythmic feel of the classic Sinatra-Riddle albums, the quarter note approach "can result in a feeling of two."

However, Finck expounds, while this rhythmic feel has little in common with contemporary approaches such as that of Keith Jarrett, it's actually quite close to the swing tradition of Count Basie. "It has to do with a feeling of weight on each beat. Frank can sing right on the beat without ever sounding stiff, even when he does 'Sweet Caroline.' It's a terrible song, but he gives it a really strong quarter-note, on-the-beat feeling. It worked really well with Count Basie. [Guitarist] Freddie Greene, who was the core of the rhythm section, always played the straight quarter notes, and Frank placed them in the same way as Freddie."

Rhythm section players praise Sinatra for digging deep into the rhythmic groove in everything he does, ballads or uptempos. There's a world of difference, Finck explains, between rhythmically aware singers like Sinatra and Nat Cole and most vocalists, whom musicians refer to as "floaters"; most singers are content to merely hang suspended over the beat without really participating in it. On the other hand, Sinatra so immerses himself in the groove that, Finck claims, "if you wipe out the orchestra and the rhythm tracks, I could tell exactly where the bar lines are. I could write down for you every rhythm that he sings, they're *that* clearly defined. His use of long and short notes, and where he stops sound, is crucial to what makes the swing feel work."

A few years ago, there was a critical movement afoot, partially inspired by some misinterpreted remarks by Sinatra himself, to categorize the singer as a classically derived vocalist. While there might be some passing similarities between the tonal qualities of Sinatra's forties voice and the *bel canto* school, it should be obvious that rhythmically Sinatra owes far less to Lauritz (as in Melchior, the crossover opera star) than Louis (as in Armstrong). As the singer once put it, "Louis Armstrong had a great deal to do with it."

Finck feels that the Popsian influence is most apparent in both musicians' use of "big, fat quarter notes." On Sinatra's "Have You Met Miss Jones," Finck says, "Every note is on the beat, and yet it doesn't feel stiff. It's the same way with Louis when he places every note on the beat." Usually swing numbers are associated more with jazz than ballads, but Sinatra is more likely to linger behind the beat, in a "jazzy" fashion, on a ballad, for dramatic effect. In Sinatra's music, rhythm and emotion are, in effect, the same thing.

Peplowski adds that by the early sixties, "as drummers loosened up, Sinatra started more implying beats rather than stating every single one. He got a lot sparser, too, as you can hear on later live versions of some of the Capitol things, such as [the 1966 Basie-backed] 'Come Fly with Me.' He leaves a lot of space, and he has a unique way of sometimes leaving out whole sections of lyrics, or perhaps punctuating them with just one word, and you know exactly what he means." The second chorus of "I'm Gonna Sit Right Down and Write Myself a Letter" also exemplifies this technique, with Sinatra outlining entire lyric lines with just a mere syllable.

Finck makes the comparison to Sinatra's and Basie's favorite trumpeter, Harry Edison. "Sweets" normally thinks in term of quarter notes right on the beat, and, even when he doesn't hit them all, the listener can still feel them all. "When Frank sings around the time, you still feel it," says Finck. "You always know where it is, which is one of the elements of a good jazz musician." Peplowski continues, "That's exactly why jazz musicians love him and [certain over-sanctimonious] cabaret singers hate him: because he can leave out great big chunks of a song and, because he's got such great time, everything else is implied anyway. You, as a listener, fill in the gaps. It's no different from what Thelonious Monk would do."

MILES, FRANKLY

One contemporary of Monk's would certainly agree. Miles Davis wrote in his autobiography, "I learned a lot from the way Frank [and] Nat King Cole . . . phrased. These people are motherfuckers in the way they shape a musical line or sentence or phrase with their voice."

Finck expounds, "I remember talking to some guys I knew who played with Miles. They swore to me that there are a couple of Miles Davis records where he plays the songs exactly the way that Frank recorded them." Davis's solos on such tunes as "I Thought About You," "It Never Entered My Mind," and "My Funny Valentine" from the mid-fifties are thoroughly Frank-ish throughout, particularly on certain passages. Finck continues. "For eight bars every note would be exactly where Frank placed them. For me, that would be the most flattering thing, to have Miles Davis copy *you*!"

Around 1984, when Bob Berg first joined Davis's band, the tenor saxophonist told his new leader that he was in the process of re-discovering Sinatra. "I had mentioned that I was listening to Sinatra, and Miles said something to the effect that he had been influenced quite a bit by Frank," says Berg. "Miles said that he was attracted to Frank's phrasing, and I agreed with him. Miles recorded a lot of the tunes that Frank was singing in the mid-fifties, like 'I Could Write a Book,' 'My Funny Valentine' and a lot of those *Pal Joey* things."

Davis's 1954 performance of another Rodgers and Hart song, "It Never Entered My Mind," reveals, in a very vivid fashion, the extent to which Davis had learned from Sinatra. Although the singer had recorded this number in 1947, Davis's interpretation anticipates the deeper, darker feelings and raw emotional edge he brought to the Rodgers and Hart classic when he re-recorded it a year after Davis for the classic *Wee Small Hours* album.

Monty Alexander first met Sinatra and his longtime sidekick, Jilly Rizzo, around 1961, only a few months after the pianist emigrated from his native Jamaica. In 1964, Alexander began playing at Jilly's, the 52nd Street nightspot that served as Sinatra's unofficial New York headquarters in the sixties. Alexander remembers the place as more of a "show-business" scene than a jazz club. But, after he started bringing in bassists and drummers on the level of Bob Cranshaw, Al Harewood, Tony Williams, and Ron Carter, pretty soon the jazz elite, among them Dizzy Gillespie and Milt Jackson, started showing up as well.

"All of a sudden, Miles—and this was still in his Italian-suit days— started coming to Jilly's," says Alexander. "That was a place where most people had no interest in hip things, and here he was, the hippest of the hip, coming in there. On one night, Miles came in and it was very crowded, because Sinatra was there. All of a sudden, the two of them were having a conversation. The place was as busy as ever with all these show people who wanted to be around Sinatra, but there he was with Miles at the piano bar, deep in conference. I wondered what these two people were talking about! I knew that Frank had hired Duke Ellington to write one of his movie scores [*Assault on a Queen*, 1966], and I thought maybe now he was going to ask Miles to do a score for him. They were putting their heads together for maybe 25 minutes, my whole set. Oh yes, Miles dug Frank."

SINATRA AND MUSICIANS

A Capitol Records producer once described Frank Sinatra as a prince among musicians. All the sidemen I spoke with, who worked with Sinatra from the thirties through the eighties, were unanimously impressed with how much the Chairman knew about their business. He personally selected all of his musicians, no less than he did his songs, and always kept an ear open for players whom he felt would fit in with his concept. "He knew more about you than you ever knew about him," said Johnny Blowers, Sinatra's drummer for roughly ten years between 1942 and 1952. "When I first met him, he knew all the things I had done since I had been in New

York. Frank is phenomenal that way. I mean, he picked guys like Hymie Shertzer, who had been the first alto man for Benny [Goodman] and also for Tommy [Dorsey], and Andy Ferretti, who was the first trumpet player with Tommy. He picked Billy Butterfield. He picked Chris Griffin [two former Goodman trumpeters]. He had guys like Will Bradley and Buddy Morrow [two trombone-playing bandleaders] and Al Klink [sax star with Glenn Miller]."

Sinatra had an elephantine retention for musical details, including not only the names of the wives and kids of nearly every sideman who played on his dates—even those he never knew socially. On one occasion in the early eighties, Sinatra happened to play a concert in New York using Chris Griffin, a trumpeter whom he hadn't worked with since he had stopped recording in the Big Apple at the end of the Columbia period in 1952. Not only did the singer instantly recognize Griffin—after not having laid eyes on him for three decades—he later remarked to another member of that particular brass section, "Isn't it great how Chris remembered me after all these years?"

Most Sinatra followers say that it doesn't matter whether or not you call him a jazz singer. The fact is that Sinatra was heavily influenced by jazz, and he influenced jazz in return (just look at how many times he won top singer in both *Down Beat* polls). Maybe today's young jazz musicians should follow the example set by the likes of Pres, Berg, Alexander, Peplowski, and Miles.

It's the Frank School, and it has everything to do with interpretation. Says Berg, "When I think of any standard, I'm always looking for the Sinatra record of it, to find out what the tune is really about!" And Monty Alexander concludes, "There are so many great young musicians coming out of the colleges. They all play so great, but I would love to give a course for them, which would be taking them aside for the next three months and playing Frank Sinatra and Nat Cole records for them. They would hear songs, they would hear lyrics, they would hear tunes, all the good, rich stuff. It would broaden everybody's repertoire and just spread good taste all around."

TOP SINATRA JAZZ CD's

As I mention earlier, there's a jazz element in everything Sinatra does, even the love songs—and even in the dozen or so songs he recorded (mainly in the '40's) based directly on classical themes. Here, however, is a sampling of the many overtly jazz recordings Sinatra has made over the last fifty-five years:

The Early Years (with Harry James and Tommy Dorsey): While the need still exists for a definitive sampler disc of the cream of the Sinatra-Dorsey sides, *Harry*

James and His Orchestra Featuring Frank Sinatra (Legacy/Columbia CK 66377) and *Tommy Dorsey-Frank Sinatra: The Song Is You* (5 discs, RCA 07863 66353-2) contain all of Sinatra's performances from his big band apprenticeship period (1939–1942).

The Columbia Years Although the forties were Sinatra's least conventionally jazzy period, at least ten percent of his prodigious output for Columbia Records could be considered uptempo rhythm tunes. While the label hasn't done a Sinatra jazz compilation since the 1958 LP *Love Is a Kick*, they recently released a single-volume set of hot highlights titled (after his first original LP) *Swing and Dance with Frank Sinatra*. The set concentrates on the great, swinging arrangements of the underappreciated George Siravo.

Songs for Swingin' Lovers **(Capitol CDP-746570-2)** If you choose to own only one Sinatra CD, let this be it. With the aid of Nelson Riddle, the one-time forties crooner reinvents himself as a heavy-duty swinger of the fifties and at the same time extends the big-band tradition with new rhythms, new instrumentation, and new energy. Containing the triumphant "I've Got You Under My Skin," this is the album that reconciled rhythm with romance and inspired a million imitations—not least of which was the entire career of Bobby Darin. (Also recommended: *Songs for Young Lovers/Swing Easy* (CDP-748470-2), *A Swingin' Affair* (CDP-794518-2) and *Sinatra's Swingin' Session!!!* (CDP-746573-2), all on Capitol and with Nelson Riddle.)

Come Dance with Me **(Capitol CDP-748468-2)** The Sinatra–Billy May brand of swing is at once more raucous and more whimsical than the Riddle variety, as evidenced by the four classic albums of their collaboration, which also include: *Come Fly with Me* (Capitol CDP-748469-2), *Come Swing with Me* (Capitol CDP-794520-2) and *Sinatra Swings/Swing Along with Me* (Reprise FS 1002-2). *Come Dance* remains a superlative collection of, as the cover announces, "vocals that dance."

Sinatra and Sextet Live in Paris **(Reprise 45487-2)** Sinatra's most intense foray into the field of small group jazz was a series of international concerts given on behalf of children's charities in the spring of 1962. Although the Paris date issued on Reprise is far from the most spirited performance of the tour (the Royal Festival Hall concert, issued only privately in England, is far livelier), this is a looser and more characteristically jazzy Sinatra than had ever been captured thus far in the studio.

The Basie Collaborations Where the Riddle and May sessions encompass an element of capriciousness, the long-awaited teamings with jazz's pre-eminent orchestra find the Chairman knuckling down in an unfrivolously streamlined, straightahead swing that brings him close to the blues tradition of Jimmy Rushing and Joe Williams. *Sinatra-Basie* (Reprise FS 1008-2), arranged by Neil Hefti, brings Sinatra into Basie's territory, albeit with a program of primarily Capitol-era remakes, while *Sinatra-Basie: It Might as Well Be Swing* (Reprise FS 1012-2), arranged by Quincy Jones and Billy Byers, renders the Basie band more suitably Sinatrian by annexing a string section. *Sinatra-Basie at the Sands*

(Reprise FS 1019-2), also conducted by Quincy Jones, proves that the pairing's electricity is even more explosive when fired by a live Vegas audience.

Strangers in the Night (**Reprise FS 1017-2**) Don't let the title track fool you—apart from that discotheque-directed ditty, this is one of the most substantial sets of Sinatra swing ever. Adding a funky organ to the mix, Sinatra and Nelson Riddle, in their climactic collaboration, concoct such *tours de force* of straight-ahead jazz as "The Most Beautiful Girl in the World," "You're Driving Me Crazy," and the masculine, metaphysical "Summer Wind."

The Jobim Collaborations Exemplifying the softer, but equally jazzy side of Sinatra swing, the bossa nova proved no less a medium for rhythmic sensuality for him than it did for Stan Getz. So far, only *The Complete Reprise Collection* (a colossal 20-CD suitcase, Reprise 2-46013) contains all twenty Sinatra-Jobim tracks, but you can get most of them on *Francis Albert Sinatra & Antonio Carlos Jobim* (Reprise FS 1021-2), arranged by Claus Ogerman, and *Sinatra & Company*, arranged by Eumir Deodato (Reprise FS 1033).

Francis A. & Edward K. (**Reprise FS 1024-2**) While not the unconditional triumph that the three Basie collaborations (and many live co-appearances) are, this once-in-a-lifetime meeting with Duke Ellington and his orchestra—history's pre-eminent musical aggregate—is an underappreciated gem. Sinatra is loose and swinging on "Follow Me" and soulfully reverent on "I Like the Sunrise," while on "Indian Summer," Johnny Hodges offers one of the most scintillating solos of his long career. Arranger/conductor Billy May does a superb job of capturing the Ellington sound throughout.

L.A. Is My Lady (**QWest/Warner Bros 9-25145-2**) Although the title track represents a failed attempt to sell Sinatra to Michael Jackson's audience, the balance of this 1984 album (paralleling 1966s *Strangers*) finds Sinatra in a dynamite, strictly jazz vein with an all-star crew of arrangers (Frank Foster, Sam Nestico, Torrie Zito) and soloists (George Benson, Lionel Hampton, Clark Terry) under the aegis of producer-conductor Quincy Jones.

Frank Sinatra and the Great American Style

RICHARD IACONELLI

If first loves remain snapshots frozen in memory, then I picture Frank Sinatra at fifty, center-stage, shoulders hunched, and that voice darting, flowing, caressing an unexpected turn of phrase, a cello-like sound floating over a sea of shimmering brass. Sinatra at his mid-century, still trim, the yet prominent cheekbones framing steely blue eyes, is the Sinatra I discovered as a teen in 1966. It was this "new" Sinatra who replaced my elixir of rock-and-roll, and with young Mia Farrow at his side, proclaimed one can be reborn at fifty. Perhaps *your* essential Sinatra is different, a bow-tied, pompadoured lad, thin as the microphone stand he clings to, voice gentle, pure, a fine violin. Or is he the reborn, finger-snapping 1950s rebel warning that "The Lady Is a Tramp," always with a devilish smile and that hat at a rakish angle? Weren't we all a part of that final audience, seeing with one pair of eyes the great star at sunset, a bit puffy, grey hair shimmering in the spotlight, the well-worn voice battling a melody but still finding in song lyrics deeper meanings than you knew? Of course, all these Sinatras are one—pieces of one broad tapestry, and yet connected by a single thread—one lonely man on a stage, telling stories into a microphone, for more than half a century.

If a singer's tone of voice is his signature, the essence of Sinatra has traveled everywhere, to the pyramids and Tokyo, down-under in Australia, and even to the moon (via tape) with the Apollo astronauts. A voice that changed so much over the years yet is identifiable in an instant. A voice that speaks to us from inside ouselves in the wee hours of the morning. It would be hard to quarrel with the box-office notion that Sinatra was the pre-eminent entertainer of his time, a credible film-actor, recording artist, and stage performer extraordinaire. As for durability, his first big record came back in 1940, "I'll Never Smile Again" with the Tommy Dorsey orchestra. Fifty-four years later, his album *Duets* sold over five million copies—the biggest-selling recording of his career.

No American performer has held center stage so long. Elvis was but a "king" for maybe three years, 1956–58; Bing Crosby was the great pop icon for about a decade (1935–45) but did not develop fans from generations beyond his own. By contrast, Sinatra was pre-eminent in parts of every decade from the Paramount Theatre Columbus Day Riot of 1944 through the 1990s. Sinatra's private lifestyle, lavish and unpredictable, had the ability to charm or shock us long before the numbing days of instant celebrity and omnipresent media. Somehow the private and public Sinatra fused in a remarkable and intricate way, enriching his art in ways no press agentry could achieve.

Fortunately, the essential Sinatra is captured on record, and the best dozen or so Sinatra albums remain unsurpassed by any pop singer. Even the finest pop performers lack Sinatra's mastery of rhythm, expression, and insight. Mel Tormé and Ella Fitzgerald swing, but never find his depth on ballads. Tony Bennett and Streisand have the emotional range, but are rhythmically much less supple. And none of the great pop stars of any era identify so closely with their material. One might even be so bold as to argue (as has the versatile critic Henry Pleasants) that Sinatra's best albums are, in variety, intensity, and consummate vocal skill, a match for the great Germans performing Schubert lieder, John McCormack singing Irish ballads, or even Caruso in Neapolitan songs.

In looking at our fractured and discordant pop culture at century's end, one might be so bold as to claim that Sinatra was *the* entertainer who most represented America to Americans. He was a superb performer who developed a rich, complex style based on the many ethnic strains of his times; he had an endlessly fascinating personality containing the constant counterpoints of toughness and tenderness; he welcomed new technology but made it bend to his needs, as he did in absorbing the technique of other performers. Sinatra embraced the big theme of "man alone," and yet retained the bite of irony and a swift sense of humor. Using all these raw materials, Sinatra refashioned himself many times over, gaining new fans with later generations, and proving Scott Fitzgerald's famous dictum wrong—there are "second acts" in American lives, and even third and fourth acts as well. Great entertainer, yes, but Sinatra is something culturally more significant, the culmination of a century's artistic progression— the great American popular stylist.

For those of us who dislike exaggeration and are wary of a society con-

stantly creating awards and trumpeting a new "number one" sedan or ce-
real weekly, we should approach the very question with reservation. Even
if we exclude those connected closely with European traditional forms, such
as composer Aaron Copeland or singer Marian Anderson, twentieth-
century American pop culture produced a rich vein of artistic styles, from
Hemingway's short stories to Edward Hopper's portraits of lonely New
York cafes to director John Ford's complex, solitary cowboys (John Wayne
as "the Ringo Kid" in *Stagecoach*). One might even consider John Kennedy's political career as a sort of pop style. Our first objective is to narrow
our focus. We will disregard the Hemingways and Hoppers, for they are
descendants of a much longer tradition, a high culture, stretching back to
antiquity. Their audience did not represent the lives of the ethnic masses
that dominated much of twentieth-century America.

Film crowned our pop culture in the 1920s and 1930s, forever reducing
the stature of the nineteenth-century theater star, and millions went to the
movies several times a week. Yet no movie star was "king" for long, not
even Clark Gable. Rising stars became falling stars, critics said, in predictable seven-year cycles. Scholars tell us the real auteurs of film-making were
directors, but directors have a hard time speaking with one voice in such
costly and collaborative efforts. What is really the essence of Frank Capra
in *Mr. Smith Goes to Washington* (1939), and what is the property of
Jimmy Stewart, or even screenwriter Sidney Buckman? A handful of film
actors have held our attention for many decades. The problem with acting
on film is that even a performance as loved as Katharine Hepburn's Tracy
Lord in *The Philadelphia Story* (1940) is static, trapped forever in celluloid.
In 1940, Tracy was already a bit dated, as *Story* had been adapted from a
1920s play. (Even "citizen" Charles Foster Kane no longer resonates in the
culture as he did in 1941.) So let us eliminate the likes of Hepburn and
John Wayne.

Sinatra in the 1950s gave us as many credible roles as any actor (including Brando), from the celebrated street-tough Maggio in *From Here to
Eternity* to drug-addicted Frankie Machine in the socially conscious *The
Man with the Golden Arm*. In fact, the edgy, chip-on-the-shoulder characters he loved to play did take on a life beyond the screen and reinforced
that public persona of a man risen from the ashes of a bobby-sox career
run dry. Sinatra became the aging kid, unbowed, street-wise, but somehow
still loyal to his roots and living by his own "Robin Hood" code, a fascinating brigand. Yet even this Sinatra is less palpable today, except when
he sings.

Great original composers appeared early in the century, such as Irving
Berlin, George Gershwin, and Duke Ellington, but their work depends on
performance style. The 1920s Gershwin, exemplified in "Someone to
Watch Over Me" as sung and recorded in a syncopated, bustling tempo
by Gertrude Lawrence (in 1927), is a lifetime's emotional distance from

Sinatra in his 1945 recording. Sinatra's 1953 remake is goose-bump time, and its painful introspection would have been an inconceivable performance to the young Gershwin. It is, after all, to the performing artist that we must turn for impact upon the public, for continued and direct communication, and for the possibility of a style that grows as we change.

We are a nation whose musical roots lie in English balladry, folksong, and both immigrant lullaby and African rhythms. Many more than Walt Whitman have "heard America singing," for we are a nation of singers. (Can one imagine a black church service or an Italian wedding without voices raised in song?) Technology served to broaden the dissemination of the song and its varied styles. Edison's phonograph, designed as a business dictaphone at century's turn, quickly became a vehicle for great opera stars like Caruso and John McCormack. In fact, opera dominated the record catalogue for the first twenty years of the century. The invention of the microphone, radio broadcasting, and (in 1925) electrical recording intertwined a new culture with the vast reach of technology and the selling of the human voice. (Think of nearly any interesting photo of Sinatra performing. The microphone is close at hand. More than a prop, it is an extension of the voice.) The hodgepodge of expressive forms that existed in the many ethnic and rural enclaves soon fed into the mainstream as people clamored into the cities. This "popular" culture found its home in the intimate world of the airwaves.

There were many giants in the performing world of pop culture in the twentieth century: Al Jolson (the first pop star), Louis Armstrong, Bing Crosby, Fred Astaire, Judy Garland, Sinatra; and later, Elvis Presley, Barbra Streisand, and Michael Jackson. Perhaps Streisand is the last universal star, the last entertainer we could agree upon before electronic overload, niche marketing, and the politics of resentment hopelessly fragmented the audience. All these stars have recorded, have been carried across the airwaves, and have resided in the homes and hearts of millions of Americans. All rose to the pinnacle of public acclaim, and all to this day have cult followings. (Yes, even Jolson has a continuing fan club over one thousand strong.) All these entertainers were products of the musical melting pot, the collision of ethnic cultures and European tradition—new rhythms, old harmony. Performance styles were borrowed, stolen, and re-blended constantly. Listen to Gene Austin, who had the first million-selling hit record, "My Blue Heaven," in 1927, and the refinements of rhythm, tone, and phrasing in any Crosby ballad from five years later. The earlier Austin now seems of another world. It surprises many to learn that even the great black jazz singer Ella Fitzgerald learned much from faraway white singers like Mildred Bailey and Connee Boswell, via the radio and phonograph. The young Boswell listened to Caruso; Louis Armstrong used Verdi opera arias as warm-up pieces for his trumpet. In a sense, all performers were propelled by a cultural and technological imperative to follow the growth of pop entertainment to a sort of culmination—that pinnacle was achieved in the career of Frank Sinatra.

Before we explore the social themes, let us set the record straight about Frank Sinatra, the performer. How good a singer was he? He was neither the singing machine, the God-gifted voice box that some claim (usually with disparagement in mind), nor simply the step-like evolution of the pop singer. Like all great artists, Sinatra hides his craft, making it all seem inevitable and, ironically, making evaluation more difficult. Sinatra's was a natural talent, but he was also gifted with the temperament of the per- fectionist—a skilled craftsman with a high musical intelligence. His usable voice (for much of his career) easily covered two octaves, important because he could embrace the modern theater song that many, such as Crosby and Judy Garland, could not sing. (Listen to his 1945 recording of "All the Things You Are," by Jerome Kern.)

Nevertheless, an oft-heard criticism is that Sinatra rarely sings "big," or that he would be nothing without the amplification of the microphone. What the casual fan often misunderstands is that Sinatra's carefully shaded dynamics allow for much greater emotional subtlety. (When your dynamic palette ranges from loud to louder, every emotion soon sounds the same.) Listen even to his explosive (1957) "Night and Day." As it builds, Sina- tra climbs to a resolution without any trace of blasting in his top notes. The simple equation of big is better, a central mid-century American adver- tising theme (think tail fins on ever-longer Cadillacs), is anathema to musical style. Bigness-equals-emotion, a necessary part of the Jolson pre- microphone 1910s theater style (and which made a comeback with the 1946 hit movie *The Jolson Story*), became the rage in the 1950s with Johnny Ray, Frankie Laine, and of course, Elvis's rock singing. Unfortu- nately, the popularity of the self-limited primal sound continues, perhaps in reaction to a culture that constructs ever more complex routes to emo- tional gratification.

By contrast, Sinatra lets the microphone overhear his voice; he does not project (redundantly) into it. The listener thus hears Sinatra intimately, like a dramatist who keeps something in reserve, and this adds both naturalism and tension to what is already an involving style. Like all great artists, when Sinatra sings, he compels you to enter *his* world. Sinatra's tone is rounded and expressive, even at mid-volume, and developed so that there would be no audible break in his upper range. Listen even to the great Ella climb the scale; the quality of her voice changes quite noticeably. Streisand blasts. Crosby rarely goes there, and likewise for good reason. Most singers sing happy-toned or sad-toned. Really *listen* to Sinatra in his 1955 record- ing of "Deep in a Dream," or the 1967 "Dindi" (from his first Jobim album); his voice contains a rainbow of emotional shadings.

One can't help but think Sinatra's keen ear was educated by his upbring- ing in the Italian streets of Hoboken, New Jersey, and further refined by the Jews, Irish, and blacks of New York City. All these peoples, whether selling pretzels in the street or running for political office, have a special feel for the turns and shadings of vocal expression. (Listen to tapes of Mayor Fiorello LaGuardia, for instance; his high-pitched vowels sing and dance, and he gives consonants vowel-like inflections.) The ethnic melting pot provided a feast of tradition in enunciation, style, and technique from which to learn. In addition to these influences, Sinatra brought his own careful study of his predecessors to the development of his style. Listen to almost any Sinatra recording, and you can sense a fine intuitive musician, and this intuition allowed him to borrow seamlessly from other great singers the many important additions that made his own style so rich. It is Sinatra alone who encompasses the best qualities from all the great vocal performance styles of our century.

Sinatra held the outline of this master style even in his earliest recordings with Harry James. Listen to even the slight "On a Little Street in Singapore," and hear a story slowly revealed, sculpted, completed, phrase by phrase. Red Norvo once told me that he had determined to sign Sinatra back in 1939 for his own avant-garde band. His wife, Mildred Bailey, one of the first jazz-pop stars, sensed even then that Sinatra was working out a special style. The mature Sinatra arches long phrases strung on vowels a la Jolson, but with proportion, as in "Old Devil Moon" (1956); he punches out key words, with Bing's onomatopoeia as he bounces the word "bounce" in "You Make Me Feel So Young" (1966 Sands concert), or uses Billie Holiday-like portamento (downward glide) in "London by Night" (1958). Even his careful use of grace notes, so common in 1920s stars like Ruth Etting, when utilized in his classic 1958 "One for My Baby" (think "ba-a-by"), is a most appropriate emotional touch.

Sinatra refined this style by constantly working in front of people. Like Jolson ("Let Me Sing and I'm Happy"), he had the passion to give generously of his voice. What Sinatra did by temperament perhaps more than design had the extra effect of both spreading his fame in a most personal way (that no film or record could match) and constantly improving his craft. By middle age, even with a well-worn voice, every concert was another brick in the building of a legend. This need to work was not so with all pop stars. Como and Crosby rarely appeared in concert in their middle years, and their voices remained unblemished and, to my ears, less interesting. Many have disdained public performance, from the early radio stylists like Annette Hanshaw, the operatic Mario Lanza, Fred Astaire, and even grande dame Streisand. But those who do not appear in public are not forced to test constantly the relevance of their style against the times. By contrast, Sinatra often saw his performances as a free-market competition against all comers. As Orson Welles once said, "Sinatra doesn't just walk on stage; he plants the flag."

It can be foolhardy to analyze a singer in regard to extra-musical qualities, but twentieth-century America elevated entertainers to the status of royalty and at the same time questioned their worthiness. Starting with the Roscoe "Fatty" Arbuckle Hollywood sex trial in the 1920s, to the tribulations of Michael Jackson, we have come to see our celebrities' private escapades as performances, too. Social critic Leo Rosten once said (in a CBS documentary on Sinatra) that Americans ask two things of our celebrities: "on stage, entertain us; off stage, excite us." The public performer and the private persona must merge, so that, even in private affairs, one seems every bit the star. Only Sinatra did this, quite remarkably, for half a century. Sinatra achieved this balance perhaps reluctantly (his disputes with the media were a precursor to today's celebrity contentiousness), but once he realized the value of achieving such a persona, he exploited it skillfully.

A critical factor to remember is that the generation that produced Sinatra shared an identity. This generation, not the celebrated baby-boomers, defined the century. They suffered the "Great Depression" (a peak of 25 percent unemployment), fought World War II (nearly ten times the casualties of our soldiers in Vietnam), and strove for dreams in the newly invented postwar suburbs called "Levittowns." Bestowing stardom was an act of community, an honor that carried responsibility. This was the last pop generation run by adults for adult tastes. (Think of Crosby or the hugely popular television evangelist Bishop Fulton Sheen.) When Ingrid Bergman left her husband to marry film director Roberto Rosselini, it was an act from which she never publicly recovered. No wonder most stars sought and found a private life outside the spotlight.

Not so Sinatra. Even apart from media invasions into his private affairs, Sinatra seemed to place himself in the middle of every great social upheaval of his time. He, along with Orson Welles, was among the first to campaign actively for a presidential candidate, Franklin Roosevelt, in 1944. This commitment was not a public-relations ploy, but a patriotism deeply felt. (Few realize that his son, born that year, is not really Frank Sinatra, Jr., but *Franklin* Sinatra.) Even the stately Eleanor appeared with Sinatra on a 1960 television broadcast, where the great lady proceeded to speak and sing "High Hopes." Of course "High Hopes," the Academy Award-winning tune from the 1958 Sinatra film *A Hole in the Head*, became John F. Kennedy's campaign song in 1960. (For Sinatra, the song did triple duty, although wisely he never made it part of his concert repertoire.) Sinatra stumped everywhere for JFK, and, given the closeness of the presidential race (Kennedy defeated Nixon by less than a one percent plurality), Sinatra helped elect a president. One saw this phenomenon repeated with Ronald Reagan.

Americans have always loved celebrities who live a little on the edge; certainly Ernest Hemingway's machismo, Babe Ruth's many appetites, and Al Capone's violent and yet charitable nature became the stuff of legend.

The darker side of Sinatra has its lure, too. Even if the underworld gang was more interested in borrowing his fame than FS was in sharing the high life with them, the Sinatra of all-night parties, playgirls, and Las Vegas gambling binges seemed to fit a certain mold of the 1950s and 1960s America, when the GI generation felt that, after the "good" war, any river could be spanned and any material want could be satisfied. When Sinatra, at fifty, openly set sail on his yacht with a teen-aged Mia Farrow, it seemed he was living a Hemingway-tinged dangerous summer, testing another boundary, waving a red flag at convention. Nearly everyone followed the Sinatra saga, and the media went to any lengths to get a story. Red Norvo recounted how the Australian media followed the Sinatra entourage throughout Australia during a 1959 tour. A reporter baited Sinatra, a prizefighter was hired to handle the singer's response, and a photographer was there—to get the photo if the fighter knocked Sinatra out.

Still, Sinatra was careful to balance the unruly side with good deeds. His public friendship with a young Sammy Davis, Jr., after Davis lost an eye in a car accident, his support in general of integration (specifically Nat Cole's tribulations with Southern segregationists), and his public philanthropy, all softened the harsher edges. Red Norvo said that Sinatra always "acted out of a sense of principle," even when he made enemies. How much of Sinatra's "principle" may have been calculated we'll never know, but we do know he took his lumps for his stands.

We should remember that other stars also had their demons. Bing Crosby sang "Temptation" and lived it, too. Bing flirted with booze in his earlier days, canceling shows and battling his ladies. Jolson unsuccessfully married the Mia Farrow-ish Ruby Keeler in his middle years. Louis Armstrong barely hid his marijuana habit. Elvis lived in bizarre seclusion with pills, booze, and a room with a carpeted ceiling, and Streisand's fits of temper rival those of any opera diva. One need hardly quote the mess that was Judy Garland's later years, nor the drug-and-booze days of Lady Day, Billie Holiday. It is Sinatra's respectable forays into civil rights, presidental politics, and philanthropy that softened his baser habits and created the intricate public-private man who fascinated us for so long.

Like so many Americans, Sinatra embraced technology. We have already seen how he saw in the microphone the opportunity to form a style encompassing the full range of subtle, expressive nuance of the human voice (something both the younger Streisand and Robert Goulet, for example, didn't understand). Yet we are fortunate that Sinatra was not seduced by more-is-better technology, and we don't have those 1950s gimmicks, like saccharine over-dubs of FS singing with himself as we do with Doris Day and Louis Armstrong. Rather, Sinatra used the microphone most tellingly in the recording studio to capture the essence of his vocal style, not to manufacture one. He sought "living" interpretations, but maintained a classical sense of form, eschewing the free-form tempos and phrasing of lesser (allegedly jazzier) singers, which wear so thin on repeated hearing. Almost all Sinatra recordings (even his parts in the *Duets* albums) were made live, the singer isolated from the musicians merely by a sound baffle or booth. The Sinatra "cooking" with a real live band is no illusion.

Moreover, Sinatra learned how to use the long-playing record (LP) format almost before anybody else did. His early Capitol albums (like *Songs for Young Lovers* and *In the Wee Small Hours*) are unified by consistent material, arrangements, the deft exploration and shifting of mood, and emotional resolution. Great singers like Ella Fitzgerald, with her composer songbooks, and Peggy Lee, with exotic themes, have made variety of the LP form, but no one has spoken in so personal a way as Sinatra. To this day, it is the early Capitol Sinatra (1953–58) that is the model for how to put together a truly musical album.

In the Wee Small Hours (1955) opened a door to one of Sinatra's major themes (as a later album put it): "A Man Alone." In this he fuses so much of what twentieth-century humanity has come to. The mass production of automobiles and, in the 1950s, the completion of a vast interstate highway system left us rootless. Our earlier migrations to the newly industrialized cities and our exodus to the suburbs and later exurbs have found no paradise. Our traditions also of independence and individuality have created institutions that perhaps leave us alone too often, and a literature of alienation has begun to develop. Like no other performer, Sinatra has touched this deep feeling of aloneness, with a hint of the irony that feeling alone in the midst of "a lonely crowd" can bring. All great pop stars sing of love and love lost, but none have dug so deeply as Sinatra. Jolson, the product of a time when stage shows were constructed around entertainers, sang in a simpler idiom. If love was lost, it was surely regained when the house lights came up. Jolson's records (especially the early ones) have the feel of a stage performance, little of the intimacy of singing for the microphone. Astaire, so believable in his 1930s classic Berlin and Gershwin songs, rarely plumbs the depths. The young Crosby, unlike the later laid-back Bing, sings love songs with passion, but by temperament he seems not to probe the dark side (and as said earlier, he certainly had one). As much could be said for the tender Peggy Lee or the buoyant Ella Fitzgerald.

Only Billie Holiday seems a match for the emotional depths plumbed by Sinatra. Her early Columbia recordings (1935–39) are sensitively sung, but she must share the focus with the fine jazz musicians who support her. Her early 1940s Commodore and Decca sides, and even the 1950s Verve years, probe deeper into her world of alienation and sorrow. Unfortunately, Holiday's limited voice (which never could sustain a long vocal line) turned sour early, and her later, often self-conscious, records are accessible mainly to aficionados. Holiday's life of drugs and booze, abuse and ill health, limited her experiences and, sadly, ended just when the world was opening up for black entertainers like the prim and proper Nat Cole.

Sinatra lived the lush life that Billie Holiday would not experience. He sang at the Hollywood Bowl with Leopold Stokowski in 1945, while being denied the stage at Philadelphia's Academy of Music. He concertized down under in Australia when a big plane was a four-propeller model. (Check the cover of the LP *Come Fly with Me*.) He married a Hollywood star, Ava Gardner, and later dated icons (Marilyn Monroe) and even Winston Churchill's granddaughter; Sinatra hobnobbed with Jack Warner, Cole Porter, and Noel Coward. Norman Rockwell painted him, and opera composer Erich Korngold wrote a lullaby for the birth of his son. Yet Sinatra spent most of his middle years unmarried and living in hotels far from any semblance of a home. It was a billboard life, played out on a grand stage, but at times it must have baffled a simple kid from Hoboken, New Jersey, who made it only to the tenth grade, and whose father tended bar and worked as a firefighter. Sinatra once made a cutting self-analysis, in the oft-quoted remarks about having "an overacute capacity for sadness," and called himself (a bit overdramatically) "an eighteen carat manic-depressive."

We should count ourselves fortunate that Sinatra felt his eventful life so deeply and took seriously the proverb that "the artist's pain is the audience's pleasure," for he set it all down for the musical record. Sinatra's "artist's pain" albums count among the darkest, yet most sublime recordings of American music. Who has better captured the bleakness of *No One Cares* (1959) or the painful introspection of *Only the Lonely* (1958)? There is much of the sadness, or perhaps what has been called the "world-weariness," in many of Sinatra's Reprise recordings, which coincided with his middle years. Certainly the great *September of My Years* is not simply about lost love, but also encompasses the pain of mortality and is most original.

We come, finally, to the main reason for Sinatra's long time in the spotlight: his ability to reinvent himself. Of course, his reinventions encompass Sinatra the singer, actor, director, businessman, master of public relations and of recording technology. But there is something more than just an accumulation of the 1940s bow-tied gentle violin, the 1950s snap-brim hipster, the 1960s Chairman of the Board, the 1970s "Ol' Blue Eyes Is Back," and the elder statesman. In truth, these are all the essential Sinatra, for the growth and changes—discovery, failure, rebirth—are the core materials of art, and resonate with the seasons of anyone's life.

Great performers in the classical arts have often grown into new and richer artists later in life. While pianist Artur Rubinstein's early (1930s) Chopin is bravura, his cycle twenty years later, when he was in his sixties and seventies, is poetic and aristocratic. Enrico Caruso lived only to age forty-eight, but in his short career he went from a lyrical tenor (hear his aria "Una Furtiva Lagrima" in 1904) to a dark baritone sound in his carefully polished final recordings from *La Juive* made in 1920. (Caruso's voice, through both overuse and choice of material, went through a change remarkably similar to Sinatra's.)

As a rule, our pop stars tend not to grow: they take the money and run. Most pop celebrities find a comfortable image and nest in it for a lifetime— if they can manage to stay in demand for a lifetime. Crosby was easily the most popular entertainer in the world for a decade, but he could not remake himself for the postwar generations; he became lazy in choosing his material and never could graduate from dixieland to swing-style rhythms. Louis Armstrong was a fully formed genius at an early age, and, though he gravitated from small bands to big bands and back again to small ensembles, his musical style and themes changed little. Al Jolson had a spectacular (albeit brief) resurgence in the late 1940s with the aforementioned film *The Jolson Story*, for which he recorded the soundtrack. Jolie became more polished, more relaxed (well, a little more), more like Crosby, but Jolson's approach to the story-in-a-song stayed cookie-cutter simple: 1920s Jolson. Judy Garland remained the little girl lost, even unpleasantly into her forties. Elvis parodied himself. Streisand has switched material (theater pop to rock, back to pop, to whatever) but her approach is remarkably like that of the young Barbra. None of these great stars gives us the sense of both a complete style and yet a work in progress. Tony Bennett did manage to grow from the overheated stylist of "Boulevard of Broken Dreams" in the early 1950s to his more subtle (and largely ignored) style in 1970s recordings with British arranger Robert Farnon and modern jazz-pianist Bill Evans. Yet Bennett, even in his tasteful 1990s "Indian Summer," is but a fine craftsman; the relationship of man, song, and performance is akin to artisan, object, and tool.

The evolution of Sinatra, the bow-tied "crooner," began early. A now departed friend once told me of a high school "penny-dance" she attended near the end of World War II. Amidst recordings by Harry James and Glenn Miller, suddenly a new Sinatra record came over the loudspeakers, one of his first since the musicians' strike of 1943–44 had ended. People stopped dancing; no one spoke. It was the boy singer, "Frankie," singing "Ol' Man River." "The Voice" (as he was known then) sustaining bravura phrases along the Mozartian lines of *bel canto* opera, digging seriously into this almost forgotten warhorse. Suddenly, he was no longer a boy, nor merely the hero of the bobby-soxers, playing himself in the aptly titled *Higher and Higher* (1943). He had grown in stature as both man and artist. After only a few years in the spotlight, Frankie had transformed himself from a lead in a vocal group ("The Hoboken Four") to band singer in 1939 with James, and, after a rewarding interlude with Tommy Dorsey (1940–42), emerged as a polished gem of a performer in 1943.

Sinatra started early in exploring the psychological implications inherent in song-stories that resonated within his own life. In retrospect, it may not be evident that Sinatra took such chances with material. He once recalled seeing Rodgers and Hammerstein's *Carousel* when it first opened in 1946 and immediately determined to record the emotionally complex "Soliloquy" (which necessitated two sides of a special long-play 12-inch 78-rpm disc). Starting in the mid-1940s, Sinatra reached deeply into forgotten stage shows for songs by Kern, Gershwin, and Berlin. He showed the world what a treasure of song our Broadway theater and Tin Pan Alley really were when this art was in danger of being buried by a return to primitive rock, blues, and bluegrass, marketed as so much product. He didn't just choose to sing these songs as historical artifacts. Rather, he immersed himself in their emotions and subtly reshaped them and, by the 1950s, had woven them through the loom of his own life and spun them out again as Sinatra whole cloth. Listen, for example, to his emphasis of the verse in "Angel Eyes." The contrast between his handling of the verse and the chorus is a microcosm of his own tough-tender persona.

No great star is intertwined so deeply with the most personal expression of our finest songwriters. Judging Sinatra merely for his choice of material, one has nothing but admiration. His catalogue has preserved the majority of the greatest American songs written in this century. For comparison, Presley (regardless of what one thinks of his style) worked with the basest of materials. Separate the songs from Elvis, and, in terms of harmonic structure and lyrical eloquence, there is precious little to analyze. Most later rock stars doubled as their own song writers, giving their work little diversity in terms of mood and expression.

When the 1950s started, Sinatra was in a fallow period. After all, being a teen idol and pop star for a decade was already a long career. After some false steps with saccharine Patti Page-style material in the period 1948–52, he broke with Columbia Records and forged a new style with Capitol. The famed "voice," now frayed and rife with unpleasant overtones, was rebuilt by disciplined study. (He even scheduled vocal practice with Metropolitan Opera star Robert Merrill.) The result was spectacular. Perhaps only clarinetist Artie Shaw (in the late 1930s) is a comparable example of an artist who improved his instrument so fast, simply by force of will.

Pop music was now devoid of new ideas and had seemingly worn out the old; rock music filled the void. Sinatra fought the competition, the bleating pop of Johnny Ray and early swivel-hipped rockers, with his famed "ballad with a beat," and the style was electric in its intensity. On stage, Sinatra conducted a subtle ballet with a microphone, a cigarette, an outstretched hand—tiny details that reinforced the idea of song as miniature stage-play. The 1950s Sinatra lived life a bit on the edge and sang about it with the same raw emotions. His divorce from first wife Nancy, and later the failed risk-it-all marriage to Ava Gardner led him to some of the most beautiful, bittersweet ballads of his career. In albums like *Where Are You?* (1957) he created a sub-genre about the flip side of fame. Angry comedian Lenny Bruce dug him, and so did Humphrey Bogart; school kids bought his albums as easily as they bought Presley.

Sinatra's need to conquer television at age fifty (after he had failed with earlier efforts) resulted in an extraordinary series of *A Man and His Music* hour-long specials, the first of which won a prestigious Peabody Award and a whole new generation of fans. Think again of the LP *The Main Event*, which appeared soon after Sinatra's brief retirement in the early 1970s. He is posed as a prizefighter.

It is therefore no surprise that Sinatra entered middle age defiantly. In 1960 he started his own record label, Reprise, recorded prolifically, bought a share in Warner Brothers films, where he even directed films such as *None but the Brave* in 1965. This is still the dream of the American entrepreneur: to succeed by controlling every aspect of your work and product. He became known as "The Chairman of the Board." As an artist, he recorded *September of My Years*, a concept new to popular music. A man at fifty (then termed the end of middle age), reflecting over his storied life and mortality. Albums like *Moonlight Sinatra, Cycles,* and the recordings with Antonio Carlos Jobim showed Sinatra reaching a more peaceful autumn, much of the tumult behind him, his phrasing ever more introspective, yet understated, with not a hint of the self-conscious. The admittedly world-weary voice actually showed the more interesting timbres one can achieve in middle age if the voice is continually explored as an expressive instrument. (Listen, for instance, to the remake of "All My Tomorrows" in 1969.) The newly introspective Sinatra may have needed time to reconcile his now superstar status with the scared kid who cradled the microphone at 1930s Jersey roadhouses. At fifty-five, still in full command of his powers, he retired. And that retirement seemed to mark the end of an era, the death of a once-great pop-culture synergy. The great songwriters, band leaders, and singers were winding down their own careers, unable (or unwilling) to compete with the bolder, more primitive pop styles of the 1970s.

After two years (which seemed an eternity of gossip and anticipation), Sinatra returned to the stage as "Ol' Blue Eyes," albeit with thicker frame and heavier rhythms, a few songs now self-conscious anthems—the king had reclaimed the throne, and perhaps we all took this Sinatra a bit too seriously. This new Sinatra recorded little, as if to acknowledge the primacy of the earlier voice, but he appeared in concert continuously, often working more than two hundred days a year. This was the "stage Sinatra," and, if the voice was a little raspy, he used it with gracious skill, borrowing new songs by Elton John and Peter Allen, but in the end returning to customary material (from Cahn and Van Heusen) and the now-classic theater songs, the "old chestnuts" as he often called them—the old matador finding new ways to handle the vocal beast in the 1970s. As a frequent concert-goer in those days, I was sometimes concerned over the voice's decline, yet continually amazed that Sinatra retained, like Caruso, Jolson, or Garland, the greatest of all performer's gifts: the urgent need to communicate to his audience.

There was that wonderful Indian Summer in 1978–82, captured in the television specials *A Man and His Music* with Count Basie in 1981 and the splendid *Concert for the Americas* with Buddy Rich in 1982, in which he slimmed down and sang with complete control. This Sinatra reinvented the voice, controlling the widening vibrato (the nemesis of all older singers) by keeping most notes in the chest. The voice was more guttural and not to every fan's taste, but oh, what phrasing. The later years were not so kind, but that made the moments of youth recaptured (the widely broadcast Dallas concert in 1987) seem so bittersweet.

In the 1990s we began to understand that Sinatra was also the end of something. The popular entertainments that grew out of immigrant ghettos and Southern cotton fields, the technology that disseminated them to a whole nation as one mass culture, the period of growth, cross-pollination, and simplicity refined to elegance, can happen only once. The rise of the city, the automobile, the ethnic voice, the middle class, patriotism, our very belief in progress, are now on the decline. Likewise, fame is now severed from achievement, becoming a kind of notoriety. One man grew up amid the cacophony of the awakening giant that was the American Century; a man who absorbed the hopes, dreams, and disappointments from its peoples, made an autobiographical style that spoke back to them, lived and loved for them, and somehow entered the quiet corners of their lives—this everyman was Frank Sinatra. One began to wonder if Sinatra would write a final chapter or merely, like MacArthur's old soldier, just fade away. But Babe Ruth in his final season still managed to hit three home runs in one game, and Sinatra still had a few swings left. He again was able to capture some of the old Sinatra electricity, singing duets with pop stars of a culture mostly foreign. What *Duets* proved is that even younger, more supple voices prove bland next to a consummate stylist; with the old man supplying superior material and technique, even youth must bend to him.

But then Sinatra was gone. Retired quietly, softly, "sotto voce."

The silence has been palpable: popular music is now truly "easy listening." If we ask music to be more, we can summon Sinatra memories, and the recordings, and they will have to suffice. The great American stylist has left a void only he can fill.

WORKS CITED

Barnes, Ken. *Sinatra and the Great Song Stylists*. London: Ian Allen, 1972.
Friedwald, Will. *Jazz Singing*. New York: Scribner's, 1990.
Lees, Gene. "Sinatra: That Certain Style." *Saturday Review*, August 28, 1971.
Norvo, Red. Personal Interview. Atlantic City, New Jersey, August 31, 1978.

Pleasants, Henry. *The Great American Popular Singers*. New York: Simon and Schuster, 1974.

Shaw, Arnold. *Sinatra: Twentieth Century Romantic*. New York: Holt, Rinehart and Winston, 1968.

Theology and Music in a Different Key: Meditations on Frank Sinatra and *Eros* in a Fallen World

EDMUND N. SANTURRI

In the widely acclaimed 1989 film *When Harry Met Sally*, we are given the story of a man and woman deeply confused about their relationship. When they first meet, they don't like each other at all, though eventually they become close friends. Beneath the surface of this friendship is a certain sexual attraction, yet both resist the attraction because they worry that making love—sexual love, erotic love—will somehow compromise or destroy or reveal as empty the friendship love they want to preserve. Based on their own previous experiences of failed relationships, they worry that if their relationship is deep down sexual—essentially erotic—it will not last, because erotic love, unlike philial love, is ephemeral. Thus they look for erotic fulfillment elsewhere, in other relationships, only to be met with frustration and disappointment. (Actually it is Harry who sleeps around. Sally sees other people but refuses to make love until she is ready.) Eventually they do give in to the erotic attraction they have for each other, make love, and, largely as a consequence of their anxieties about sex, become alienated from each other temporarily. Yet Harry comes to realize that he is in love with Sally, and, at the culminating point in the film, runs to her to declare that fact at a New Year's Eve party. Sally reciprocates Harry's expression of love, and we are left with the impression that they live happily ever after, the implication being that genuine erotic love, *eros*, is both sexual and enduring. The film, then, after registering a good bit of cynicism and anxiety about the possibility of romantic love, comes around finally to reaffirming what might be called the contemporary cultural myth of *eros*.

The soundtrack of the film is filled with standard love songs sung by some of the great American popular singers of the century: Ella Fitzgerald, Ray Charles, Louis Armstrong, Bing Crosby, Harry Connick, Jr. But at the film's climax, the point in the narrative where Harry realizes that he truly loves Sally, the point where the myth of *eros* is reaffirmed, we hear in the background the voice of sixty-four-year-old Frank Sinatra singing "It Had to Be You" from his 1980 album *Trilogy*. It seems fitting that we hear Sinatra's performance at this point in the story because, as the film apparently recognizes, it is Frank Sinatra who has been the most enduring of our culture's many musical priests and priestesses of erotic love. Indeed, Sinatra has been the musical high priest of *eros* in our culture for the past fifty years or so, even if in particular periods during that span he has been overshadowed by other singers of love songs. Every period in that time span has its own Sinatra and its own Sinatra songs. No other singer of love songs during this fifty-year span can match Sinatra's longevity and influence on popular culture. And the film seems to say as much in its choice of Sinatra as the singer privileged to consecrate the erotic relation of Harry and Sally.

As the cultural high priest of *eros*, Sinatra has given powerful musical expression to the culture's myth of erotic love, a myth reflected in the lyrical theme of the song sung by Sinatra in the film soundtrack. According to this myth, human beings have their erotic destinies determined by forces beyond the lovers' control. Moreover, there is just one person in the world for whom each individual in the world is erotically destined. No other person can take the place of one's beloved in fulfillment of one's erotic destiny. (The plot line of the film *Sleepless in Seattle* comes to mind here.) Erotic attraction to the person for whom one is destined bears witness to a metaphysical force, the force of *eros*, exerting its control over the erotic careers of all. This erotic attraction to the predestined one has nothing to do with his or her intrinsic moral virtues. Indeed, erotic power is utterly indifferent to virtue. It may propel even in the direction of a morally questionable character. From all of this presumably comes erotic fulfillment, which paradoxically is so overwhelming in its effect that it makes *happy* the occasional sorrow bred by the intermittent trials and tribulations of a love relationship. The force of *eros* does not simply transform sorrow into happiness. In the world view of the song, *eros* metaphysically and paradoxically *makes sorrow happy*.

As high priest of *eros*, Sinatra characterizes its force as ultimately mysterious, resisting the explanations of philosophers, theologians, and natural scientists. Consider his 1956 rendition of "How Little We Know," a recording which surely stands as one of his most deeply erotic musical performances. In that song, Sinatra, the high priest, instructs that love is a mystery and that, since it is, theological or philosophical or scientific understanding is utterly beside the point. (Priests, of course, are always at loggerheads with the theologians and philosophers and scientists who want to understand mysterious things that cannot be understood.) The important thing, the priest proclaims, is not to understand erotic reality but to gain access to it, to participate in this reality, to partake of its cosmic significance, its cosmic power. And it is the high priest of *eros*, the singer Sinatra, who mediates this cosmic force through the singing of song. The high priest initiates us into this mystery. We gain access to the reality through hearing the song. The song is, in other words, sacramental—a sign of, but more importantly a means of participating in, this erotic reality. One cannot hear Sinatra's performance of "How Little We Know" without sensing that one is in the midst of love-making, in the midst of the erotic. The song is not only about love, then; it is also a kind of love-making in which the listener shares, and Sinatra, the high priest, the singer of the song, makes it all possible through his lush, sensuous interpretation. We are made to feel the physical sensations of erotic engagement through Sinatra's exquisite articulation of the lyric's words. We are made to sense the transmission of erotic power between the lovers by Sinatra's renowned seamless legato delivery enhanced by his extraordinary breath control. We are made to hear the universe disintegrate, a consequence of the lovers' kiss, through Sinatra's ecstatic delivery and consummate phrasing of the line describing this cosmic effect. Once again, the singer is the priestly mediator of erotic reality.

Let's hold on a bit longer to these images of Sinatra as singer-priest, song as sacrament, singing as a kind of love-making, the singer-priest as mediator of erotic reality and turn to another of Sinatra's products, this time the song "Nice 'n' Easy" from the album of the same name, recorded by Sinatra at the age of forty-four in 1960. On the surface, the song is one sung by a lover, who is gently recommending to his beloved that they slow things down. The relationship is developing too quickly, or perhaps, she is expecting too much, too fast. Eventually we'll fall in love, he seems to say, but we should go slowly and enjoy the trip. Again, this is the message on the surface. Yet, as some have hinted and as is apparent especially in Sinatra's rendering, the whole song is really a *double entendre*. In the second meaning, what the singer recommends to his beloved is not to slow down the relationship's development but rather to slow things down when they are making love physically. Sinatra's interpretation highlights this second meaning with maximal effectiveness. Indeed, in Sinatra's rendering, the sexual meaning arguably becomes the primary one. The singer achieves this effect in substantial measure by singing at points behind the beat of the song, lagging behind the orchestral pace (maybe by holding onto a note or by coming in late), virtually urging the orchestra to slow down, and thus expressing musically the principal lyrical message of the song. Over all,

Sinatra's phrasing of this song achieves a perfect marriage of sound and sense, of form and content. The singer recommends patience, erotic patience, and simultaneously practices such patience in the singing of the song by singing behind the beat, in effect musically urging the orchestra to take its time. Indeed (except for fear of being misunderstood!), one is tempted to say that Sinatra is making love to the band since there is a kind of play between the singer and orchestra in the song which simulates the rhythms of erotic engagement, and the attentive listener is inevitably drawn into the dynamic. Again, we have an instance of Sinatra, the singer as high priest, not just singing about the erotic, but singing erotically, mediating in a sense erotic reality.

Naturally I have been playing here with the metaphor of Sinatra as erotic priest in the way of making some points about his extraordinary power as a singer and about the view of erotic love that his singing often expresses. But from the perspective of Christian conviction, what do we make of the eroticism that Sinatra so attractively depicts and commends in so many of his songs? Of course, for a good bit of its history Christian tradition has harbored deep suspicions about the erotic sensibility. For Augustine, to take one example, that sensibility in its sexual expression was no more than the worst form of lust, libido, the disposition to prefer worldly to eternal goods, a spiritually pathological disposition, whose perversity was signaled, among other ways, by the lack of rational control over the sexual functions and by the shame that humans feel about the sexual act. At times the tradition has indicted erotic love by contrasting it with genuinely Christian love, *agape, caritas. Agape* is universal in its scope; we are to love all humans. Yet *eros* is partial, limited, exclusive, elitist. *Agape* is unconditional; we are to love irrespective of the other's individual characteristics. But *eros* is irredeemably conditional. We love the other erotically because there is something about the other that attracts us. If the beloved lacked the thing that attracts us, we would not love. *Agape* is unequivocally altruistic—other-regarding, it is sometimes said—but *eros* is at bottom egocentric. In erotic relations we want to get something out of the relation; we want to possess the other; we want erotic satisfaction. *Agape* is eternal, but erotic love is transient, unreliable, untrustworthy. Thus erotic love is to be distrusted, seen for what it is essentially, an occasion for human corruption.[1] Like most others today, I regard such traditional worries as exaggerated and out of keeping with what I take to be the biblical legitimation of the erotic in the Song of Songs, which is, in my view, the principal canonical affirmation of the erotic's place in any Christian doctrine of creation, notwithstanding the tradition's frequent attempts to explain away the eroticism of this biblical text, through allegorization, for example. We are created as erotic beings. God sees our eroticism, one might say, and it is good.

Having said this much, we must also say that Christian theology rightly notices that the erotic can go wrong. There is, after all, sin as well as creation, finitude as well as capacity; and thus Christians will resist glorifications of the erotic and will be resistant especially to elements in the myth of *eros* that present erotic love as providing the key to human happiness, as establishing the meaning of one's life, as though meaning or happiness could ever be secured in erotic consummation. This point may seem obvious, transparent to common sense as well as to Christian conviction, particularly in our culture, which is so deeply cynical in so many ways, but I don't think one can overestimate the power of this element in the myth even in our cynical times. Indeed, what does seem obvious to me is that in no insubstantial measure the problem of marriage in our culture, the fact that it seems frequently not to work, is a function of unreal expectations about the kind and degree of happiness erotic love can bring. These unreal expectations are buttressed by the popular culture in a variety of ways, for example, in the creation of films like *When Harry Met Sally* for all its apparent realism or *Sleepless in Seattle*, which gives up on realism altogether but still manages to proclaim the myth as true.

My main point here is to suggest that if Sinatra's music were limited to priestly celebration of erotic consummation, he would be, from the point of view of Christian conviction, little more than a popular ideologue, a propagandist for a social fiction, an artist maybe suited, ironically enough, to certain New Age sensibilities. Yet Sinatra is not simply a priestly celebrant of erotic love; he is also a prophetic critic of erotic love, one who often presents erotic engagements and interactions not as occasions for life's fulfillment but as parables of the world's corruption, its "fallenness."

A perfect instance is a song he recorded in 1957, "I Wish I Were in Love Again," from the album *A Swingin' Affair*. The marvelously inventive lyrics of this song written by the great Lorenz Hart undermine love's sentimental pretensions with a series of startling images. The singer wishes that he were in love again. He misses "the sleepless nights, the daily fights . . . the broken dates, the endless waits, the lovely loving and the hateful hates, the conversation with the flying plates." (In singing that last line Sinatra nicely simulates the rhythm of a flying plate.) The singer misses "the pulled out fur of cat and cur," an image that suggests naturalistic continuity between erotic conflict and beastly violence but also intimates that the struggle between the sexes is akin to a struggle between biologically alien species— cat and cur (images that also have morally critical overtones—a cat is sly, deceptive; a cur is a scoundrel—that's what you find in love). The alienation between man and woman runs as deep as the alienation between members of different species. The singer longs for "the fine *mis*mating of a him and her" [italics added]. Erotic connections are *mis*matings, biological accidents, evolutionary anomalies. From such *mis*matings come grief, pain, loss, humiliation, delusion, betrayal, death:

> The furtive sigh,
> The blackened eye,

The words, "I'll love you till the day I die,"
The self-deception that believes the lie,
I wish I were in love again.

As Philip Furia has intimated, a good number of these figures amount to ironic reversals of classic love images.[2] The traditional love sigh now becomes the "furtive sigh," the duplicitous, calculated sigh, or the hidden sigh, the sigh out of sight, occasioned perhaps by "the blackened eye," an image which gives new meaning to a long-standing verbal expression of eternal love, "the words, 'I'll love you till the day I die.' " Here the words have the ring of an erotic death wish. Love is not all it pretends to be. Indeed, after the fact of erotic consummation, love is shown to be what it truly is, the coming together and settling of evolutionary slimes. "When love congeals, it soon reveals, the faint aroma of performing seals," this grotesque image playing, almost pornographically, with the physical materials of the sexual act, but also affirming, again, the close connection between erotic love and the beastly world. At the same time, the moral indictment of love is preserved despite the naturalism. "When love congeals, it [also] reveals . . . the double-crossing of a pair of heels," the metaphor here transfiguring a classic trope of erotic attraction (a woman in high heels crossing her legs) into an image of moral indictment by depicting the lovers as a "pair of heels" who deceive, who *double-cross* each other. As Furia nicely summarizes the effects of the song's lyrics over all, love here "is seen not through the eyes of Romeo and Juliet but through the baggy lids of Antony and Cleopatra" (Furia 121), or, we might add, love here is seen not through the eyes of Harry and Sally, but through "the blackened eye[s]" of the abused spouse Tina Turner in the film *What's Love Got to Do With It?* Indeed, we have moved into the lurid world of Nicole and O. J. Simpson: "The furtive sigh/the blackened eye/the words, 'I'll love you till the day I die.' "

These are bleak themes projected in the song's lyrics, but for a good bit of Sinatra's performance, the music, the singer's lighthearted and relaxed delivery, the Nelson Riddle orchestra's swinging accompaniment, all set a mood that seems out of keeping with the lyrics' thematic content. Sinatra and the band and the music lead the listener on, create at the outset a false impression. If the listener is taken in by the singer and the music at the beginning, if the listener is not attending carefully to the lyrics, she'll have the sense that this is just another swinging, if somewhat wistful, celebration at a distance of the joys of love. Yet what we get in Sinatra's performance is the musical expression of an *argument* exposing the ideal conception of erotic love as ideology. On its surface, in its ideal conception—a conception represented in most of the song by the music and principally by Sinatra's exceedingly effective vocal interpretation—love is blissful. That is the ideology. That's what the *music* and the *singer* seem to say for most of the song. But underneath the ideology, in this case underneath the music and

Sinatra's voice, is an unseemly reality exposed in the lyrics. It isn't until midway through the song, a point marked by a modulation in key, that the singer and music begin to signal something other than the message of blissful love. The intensity of the music increases. A tone of urgency, anxiety, begins to creep into Sinatra's voice. By the time we get to the end of the song, the tone of the singing expresses a disturbed excitement, matching the disturbing sense of the lyrics:

> Believe me, sir,
> I much prefer
> The classic battle of a him and her.
> I don't like quiet, and I wish I were in love again.

Then, as though exhausted, Sinatra trails off in repeated, subdued tones of "in love, again." This is a song, not only about erotic disappointment, erotic longing, and erotic corruption, but also about erotic pathology. The singer misses the "kisses" and "the bites" of love. True, he's "learned" his "lesson." He's learned that without love there's "no more care/no, no despair." "Now [he's] sane." "[He's] all there now," "but [he'd] rather be punch drunk," a declamation that Sinatra delivers toward the end of the song with a quasi-grunt and with the force of a one-two punch, accentuating the violence of *eros* and the ringing disorientation that marks the singer's obsession with love.[3] Here we have a musical critique of *eros* as ideology, as pathology, as moral corruption, as sin—a musical critique that is as powerful as any social, psychological, philosophical, or theological analysis. And the effect is maximized by Sinatra's consummate vocal interpretation. Indeed, one appreciates the quality and depth of Sinatra's performance especially when one compares it to relatively innocent or playful renderings of the song, such as Ella Fitzgerald's in her Rodgers and Hart songbook, or Mel Tormé's in his Crescendo Club performance of 1954.

So many of Sinatra's performances advance this prophetic critique of *eros* that I can hardly do justice to the breadth or depth of the treatments here. There are songs of innocent love deceived, songs of erotic self-deception, self-deception about the intentions of the beloved, self-deception about the lover's own intentions, self-deception about the lover's capacity to weather the storm of romantic loss. There are songs about erotic disappointment and erotic obsession. In some instances, our interest in the subject matter is heightened by a thematic ambiguity created by the special nuances of Sinatra's renderings. As an example of this last, consider his 1963 performance of the song "Please Be Kind" with the Count Basie orchestra. If one attends exclusively to the lyrics, this song would appear to be sung by an erotic ingenue, who is anxious about the tenuousness and transience of erotic engagements. The ingenue has somehow grasped prior to experience (perhaps through parents' or friends' warnings) that in love there is the high likelihood of disappointment and betrayal. In the song, the ingenue entreats the lover to be gentle, compassionate, forthright, and confesses that this relationship offers an *initial* erotic experience, a confession that reveals the singer's erotic innocence and vulnerability but perhaps also signals the ingenue's fatalistic expectation of eventual disappointment since this is at best an inaugural experience in a series of subsequent erotic relationships. Again, such is the meaning suggested by the lyrics, and, when the song is sung with the kind of sweet tenderness conveyed by, say, Sarah Vaughan in her 1958 performance with Quincy Jones, the reading of the singer as a vulnerable, erotic ingenue is eminently plausible.

With Sinatra at the helm, however, that reading is quite implausible, partly because we know a bit about his own, real-life, swinging history. Yet, quite independent of the singer's erotic biography, Sinatra's perform-ance of the song, supported by the swinging Basie accompaniment, is too hip, too smooth, too self-assured, for the reading of erotic innocence to hold. Now the singer's knowledge of erotic transience and ephemerality seems to be evidence of wisdom born not of mother's teaching but of many affairs, a deep and multifaceted erotic experience. In this reading the ap-pearance of erotic innocence generated by the lyrics is exposed as just that, an appearance. This is not really the singer's initial erotic encounter, after all, and the semblance of erotic innocence is now easily taken as part of a strategy, a strategy of seduction. On this reading, the singer is not the ingenue but the seducer, and among those who may have been seduced are the listeners of the song.

Let's move to another form of erotic corruption, a form I shall call "erotic apocalyptic." By "erotic apocalyptic" I mean to denote the sensi-bility of an individual who is drawn to erotic self-destruction and acts as though the destruction will be redeemed by the sheer intensity of the erotic experience, no matter how ephemeral. Examples of such include persons immersed in risky, illicit love affairs. Such persons will sometimes confide that what they are doing is crazy, irrational, likely to be tragic for them-selves, their families, friends, and their lovers, but they persist anyway be-cause they seem to find ultimate meaning in the erotic encounter, even knowing full well that the experience is transient or dangerous. Indeed the virtually certain impending disaster often seems to serve as an aphrodisiac for such persons. It is this sensibility that I mean to denote by the expression "erotic apocalyptic." Here I'm reminded of Woody Allen's film *Husbands and Wives*, where he plays a college professor drawn to a student consid-erably less than half his age. The Allen character is interviewed in the movie and talks about his irresistible attraction to destructive erotic relationships. Of course, the film's sequence is painfully ironic, given later revelations of the real-life scandal involving Allen and Mia Farrow's adopted daughter. Both the film and real-life stories give us a perfect expression of "erotic apocalyptic" as I am using the term.

One song of Sinatra's that illustrates this erotic-apocalyptic sensibility is Irving Berlin's "Let's Face the Music and Dance." Sinatra recorded the song at least twice in his career, once in 1960, at the age of 45, and again in 1979, at the age of 63. The song's lyrics suggest the circumstance of an impossible, if not illicit, love affair, one that will have to end soon. The singer is saying to his lover, "This is the end. We need to acknowledge that. But we should enjoy each other now because tomorrow the jig is up." The respective tones of Sinatra's two recordings of the song are very different. In the earlier version, the singer conveys an attitude of carefree, hip, swinging, nonchalant, relaxed, almost indifferent, irresponsibility toward the whole business. "Hey, we should live for the moment," he seems to say. "We'll worry about tomorrow, tomorrow." The tone of this earlier version leaves the impression that the consequences of the affair will not be all that serious—a few tears, a few debts that will be hard to settle. But in the later performance the tone is much more ominous than in the earlier, made so in part by conductor Billy May's distinctive arrangement but also by Sinatra's delivery, enhanced by a voice, here in 1979, that is older, heavier, coarser than it was in the 1960 performance. The mood of the second version is one of imminent destruction, apocalyptic, and one gets the sense that here the singer's call to his lover reflected in the song's title has the ring of a desperate but futile attempt to salvage the situation through one last defiant act of erotic consummation—as though the disaster could be legitimated, redeemed, made ultimately meaningful by this one final experience. This sense is created not so much by the lyrics' explicit meaning but by the musical tone set by the May arrangement and by the grave, urgent intensity of Sinatra's vocal, existentialist, interpretation of the song. While the singer in this 1979 version of "Let's Face the Music and Dance" seems to recognize the imminence of the relationship's end, his desperate plea at the song's conclusion for one last escapade (a plea conveyed through his insistent and persistent reiteration of the title line) indicates a deep-down unwillingness to let go, a deep denial of the reality of erotic loss.

Of course, after the dance, or the morning after, the reality of erotic loss sets in, and Sinatra's music arguably reaches its greatest heights when it depicts the loss of love fully and unequivocally confronted by the lover. I am referring here to the ballads, the torch songs, but especially the so-called "saloon songs." Over the years Sinatra has often characterized himself as a saloon singer, meaning in part that he sings in saloons (nightclubs) but also that he sings saloon songs, songs which frequently, though not always, have bars as their explicit dramatic settings and which, more importantly, present characters in dramatic monologues singing about their romantic disappointments, about their pain, their sorrow, their sense of betrayal, their sense of loss, their loneliness, their emptiness, their erotic despair. What makes so much of this music great, in addition to the characteristi-

cally superb selection of material and the masterful arrangements, is Sinatra's extraordinary capacity to bring these dramatic situations to life, to
convey in song an impressive range of emotions in utterly believable ways,
to create a mood of despair, of sorrow, of emptiness, to render musically
but conversationally. We really do have the sense, when we're listening to
these songs, that someone is there talking to us about his hurt. Many observers agree that the greatest of all the Sinatra saloon songs is his 1958
performance of "One for My Baby," on what many think is his greatest
album—*Frank Sinatra Sings for Only the Lonely*, recorded when he was
forty-two years old. There are many other great saloon songs—"Angel
Eyes," on the same album, or the 1967 "Drinking Again," to name just
two—but the one I want to consider is a relatively recent song from what
I regard as Sinatra's last really great album, the 1981 *She Shot Me Down*,
a saloon-song album whose dust jacket pictures the sixty-five-year-old Sinatra sitting at a bar with a drink and cigarette looking pretty grim. The
song is "A Long Night," written explicitly for Sinatra by Alec Wilder and
Loonis McGlohon. Jonathan Schwartz once said that "A Long Night"
"takes the pain of 'One for My Baby' all the way to the bottom of the
glass,"[4] but I find the song particularly interesting because of what it does
with the genre of the saloon song. As all saloon songs are, this song is
about the brokenness of the singer's existence, but the theme of erotic loss
has receded considerably. There is only the slightest hint that the singer's
despair might have some connection with failed romance. In short, I think
that in this performance Sinatra and his collaborators transform the genre
from within. The saloon song now becomes a plaint, a lament, not essentially about erotic loss but about the brokenness of human existence generally, the fallenness of the world, a brokenness of which erotic loss is just
one element or expression.

Sinatra performs the song* as a kind of anti-hero in a postmodern tragic
drama. The singer of the song is both fashioner and victim of the world's
corruption. "I rarely paid debts that I owed but I sure have paid my
dues"—paid those dues, that is, in profound, desolate suffering ("the bus
rides and the nowhere to go"), suffering partly at the hands of the world's
manipulators, the "wheelers and the dealers," who "win." But he's also
done himself in on the "street corners," which wreck "love and dreams"
(there's the one hint of connection with love) and with booze, which de-
stroys "hope" and "schemes," but is embraced, nevertheless, as the one
comfort: "I've tasted the 90-proof gin and chased it away with the blues."
In fact, the despair is unrelieved ("the barrooms and the back streets, dead
end"). The singer's existence is "a long night," "no daylight." His vision

---

*All of the excerpts in this paragraph are from "A Long Night." Words by Loonis McGlohon;
Music by Alec Wilder. TRO—© Copyright 1981 and 1982 Ludlow Music, Inc. New York
and Saloon Songs, Inc., Los Angeles, CA.

is empty, his tone virtually nihilistic. The mood of the song almost convinces us that the singer is utterly alone precisely because he lives in a universe utterly alone. The song seems to say that this is a *world* without hope, despite the apparent victories of the "wheelers and the dealers." Again, what we have here is the genre of the saloon song transformed from within, issuing in a vivid and profoundly disturbing depiction of human life morally and spiritually deadened. And the rough edges of Sinatra's aged voice here only heighten the effect.

So Sinatra sings about despair as well as fulfillment. Does he sing about redemption as well? And particularly does he ever project an image of *erotic* redemption in his music, recovery from romantic loss, sorrow, pain, guilt? Or when he sings of erotic loss is his vision essentially tragic such as the vision of Shakespeare's *Othello*, a play about one who "loved not wisely but too well" (V. ii.) and consequently destroyed himself, the wife he loved, and his faithful lieutenant, as well as others? In the play the tragedy is unrelieved. Is this also Sinatra's musical vision of romantic loss?

Certainly it cannot be the Christian vision. Christianity denies that the tragic denouement of *Othello* can be the last word on erotic loss even in the most catastrophic of circumstances. If the erotic is a dimension of created humanity, as I think Christians must believe, then one has reason to expect that creation's restoration will involve in some way the restoration of *eros*. In part, this means that the Christian rightfully will seek, even in the experience of erotic loss, signs of God's eternal *yes* to humanity in Christ, creaturely analogs to or anticipations of the world's full restoration—for example, erotic relations scarred but repaired or rejoined, even strengthened by earlier troubles, persons who have loved and lost and who move on, who find some sustenance in the memory of a failed relation, or, more likely, who are able to forget. On occasion Sinatra will sing about these sorts of things. I find him most effective, interestingly enough, when he sings about love from a perspective assumed after the passage of considerable time, young love, for example, seen from the vantage point of middle age, a theme struck a number of times in the 1965 album *September of My Years* (cut in celebration of Sinatra's fiftieth birthday). That album includes a song entitled "Man in the Looking Glass," a funny, wistful song about a middle-aged man looking at himself in a mirror and wondering whatever happened to the youthful looking guy with all the hair. Now what he sees, among other things, is an older man whose sexual desire comically lives in uneasy and unseemly relationship with his age. Yes, old age brings erotic deterioration and decadence and the comedy of the old fool. Yet age can also have its erotic compensations. Time, after all, heals erotic loss. What at one time seemed to the singer to be a catastrophic denouement to a love relationship, a denouement signifying the destruction of his life, now is an event without readily discernible traces, an episode recalled only with a sense of irony and bemusement. Time can heal. Humor about the past is often a sign of the healing. And Sinatra's ironic rendering delightfully displays the power of time to redeem erotic loss and the significance of comedy as a mark of erotic redemption.

Of course, time does not always heal. It cannot help Othello or Desdemona or other casualties of fallen *eros*. Yet for Christianity, again, tragedy cannot be the last word, even in cases like these. Eschatologically it is not the last word. In Christian belief creation will be restored in eschatological time, and this includes creation in its erotic dimension. It is fruitless, of course, to speculate about what all of this might mean in detail (though it might be fun to speculate about what an eschatologically redeemed eroticism might be like). Nevertheless, if Jesus promises, "Blessed are you who weep now, for you will laugh" (Luke 6:21), must he not be talking to those who have wept lover's tears? Must he not have in mind those who have "loved not wisely but too well" (at least Desdemona if not Othello)? When Revelation promises that "God will wipe away every tear from their eyes" (Revelation 7:17), must we not include the eyes of all losers in love?

It seems only fitting to end with the lyrics of an exhilarating Sinatra song that can be read as answering "yes" to all these questions—a saloon song of a sort, but this time one that lifts the glasses to transfigure the recognition of erotic loss in an ecstatic proclamation of beatitude and hope. Appropriately enough, the song echoes Othello's famous lines as point of departure:

Here's to those who love not too wisely, no, not wisely but too well,
To the girl who sighs with envy when she hears that wedding bell,
To the guy who'd throw a party if he knew someone to call,
Here's to the losers.
Bless them all.

Here's to those who drink their dinners when that lady doesn't show,
To the girl who waits for kisses underneath that mistletoe,
To the lonely summer lovers when the leaves begin to fall,
Here's to the losers.
Bless them all.

Hey, Tom, Dick, and Harry,
Come in out of the rain.
Those torches you carry
Must be drowned in champagne.

Here's the last toast of the evening.
Here's to those who still believe
All the losers will be winners,
All the givers shall receive.

Here's to trouble free tomorrows.
May your sorrows all be small.

> Here's to the losers,
> Here's to the losers,
> Here's to the losers,
> Bless them all.

But this is a toast to be heard, not just read. And those who *have* heard Frank Sinatra's inspired performance of "Here's to the Losers" might be forgiven for thinking that the music of redemption is a varied genre indeed.

NOTES

1. On the relation between *agape* and *eros* in Christian tradition, see Gene Outka, *Agape: An Ethical Analysis* (New Haven and London: Yale University Press, 1972).

2. Philip Furia, *The Poets of Tin Pan Alley: A History of America's Great Lyricists* (New York and Oxford: Oxford University Press, 1990), pp. 120–21.

3. In Sinatra's rendering, he alters Hart's lyrics slightly, which I have also quoted out of sequence. In the first verse of Hart's original, we find:

> No more pain,
> No more strain,
> Now I'm sane, but
> I would rather be ga-ga!

And in the second verse of Hart's original:

> No more care,
> No despair.
> I'm all there now.
> But I'd rather be punch-drunk!

Among other things, Sinatra replaces the relatively light "ga-ga" of Hart's first verse with the "punch-drunk" of the second and sings the second verse unaltered, thus sounding the relatively grim "punch-drunk" phrase twice in the song.

4. Jonathan Schwartz, "The Songs: An Introduction" (Palm Springs, California, August 1990), p. 33. These are the liner notes for *Frank Sinatra: The Reprise Collection* (Burbank, CA: Reprise Records, 1990).

PART III

Personal Reminiscences

Eye Witness

STAN CORNYN

Frank is the last to walk in.

Things, they always knew how to get themselves arranged and into place before Frank Sinatra walks down the corridor, in the two-inch thick recording studio door. Our list of those things that all get themselves into place begins with Ernie.

Ernie the piano tuner is there an hour before everyone, going thwang-thwang-thwang on each note of the coffee-cup-scarred grand piano, laboring one by one up each of its 88 keys. Thwang-thwang, then down one octave, thwong-thwong. Ernie knows he's to finish before anyone gets there. Thwang-thwang. An anonymous life, leads Ernie. Who can remember any pianist hushing a crowd to say, "And mostly, I owe all this to Ernie, my tuner"? Only in Ernie's dreams. Thwing-thwing, then exit.

The hallway, where they have vending machines and linoleum and, on the walls, dusty gold records. To this pretension-free corridor, tonight are added two guards with clipboards. Smell of pizza in cardboard boxes off to one side. The guards wait. They wonder what to do with their hands. As good Rent-a-Cops, they will not ask Sinatra for his ID. They will edge out of his way.

Behind that thick door, the one with the red light that will later light up and say "Recording. Do Not Enter," sits tonight's recording studio. This big room looks as if it will be caught by surprise, not expecting guests. Like somebody maybe emptied the ash trays, but when was the last time anyone around here thought to wash an ash tray? This studio, its piano in tune but everything else less-than-coordinated, this studio is not a ceremonious place.

By definition, this studio is to listen in, not to look at. It looks born for that role. You want looks, whyncha try down the street, some Italian place, Chianti bottles hangin' from the rafters, you want looks. You want sound? That you get here. Tonight, we got pock-holed acoustic tile and wood panel baffles.

Overhead, hard lights, bright, lights to read all those little, specky C sharp quarter notes. And, taped across those ceiling light fixtures, fading magenta gels, no fancier than those generally found in a North Dakota Holiday Inn piano bar. The tape holding these gels has, half of it, loosened, leaving the gels to dangle.

Underfoot: red commercial carpeting, aluminum-duct-taped to the floor. The freshest feature in the whole place is the new sign reading "Fire Hose."

Musicians have gathered, according to union custom, before the second hand swings past o'clock. Hollywood studio musicians, by definition, have mileage on them. Look at them, you see jaded. The jadedest of all play violin.

Violinists are here tonight for the ballads. These are professional violinists, mostly men, very trained. They can sight read Schoenberg scores while upside-down. Put the score upside-down, they play it perfectly. Hang the violinists upside-down, they play it perfectly.

These violinists get paid scale, good money, for playing these "pop" sessions. Mostly, they play fills behind the singer. Not too taxing. So they're jaded. They being Hollywood studio violinists, they're happy to take the money and strum. Tonight, however, they behave differently.

There are about 16 violinists here tonight. Tonight, they bring their wives, who sit to one side, in black, beaded sweaters.

They pay attention.

Brass is here, too. You don't do an up tempo "Mack the Knife" with just strings.

These guys—trumpets and trombones—are always fatter than the violinists. They maybe get that from sitting in the back row in big bands? They have bellies. They make jokes that sound as if they must be inside jokes. Seen it all jokes. Maybe because there is no way to insure your lip with Lloyds of London, jokes.

And these brass players, they think, dream to themselves, one of them admits, of chucking it all, of working in comfortable chairs, the kind that don't fold, padded chairs, yeah, and doing something sane for a living, like open a travel agency.

Reed men less often have bellies. They are built like football ends, in contrast to the brass guys, who are interior-lineman-shaped. Sax players are thinner and, unlike trumpet players, they sit stooped over. These men who play several instruments—assorted saxes, clarinets, oboes, flutes of many dimensions—perhaps they hunch over from reaching down to grab the next instrument for the next eight bars? Who know, but stooping, that's a fact of life about the reeds players.

Across the room, behind some shoulder-high sound baffle that prevents one section from bleeding into another section, for those of you stereo separation addicts, perches the evening's drummer. The key man, driving his teammates with a thwack-thwack-a-thiddly-thack beat. Occasionally, because it's that kind of night, grasping two drum sticks in each hand, the four sticks pounding the point.

This orchestra, assembled here with much the same care that went into assembling the Invasion of Normandy, is ready. For those rooms accustomed more to laborious, rock-and-roll recordings, sessions where getting just the drum track on one song can take a day or so, there is here a Major Difference. This is an adult orchestra. It has been assembled to get it right on first take, because the baritone has been known to get impatient.

This roomful of 40 musicians, linked by a common delight in a well-smeared 8th note, an elite fraternity. These musicians are hard core, although not so hard core tonight as to forget to slip Instamatics into their instrument cases.

Running down the charts is done in earnest, as these sheets of music show no dog ears, but feel as if they were wet ink still. This is the era before rapid copying. This is an era when a nervous fellow known as the Copyist has transferred the arrangements of whoever, of Gordon Jenkins or Billy May, say, in ink onto some translucent vellum paper, instrument by instrument: he does one page for First Tenor Sax, then he transfers a new page for Second Tenor Sax, that times 30 or 40 instruments. And those 30 or 40 instruments times 10 or 12 song arrangements. Pre-Gutenberg torture. A mound of pages of staves filled with notes, copied by one man who would have to be inhuman if he got every note right.

Rehearsal is run down to check for wrong notes, this Copyist scurrying through the tangle of music stands, cables and mikes, open instrument cases, and the occasional tin Fedora.

Get it right before he . . . Get it right before . . . "—hey Billy? Bar 4 after letter G, third note an E Flat?"

Engineers tapping on mikes, pointing them five degrees to the northeast.

Conducting these musicians takes a different kind of conductor skill than that used by, say, the conductor for Jr. Band at Roosevelt High. The musicians gathered here know how to count. They can read ppp and play ppp when it says ppp. Instead, the conductors here get the tempo started, then move with the music, indeed personify the music as it is played, swaying and being swept up in it and being the orchestra up there. These are conductors' best hours. Often, they will close their eyes as the orchestra plays their arrangements.

They will beam down at their singer, in his booth, like a successful marriage broker who has mated instrumentation to voice, and it works.

All of these conductors have one thing in common. Their bodies show signs of neglect. For soft and strings, no one better than the posture-free Gordon Jenkins. For brass and sass, Billy May, wearing decade-old tennis shoes and cigarette ashes down his front.

Accompanying is always performed by a piano player. Often, this man was a white-haired, sallow-from-no-sun man named Bill Miller. Sinatra clears his throat. "Think I just swallowed a shot glass." Miller does not laugh; he has heard this line before. He mostly talks privately, only to Frank, covertly, as if passing exam answers in class.

Co-stars figure heavily in the Sinatra discography. At times, co-performers, ranging from daughter Nancy to guitarist Antonio Carlos Jobim, get to co-star. Jobim particularly made a dramatic co-performer in 1967. Their album together was anything but ring-a-ding-ding. More like the World Soft Championships. Slap one of Jobim's fragile songs on the back with a couple of trumpets? Like washing crystal in a cement mixer. The two men out-hushed each other.

But more often, it rang-a-dang-dang.

Two jazz band guys become most memorable: Basie and Ellington. Ellington, six feet plus, dressed with wry urbanity, his blue sox rolled down to an inch above the ankle, and zoot! three-inch cuffs on his slacks.

Basie, seemingly glued to his piano bench, or piano throne you could say, moving as little as need be, playing with one finger when two are not needed. But the eyes, always alive, seeing everything in the place. And little nods when it, as expected, goes right.

It's maybe 8:20. A car drops Sinatra off out front. He and friends alight, and head into the studio. In the corridor, he passes the two guards, who have stepped back out of the way.

"Good evening, gentlemen. Who's got the ball game on?" Two guards look around for a transistor radio.

Sinatra enters, about half an hour after the orchestra has been running down the songs. He looks natty, his wide-banded hat tipped back, an inch off straight flat. Tie and collar loosened. He strolls through the studio obstacle course. His eyes are on his colleagues for the evening, musicians who've worked his sessions for years.

"Hiya, Sweets." "Evenin', Sunshine."

He looks professionally shaved.

He turns to the string section: "Hello, Sidney, how are ya? What's happening in the music business?"

Guests, but a handful only, sit against one wall, silent, their eyes on him as he moves across the studio. Each guest awaits her or his own personal wink. Ladies with Revlon Red fake nails; men with Countess Mara ties and gold cuff links, looking as if they've chipped in for a pavilion or two at Cedars-Sinai.

Like Ed McMahon, who after a song'll say, "Let's have a drink on that one." And others. White-haired, expensive men, in black suede loafers with gold, tiger-head buckles on them. They sit upright, alert for introduction possibilities.

Rehearsing is efficient, the arranger up on a platform, still running through voice-empty arrangements to check they've been written out note perfect. The conductor remains intent on getting everything into the state of no-kinks before the impatience of recording begins. Sinatra will stroll up behind the conductor and listen, feel, then turn to someone sitting over there in the celeb section.

He turns to a saggy face restaurateur named "Prince" Mike Romanoff, and gestures at the conductor intent behind Sinatra. "The way this guy writes strings," he says, "if he were Jewish, he'd be unbearable." At this, the Prince wakes up a bit.

If rehearsal is not going well, Sinatra mother hens more intently. "Let's have an 'A,' huh?" he asks the orchestra. The "A" passes around the infield. Piano to strings to reeds.

The arranger-conductor hustles to get in as many fixes as possible before the baritone says it's time to sing. "See if we can fix that 'bone right there," is said in a hurry.

"Let's make one" is Sinatra's way of signaling it's time to roll tape and record. "Let's not over-rehearse it," he urges. Readiness.

He steps into the singer's booth, a three-sided arrangement of particle board walls with windows. His music stand has his name engraved on it, a moment of pride by the owners of the recording studio, useful to point out to others, months later, with offhands like, "That, oh yeah, well Frank, yes, he records here."

Sinatra takes a second to shuffle through pages of music. His piano player, keyboard or not, stands close by, in case.

Sinatra grasps and un-grasps the music stand. Pinkie ring on his hand. Sinatra shoots his cuffs, three-quarters of an inch, as if looking fine helps singing fine, but who are we to complain. Probably it is just instinct, because the man is definitely here to sing. Still, I am clearly not a sophisticate, because I wonder why his shirt cuffs have three buttons on them.

He speaks straight into his mike, with a casual smile, deliberately easing the tension that surrounds this session.

"Everybody straight?"

Singing happens out of sight in that isolation shed. For those in the room, singing is also out of hearing, the voice being drowned out by the orchestra. The voice is for you to hear later, Sinatra being a prime example of why records were invented.

The booth is where the engineers and producer sit on the other side of a big glass window. From the studio outside, you can't see in at them. Cannot see all of those engineers, and other workers, like men who watch to make sure the tape does not run out in the middle of something, and like the union rep, watching the minute hand.

Producers also sit in the booth. During Reprise, they mainly are two contrasting men. One, the genteel Sonny Burke, soft-spoken, ready to pour oil on any troubled waters, the consummate of the flawless take. Other nights, in contrast, the younger Jimmy Bowen, with a drawl, with savvy and the ability to sneak in back-beat and triplets at a time those devices were thought, by many, somewhat criminal to better music.

From the booth issues a well-behaved voice over Talk Back: "Any time you're ready." And then, to identify what is about to happen in less-than-artistic terms, the speaker rattles off "G, One Thousand Four Hundred and Sixty-Seven, Take One."

The first silence—records begin in silence. Fifteen yards away, the arranger stands before his orchestra, waiting. A trumpeter tucks a mute between his knees, because to pick it up from the floor might mean dropping it, blowing a take, maybe a possible explosion. This is not time for nerves.

The room is silent, and you become aware how silent it really is. Quiet enough to hear the fluorescents. A vacuum of silence can be felt in your ears.

The orchestra wives in their black, beaded sweaters muffle their charm bracelets.

Sinatra's hands stuff into his pants pockets. His knees bend half an inch, like a tennis pro waiting for his opponent's best serve. He studies the microphone. Friend or enemy? Fiddles with it, moving it maybe a quarter-of-an-inch closer.

He balances on the balls of his feet, his eyes feeling their way through the already-memorized poem before him.

The Arranger sets tempo: "One . . . two. Uh-One . . . two . . . three" (and no "four," for reasons of silence).

The orchestra starts on take G1477-1, the drummer often in the lead. Doesn't he seem too loud? But Sinatra likes that, and anyway, in the booth, they have all those sliders to balance mikes, louder, softer. Drummers are always loud at Sinatra dates, because, maybe, that's a hangover from the dance band dates at the beginning.

Coming in on cue means the others—brass, reeds, all of them—tick off the bars in their heads, counting till their time to toot.

They are specially alert tonight, like they're counting time in, what?—in Roman numerals maybe. Special? Later on, after the session, these are musicians who'll drive home and have to explain to their sleepy wives how it had been just to Be There, three hours in the same room with . . . with Roosevelt, maybe.

The orchestra, rehearsed, plays well, avoiding the mistakes that once were in the Sixties referred to as clams, then in the Eighties, through some Darwinian leap, called anchovies. The anchovy tonight is an endangered species.

Singing begins. He leans into the words, like a high jumper loping down the gravel path to liftoff. The woman in the crowd, the one against the wall, forgets to wonder if he notices her.

He sings. Everyone feels that rhythm. Thirty right feet silently tapping.

But in this room, while he's recording, people cannot hear that voice, which is projecting all of eleven inches, lip-to-mike.

Usually, it's straight through, but occasionally, Sinatra just stops himself singing. Long silence. Long. Sinatra points to himself as the culprit. "That was an old Chesterfield that just came up on me. Around 1947 it felt like."

Another take begins, same tempo exactly, in case they later want to cut the two takes together. You feel for anybody who will blow it on this next take.

The long, long. Controlled breathing all around. About a minute and a half in, a trombonist makes a bleecchh on his horn. So he sits there, a blush-colored felt hat sagged across the bell of his horn, there to keep it soft. Poor Trombone Player knows: the music said B and he played F and Jesus was it wrong!

Sinatra looks over. "Don't sweat it," he says.

In the booth, where the sound gets balanced, they listen and only listen. Sitting in the mostly-dark, a few pin spots in the ceiling aimed down through cigarette smoke whirls onto the console below, where engineers move dozens of sliders up or down a quarter of an inch. Where producers let their eyes move across the hand-notated scores, but that's just something to do with their eyes while their ears are busy. These men, who know not suntans, attend not to what's to be seen, but what is heard.

Sinatra, if you were to listen analytically, as these sallow men now do, to what Sinatra is doing with his voice, is singing like few can. It's like he makes a contest out of singing without breathing.

If he runs out of gas on a phrase, which is a very rare bird for this man, then he runs out of gas two-and-a-half miles after anybody else would. He sings like there's extra Texaco in his tummy.

His approach to song is belly to belly. He is no teen at the mike. He has sung and lasted through the Age of Anxiety, the Age of the Atom, and the Age of Acne.

See him at the mike, up close. When he sings, it's not to you. It's to about six inches behind your eyes. His own eyes a little far away, where the Truth lives.

No other singer sings quite so honest.

The songs, which are just songs, not to be confused with poetry, become in his voice anthems. Anthems to love, and anthems to the lack thereof or the goneness thereof. Anthems about "my baby" bein' gone and it's "just you an' me, Joe."

Songs used to remember, with softened pain, of the penny days. Of the rose-lipt girls and candy apple times. Of green winds, of a first lass who had perfumed hair.

Songs destined-at-birth to romp and roar, songs about Cheeekagoh or New Yooork and "look out! ol' Mackie is back!" Ka-da-thump.

Followed, occasionally, by a "doobie-doobie-doo."

And then, somewhere in the third or so minute, the musicians run out of their notes and the conductor crashes down both his arms like he's ripping down drapes in one big whoosh.

Ka-da-THUMP, then the sound stops, it just stops coming out, yet lingers for a moment in the air, echoing in the still.

That second silence. The studio waits for the ring of the last cymbal crash to die out.

Sinatra puts up his hand, so no one squeaks. Morgue quiet. Those fluorescent lights again. Egg shell city.

No mistaking it: this, from a man of no little self-confidence, is to be The Take.

Sinatra, a born peeker, looks over the top of the music stand. Into the control booth, he peeks, unwilling to wait for the endless cymbal overhang to end. Peeking in at the engineers, as if daring them to confess Electronic Irreverences. They reveal none.

"That," says Sinatra, "*should* be the record." He leans into the mike with the boyish pride of a kid, one who's just made his first no hands ride about the whole block!

"Any questions?" he asks.

From the booth: "No questions."

"Groovy."

Following each recording, the verdict is announced by Mr. Sinatra simply: either "Next tune" or "One more." His verdict is spoken quietly, but is heard well.

Then, to start the transition, Sinatra will turn to the two rows of audience and say things probably said before, like "Anybody got any oxygen?" Taking a towel and fanning the trumpet section.

One more song sung. The room unbends. The semi-pros on the sidelines chatter softly, feeling proud as if they too had all just cleared the bar at six-foot-six. The women sit up straighter. No matter what Sinatra says next, they'll all laugh. He always has a funny throw-away when another tune is in the can. "Any more like that, we'll have to call 9-1-1."

Making it look easy.

The engineer, usually Lee Herschberg, walks in and gets the evening's understatement award: "Gee, I hope we got that on tape."

Playback comes fast. Sinatra has moved out from behind the mike, up next to the conductor, equilateral from the playback speakers. He leans on the conductor's vacant podium. The only parts of him you see are just those popped white cuffs and worry lines in his brow. He bears down listening, like it's the last reel of "The Greatest Birth Ever."

His eyes, during playback, shift from chair to table top but not to another eye. Hearing only.

Around him circle the others. That circle, too, listens to the playback. They put on faces gauged to be intent. They too listen hard, as if halfway through someone whispers buried treasure clues.

String men, violins, violas, who don't get called in to record as they once did, since the amplification of the guitar, they stand around the speakers now, listening, when years back they were out in the hall, phoning their service.

Playback over, Sinatra walks away. "Next tune," he says.

Around him, the circle. Half-stammering, half-silent, because they cannot think up a phrase of praise that's truly a topper. The white-haired, expensive men stay sitting upright, applauding on their knees and saying, "Magnificent."

Quincy Delight (that is his real middle name) Jones is a born hugger. He relaxes after the take. It is good. He hugs everyone more animate than a water cooler.

In the end, the arranger turns to the singer, and the singer to the arranger. "Elegant record, Francis," says the arranger.

Francis replies, "Always glad to hear about that kind of carrying on."

The session is over. After four tunes, this session, this full album, is over and on tape. You look at this man, who's lasted so long, sung so many, started and stopped so many times. He puts on his coat. Sinatra tells the orchestra, "Take a long ten."

"One more time, Frankie," says Hamp, those words meaning more than first they sound like.

The album in the can, a party is called for. Sinatra wants it *all* played back, three nights' worth. By now, the two-row audience is four deep and stacked into the hallway.

The room is crowded, pros and guests milling about during playback, watching one another listen to the first play through of the newest Frank Sinatra Cook Book. People smiling at each other, shaking hands with vigor, more Instamatics out than the last night at Summer Camp.

"I figure," he says, "we got a record."

Perhaps out of habit, he doesn't say goodbye. It's just that . . . wait a minute . . . where's . . . ?

Sinatra slipped out a minute ago, down the hall with Jilly and a younger man they call Nifty. Past the rent-a-cop guards, who now are prepared with the answer "9-to-2 Dodgers," but don't get asked.

An hour later, the rented recording studio stands empty. Lights've been left on, but no one is in there. All gone home. The piano sits there, another coffee ring scar on its dashboard. Ash trays still beg to be scrubbed, but will not be. Those pock-holed studio walls, they produce no echo, no memory of a hour before. Those walls are, face it, just plain plain.

Nobody's got the ball game on. It's all gone, except for what was saved on tape.

Sinatra and the Atlantic City Connection

RICHARD APT

The 500 Club, Atlantic City, New Jersey. He winked at me from the stage. It was my tenth birthday—July 1959. It was the dinner show. Roast turkey and Frank Sinatra. The smoke bothered my eyes. Ventilation was a rumor in 1959. I consistently dipped my cloth napkin into my water glass, dabbing my eyes over and over. More than six hundred people were packed into the little saloon. Next to us were two nightclub owners from Boston. I remember them saying that it was their sixth night in a row and that they were getting tired of eating bad steak. I sat there in my white "ice cream" suit with matching white bucks and crew cut, looking like a spiffed up Jewish Huckleberry Finn. I knew of Frank Sinatra from *Pal Joey* and *A Hole in the Head*, and of course, from all the Capitol songs played on Atlantic City Top-40 radio.

Red Norvo was introduced, and the music started. Before this the only live music I'd ever heard was played behind Paul Anka at the Steel Pier, and I really loved the sounds now coming from the stage, especially the vibraphones. Then Red Norvo said, ". . . now our boy singer," and out from the wings came Frank Sinatra. Somewhere in between "High Hopes" and "All the Way" he noticed me and leaned over to our ringside seats and gave me a couple of exaggerated winks. My mother later told me that I blushed quite deeply.

This was my first exposure to Sinatra in Atlantic City. His first exposure, as he told his audience at Resorts International in 1979, occurred when he stayed in a Pennsylvania Avenue rooming house, vacationing with his parents in the early 1920s during Atlantic City's heyday. Famed Broadway producer George White broke in his famed *Scandals* reviews every summer on the majestic Boardwalk. W. C. Fields did his juggling act at the Steel Pier. Al Capone held one of the first gatherings of crime families in Prohibition-era Atlantic City. Al Jolson, Eddie Cantor, and Fanny Brice were among the top entertainers appearing at Boardwalk theaters and vaudeville houses. (Perhaps young Frank Sinatra witnessed the magic of Jolson in *his* ice cream suit!) People would "dress" to walk the boards, and Atlantic City's Easter Parade rivaled the one on New York's Fifth Avenue.

Twenty years before my first encounter with Sinatra, he played the Steel Pier in Atlantic City with Harry James in the summer of 1939. The Steel Pier, which extended a half-mile out to sea, featured several theaters showing movies, live stage shows, and the water circus that starred the famous high-diving horse. Located directly in front of the horse's stage was the Marine Ballroom. Here, Sinatra played with Harry James and, later, Tommy Dorsey. The ballroom had no chairs, just a huge dance floor fronting the bandstand, which crowds of kids would press against, listening to Frankie's easy, gentle song renderings.

It was 1946 when Paul "Skinny" D'Amato, owner of the 500 Club, first partnered Dean Martin and Jerry Lewis. The following year, Skinny was approached by the father of a young, crippled bobby-soxer from the neighborhood, a girl whose only desire was to meet her idol, Frankie Sinatra. Skinny made the right calls, arranged the meeting and, most importantly, met Frankie himself for the first time, beginning a lifelong friendship.

Frank started playing Skinny's saloon in the fifties, during the turbulent Ava years when his career was in a downward spiral, and continued to play there well after his Oscar-winning return to prominence. These were the "salad days" of Skinny and Sinatra. The "5," as it was known, hosted Milton Berle, Sophie Tucker, Jimmy Durante, Louis Prima and Keely Smith, and all the top acts of the mid to late 1950s. Frank would often work the club just for expenses, refusing any compensation from his good pal. While filming *The Pride and the Passion* in Spain, he sent Skinny a telegram that read simply, "How about August 24, 25, 26, 27?" and it was signed "El Dago." (Skinny later had this telegram framed and hung in his bedroom.)

Sinatra's appearances at the 500 Club became legendary. Skinny's billboard and print ads simply read "HE'S HERE." Upon the close of the engagement, those same billboards and print ads read "HE WAS HERE." Skinny often said, "Many entertainers can fill up a room, but Frank filled up the town." This was proven true when Sinatra did six shows in one night, and people kept lining up along Missouri Avenue throughout the early morning hours. Each performance was packed to overflowing.

Frank loved the informality and easy-going, unstructured, saloon-like environment of the "5." He always thought it was a great place to break in new material, and he would also have great fun translating some of his most famous standards into hip "Sinatra-ese":

We did it in Monterey, in old Mexico;
Stars, guitars, big fat lips, red as wine;
They grabbed somebody's bird,
And I'm afraid that it was mine.

Often he was joined on stage by other famous performers, including Jack E. Leonard, who would interrupt Frank's act, hurl one bombastic insult after another, and break Frank up. Jack E. would often kid Frank about his thin appearance, his womanizing, his Italian heritage, and his gangland associations. One night while Dean Martin was headlining at the "5," Frank and Sammy Davis, Jr., flew in to do a special 4:00 A.M. show with Dean. Someone recorded it for posterity. Listening to it now, one gets the feeling that perhaps you had to be there to appreciate it. It's hard to tell which performer was the most inebriated that morning, although everyone seemed to be having a great time. Perhaps it was the magic of the "5" or the performers' love for each other and Skinny.

After the shows, Frank and Skinny would usually retire to Frank's Claridge Hotel penthouse suite, often with visiting celebrities who included Robert Wagner, Natalie Wood, Joe DiMaggio, and Leo Durocher. This is where the action was. It was as if Mack Heath was back in town and the party was just starting.

There were also frequent visits to the black section of town. Kentucky Avenue was Atlantic City's answer to New York's West Fifty-Second Street, and scattered among the many jazz clubs was the Club Harlem, featuring a chorus line of beautiful "sepia" dancers. Larry Steele produced a Ziegfeld-like review every summer featuring lavish production numbers bookended by dance acts, ventriloquists, acrobats, comedians, and prominent black headliners such as Billy Eckstine, Pearl Bailey, Sarah Vaughan, and Billy Daniels. Often Frank attended the Club Harlem's once-a-week Sunday morning 4:30 A.M. breakfast show, done primarily for the entertainers performing elsewhere in town.

In those days, Atlantic City offered a great deal to satisfy Sinatra's epicurean tastes. Frank sampled the best of Atlantic City's culinary delights. He often visited "Jimmy's Just a Hobby." Jimmy was an eccentric restaurateur, who, it was said, fed you what he felt you should have, rather than what you wanted to order, and kept his cheesecake in a refrigerated safe in the back kitchen. Hackney's Seafood Restaurant, located at the inlet of Atlantic City, would stay open well past closing time to serve Sinatra and his entourage. And what about women—or in the Sinatra jargon the "chicks" or the "broads"? Yes, there were plenty. Skinny's brother, Willie

D'Amato, often boasted about getting his "bird" serviced from any number of women just by getting them an opportunity to say hello to Frank. Sinatra was partial to showgirls and cocktail waitresses, and sometimes he imported Hollywood girlfriends to fill the ring-a-ding hours.

History has shown Sinatra to be a complex man, and the complexities have often shown themselves in his singing. It is only natural, therefore, that, in addition to all of his carousing, there were also reflective and contemplative times as well. One longtime Atlantic City cab driver, known to everyone as Herbie, was well known for the time he took Sinatra on a 4:00 A.M. cab ride. Stopping at a local tavern, Sinatra picked up sandwiches and beer and asked Herbie to drive him to the extreme end of the island, at Longport, where Frank sat solo on the jetty, ate his food, and contemplated the isolated tranquillity of the bay meeting the ocean. He didn't say much that night. He just muttered something to Herbie about clearing out the cobwebs.

Interestingly, Sinatra's relationship with Skinny D'Amato went beyond the boundaries of Atlantic City. Rumors circulated about the involvement of Skinny and Frank with Chicago capo Sam Giancana. Skinny was, in fact, managing Frank's Cal-Neva Lodge and Hotel in Lake Tahoe, Nevada, when Giancana—then on the blacklist in Nevada—was spotted by the FBI visiting Phyllis McGuire. Phyllis, a member of the singing trio the McGuire Sisters, was involved in a longtime love affair with Giancana. This romantic encounter became the catalyst to Sinatra's losing his Nevada gaming license. Many years later, in 1981, Frank finally got his gaming license back. His testimony to the Nevada Gaming Commission was broadcast on CNN, and I brought a copy of the video of this testimony to Skinny's house that year. As we watched it together, Skinny laughed throughout Frank's testimony, and, when I asked Skinny what struck him so funny, he said, "He should have gotten the Oscar for *this* instead of *From Here to Eternity*."

There were other connections, too. As depicted in the 1992 TV miniseries *Sinatra*, Joseph Kennedy asked the singer for assistance in winning over the West Virginia electorate for his son's presidential bid—an electorate that was largely controlled by the labor unions. The assistance the elder Kennedy purportedly requested was for Sinatra to ask Giancana to sway the union leaders to support JFK in the West Virginia primary. Frank agreed, and Giancana sent Skinny to West Virginia to assure success.

Fire destroyed the 500 Club in 1973. By then the major boardwalk hotels had become sad relics of the past. Economical jet travel led people to more glamorous destinations. The boardwalk had become a second-rate Coney Island, made up largely of T-shirt shops and hotdog stands. It was proposed that casino gambling could bring the town back from certain extinction, but gambling was initially voted down in a referendum. Its proponents fought hard, however, and the measure eventually won. In 1978, the Resorts International Casino and Hotel opened. Sinatra, who hadn't appeared in Atlantic City for almost fifteen years, returned in the fall of 1978 for a major benefit performance, raising $600,000 for the Atlantic City Medical Center. Backstage at the benefit concert Skinny and family were welcomed by Frank and Barbara Sinatra. Sinatra signed a four-year contract with Resorts International and started appearing there in April 1979. Skinny attended every opening, partying with Frank into the wee small hours.

When Skinny was named Atlantic City Man of the Year in 1982, Sinatra chaired the event. After dinner Frank spoke in reverent tones of his "pallie" Paul D'Amato and all the fun and good times that were had at that little joint on Missouri Avenue. Also present that poignant evening were 500 Club alumni Jerry Lewis and comedian Pat Henry. Video messages were sent by Dean Martin, Danny Thomas, and Sammy Davis.

Some months later, Skinny died. Perhaps years of living on cigarettes, black coffee, and very little sleep had finally taken their toll. Skinny was Runyonesque, a real character. Longtimers still feel his absence. The funeral was difficult for pallbearer Sinatra. Upon exiting his limousine, Frank was clearly overcome with grief. He retreated back to the isolation of the limo for a few moments before being able to help bury his close pal.

At the beginning of the nineties, Sinatra's relationship with Atlantic City continued, but there was a marked difference in the man who'd been playing this city beginning some four decades earlier. After a few years at Steve Wynn's Golden Nugget and Bally's Grand, Sinatra inked a long-term contract with the Atlantic City Sands Hotel in 1990. During one engagement, he eluded his security guards, took the elevator down to the food court, and waited in line to buy a Nathan's frank, sharing a table with several bewildered fans. The years were starting to catch up with Frank. One night in 1991, I asked the Sands entertainment director, the late Jay Venetianer, how Frank was doing. "He's acting like a seventy-five-year-old pain in the ass," Jay snarled.

Sinatra made his last nightclub appearance at the Sands in November of 1994. It had been fifty-five years since the skinny kid singer with the Harry James band made his first professional appearance in town, and thirty-five years since the ice-cream-suited boy first witnessed the grandeur of a Frank Sinatra performance. I found it difficult to watch. Lyrics were forgotten, and I struggled with him. We all did. There was the occasional flash of brilliance. "My Kind of Town"—in the pocket! We roared our appreciation. Some of us helpfully shouted forgotten song lyrics. Our support moved him to tears, as his passion and artistry had so often done to us.

He belonged to us. We belonged to him.

A Kid in Line Who Made It Backstage

BILL BOGGS

Anse Chastanet Hotel, St. Lucia—I'm sitting on a lounge under a thatched hut looking at the sun sparkle on the sea. I've just removed the small Walkman speakers from my ears as the audience applause started to fade after Frank Sinatra's last number on the *December Down Under* CD, which was recorded on the evening of December 2, 1961, in Sydney, Australia. It's one of the best recordings of a Sinatra live performance I've ever heard.

The air here is sweet from the rain forest, and the blue sky is as cloudless today as it was yesterday. The only sound I hear is the quiet rhythm of the sea playing with sand. I'm in paradise, but, ironically, if I could be beamed up the way they do on *Star Trek*, I'd be happier to be in a smoke-filled saloon anywhere in the world . . . if I could see Frank Sinatra in person just one more time.

Not that I haven't witnessed my fair share of performances. By my best estimate, I figure I've seen about a hundred and fifty shows spread out from August of 1960 at the 500 Club in Atlantic City to one of Frank's final performances thirty-four years later at the Sands Hotel in the same town. To think I did all that.

I saw the swaggering, macho, intimidating Sinatra of the sixties—the one who snapped the microphone cord like a bullwhip—slowly evolve into the white-haired performer of the nineties—the one who held a golden wireless mike and expressed misty-eyed gratitude for the cheers at the close of his shows. The audiences and Frank, I think, found it harder and harder to say goodbye. And why not?

Sinatra's audiences shared a collective loyalty, not unlike patriotism, from all the past individual associations with his songs. Whether he was singing about romping through the meadows picking flowers or losing love and sucking up the third drink too many, he brought the audience's energies to a common point. The Voice—sometimes a whisper, sometimes a territorial roar—held tender memories.

Seeing Frank Sinatra in person gave me a fix, like a junkie. I got high on all those autobiographical associations that I had with the songs and that Frank himself had with the songs. I needed that heart-pounding feeling before the start of a show. I craved the tingle from feeling the vibrations coming from the stage, because part of Sinatra's great success is that he exudes uncommonly powerful energy from his body. You can't get it by watching him on TV or listening to recordings. You have to be in his presence to feel it. The United States Marines call that quality "command posture." It's a term they reserve for the rare leader whose physical presence and personal authority dominate others in a group. When Frank Sinatra appeared on stage he conveyed all that concentrated power. He was a force, a hearable presence, even in silence. Combine the charisma with his voice, dramatic acting ability, a full orchestra, and some of the greatest songs of the twentieth century, and wowie! You're in for a show!

My love of seeing Frank Sinatra perform live started for me as a teenage caper, when I dressed as a busboy and sneaked into the "500 Club" in Atlantic City. Frank's show didn't start for an hour after I got in, so I set up tables and kept roaming around so as not to arouse suspicion. When Frank came on he transformed a rowdy group of drinkers and smokers into one utterly attentive audience. I watched from just a few feet away and fell in love with him, with his artistry and the feeling of being transported into the ebb and flow of the emotions in each song. I was happily hooked. Ever after, being right there in the same space with Frank always lifted my spirits. After watching some of the later-day shows of the early 1990s, I said that watching him perform was like going to church. My perceptions of Frank's life and the way he lived it became intermingled with my sheer love of the music.

As a young man I believed there were lessons to be learned from Frank. As an older man now, I know that his inspiration to me far transcends the music. I found a role model who was steamroller ambitious and a man who was in control of his own destiny. I needed the influence of someone who spoke his mind directly and appeared to be honest in his dealings with others. I liked the idea of a man who goes after the woman he wants. Frank was someone who'd known pain and used the experience to grow. That inspired me not to be too afraid of the darkness that entered my life at times. Frank is a man who will tell you that you have to scrape bottom to really appreciate living. Knowing about his tenacity, his belief in himself and his comeback, I found a source of inspiration, especially when I was near the bottom a couple of times. Above all, I admired Frank Sinatra as a man who liked to have fun. He said, "Live each day like it might be the final day."

I can state, without hesitation, that some of the greatest fun I've had in my life came when I went to see Frank perform. I can assemble a mental montage of the shows and the venues over the years:

- Frank sharing the bill with Lena Horne at Carnegie Hall with Nelson Riddle conducting and Martin Luther King speaking at intermission.

- The balmy summer evening at the Forest Hills Tennis Stadium when the audience applauded his breath control at the beginning of the song "Don't Worry 'Bout Me."

- The wild night when I first saw Frank in Las Vegas. I sat ringside at Caesar's Palace with Ed McMahon and three marines in full dress uniforms whom Jilly Rizzo invited to the show at the pool that day. Ed outdrank all three marines.

- I remember many shows from Radio City Music Hall but particularly one with New York Governor Hugh Carey in the audience and Frank blasting "New York, New York" as his opening and getting a standing ovation at the top of the show.

- There was a long, cold night in the back of a limo when Sylvia Syms, television producer Richard Dubin, and I went from Manhattan to Cherry Hill, New Jersey, to the Latin Casino to see Frank's late show. Frank was sensational, and he really turned up the heat when he spotted Sylvia ringside. She was on her feet cheering for half of the show.

- I'll never forget the Mother's Day Sunday afternoon when I took my mother (a former bobby-soxer) to the Valley Forge Music Fair and the beautiful Barbara Sinatra graciously introduced her to Frank in his dressing room. My mother said, "Thanks for the music; it's helped us over some of the hard times." Frank gave her a hug, and she squealed like a teenager. Afterward, when we took our seats, she said, "I'm one of the kids in line who made it backstage."

- Years later I took my mother and girlfriend Ishbel Burnet to London, where we saw Frank's opening night at Royal Albert Hall. It was an uncommonly hot spring evening, and, unfortunately, Frank was wearing a heavy three-piece tuxedo. During the show, my mother said that she felt sorry for the seventy-seven-year-old singer working in the heat. The next day one London newspaper ran a large color picture of a dripping Sinatra with the caption "Heavy-weight Goes the Distance."

- At Carnegie Hall, I watched three of my guests—jazz piano great Walter Bishop, Jr., rocker Ian Hunter, and fifteen-year-old Brooke Shields—sink back in their seats after giving Frank a standing ovation for a panoramic interpretation of the ballad "Autumn Leaves."

- At the Uris Theater (now the Gershwin) with Count Basie in 1975, Frank sang a particularly rousing interpretation of "Nice 'n' Easy." I can vividly recall one person leaping to his feet and delivering a solo standing ovation. It was Elton John.

- After another performance at the Uris during that same gig, I went back to Frank's dressing room and met Jacqueline Kennedy Onassis, who'd been in the audience as Sinatra's guest. I said, "Wasn't the show wonderful?" And she gave me a terrific, wide-eyed, little-girl reply: "Don't you wish it was just starting all over again!"

I wish the whole adventure of seeing Frank was starting all over again for me. It's been a thrilling ride. I went from being the kid who sneaked into a nightclub dressed as a busboy to being the first person ever to interview Sinatra on a daytime talk show.

But the first time I ever spoke to Frank Sinatra was several years before I even began my career as a television host and producer. The year was 1965, and Frank was to open at the Eden Roc Hotel in Miami Beach. This was to be his first appearance on the East Coast in a couple of years, in fact, the first since my friend Norman Steinberg and I had shaken hands at the end of the summer of 1963 and made a pact: "If Frank ever comes East, no matter where we are, we'll go to see him." After that, Norman and I went in different directions. By 1965, I'd finished college and was working as a writer in Lancaster, Pennsylvania, and Norman was in basic training for the Army someplace in the deep South. As soon as I heard about the show, I sent a letter to the maitre d' at the hotel with some cash as a "tip" in an effort to get a reservation. Norman wrote to say that the date of Frank's opening night coincided with his last day of basic training. We were going. The only problem was that, after sending even more "tips," I'd gotten no answer from the hotel, and we had no reservation for the show. I called and was told that the engagement was sold out.

I packed two white busboy jackets just in case we'd need them. We wouldn't. Norman and I got in the line for the early show. When the captain asked for our names, I told him I was the person who'd written him and mailed the tips. He said, "You came! And this is your friend who is just getting out of the Army." "That's it. We're here," I replied. He snapped his fingers and showed us to a ringside table. The show featured

Joe E. Lewis as the opening act, and young Quincy Jones served as Frank's conductor. How happy do you think we were? But it gets better.

After the performance, we learned from a couple of girls who were singers in the lounge that the man himself would be partying that night. Frank was set to host a small group in the Mona Lisa Room around two in the morning. "Was the room open to the public?" we asked. "Yes" was all we needed to hear. So a few minutes before two, Norman and I took seats at the bar. The only other people in the place were a honeymooning couple a few stools away. At two on the dot, Frank arrived with eight people including Bill Miller, his pianist. There was Frank having dinner, just a few feet away! Norman and I ordered two Jack Daniels mists and casually watched. The honeymoon couple stayed put. At one point, Jackie Gleason waltzed through the room, greeted Frank, and then headed off.

Around three-fifteen, the unimaginable happened. A baby grand piano was wheeled near the table and a lighted candelabra placed on it. Bill Miller got up and played. Then, a singer ambled over to the piano, and, with the candlelight glowing on the side of his face, Frank Sinatra closed his eyes and started "The Girl Next Door." The first thing that struck me was the muscularity of his voice, unamplified by a microphone. It seemed that he was singing to himself, not performing at all, and he was very intense. When the song was over and we applauded, he appeared slightly embarrassed that he'd become so wrapped up in his own feelings. He sang "Little Girl Blue" next, and at one point needed a line of the lyric. From my perch on the barstool, I gave it to him. He was singing brilliantly. Next he wove his way through "My Funny Valentine." His last song was "Violets for Your Furs," and again I pitched in a needed lyric.

Frank walked back to his seat at the table while we were still applauding. Norman and I shook hands again. The honeymoon couple had their mouths wide open. In a few minutes it was evident that the party was breaking up, and so Norman and I left the Mona Lisa Room to watch Frank and his guests depart. As Frank walked past me, I said, "Thanks for the singing." And he said, "That was fun, wasn't it?" And that's the first time I spoke to Frank Sinatra.

The next time was also around four in the morning. It was on Easter Sunday, ten years later, at Caesar's Palace in Las Vegas. How did I get to meet Frank Sinatra in Las Vegas? Well, I can say with certainty that I was introduced to Frank in the way I was that night because of events that took place at the University of Pennsylvania in the spring of 1967.

At the time I was Assistant Dean of Men at Penn, while also managing the comedy team of Tom Patchett and Jay Tarses. One afternoon, I had a phone call from Ken Roberts, who has since gone on to become a radio mogul. Back then, he'd created University Concert Productions, one of the first organizations to book big-time acts on university campuses. He called to see if there was interest in having Sammy Davis, Jr., at Penn. My fellow deans and I agreed that Sammy would be an excellent attraction, but the student board wanted absolutely nothing to do with Sammy. They turned him down in favor of some white-bread folk act.

Now normally that would have been it—no Sammy Davis, Jr., at Penn. However, I pressed on because I thought it would be good for both the university and the city of Philadelphia to have Sammy come to town. To make it happen, I enlisted the help of another dean, Paul Hiller, and together we went to the Interfraternity Council to stage the show. The fraternity men loved the idea, particularly of having the opportunity to outshine the student board and their spring event. And even though the Interfraternity Council had never staged an event of this kind in its ninety-year history, they put up the money to book Sammy.

For my ground-breaking actions, I found myself in the middle of an ugly political battle with the student board and many of its patrons on the faculty. I stuck to my guns and the show was staged at the Palestra. It got rave reviews. Somehow, Ken Roberts got word of my strong stand for Sammy, and we became good friends. A couple of years later Ken introduced me to his and Frank Sinatra's mutual friend, Jilly Rizzo, and, a couple of years after that, it was Jilly who presented me to Frank.

There have been many seemingly mystical coincidences related to Frank and his music in my life. Certainly meeting him that Easter Sunday morning in Las Vegas and his subsequent appearance in 1975 on my television program was just one of them. By the time I met Frank, I was well established in my career on television, hosting a show called *Midday Live with Bill Boggs*, which aired on WNEW-TV in New York City. In fact, it is likely that I would not have gotten my job on that show in New York were it not for a coincidence related to one of my trips to see Sinatra perform. The previous year I was hosting and producing a show in High Point, North Carolina, called *Southern Exposure with Bill Boggs*. I heard that Frank was going to be appearing at the Spectrum in my hometown of Philadelphia, so I got tickets and flew up for the Saturday night show. That afternoon, while walking across Chestnut street, I bumped into Judy Licht, who worked at WNEW-TV. Judy told me to call a man named Noble to see if I could audition for the *Midday* show. I made the call, did the audition, and got the job. If I hadn't seen Judy on my way to see Frank, I would have taken an offer on the table to host a program in Miami, Florida.

I went to Las Vegas that Easter weekend at the suggestion of a girlfriend who lived in Los Angeles. She called to say that both Frank Sinatra and Elvis Presley were performing in Vegas on the very weekend when she'd be celebrating her birthday. She wanted to meet there and see both shows on the same night, and we did.

Before I left on the trip, I told Paul Noble that I was going to meet Frank Sinatra over the weekend and that Frank would say he'd appear on *Midday*. I assume Paul thought I was nuts. But I'd been having recurring dreams for years that I was sitting having a conversation with Frank, and, two days before leaving for Vegas, I had such a dream again. I took it to be an omen of things to come, and it was exactly that.

My friend and I saw Elvis in the early show and Frank at the late show. When my date retired at about two in the morning, I set out somehow to meet Frank. As I had ten years before at the Eden Roc, I'd heard that he was supposed to be hanging out at a particular lounge at Caesar's. At around 3:30 A.M., I saw Jilly, who'd been helpful in getting us excellent ringside seats for the show, and we talked for awhile. Jilly asked if I would like to say hello to Frank, and, of course, I said yes. He told me to come back at around four, and so I walked around for a little while, concentrating on my deep feelings for Frank. I remembered how I used to listen to him on *Your Hit Parade* on a tiny white Bendix radio when I was a little boy.

We met leaning over the rail of a lounge. And the first thing I said was, "Thanks for all the great music you've put in my life." I told him the busboy story. He told me how he felt he was doing on his way back from his retirement. "The whole thing dropped," he said, referring to his voice, "and now I'm fighting my way back." I told him how much I thought audiences liked the song "Cycles," and he said that they still had it in the performance book. We talked about other things, too, like the fact that my date had passed out from drinking too much and that I thought Elvis looked unwell.

After a little more conversation, he said, "Jilly tells me you've got a show on [channel] five in New York. I'm going to be in town this fall. I'm not promising anything, but maybe I can come by and do your show." I replied, "That would be great, but I'm not asking for anything." He looked me straight in the eye and said simply, "I know that."

We never discussed it any further. Seven months later, his lovely secretary Dorothy called to make the arrangements, and it happened! For me, the experience of sitting down and talking with Frank Sinatra on television was straight out of the song "Where or When," which addresses the idea that things that seem to have happened before were happening all over again.

For years people have asked me how I got Frank Sinatra to do my talk show. If I think they couldn't understand the real answer, or if I didn't like the way they asked me in the first place, I'd give a joke response like "I made him an offer he couldn't refuse . . . a year's free meals at Pizza Hut." Certain people would not appreciate the purity of the truth, and I didn't want to waste its intimacy on them. But since you have this book and are reading this article, I'll tell you clearly why it happened. It was quite simple. When he met me, he knew that I loved him.

On a Sunday in early November 1992, Frank Sinatra did a rare matinee performance at Radio City Music Hall. It was a make-up date for a show that had been canceled because of his illness. That afternoon, the audience had a particularly interesting buzz—there were many children in attendance. Among them was my seven-year-old son Trevor.

After Shirley MacLaine finished the first half of the show, there was a racehorse-like rush by many people backstage to say hello to "Mr. S" before his performance. I joined the pack and somehow, together with Trevor's mother, the actress Linda Thorson, made it over several hurdles to meet the man backstage. When we showed up, Frank was on his way to the stage but had stopped to have his picture taken with someone's fluffy white dog. (It's never exactly like you think it's going to be backstage anywhere.) After the flash popped and Frank handed the startled dog back to its glowing owner, I had the opportunity to do something that was very important to me—introduce my son to Francis Albert Sinatra. I seized the moment and said, "Frank, Linda and I would like you to meet our son, Trevor." Frank, wearing a dark suit and tangerine-colored shirt, studied Trevor and beamed at us, "He's marvelous, just marvelous." Then he slowly bent over, looked Trevor in the eye, and said, "Never get old. Never get old."

With the gift of good health and some luck, I hope that my son will live a very long life. I see him near the end of the twenty-first century recalling that long-ago day when he met Frank Sinatra. He's telling his children's children about what Frank said to him at Radio City Music Hall. Then I'd like to think that he'd put on the CD of that live performance in Sydney, Australia, and say, "This was one of your great-grandfather's favorites. It reminded him of all the times he saw Frank Sinatra perform. Let's listen."

Sounds of Sinatra: A Conversation with Sid Mark

CHARLES L. GRANATA

The first thing to impress you upon meeting Sid Mark is his size. At well over six feet, if he hadn't gone into radio, he would have been a natural as a center for the Philadelphia Seventy-Sixers. The second distinguishing feature is the rich, booming voice that genially greets you. The voice is, by the way, perfectly natural. The sound you hear in your living room, or in your car, or on your portable Walkman is not enhanced or sweetened by any electronic means. The profoundly deep, velvety-smooth instrument that sets Sid Mark apart from all other radio personalities is, in fact, a resonant reflection of his confidence and knowledge, which are eloquently displayed in the interludes between records by his friend, Frank Sinatra.

In many ways, Sid Mark is a man to be envied. Could any other word appropriately describe the way some people must feel about a guy who has spent the last forty-two years of his life playing Frank Sinatra records on local and national radio? To be sure, Sid has a job that most Sinatra devotees could only dream of—except, few would have the perseverance or inner drive to stay in the race and excel on the level that Sid has for lo these many years. The word *envy* connotes desire, and it is used here with the greatest respect for this man.

Putting your finger on exactly what it is about Sid that makes his Sinatra radio programs so downright appealing is tricky. The made-for-radio voice aside, he is a master programmer who scrupulously avoids all unauthorized

Sinatra recordings and bootlegs. Moreover, he broadcasts each and every show, even the ones committed to tape for delayed airing, in real time: listening to the music as it rolls along, commenting on songs, extemporizing in commercial announcements and allowing them to emerge as custom-crafted advertisements worthy of the most prestigious Madison Avenue ad agency. His gentle on-air persona is genuine, and perhaps that is what catches your attention and reels you in . . . that and the love and respect and passion that Sid obviously feels for the focus of his attention, the man he affectionately calls "Mr. S."

In my own experiences with the music of Frank Sinatra, Sid Mark's *Saturday with Sinatra* program was, from its 1979 inception on WYNY in New York, a comforting companion. In the beginning, it served to broaden my "Sinatra horizon," as it was through Sid's show that I learned of the versatile catalog of Sinatra recordings that existed outside my small collection of Columbia and Capitol gems.

In a way, I guess that I, too, was one of those who secretly wished that I were like Sid Mark, being able to pursue a vocation that I loved, sharing music that I thoroughly enjoyed with listeners who were equally as enamored of "The Voice." Little did I know that years later, I would be invited to share Sid's microphone a couple of times to talk about our mutual love for the music of Frank Sinatra—an experience that has thrilled me and that I count among my warmest Sinatra memories. The folks who surround Sid—his producer/engineer, Steve Johnson, his friend/partner Jon Harmelin, his son/business associate Brian Mark, and of course, his devoted wife Judy, sons Andy and Eric, and daughter Stacey—are all major supporting players in his ability to thrive gracefully in an industry that floats in shark-infested waters.

Coming to know Sid Mark, I honestly feel that he is among the most passionate people I have ever known. His dedication to and enthusiasm for all things Sinatra is infectious and has evolved from very simple roots. His reminiscences of years in jazz clubs and on radio and television are interesting and entertaining. In fact, they could easily fill a book, and I'm sure that someday they will! Until then, I'd like to share some of Sid's recollections, in his own words:

Q: It was an unusual path that brought you to the radio microphone. How did you become interested in radio?

A: My Dad had a clothing business in Southern Jersey, and I was working in the "family" business. My best friend, Harvey Husten, was in radio (he was the program director at WKDN in Camden New Jersey, a very powerful AM station whose slogan was "From the Capitol to the Cape!"). Harvey used to do a program called *Harvey's House*—it was all jazz. Once in a while, I'd take a break from working and go over to the station while he was broadcasting and just sit there and watch. He was playing June Christy and Basie and Ellington—he was playing it all!

A bit later, I became a student at the Columbia Broadcasting School. There's a funny story about my very first "interview," with Nat Cole, who was appearing at the Earle Theater in 1950. I got in by going to the Earle with a microphone that had CBS on it and a big tape recorder that said WCAU on it. During our conversation, Nat began asking me about people that worked at WCAU [Philadelphia's CBS affiliate], and I knew no one! Finally, he asked me, "Do you work at WCAU?" And I told him, "No, sir, I don't." He asked me what the WCAU stood for on my tape recorder, and I told him, "Webcor Audition Unit." Quick thinking. "And the CBS?" he asked. "Columbia Broadcasting School." I got thrown out! Nat was very gracious, but I had been going there every show. I had a big long trench coat, and I'd come in there with the big WCAU on there. I looked pretty good! The clincher was when Nat asked me, "How's Bill Sears?" And I said, "Fine!" Nat looked at me and dead panned: "He died a year ago."

In the early 1950s, I went into the service, and, while I was gone, Harvey had opened a jazz room, the Red Hill Inn. When I returned, he asked me if I'd like to work for him. I told him, "I'd love it! What am I going to do?" And he said, "You're going to be a gopher." So my primary job became that of chauffeur: I would pick up the artists and make sure that they got to the club. He also had two record boutiques at farmers' markets in Bridgeton, so I ran that. Of course, the best part of the job was that I got to know all of the artists. I drove Ellington in, I drove Lester Young in, Carmen McRae, Sarah Vaughan . . . the stories they used to tell me when they were in the car! And I used to ask them all, "Do you know Frank Sinatra?" It was always, "Yeah." Me: "Would you please tell him that there's a kid in Philadelphia . . . ?" The guys in the Basie band all knew Sinatra. The first one to ever talk to Frank about what I was doing in Philly was Al Grey, the trombonist. They all loved Frank.

Q: It must have been incredible to spend time with Lester Young.

A: Actually, my encounter with Lester was rather unusual. I had been working at the club about two weeks, when they told me I had to go pick up Lester Young, and I said, "Lester Young? Prez? Fine!" I go to the hotel, and I've got my car outside, and it's starting to snow. We were about ten miles out from the club. "Hello, Mr. Young." Not a word. "The car's over here." Nothing. He's wearing a black cape and that porkpie hat. Now we're driving—out on old New York Highway. It's snowing, and I'm worried. Not for me, not for my car—but I've got *Lester Young* in my car, in the front seat . . . and there were no seat belts at the time. And we're driving, and nothing. Not one word of conversation. Who am I? I'm a punk kid; I'm a driver! We come up to the club, and I hit the brakes, and the back end of the car goes out. And I turned around and said, "My God, Prez, what should I do?" And he looked at me, took his hand and put it on top of his porkpie hat, and said, "I'm just followin' and swallowin'!" He said not one other word to me for the entire weekend. One thing I never realized was that one of Frank Sinatra's favorites was Lester Young, and that one of Lester Young's favorites was Frank Sinatra, which no one knew either. Lester used to go home and listen to Frank Sinatra!

Q: Working at the Red Hill Inn was a tremendous opportunity. There is definitely a strong connection between Frank and the jazz greats that appeared there: Lester, Basie, Billie Holiday.

A: I spent a week with Billie at the Red Hill Inn, toward the end. She was in bad shape already—such bad shape, that she had to sleep upstairs at the club. My only job that week was to make sure that she was a hundred percent happy and to keep everyone away from her. She'd call me at three o'clock in the morning. "Would you go out and get me some white bread and orange juice?" she'd ask. I'd say, "Absolutely." I adored her. One Friday night, she was so sick, I brought in my Mother's chicken noodle soup, and we sat in the dressing room—me, Harvey, and Billie Holiday, and she ate this chicken noodle soup, and it was like someone was giving her gold.

Q: This must have been around the time she was planning the Columbia album *Lady in Satin*, on which she does a searing rendition of "I'm a Fool to Want You."

A: Yes, it was. I remember she said, "Sidney, I want to do an album for Frank." Years later, I brought Frank a copy of her last album, the one on MGM with Ray Ellis, he hadn't heard that. He said, "Wow!" It really was, in a way, a tribute to Frank because she did "All the Way," "Don't Worry 'Bout Me," and "Polka Dots and Moonbeams."

Q: So where were you, radio-wise, while you were working at the Red Hill Inn?

A: I was at WHAT in Philadelphia (now WWDB, the same station I've been at for my entire career). The guy who hired me was Charlie O'Donnell, who is now a staff announcer at ABC in Los Angeles.

Q: With the name Sid Mark inextricably linked to that of Frank Sinatra, it's almost hard to believe that your creation of a Sinatra radio show was utter happenstance, one of life's serendipitous occurrences. Why Sinatra? When did Sinatra, as a vocalist, first affect you?

A: My first Sinatra "memory" was actually buying the 78's for my sister. To be a teenaged boy and go into a record store and buy a Sinatra 78 was almost like the first time a teenage boy goes in to the drugstore to buy a prophylactic! It was almost embarrassing, because they'd say, sneeringly, "Is this for you?" "No, it's for my sister." And she would always say to me, "Make sure you don't drop it on the way home," because they were in paper-thin bags, and, if you dropped it, it was gone.

In 1955, I was handling the overnight shift (for free) at WHAT, doing a jazz show called *Sounds in the Night*, from 2 to 3 A.M. The show that was supposed to follow mine was *Rock and Roll Kingdom*, but the guy that did that show wasn't going to make it, and I got a call that I was going to be on for the remainder of the evening. When the call came, I wasn't prepared, so I went on the air, and said, "What do you folks want to hear? I'm going to be here until six, and this is what I have: Miles Davis, Dave Brubeck . . . and, oh, I've got a couple of Sinatra things here as well." A guy called, and said, "Why don't you do an hour of Sinatra?" This was a Friday night, so I said, "Great. I'll call it *Friday with Frank*." I did—and the phones lit up like crazy! People loved it, and said "This is great. Why don't you do it again?" I explained that it was only for the one night, because I was only filling in. On Monday, I received a call from management, telling me that the all-night guy had been fired and that I'd be doing all-nights, never asking me what I was going to do. "Just do it," they said.

So I continued to do jazz all night long, and, on Fridays, I'd do my one hour of Frank Sinatra. It must have been about six or eight months later when I got called in, and they asked, "What are you doing overnight? You're not doing *Rock and Roll Kingdom*?" They'd been hearing about the jazz show from kids at Temple University and Penn who thought it was a great show to study to! And the overnight workers from the post office had called and said that they were listening to us, as opposed to the "big gun," which, at that time, was WIP in Philadelphia. So I told them, and they said, "Obviously, it's working. Do you want to do the job?" They gave me thirty-five dollars a week (it cost me twenty-five to get there), but I was working at the Red Hill Inn, so it really tied in beautifully. Now, I could not only be with the people, but I could play their music . . . and they started coming over as guests on the program. And everyone used to say, "Yeah, I'm going to go do the show . . . you know, with Frank's kid . . . the kid that likes Sinatra."

Q: This is the mid-1950s. Was Frank even aware of what you were doing then?

A: No. I had started writing to Capitol, in long hand: "Dear To Whom It May Concern. This may be of some interest to you . . . I do a show . . . three o'clock in the morning . . . *Friday with Frank*." Nobody ever answered. Never!

Q: But the show took off anyway!

A: Well, some years later, when FM came into being, we moved the show back to six o'clock in the evening, and it went 'til eight. But the station had a strange rule. They told me, if I was going to do two hours, I couldn't play two successive Frank Sinatra recordings—people wouldn't want to hear that. So I had to do Sinatra, then a Basie, a Sinatra, then a Kenton. I kept it all big band. I was only playing the swingin' stuff at that time. And the rest just happened. It caught on, and the station caught on. We became the first twenty-four hour full-time jazz station, with national recognition. WHAT was called "a breath of fresh air on the FM dial."

Q: There was one very special lady that helped move things along, too.

A: I was still at the Red Hill, booking acts (once I went to the station full-time, they asked me to quit working at the club, because I was playing the records of the artists that were appearing, and they thought it smacked of payola), and Erroll Garner was supposed to be in. But the afternoon that he was scheduled to arrive, he was involved in a cab accident in New York. We didn't know what to do. There was a girl that had a hit record with "I Could Have Danced All Night" on Decca. Someone said, "We can get her for you, but it's going to cost you 'X' amount of dollars (I don't remember the figure), and I figured that I really didn't have much choice, so we brought her in, and it was Sylvia Syms. Now I was doing everything at the club: I put up the microphones and set the levels and did the gels on the lights. We started talking, struck up an immediate friendship, and, when the Sinatra things came up, that was the home-run. Sylvia became my "guardian angel" from there on out.

Q: Sinatra and Syms were friends, weren't they?

A: Old friends. They used to go see Billie Holiday together, on 52nd Street. (Sylvia told me that she was in the dressing room when Billie burned her hair with a curling iron and that she, Sylvia, suggested that Billie cover the spot with white gardenias.) It was Sylvia that started telling Frank about me, and I met some folks that were friendly with Jilly, and he started telling Frank. So he was hearing about what we were doing, which was still confined to Philadelphia at the time.

Q: Were you limiting yourself to just Sinatra yet?

A: No. I was doing a whole series of shows, each night of the week. I had *An Evening with Ella, A Night with Nat, Saturday with Sarah* . . . block programming, shows like that.

Q: What was the turning point for the Sinatra show?

A: In 1966, the album *Sinatra at the Sands* was recorded. The record was supposed to be released on the weekend; since we were a jazz station, we got the album on the Wednesday before. I figured, "It's Basie! I'm going with it now," and played it top-to-bottom all day Wednesday and all day Thursday. We had arranged a sale on the album at one of the record shops, and the sale was to begin on Friday afternoon, to carry through into the weekend. We were playing the record so much, they sold out on Friday night! They called me, and asked, "Could we get the distributor to open, to bring more product in? We want a hundred mono and a hundred stereo." The distributor said, "I'm not coming in for a hundred mono and a hundred stereo," so I said, "Fine—send them what you want." So he sent them a *thousand* of each, and they immediately sold those out!

The following Monday, I received a call from Warner Brothers, saying, "We heard what you did. That was very nice. Is there something we can do for you?" And I said, "Yeah, I want to meet Frank." They told me that wasn't really possible, but "thank you very much." Then, on Thursday of that week, I got a call that we were to fly to the Sands and be Frank's guests for the weekend.

Q: This is the moment you've been waiting for. The call comes, and you're going to be Sinatra's guest, for the weekend. What were your very first thoughts?

A: First, that my clothes probably had gotten moldy—they'd been packed for ten years. They were in the back of the car. I mean, I was ready to go on a moment's notice! I said, "Jeez, how am I going to get airfare?" They said, "It's all been taken care of. You just show up at the airport, and you go."

I really wondered, what would it be like? Would I be able to speak with him? Would I stutter? Would he know who I am? Would I even see him? (I had been to the 500 Club a trillion times, and you couldn't even get in through the kitchen, and I was with the Capitol people then. You'd be with them, but you could not get to see Frank. It was impossible.) So here I am, going by myself. I don't have anybody that's going to walk up and say, "Frank Sinatra, I would like you to meet Mr. and Mrs. Mark. They're from Philadelphia." We were on our own.

My wife and I arrived at the Sands, and checked in. I said, "Let's go down and make sure we have reservations for the show," and, when we did, there were no reservations in our name, for any shows—for the whole weekend. No early shows, no late shows—everything was sold out. "Sorry sir," they said. "I'm a guest of Mr. Sinatra's . . ." "Yeah, well, *everybody's* a guest of Mr. Sinatra's." I didn't know what to do. I was really embarrassed. Then I remembered that Sylvia said she would call ahead for me, and, if there were a problem, she'd call Jilly. So I called Sylvia, she called Jilly, Jilly called me and said, "They're having dinner. He's waiting for you. He knows you're here."

Q: What was the moment of truth like?

A: It was just a bit better than incredible! Jilly had told us to go to a certain restaurant, and we walked into the restaurant and did not see anybody. There was nobody in there. I was getting nervous, and my wife said to me,

"Now, don't get upset, but turn around and look to your left . . . he's standing right next to you." I turned around, and he was right there. The blue eyes met with mine. "Hi, Sidney, how are you? Come on in," he said.

We walked into the room, and seated at the table were Jack Benny and Mary Livingston, Milton and Ruthie Berle, Nancy Jr. and James Darren, Leo Durocher, Jack Entratter. Frank introduced us around to everyone and proceeded to give them the time the program was on and the call letters of the station (which floored me—he was so prepared). I was so nervous. They asked if we had eaten: I said "yes," my wife said "no." They asked if we wanted a drink: I said "no," my wife said "yes." It was almost comical! Then, Frank came over and gave me a little tweak on the cheek and said, "You'll have to excuse me. Please sit here with my friends. I'm going to go change and get ready. You'll come to the show." I remember saying, "I don't have tickets." He laughed and replied, "You don't have tickets! You're sitting at our table. And don't forget, you're coming to the party afterward as well."

It was fantastic! Frank couldn't have been any nicer. Jack Benny was delightful, Nancy was superb, Jimmy Darren was gracious, Jack Entratter couldn't do enough . . . to go to the show and enter the showroom where everyone was seated, preceded by all these people, and here are these two civilians. Everyone knew who *they* were, but I'm sure they were wondering, "Who are these people?" Afterward, at the party, we sat with Mia, and Frank kept coming over, making sure we were okay. It was quite a kick!

Q: Any drawbacks to the weekend of a lifetime?

A: The difficult part was flying back and getting back into the normal routine. I remember coming back, and it was garbage day, and here I was, taking the garbage out, saying, "What is *this* all about? How could I have just been with Frank Sinatra, and here I am? It's cold in Philadelphia, and I'm taking the garbage out and driving to work. I'd rather be there! I think I want to go back. It was just unbelievable to finally meet somebody that you've wanted to meet since you were a kid, but professionally for ten years, and to see him in person. He did an incredible show that night. I remember he did "Nancy," and sang it to Nancy. It was brilliant. And he had this kid with him conducting—Quincy Jones. And I had known Quincy from before, at the Red Hill Inn, and from when he worked with all the other jazz bands.

Q: After that first meeting in 1966, the Philly show evolved to include a Sunday program, and, in the late 1970s, you hit New York with *Saturday with Sinatra*, and began your national syndicated show.

A: Frank and I had letters going back and forth through the years. He'd come to do the Spectrum here in Philly, and it would be a nod and introduction from the stage. Then, we decided to try to syndicate the show. The first station we picked up after WWDB was KGIL in Los Angeles, which excited me, because I knew they [the Sinatra people] could hear it! And then we got WGN in Chicago, which is an enormous station. Then, in 1979, I got a call to audition for WYNY (NBC) in New York. I said, "Audition? I've been on the air since 1955!" They said, "No, you have to audition," but I got the job. They made me wait from June to August until they gave me the response.

WYNY told me they were going to run an ad in the *New York Times*— full page, with Frank's picture. The banner was "Saturday nights will never be the same." The phone rings, and it's Dorothy, Sinatra's secretary. "Hold on a second. The boss wants to talk to you." You get a call like that, your heart's in your mouth! "Saw the ad—great! Can I do anything for you?" he asked. I said, "They don't know me up there." And he said, "Well, number one, you've got to go meet Willie [the late William B. Williams, then the dean of New York Sinatra radio]. Go to lunch with him at the Friar's Club." "Just like that?" I asked. "Just like that," he said, giving me Willie's home phone number. Then, he added, "What can I do?" "You could be on the show," I suggested. Without hesitation, he said, "Fine, set it up with Dorothy." "Just like that?" I asked. "Just like that."

I went up to the Waldorf, and he was incredible. I told him that I wanted to do the show as though he were there, commercials and all, so he said, "Okay, let's do it." So I'm reading the copy, which was for so-and-so on Houston Street, which I pronounced "Hugh-ston Street." And he fell on the floor. I mean, he fell out completely! I said, "What's the problem?" He said, "Do you want to make it in New York? Well, you better learn the sayings. It's pronounced 'How-ston Street.' It's in the Village. Let's go through all the sayings." Then, he said, "Give me the copy. I'll do the commercials!" He did a commercial for the Clam Broth House in Hoboken and told everybody about how he used to go there as a kid. It was incredible.

Q: This was pretty personal—just you and Frank, at his home in the Waldorf Towers.

A: He was so loose, he was so gracious, he was so kind. You sit there, and you're amazed that this guy that no one seemingly can get to can be so genuine, so kind, and take such an interest in what you're doing. It was then that I realized that, if Frank had never sung a note, I'd still have wanted him to be my friend. He's just a guy's guy.

A year or two later, we did a full network New Year's Eve show on Mutual, and I met him down in Atlantic City, where we were going to tape the interview, between his shows. We ended up waiting until after the last show, and, from midnight until three A.M., it was just me, Frank, and Jilly in the dressing room at Resorts. Frank changed into a sports jacket, got a cup of tea, and, when we finished, he asked, "Do you have everything you need? Are you sure?" He was in no hurry to go. People were waiting for him, and he kept saying, "I know . . . I'll be there." We talked about all of the arrangers and all of the writers. It was very special.

Q: Frank probably spoke more with you about his collaborators than he did with anyone else. It's obvious that he had a special affection for them.

A: When Gordon Jenkins was sick, a friend of mine told me that he was gravely ill and didn't have long to live. Frank was appearing at the Spectrum in Philadelphia, and I wanted to do an interview to use as a tribute, for Gordon to hear. So we arranged to talk backstage, before the performance. Originally, Frank had said, "I think I'll pass on this one. We're having a dinner for Gordon when I get back to Los Angeles." I said, "Frank, I don't think you realize how seriously ill he is."

On the master tape, you can hear the band in the background. Frank wouldn't sit down; he had his tux on and didn't want to wrinkle it. And he was out of sorts because he knew that he would never see Gordon again. We sent the tape right out to the Coast, and Gordon heard it. I believe I got the last letter he ever wrote—it's written in the most stumbling handwriting—and I gave it to Frank. In the note, Gordon said that he wouldn't trade any of the pain of his illness for the opportunity to have worked with Frank Sinatra, Steve and Eydie, and Nat Cole. When Frank read that, he broke down. Shortly after we aired the special, Gordon passed away. When I spoke with his wife, Beverly, she told me that Gordon was moved to tears by Frank's words and that it really meant a lot to him in the last days of his life.

Q: You've also been confident enough to discuss with Frank issues that most people would assiduously avoid—like politics.

A: One of the most enjoyable times we spent together was back at the Waldorf, on a gorgeous afternoon. I had gotten there early. Barbara was going out shopping, and the two of us sat in the living room, which faced out onto Park Avenue, and just talked and talked. It was one of those clear, crisp winter days. We didn't stop talking until it was almost dark (I didn't have to be on the air until seven), and Barbara came home and said, "Frank, we have to go out." I'd bring him cassettes sometimes, and he'd listen to them and then ask, "May I have this?" slipping it into his pocket. I always wondered where all the tapes went. Did he have a file somewhere? Always in the pocket! I liked when he did that.

From that visit, I have a whole hour that I never aired because we didn't talk about anything having to do with music. We talked about a U-2 plane that had been shot down and how difficult it must be for the President. Frank talked about going to Israel to do a concert for orphans, and how he realized (while he was there) that the diplomatic thing to do would be to go to Egypt as well because he was friendly with Mrs. Sadat. So he flew to Egypt and did a concert there as well. He was so well versed on politics and sounded like he was going to run for office. At one point on the tape, I said, "You mean you choose not to run?" and he just laughed.

Q: Forty-plus years of playing Sinatra—and only Sinatra. That amounts to countless thousands of hours, with a finite number of commercial record-ings at your disposal. Most radio people think you're crazy for doing each and every show in real time, whether live on the air, or live-to-tape. How do you keep it fresh?

A: I wouldn't do it any other way. It's more honest this way, and, I have to do it this way because that's how Frank would do it. It is always just a bit different; it never sounds the same to me. I can play a song on *Friday with Frank*, and then play the same song on *Sunday with Sinatra*, and, even though it's the very same performance, I hear it differently. It all has to do with the mood I'm in. If I come on swinging and I'm feeling really great, I may hear something that I've never heard before. With CD's, it's very refreshing, almost like hearing Frank again for the very first time.

I sit down early on Saturday mornings, while everyone in the house is asleep, and I can just relax and program the syndicated shows, which we tape on Mondays and Tuesdays. For the Friday and Sunday shows at WWDB, which are live, I just program the shows according to how I'm feeling at that moment.

Q: Have you ever seen a sensitive side of Sinatra that maybe not too many others get the chance to see?

A: One night, we were backstage at the Latin Casino, and Nancy was there with A. J., who was in her nightclothes, lying in her carriage. Frank came out of his dressing room in his tux. The band was vamping already, and he was shooting his cuffs . . . you know, that little thing that he likes to do? And, as he was getting ready to go on, A. J. said, "Pop-Pop," and he stopped. The band kept on vamping, and he turned around, and I wish I had a camera because I've never seen a smile like that Sinatra smile. He came over and gave that baby a little hug and a kiss, and then he went out on stage. He was bounding. I don't think his feet touched the floor! And he gave a show like I've never seen; he was roaring. I think it was the energy, kind of like an infusion, from the baby!

Q: But your friendship also went beyond casual sit-downs and backstage meetings.

A: The dinners were always very enjoyable, depending upon who else was at the table. If he was relaxed and had done a good show and he knew he had done a good show, it was fabulous! I always liked when Frank sat directly across from me, because you knew that, when he talked to you, your eyes connected.

Not too long before he stopped performing, I was at dinner with him, and he asked, "How's *Duets* doing, Sidney?" I said, "It's number one in Philadelphia." Frank said, "Well, it's number two nationally!" I repeated that it was number one in Philly, and someone said, "Well, how do you know that?" It was in the paper that day, "Sinatra Knocks Out Pearl Jam," so I told Frank that I had the headline in my hotel room. "Would you like me to get it?" I asked. Frank said, "Would you?" So my friend and business partner, Jon Harmelin, said, "Sit here, Sidney. I'll go get it," and he brought the paper down. "Sinatra Knocks Out Pearl Jam." Frank was thrilled. That's what I enjoyed—returning something to the man who's given me so much.

Q: As someone who is so intimate with this music, with this man, why do you feel Frank's music is so special and enduring?

A: Quality. The music is every bit as fresh today as it was when it was recorded. Every time you hear it, you hear it for the first time. And each recording is like a building block. Take the Columbia recording of "Don't Cry Joe" [1949], for example. When you listen to it, you realize that every single thing on that recording is a precursor of where Frank Sinatra would be in five years, ten years—as if there were a fortune teller there. Take it all the way up to Frank re-doing it on the *Swing Along with Me* album, with Billy May [1961], and you can hear that the new chart came right out of the original chart. The same applies to "I'm a Fool to Want You." Comparing the Columbia version with the later Capitol, you realize that the original is every bit as good and that Frank built his later work on the foundation of his earlier work. You can make these comparisons with dozens of songs, and it is interesting to do that. When Frank Sinatra sings a song and I feel what he's feeling . . . well, it doesn't get any better than that.

Q: Loyalty. Friendship. Two very important words in Sinatra's vocabulary—not just words, but the very principles upon which your relationship with him are predicated.

A: There is no doubt that Frank Sinatra is the most loyal of friends. We spent one entire night together, after a concert. It got to be pretty late, around four-thirty A.M., and my cheeks were numb, my legs felt dead. I'm not a drinker! By about five-thirty, Frank and I were the only ones still sitting at the table. I'll never forget it: the sun was coming up, and Frank looked at me, and said, "Is there anything I can do for you?" I said, "The only thing I ever wanted from you was your friendship." With that, he leaned over, hit me on the leg, and said, "You got it." He gave me a hug, and said, "If anyone ever hurts you, call me." I've always felt as if he were just a phone call away.

I guard my friendship with him cautiously. I always was concerned about doing anything that would offend Frank Sinatra. How in the world could I go on and do this show if he were angry at me? And I have never seen him angry. I admire this man for what he has accomplished. There will never be another Frank Sinatra.

For me, Frank Sinatra is an original, not unlike Picasso or Van Gogh. There's no question that, when Frank Sinatra paints a portrait, the tones and colors are his alone. Isn't it true that whether it's on record or on stage that he's singing to all of us individually—to you and me—who wanted it all? I think everyone knows that Frank Sinatra is the consummate performer. To me, he has been the consummate friend. There are no boundaries to his loyalty, whether it's an introduction on stage or a phone call or just a congratulatory note.

We've broken bread together, even lifted one or two. And the only thing I've ever asked for, he's given me—his friendship—a gift I'll treasure forever.

Appendix: Career Highlights

What follows is a chronological listing of Frank Sinatra's major accomplishments and recognitions in his seven decades as a recording artist, actor, concert performer, and mass-media personality. It includes information in seven general categories:

1. *Recordings*—The number of individual songs recorded in studio sessions, whether or not they were released at the time of their production.

2. *Albums*—The titles of major authorized releases, both those conceived of as unified theme albums and collections.

3. *Concerts*—A selected list of major concerts and benefit performances.

4. *Films*—Sinatra's appearances in motion pictures, whether as featured star or in a cameo role.

5. *Radio*—Regular radio programs, excluding appearances as a guest star on other programs.

6. *Television*—Regular series and specials starring FS. The list does not include guest appearances on other programs.

7. *Honors*—Awards and recognitions of Sinatra's work as an artist and humanitarian.

Despite its length, this listing is far from exhaustive.

1935

FS and The Hoboken Four appeared on *Major Bowes' Original Amateur Hour*. They were very successful and, as a result, joined Major Bowes's national touring company. They also appeared in two film shorts for *Major Bowes' Amateur Theatre of the Air*.

1937

FS took a job as a singing waiter at the Rustic Cabin in Englewood, New Jersey, remaining there until June of 1939, when Harry James hired him as the singer for his band.

1939

Sinatra joined The Harry James Orchestra, making his first appearance at the Hippodrome Theatre in Baltimore (June 30) and remaining with the band through the end of the year. He made 10 studio recordings with the orchestra on the Brunswick and Columbia labels.

1940

FS joined Tommy Dorsey's Band, appearing first in Rockford, Illinois, on January 25. During this first year of his 18-month tenure with the band, FS made 45 recordings on the Victor label, including his first #1 single, "I'll Never Smile Again."

1941

Recordings: 29 songs on the Victor label.

Film: Las Vegas Nights.

Honors: Outstanding Male Vocalist, *Billboard* magazine; Outstanding Male Vocalist, *Down Beat* magazine.

1942

FS decided to leave the Dorsey Band to pursue a solo career. He recorded only 15 songs that year with Tommy Dorsey, and he made four solo sides on the RCA subsidiary label Bluebird. His last recording session with the band took place on July 2, and his final live concert occurred in September. He made his first solo appearance at the Paramount Theatre in New York City as the "extra added attraction" to Benny Goodman's Band on December 30.

Film: Ship Ahoy.

Radio: Reflections; Songs by Sinatra.

Honor: Outstanding Male Vocalist, *Down Beat* magazine.

1943

Recordings:

FS signed on with Columbia Records, with whom he would remain until 1952.

However, during his first year with the label, a recording ban by the American Federation of Musicians prevented him from making records with orchestral backing until November 1944. As a result, he made only 12 a capella sides during this first year. To capitalize on the enormous popularity of their new artist, Columbia re-released the 1939 Harry James recording of "All or Nothing at All," which went all the way to #1 and remained on the *Billboard* charts for 21 weeks. Sinatra also made 12 recordings for the military's Overseas Victory-Disc Program.

Concerts: First solo nightclub appearances at the Riobamba Club (March 11) and the Waldorf-Astoria's Wedgwood Room (October 1); appearance in New York's Central Park for a World War II bond rally, singing "God Bless America" (May 16); appearance at Madison Square Garden in New York for Greek War Relief (May 18); FS performed with various philharmonic orchestras to help raise money and attendance at their concerts (June–August); first solo concert on the West Coast at The Hollywood Bowl (August 14).

Films: Higher and Higher; Reveille with Beverly.

Radio: Broadway Bandbox; Songs by Sinatra; Your Hit Parade.

Honor: Outstanding Male Vocalist, *Down Beat* magazine.

1944

Recordings: 17 songs for Columbia; 30 V-Discs for the U.S. Army and Navy.

Concerts: Toured the country with Bob Hope, Bing Crosby, and others, entertaining American uniformed personnel (January); benefit performance in Los Angeles for the Jewish Home for the Aged, where MGM chief Louis B. Mayer first heard him sing and decided to sign him to a long-term motion-picture contract; Columbus Day Riot at the Paramount in New York. Young fans on a school holiday crowded the streets outside the theater, and, when many found out that they would not be admitted to the show, they rampaged through Times Square, causing property damage, traffic jams, and widespread mayhem (October 12).

Films: The Road to Victory; Step Lively.

Radio: For the Record; The Vimms Vitamins Show; Your Hit Parade.

Honor: Most Popular Singer, *Metronome* magazine.

1945

Recordings: 40 songs for Columbia; 13 V-Discs.

Concerts: USO Tour of North Africa and Italy with comedian Phil Silvers (June); concerts and lectures to promote civil rights (November).

Films: All-Star Bond Rally; Anchors Aweigh; The House I Live In.

Radio: The Max Factor Frank Sinatra Show; Old Gold Presents Songs by Sinatra.

Honors: American Unity Award; Commendation, The National Conference of Christians and Jews; Most Popular Singer, *Metronome* magazine.

1946

Recordings: 56 songs for Columbia; 8 V-Discs.

Albums: Songs by Sinatra; The Voice of Frank Sinatra.

Film: Till the Clouds Roll By.

Radio: Old Gold Presents Songs by Sinatra.

Honors: Special Oscar for the film short *The House I Live In*; America's Favorite Male Singer, *Down Beat* magazine; Most Popular Screen Star, *Modern Screen* magazine.

1947

Recordings: 70 songs for Columbia; 1 V-Disc.

Album: Frankly Sentimental.

Concerts: "Command Performance" in Miami for military personnel (February 8); benefit performance for the Damon Runyon Cancer Fund (March 27); afternoon concert at Carnegie Hall in New York with Skitch Henderson conducting the orchestra (April 20); benefit concert in Galveston, Texas, for the victims of the Texas City petroleum explosion (April 28).

Film: It Happened in Brooklyn.

Radio: Old Gold Presents Songs by Sinatra; Your Hit Parade.

Honors: Thomas Jefferson Award for his work against ethnic intolerance; "Frank Sinatra Day" celebrated on October 30 in Hoboken, New Jersey; Outstanding Male Vocalist, *Down Beat* magazine.

1948

Recordings: 10 songs for Columbia.

Album: Christmas Songs by Sinatra.

Concert: "Music for the Wounded" benefit in Hollywood (August 5).

Films: The Kissing Bandit; The Miracle of the Bells.

Radio: Your Hit Parade.

1949

Recordings: 27 songs for Columbia.

Films: On the Town; Take Me Out to the Ball Game.

Radio: Light Up Time; Your Hit Parade.

Honor: Hollzer Memorial Award, Los Angeles Jewish Community.

1950

Recordings: 35 songs for Columbia.

Albums: Dedicated to You; Sing and Dance with Frank Sinatra.

Concerts: Benefit performance at the Biltmore Bowl for the Jewish Home for the

Aged (February 26); while appearing at the Copacabana in New York, he suffered a vocal hemorrhage and was unable to complete the performance run (April 26); first appearance at the London Palladium (June 10–23).

Radio: Light Up Time; Meet Frank Sinatra.

Television: TV debut on Bob Hope's *Star-Spangled Review; The Frank Sinatra Show.*

1951

Recordings: 14 songs for Columbia.

Concerts: First appearance at a Nevada casino—Reno's Riverside Inn and Casino (August 11); first appearance at a Las Vegas casino—The Desert Inn (September); Royal Command Performance at the London Coliseum for Prince Philip and Princess Elizabeth (December).

Film: Double Dynamite.

Radio: Meet Frank Sinatra.

Television: The Frank Sinatra Show.

1952

Recordings: 12 songs for Columbia.

Film: Meet Danny Wilson.

Television: The Frank Sinatra Show.

1953

Recordings: 26 songs for his new label, Capitol.

Concert: Appeared for the first time at his new Las Vegas "home," The Sands (October 19).

Film: From Here to Eternity.

Radio: Rocky Fortune; To Be Perfectly Frank.

1954

Recordings: 23 songs for Capitol.

Albums: I've Got a Crush on You (Columbia); *Songs for Young Lovers* (Capitol); *Swing Easy!* (Capitol).

Films: Suddenly; Young at Heart.

Radio: The Bobbi Show; Rocky Fortune; To Be Perfectly Frank.

Honors: Academy Award, Best Supporting Actor, *From Here to Eternity*; Top Male Singer, *Billboard* magazine; Most Popular Vocalist, *Down Beat* magazine; Singer of the Year, *Metronome* magazine.

1955

Recordings: 38 songs for Capitol.

Albums: Christmas with Sinatra (Columbia); *Frankie* (Columbia); *Get Happy!* (Columbia); *In the Wee Small Hours* (Capitol); *The Voice* (Columbia).

Concert: First Australian Concert Tour (January).

Films: Guys and Dolls; The Man with the Golden Arm; Not as a Stranger; The Tender Trap.

Radio: The Bobbi Show.

Television: Our Town (September 19).

1956

Recordings: 63 songs for Capitol.

Albums: High Society (Capitol); *Songs for Swingin' Lovers!* (Capitol); *That Old Feeling* (Columbia); *This Is Sinatra!* (Capitol); *Tommy Plays, Frankie Sings* (RCA Victor).

Concert: Reunion appearance at the Paramount Theatre in New York with Tommy and Jimmy Dorsey (August 15–21).

Films: Around the World in 80 Days; High Society; Johnny Concho; Meet Me in Las Vegas.

Honors: Academy Award Nomination, Best Actor, *The Man with the Golden Arm*; Special Award, British Cinematography Council, *The Man with the Golden Arm*; The Musician's Musician of the Year, *Metronome* magazine poll of jazz musicians; Top-10 Money-Making Star, *Motion Picture Herald* magazine.

1957

Recordings: 56 songs for Capitol.

Albums: Adventures of the Heart (Columbia); *Christmas Dreaming* (Columbia); *Close to You* (Capitol); *A Jolly Christmas from Frank Sinatra* (Capitol); *Pal Joey* (Capitol); *A Swingin' Affair!* (Capitol); *We Three: Frank Sinatra with Tommy Dorsey and Axel Stordahl* (RCA Victor); *Where Are You?* (Capitol).

Films: The Joker Is Wild; Pal Joey; The Pride and the Passion

Television: The Frank Sinatra Show.

Honors: Top Male Vocalist, *Playboy* magazine; Entertainer of the Year, *American Weekly* magazine; Mr. Personality, *Metronome* magazine.

1958

Recordings: 46 songs for Capitol.

Albums: Come Fly with Me (Capitol); *Frank Sinatra Sings for Only the Lonely* (Capitol); *The Frank Sinatra Story in Music* (Columbia); *Love Is a Kick* (Columbia); *Put Your Dreams Away* (Columbia); *This Is Sinatra, Vol. 2* (Capitol).

Concerts: Benefit performance for the Palm Springs Police Department (March 29);

benefit concert in Monaco for the United Nations Fund for Refugee Children (June 7); benefit performance for Cedars of Lebanon Hospital (July 2).

Films: Kings Go Forth; Some Came Running.

Television: The Frank Sinatra Timex Show (October 19).

Honors: Grammy Award for Best Album Cover, *Frank Sinatra Sings for Only the Lonely*; Grammy nominations for Record of the Year ("Witchcraft"), Album of the Year (*Come Fly with Me* and *Frank Sinatra Sings for Only the Lonely*), Song of the Year ("Witchcraft"), Best Male Vocal Performance ("Come Fly with Me" and "Witchcraft"), Best Arrangement ("Come Fly with Me" and "Witchcraft"), Best Engineered Record ("Come Fly with Me" and "Witchcraft"), and Best Album Cover (*Come Fly with Me*); Top Male Vocalist, *Playboy* magazine; Entertainer of the Year, B'nai B'rith.

1959

Recordings: 21 songs for Capitol.

Albums: The Broadway Kick (Columbia); *Come Back to Sorrento* (Columbia); *Come Dance with Me* (Capitol); *Look to Your Heart* (Capitol); *No One Cares* (Capitol).

Concerts: FS and Dean Martin appeared together for the first time at The Sands in Las Vegas (January 28). By the following year, Sinatra, Martin, and the other members of "The Clan" would be virtual fixtures at the hotel-casino; Australian and U.S. Concert Tour with Red Norvo and a small jazz combo (March and April).

Films: A Hole in the Head; Never So Few.

Television: The Frank Sinatra Timex Show (October 19); *An Afternoon with Frank Sinatra* (December 19).

Honors: Grammy Awards for Album of the Year, Best Male Vocal Performance, and Best Arrangement for *Come Dance with Me*; Grammy nominations for Record of the Year ("High Hopes") and Song of the Year ("High Hopes"); Top Male Vocalist, *Playboy* magazine.

1960

Recordings: 21 songs for Capitol; 17 songs for his newly formed record company, Reprise.

Albums: Can-Can (Capitol); *Nice 'n' Easy* (Capitol); *Reflections* (Columbia).

Concerts: First concert tour of Japan (May and June); FS and Judy Garland appeared in Chicago at a fundraiser for John Fitzgerald Kennedy's bid for the Presidency (July 10); Sinatra sang the National Anthem at the Democratic National Convention in Los Angeles (July 11). After JFK received the party's endorsement, Sinatra would do many fundraisers throughout the campaign that fall; FS appeared at the Urban League's Jazz Festival in Comiskey Park in Chicago (August 27).

Films: Can-Can; Ocean's Eleven; Pepe.

Television: The Frank Sinatra Timex Show (February 15 and May 12).

Honors: Grammy for Best Soundtrack Album for *Can-Can*; Grammy nominations for Record of the Year, Album of the Year, Song of the Year, Best Male Vocal Performance (Single and Album), Best Arrangement, and Best Performance by a Pop Single Artist, all for *Nice 'n' Easy*; Top Male Vocalist, *Playboy* magazine; Top Box Office Star of 1960, Film Exhibitors of America; Honorary Doctor of Humanities Degree, Wilberforce University.

1961

Recordings: 24 songs for Capitol; 46 songs for Reprise.

Albums: All the Way (Capitol); *Come Swing with Me!* (Capitol); *I Remember Tommy* (Reprise); *Ring-a-Ding Ding!* (Reprise); *Sinatra's Swingin' Session!!!* (Capitol); *Swing Along with Me* (Reprise).

Concerts: FS produced and starred in JFK's Inaugural Concert at the National Guard Armory with orchestra conducted by Leonard Bernstein (January 19); with Sammy Davis and Dean Martin, Sinatra appeared at a Carnegie Hall benefit for Martin Luther King's Southern Christan Leadership Conference (January 27); benefit concerts in Mexico City (April 19–21); benefit perform-ance at the County Sheriff's Rodeo at Memorial Coliseum in Los Angeles (June 24); benefit performance for Cedars of Lebanon Hospital (July 9); in his ap-pearance at The Sands in Las Vegas with Antonio Morelli conducting the or-chestra, Sinatra recorded his first live album for Reprise, though it was later decided not to release it (November 5); FS drew record-breaking crowds in his 4-day series of concerts at Sydney Stadium in Australia (November 29–Decem-ber 2).

Film: The Devil at 4 O'Clock.

Honors: Grammy nomination for Record of the Year ("The Second Time Around"); Top Male Vocalist, *Playboy* magazine.

1962

Recordings: 51 songs for Reprise.

Albums: All Alone (Reprise); *The Great Years* (Capitol); *Point of No Return* (Cap-itol); *Sinatra & Strings* (Reprise); *Sinatra and Swingin' Brass* (Reprise); *Sinatra Sings Great Songs from Great Britain* (Reprise); *Sinatra Sings . . . Of Love and Things* (Capitol).

Concerts: On April 18, Sinatra kicked off a 30-concert world tour to raise money for children's charities, including stops in Japan (April), Hong Kong (April), Israel (May), Greece (May), Italy (May), England (May and June), and France (June). The final concert of the tour occurred in Monaco on June 9; Sinatra headlined a show at his own Cal-Neva Lodge, which had been remodeled and expanded since he acquired it the previous year (June 29–July 5); along with Dean Martin and Sammy Davis, Sinatra played the Villa Venice, a club owned by Sam Giancana, in Northbrook, Illinois (November 29–December 2).

Films: The Manchurian Candidate; The Road to Hong Kong; Sergeants 3.

Honors: Medal of Honor, conferred in Athens, Greece; Italian Star of Solidarity Award, conferred in Rome, Italy; Gold Heart Award, Variety Club of Great Britain, conferred in London, England; Gold Medal of Paris, conferred in Paris, France; dedication of the Sinatra wing of the Summer Home of St. Jean De Dieu for Crippled Boys, Bruyeres le Chantel, France; Top Male Vocalist, *Playboy* magazine.

1963

Recordings: 41 songs for Reprise.

Albums: The Concert Sinatra (Reprise); *Reprise Musical Repertory Theatre* (Reprise); *Sinatra-Basie: An Historic Musical First* (Reprise); *Sinatra's Sinatra* (Reprise).

Concerts: Benefit concert for the blind at Carnegie Hall (May 19); another attempted live album from the Sands with orchestra conducted by Antonio Morelli (September 6–8). One excerpt from this date, "The Summit" with Sammy Davis and Dean Martin, was released on the Reprise album *Sinatra: A Man and His Music* in 1965; benefit performance at Carnegie Hall for Martin Luther King's Southern Christian Leadership Conference (September 12); benefit concert at the United Nations with Skitch Henderson conducting (September); benefit concert with Jerry Lewis in Rockford, Illinois, for the family of a fireman killed in the line of duty (September); concert with Lena Horne at Carnegie Hall (October 5–6).

Films: Come Blow Your Horn; 4 for Texas; The List of Adrian Messenger.

Honor: Top Male Vocalist, *Playboy* magazine.

1964

Recordings: 45 songs for Reprise.

Albums: America, I Hear You Singing (Reprise); *Frank Sinatra Sings "Days of Wine and Roses," "Moon River," and Other Academy Award Winners* (Reprise); *Frank Sinatra Sings Rodgers and Hart* (Capitol); *Frank Sinatra Sings the Select Johnny Mercer* (Capitol); *Robin and the 7 Hoods* (Reprise); *Sinatra-Basie: It Might as Well Be Swing* (Reprise); *Softly, As I Leave You* (Reprise); *12 Songs of Christmas* (Reprise).

Concerts: Benefit for the NAACP at the Cow Palace in San Francisco (July 31); first appearance by Sinatra and Count Basie at The Sands in Las Vegas, with Quincy Jones conducting the band (November 27–December 10).

Film: Robin and the 7 Hoods.

Honors: Grammy nomination for Best Original Score, *Robin and the 7 Hoods*; dedication of the Frank Sinatra International Youth Center for Arab and Jewish Children in Nazareth, Israel; Top Male Vocalist, *Playboy* magazine.

1965

Recordings: 35 songs for Reprise.

Albums: Sinatra: A Man and His Music (Reprise); *My Kind of Broadway* (Reprise);

September of My Years (Reprise); *Sinatra '65* (Reprise); *Tell Her You Love Her* (Capitol).

Concerts: Closed-circuit television performance with Dean Martin and Sammy Davis to benefit Dismas House in St. Louis; FS appeared at Newport Jazz Festival with Count Basie (July 4). Following this appearance, he made a brief U.S. concert tour with stops in New York, Chicago, and Detroit (July 8–18).

Films: Marriage on the Rocks; None But the Brave; Von Ryan's Express.

Television: Sinatra: An American Original (November 16); *Sinatra: A Man and His Music* (November 24).

Honors: Grammy Awards for Best Album of the Year (*September of My Years*) and Best Male Vocal Performance ("It Was a Very Good Year"); Special Grammy—the Lifetime Achievement Award (Bing Crosby Award); Emmy Award for Outstanding Television Musical Program, *Sinatra: A Man and His Music*; Peabody Award for Distinguished Achievement for Video Programming, *Sinatra: A Man and His Music*; Commandeur de la Santé Publique, presented by French President Charles de Gaulle; Entertainer of the Year, Conference of Personal Managers, Los Angeles; 150th celebrity to join the walk of the "Immortals" at Grauman's Chinese Theatre in Los Angeles; Top Male Vocalist, *Playboy* magazine; Outstanding Male Vocalist, *Down Beat* magazine.

1966

Recordings: 19 songs for Reprise.

Albums: Forever Frank (Capitol); *Frank Sinatra at the Movies* (Capitol); *Frank Sinatra's Greatest Hits: The Early Years* (Columbia); *Frank Sinatra Sings the Select Cole Porter* (Capitol); *Frank Sinatra Sings the Select Harold Arlen* (Capitol); *Moonlight Sinatra* (Reprise); *Sinatra at the Sands* (Reprise); *Strangers in the Night* (Reprise); *That's Life* (Reprise).

Concerts: Sinatra and Count Basie appeared at The Sands in Las Vegas, and the live album that was twice attempted there was finally made—a wonderful 2-LP Reprise set titled *Sinatra at the Sands*. Quincy Jones conducted the orchestra and wrote the arrangements, along with Billy Byers, and the album is an edited compilation from 10 performances given between January 26 and February 1; FS appeared at a number of fundraisers for California Governor Edmund Brown's reelection campaign (August–October); benefit performance in Las Vegas for Danny Thomas's St. Jude's Children's Research Center (November 20).

Films: Assault on a Queen; Cast a Giant Shadow; The Oscar.

Television: Sinatra: A Man and His Music, Part II (December 7).

Honors: Grammy Awards for Album of the Year (*Sinatra: A Man and His Music*), Best Liner Notes (*Sinatra at the Sands*), and, for his hit song "Strangers in the Night," Record of the Year, Best Male Vocal Performance, Best Arrangement, and Best Engineered Record; Emmy nomination for *Sinatra: A Man and His Music, Part II*; Top Male Vocalist, *Playboy* magazine; Outstanding Male Vocalist, *Down Beat* magazine.

1967

Recordings: 31 songs for Reprise.

Albums: The Essential Frank Sinatra (Columbia); *Francis Albert Sinatra & Antonio Carlos Jobim* (Reprise); *The World We Knew* (Reprise).

Concerts: Benefit performance on behalf of the library at the University of Southern California (February 12); benefit performance at a rally for Israel at the Hollywood Bowl (June 11); benefit performance at New York's Madison Square Garden for the Italian-American Anti-Defamation League (October 19).

Films: The Naked Runner; Tony Rome.

Television: Sinatra: A Man and His Music + Ella + Jobim (November 13); *Movin' with Nancy* (December 11).

Honors: Grammy nominations for Record of the Year ("Something Stupid") and, for the album *Francis Albert Sinatra & Antonio Carlos Jobim*, Album of the Year, Best Male Vocal Performance, and Best Liner Notes.

1968

Recordings: 19 songs for Reprise.

Albums: Cycles (Reprise); *Francis A. & Edward K.* (Reprise); *Frank Sinatra's Greatest Hits!* (Reprise); *The Sinatra Family Wish You a Merry Christmas* (Reprise).

Concerts: Beginning on May 22 and extending throughout that summer, Sinatra appeared at a number of fundraisers on behalf of Hubert Humphrey's bid for the presidency; Sinatra's first appearance at his new Las Vegas "home," Caesar's Palace (November 26–December 19).

Films: The Detective; Lady in Cement.

Television: Francis Albert Sinatra Does His Thing (November 25).

Honors: Top Male Vocalist, *Playboy* magazine; induction into the Playboy Hall of Fame.

1969

Recordings: 50 songs for Reprise.

Albums: Frank Sinatra in Hollywood, 1943–1949 (Columbia); *A Man Alone* (Reprise); *My Way* (Reprise).

Concert: Performance at an all-star tribute in Houston's Astrodome to honor the Apollo 11 astronauts—Neil Armstrong, Buzz Aldrin, and Michael Collins (August 16).

Television: Sinatra (November 6).

Honors: Grammy nomination for Best Male Contemporary Vocal Performance for "My Way"; Honorary Alumnus, UCLA; Top Male Vocalist, *Playboy* magazine.

1970

Recordings: 11 songs for Reprise.

Album: *Watertown* (Reprise).

Concerts: Performance at the White House in tribute to Senator Everett Dirksen (February 27); charity concerts with Count Basie at Royal Festival Hall in London (May 4–8); benefit performance at the Coliseum in Memphis for Danny Thomas's St. Jude's Children's Research Center (May 30); benefit performance at the Chicago Civic Opera House for Villa Scalabrini (August 15); benefit performance at the Hollywood Bowl for Nosostros, an Hispanic-American charitable organization (August 16); benefit performance with Jerry Lewis in Richmond, Indiana, on behalf of the family of Dan Mitrione, an American killed overseas (August 29); benefit performances in Los Angeles, San Francisco, and San Diego on behalf of Ronald Reagan's bid for the governorship of California (October); introduced by Princess Grace of Monaco, Sinatra performed at Royal Festival Hall in London (November 15–16). The second performance was taped and shown on BBC television and subsequently released as a videocassette.

Film: *Dirty Dingus Magee*.

1971

Album: *Sinatra & Company* (Reprise).

Concerts: Performance at the gala celebration of Ronald Reagan's election as Governor of California (January 4); performance at the Songwriters Guild Hall of Fame ceremony to honor Richard Rodgers. Sinatra also presented the award to the composer (March 8); retirement concert at the Los Angeles Music Center to benefit the Motion Picture and Television Relief Fund (June 13); although officially retired, he performed a dozen songs at a fundraiser at New York's Madison Square Garden to benefit the Italian-American Civil Rights League (November 20).

Honors: Award of the Century, The City of Paris, France; dedication of the Martin Anthony Sinatra Medical Education Center at Desert Hospital in Palm Springs; Special Oscar—Jean Hersholt Humanitarian Award; Distinguished Service Award, The City of Los Angeles; tribute read into the Congressional Record by Senator John Tunney.

1972

Albums: *The Dorsey/Sinatra Sessions* (RCA Victor); *Frank Sinatra: Greatest Hits, Volume 2* (Reprise); *Frank Sinatra: In the Beginning* (Columbia); *This Love of Mine* (RCA Victor).

Concert: Although officially retired, he did a brief performance at a Young Voters for Nixon rally in Chicago (October 20).

Honors: Medal of Valor, The State of Israel; Humanitarian Award, The Friars Club; Highest Achievement Award, The Screen Actors' Guild.

1973

Recordings: 15 songs for Reprise.

Album: Ol' Blue Eyes Is Back (Reprise).

Concert: At President Nixon's request, the "retired" Sinatra performed at the White House for Italian Prime Minister Giulio Andreotti (April 17). Shortly thereafter, he emerged from retirement.

Television: Ol' Blue Eyes Is Back (November 18).

Honors: Entertainer of the Century Award, The Songwriters of America; Man of the Year Award, The March of Dimes; Splendid American Award, The Thomas A. Dooley Foundation; Man of the Year, The All-American Collegiate Golf Association.

1974

Recordings: 14 songs for Reprise.

Albums: The Main Event (Reprise); *Some Nice Things I've Missed* (Reprise).

Concerts: First post-retirement concert appearance at Caesar's Palace (January 25–31); benefit performance to build a gymnasium at the University of California, Santa Clara (March 9); concert tour to benefit Variety Clubs International, with stops in New York, Providence, Detroit, Philadelphia, Chicago, and Washington, DC (April 8–27); benefit performance for the Las Vegas Sheriff's Department (June 19); tour of the Far East, with concerts in Tokyo, on the USS *Midway* off the coast of Japan, and in Australia (July 4–17); FS appeared in concert with daughter Nancy and son Frank Jr. at Harrah's in Lake Tahoe (September 4–18); benefit concert for Cedars-Sinai Medical Center at the Universal Amphitheater in Los Angeles (September 27); nine-city East Coast tour with Woody Herman and His Young Thundering Herd (October 2–29)—the high point of the tour was his appearance on October 13 at Madison Square Garden, billed as "The Main Event" and televised live around the world; fundraiser at Madison Square Garden to benefit Hugh Carey's bid for the governorship of New York.

Film: That's Entertainment.

Television: The Main Event.

Honor: Man of the Year, The City of Las Vegas.

1975

Recordings: 12 songs for Reprise.

Concerts: European concert tour—the first since 1962—with stops in Paris, Vienna, Munich, Frankfurt, London, Brussels, and Amsterdam (May 13–June 2); FS and John Denver performed to capacity crowds at Harrah's in Lake Tahoe (August 1–7); performance on Jerry Lewis's Telethon for Muscular Dystrophy (August 31); with Count Basie and Ella Fitzgerald, FS did a two-week run at the Uris Theater on Broadway in New York (September 8–20) (after this very successful engagement, the trio took their show to Philadelphia, Cleveland, and Chicago [September 22–24]); benefit performance for St. Jude's Children's Research Center honoring Danny Thomas (October 5); concert at the London Palladium with Count Basie and Sarah Vaughan (November 13–20); benefit concert tour of the Middle East, with stops in Iran and Israel (November 23–30).

Television: *A Conversation with Frank Sinatra and Bill Boggs* (November 30).

Honors: Cecil B. DeMille Award, The Hollywood Foreign Press; Lifetime Achievement Award, The American Film Institute; dedication of the Frank Sinatra Child Care Unit at St. Jude's Children's Research Center in Memphis; Gold Medallion of Citizenship, The City of Chicago.

1976

Recordings: 10 songs for Reprise.

Concerts: U.S. and Canadian Tour with Count Basie, including a stop at Nashville's Grand Ole Opry (May 1–15); performance at the Canadian National Expo in Vancouver (August 24); FS appeared from Caesar's Palace in Las Vegas on Jerry Lewis's Labor Day Telethon, bringing along a surprise guest—Lewis's former partner, Dean Martin (the two men had not seen or spoken to each other in more than 20 years); concert tour with stops in Lake Tahoe, Tarrytown (New York), Hartford, Binghamton, Pittsburgh, Providence, New Haven, Montreal, Syracuse, Norfolk, and Richmond (September 10–October 20).

Film: *That's Entertainment, Part II.*

Television: *John Denver and Friend* (March 26).

Honors: Top Box-Office Name of the Century, The Friars Club; Honorary Doctor of Humane Letters, University of Nevada at Las Vegas; Scopus Award, The American Friends of the Hebrew University of Israel; Jerusalem Medal, The City of Jerusalem, Israel.

1977

Recordings: 9 songs for Reprise.

Concerts: Benefit concerts in London for the National Society for the Prevention of Cruelty to Children (February 28–March 5); performance at the Concertgebouw in Amsterdam (March 7); benefit performance at the Gene Autry Hotel in Palm Springs for the Friends of the Eisenhower Medical Center (April 1); FS sang the National Anthem at the home opener at Dodgers Stadium (April 7). A week later, he threw out the first ball at San Francisco's Candlestick Park when the Giants played the Dodgers; benefit at New York's Carnegie Hall for the Institute of Sports Medicine and Athletic Trauma (April 27); benefit performance at the Aladdin Hotel for the University of Nevada, Las Vegas (August 25); performance on Jerry Lewis's Muscular Dystrophy Telethon (September 4); with John Denver, FS performed at the Beverly Hilton Hotel in a benefit honoring Jane Levintraub as the Mother of the Year (October 1). Earlier that year, in January, Sinatra lost his own mother in a plane crash; benefit performance in Washington, DC, for Hubert Humphrey (December 2).

Television: *Sinatra and Friends* (April 21); *Suzy Interviews Ol' Blue Eyes* (May 24); *Contract on Cherry Street* (November 19).

Honors: Freedom Medal, The City of Philadelphia; Cultural Award, The State of Israel.

1978

Recordings: 3 songs for Reprise.

Concerts: Benefit performance at the Century Plaza Hotel for the Los Angeles Sheriff's Office (January 23); benefit performance in New York honoring Hugh Carey (April 2); with Dean Martin and Sammy Davis, FS did a benefit performance at the Santa Monica Auditorium for SHARE, a group dedicated to helping emotionally challenged children (May 20); concert with Sarah Vaughan at the Universal Amphitheater in Los Angeles (July 31–August 10); appearance at the New York State Fair in Syracuse (August 27); benefit performance at New York's Waldorf-Astoria Hotel for the World Mercy Fund (October 13). The following week, he did a one-week engagement at Radio City Music Hall; performance at a tribute to former heavyweight champion Joe Louis (November 9).

Honor: Dedication of the Frank Sinatra International Student Center, Mount Scopus Campus of the Hebrew University, Jerusalem.

1979

Recordings: 35 songs for Reprise.

Concerts: Inaugural performance at Resorts International Hotel Casino in Atlantic City, New Jersey (April 12–21); benefit performance at the Aladdin Hotel for the University of Nevada, Las Vegas (May 30); benefit in Denver for the Juvenile Diabetes Foundation (June 9); benefit performances at the Pyramids in Cairo, Egypt, for the Faith and Hope Rehabilitation Center (September 24–27); benefit performance at the Waldorf-Astoria in New York for the World Mercy Fund (October 12); with Robert Merrill and Beverly Sills, FS performed at the Metropolitan Opera House in New York to benefit the Memorial Sloan-Kettering Cancer Center, New York (October 28); with Dean Martin, benefit performance on behalf of Ronald Reagan's bid for the presidency (November 2); celebration of his fortieth year in show business, Caesar's Palace, Las Vegas (December 12).

Honors: Pied Piper Award, The American Society of Composers, Authors, and Publishers; Trustees Award, The National Academy of Recording Arts and Sciences; Primum Vivere Award, The World Mercy Fund; International Man of the Year Award, presented by President Gerald Ford; Grand Ufficiale Dell'Ordine al Merito Della Repubblica Italiana—the highest civilian award conferred by the Italian government; Grand Marshal of the Columbus Day Parade, New York City; Humanitarian Award, The Columbus Citizens' Committee, New York City; dedication of the Frank Sinatra Wing of the Atlantic City Medical Center, New Jersey.

1980

Album: Trilogy (Reprise).

Concerts: Four shows at the Rio Palace in Brazil (January 22–25); concert at Mar-
acana Stadium in Rio de Janeiro, Brazil (January 26). With over 175,000 people in attendance, it was the largest live paid audience for a concert for a solo
performer until Paul McCartney broke the record in the same stadium in 1990;
benefit performance for the University of California, Santa Clara, which established an endowed chair in his honor—The Frank Sinatra Chair in Music and
Theater Arts (February 2); with Dean Martin, performed at the Shrine Auditorium in Los Angeles to benefit Ronald Reagan's campaign for the presidency
(February 3); benefit performance at the Canyon Country Club and Hotel in
Palm Springs for the Desert Hospital (February 15); two-week engagement at
New York's Carnegie Hall (June 13–26). Tickets for the series sold out in one
day, breaking all of the theater's previous sales records; benefit performance
in Los Angeles for St. Jude's Children's Research Center (July 11); benefit performance in Monaco for the Red Cross (August 8); from the stage at Resorts
International in Atlantic City, FS appeared on Jerry Lewis's Labor Day Telethon (August 31); concert in London at Royal Festival and Royal Albert Halls
(September 8–20); with Dean Martin, FS appeared at New York's Waldorf-
Astoria Hotel in support of Ronald Reagan and George Bush (September 30);
campaign appearance for Ronald Reagan in Syracuse, New York (October 22);
benefit performance at the Aladdin Hotel for the University of Nevada, Las
Vegas (November 11); benefit in Las Vegas for St. Jude's Ranch (November 14).

Film: The First Deadly Sin.

Television: Sinatra: The First 40 Years (January 3); *Sinatra in Brazil* (January 12–
26).

Honors: Grammy nominations for Album of the Year (*Trilogy*) and, for his hit
song "New York, New York," Record of the Year, Song of the Year, Best
Male Pop Vocal Performance, and Best Arrangement; Special Trustees Award,
The National Association of Recording Arts and Sciences; Grand Marshal, The
Tournament of Roses Parade, Pasadena; Metromedia Certificate of Achieve-
ment, The Los Angeles Bicentennial; First Member, The Simon Wiesenthal
Center Fellows Society; Entertainer of the Year, *Atlantic City* magazine; Johnny
Mercer Award, The Songwriters Hall of Fame; Humanitarian Award, Variety
Clubs International; National Campaign Chairman, The National Multiple
Sclerosis Society (1980–83); award for work with St. Jude's Children's Re-
search Hospital, Memphis; The Frank Sinatra Chair in Music and Theater Arts
established at the University of California, Santa Clara.

1981

Recordings: 12 songs for Reprise.

Album: She Shot Me Down (Reprise).

Concerts: Benefit at New York's Radio City Music Hall for Memorial Sloan-
Kettering Cancer Center (January 10); FS produced, directed, and headlined at

President Reagan's Inaugural Gala at the Capitol Center in Landover, Maryland (January 19); with Sammy Davis, FS performed in a benefit concert at the Atlanta Civic Center to help finance the investigation into the serial murders of children in that city (March 10); performance at the Congressional Club in Washington, DC, at a luncheon honoring Nancy Reagan (May 7); benefit performance at the Aladdin Hotel for the University of Nevada, Las Vegas (June 10); controversial concerts at Sun City in Bophuthatswana (July 24–August 2). Anti-apartheid groups opposed his appearance in the South African venue; concerts in South America, including Luna Park Stadium in Buenos Aires, Argentina, and the Maksaud Plaza Hotel in Sao Paulo, Brazil (August); a two-week concert appearance with pianist George Shearing at New York's Carnegie Hall (September 8–20); benefit performance at the Carousel Ball in Denver for the Juvenile Diabetes Association (October 18); benefit performance for Los Angeles County Sheriff Sherman Block's re-election campaign (October 25); benefit performance at the Beverly Hilton Hotel in Los Angeles for St. John's Hospital; with Johnny Carson, benefit performance in Los Angeles for Jack Benny's Diabetes Foundation (October 31).

Television: All-Star Inaugural Gala (January 19); *Sinatra: The Man and His Music* (November 22)

Honors: Order of the Leopard, The Republic of Bophuthatswana; Entertainer of the Year, *Atlantic City* magazine; Tribute to Men and Women of Achievement, Metromedia; Sinatra/UCLA Music Scholarship established; appointed to the President's Council on the Arts and Humanities.

1982

Recordings: 2 songs for Reprise.

Concerts: Benefit performance at the Sheraton Plaza in Palm Springs for Temple Isaiah (January 10); benefit performance in Washington, DC, honoring Simon Weisenthal (January 17); with Luciano Pavarotti and George Shearing, benefit performance at Radio City Music Hall in New York for the Memorial Sloan-Kettering Cancer Center (January 24); with Bob Newhart, benefit performance for the Myasthenia Gravis Foundation, in honor of Ed McMahon (February 20); two-week engagement with Nancy Sinatra at Caesar's Palace in Las Vegas (March 4–17); with Perry Como, FS did a performance at the White House at a state dinner for visiting Italian President Sandro Pertini (March 25); with Bob Hope, Sinatra performed in Philadelphia in a tribute to Pricess Grace of Monaco (March 31); benefit performance at the Aladdin Hotel in Las Vegas for the Musicians' Emergency Benevolent Fund (April 28); benefit performance at the Aladdin Hotel for the University of Nevada, Las Vegas (June 3); benefit performance at the inauguration of the newly enclosed Universal Amphitheater in Los Angeles (July 30) (he then played the same venue with Nancy Sinatra and comedian Charlie Callas through August 7); performance at Chicago Fest (August 10); with Buddy Rich, concert performance in the Dominican Republic (August 20) (the concert was taped and subsequently shown on television under the title *Sinatra: The Concert for the Americas*); with Rich Little, FS did a benefit performance for a hospital in Ottawa, Canada (September 11); with

Buddy Rich and Charlie Callas, FS did a benefit performance at Carnegie Hall for the World Mercy Fund (September 13); following the benefit, he remained at Carnegie Hall for a concert engagement that extended through September 23; benefit performance at the Irvine Meadows Amphitheater in California for the developmentally disabled (September 25); benefit performance in Washington, DC, for Nancy Reagan's Grandparents Program (October 19); benefit performance at the Beverly Hilton Hotel for the American Cancer Fund's Tri-State Branch (December 2); first performance at The Golden Nugget in Atlantic City (December 8–10). By early the following year, he also became a paid commercial spokesman for the casino-hotel.

Honors: Special Recognition Award, The National Multiple Sclerosis Society; inductee, The Broadcasters' Hall of Fame; "I'll Never Smile Again" inducted into the Grammy Hall of Fame.

1983

Recordings: 6 songs for Reprise.

Concerts: With Victor Borge, benefit performance at Radio City Music Hall in New York for the Memorial Sloan-Kettering Cancer Center (January 23); with Dean Martin, Sammy Davis, George Kirby, and Nancy Sinatra, benefit performance at the Canyon Country Club and Hotel for the Desert Hospital (February 12); FS performed for Queen Elizabeth of England at Twentieth Century Fox Studios in Los Angeles (February 27). Fellow performers included Perry Como, Dionne Warwick, and George Burns; performance at Arizona State University in Tempe (April 8); with Dionne Warwick and Marvin Hamlisch, benefit performance in Boston for Red Sox outfielder Tony Conigliaro (April 15); performance at The Kennedy Center in Washington, DC (April 18–21); with Red Buttons, benefit performance at the Waldorf-Astoria Hotel in New York for the Hospital for Special Surgery (May 20); with Perry Como, benefit performance in Durham, North Carolina, for Duke University's Children's Classic (May 22); with Sammy Davis, benefit performance in Monte Carlo for the Red Cross (August 5); with Count Basie and Sarah Vaughan, benefit performance at the Beverly Wilshire Hotel for the City of Hope BRAVO Chapter (December 12); performances at the San Diego Sports Arena (December 14) and Long Beach Convention Center (December 15); with Sammy Davis, Dean Martin, and Diana Ross, benefit performance for the University of Nevada, Las Vegas (December 16); with Alan King, benefit performance for Temple Isaiah (December 18).

Honors: Kennedy Center Honors Award for Lifetime Achievement; the Spirit of Life Award, The City of Hope BRAVO Chapter; dedication of the Sinatra Family Children's Unit for the Chronically Ill, Seattle Children's Orthopedic Hospital.

1984

Recordings: 14 songs for QWest.

Album: *L.A. Is My Lady* (QWest).

Concerts: Sinatra performed in a number of large venues between January and July. Included among his stops were the Reunion Center in Dallas (January 12), the Sun Dome Theater in Tampa (January 21), Riverfront Coliseum in Cincinnati (March 15), Veterans Memorial Coliseum in New Haven (March 20), the Premier Entertainment Center in Detroit (March 23–24), the Civic Center in Pittsburgh (April 11), the Spectrum in Philadelphia (April 14), the Devany Sports Arena in Nebraska (April 19), the Golden Nugget in Atlantic City (May 1–5), the Arie Crown Theater in Chicago (May 8–12), the Mecca Arena in Milwaukee (May 14), the Pacific Amphitheater in Costa Mesa, CA (July 17), and the Garden State Arts Center in New Jersey (July 25); with Buddy Rich, benefit performance at the Hyatt Regency Hotel in Houston for the Wortham Theater Center for the Arts and Humanities (January 11); with Dean Martin and Sammy Davis, benefit performance at the Century Plaza Hotel in Los Angeles for St. John's Hospital (February 16); with Luciano Pavarotti, Monserrat Caballe, Diana Ross, and Buddy Rich, benefit performance at New York's Radio City Music Hall for the Memorial Sloan-Kettering Cancer Center (March 18); with Dean Martin, Sammy Davis, and Lionel Richie, benefit performance at UCLA for SHARE Boomtown (April 28); AT&T-sponsored Sinatra concerts at Constitution Hall in Washington, DC (May 15), the Fox Theater in Atlanta (June 1), and Davies Symphony Hall in San Francisco (July 15); with President Reagan in attendance, FS performed at a fundraiser in New Jersey for the Republican Party (July 26); with Elton John, benefit performance in Monte Carlo for the Red Cross (August 10); with Buddy Rich, FS performed at the Canadian National Exhibition in Toronto (September 2); six shows at Royal Albert Hall in London (September 17–22); performance at the Moulin Rouge in Paris (September 25); concert at the Stadthalle in Vienna, sponsored by the U.S. Embassy to benefit children's charities in Austria. Sinatra not only waived his own fee, but paid the expenses for Buddy Rich and his band to perform with him (October 1–2); fundraiser for Ronald Reagan's reelection campaign in Chicago, Cincinnati, Hartford, Westchester (NY), New York City, Washington, DC, Sacramento, and San Diego (October 16–20 and November 5); performance at the Hollywood Park Horse Breeders Cup Gala, held at Twentieth Century Fox Studios (November 8); performance at the Universal Amphitheater in Los Angeles (November 14–18).

Film: Cannonball Run II.

Honors: In the Wee Small Hours album inducted into the Grammy Hall of Fame; Honorary Doctor of Fine Arts, Loyola Marymount College, Los Angeles; Distinguished American Award, The Boy Scouts of America; Medal of Honor for Science and Art First Class—Austria's highest civilian honor.

1985

Concerts: Performance at Vice President Bush's Inaugural (January 18); FS produced and headlined at President Reagan's Second Inaugural Gala (January 19); benefit performance at the Miracle Ball in Miami Beach for St. Jude's Children's Research Center (February 12); with Pete Barbuti, FS appeared at the Summit Arena in Houston (March 27) and the Kemper Arena in Kansas City (March 28); performances at the Budokan (April 17–19) and the Imperial

Hotel in Tokyo (April 22); performance at the Coliseum in Hong Kong (April 25); nine performances at New York's Carnegie Hall (September 5–14); benefit performance at the Universal Premier Hotel in Los Angeles for the Entertainment Industry Council Against Drug Abuse (September 26); benefit performance in Palm Springs for the Barbara Sinatra Children's Center (November 30).

Honors: Honorary Doctor of Engineering, The Stevens Institute of Technology, Hoboken, New Jersey; The Medal of Freedom, Washington, DC; Entertainer of the Year Award, The Italo-American Coalition; Special Recognition, The Players Club; Lifetime Achievement Award, Washington, DC; "Thank You, Frank, Gala," Temple Isaiah.

1986

Recordings: 3 songs for Reprise.

Albums: Sinatra Rarities—The Columbia Years (Columbia); *The Voice: The Columbia Years, 1943–1952* (Columbia).

Concerts: Performance at the Providence Civic Center to celebrate Rhode Island's 300th Anniversary (May 16); benefit performance at the Universal Amphitheater in Los Angeles for the victims of an earthquake in Mexico (August 12); benefit performance at the Anatole Hotel in Dallas for the Princess Grace Foundation's Third Annual Arts Awards Gala (October 18); benefit performance at Caesar's Palace in Las Vegas for St. Jude's Children's Research Center (November 21); performance at Carnegie Hall's 100th Anniversary Show (December 15).

Honor: Coachella Valley Humanitarian Award.

1987

Album: Hello, Young Lovers (Columbia).

Concerts: Performance at the Marriott Desert Springs Hotel for the Dinah Shore/ Nabisco Golf Tournament (April 1); benefit performance at the Las Vegas Convention Center for the United Way's 75th Anniversary (October 18); benefit performance at the Universal Sheraton for the Juvenile Diabetes Foundation (November 29); performance at the Century Plaza Hotel in Los Angeles to honor industrialist Armand Hammer (December 2); performance at the Kennedy Center in Washington, DC, to honor Perry Como (December 6).

Honor: Lifetime Achievement Award, The NAACP, Los Angeles Chapter.

1988

Recordings: 3 songs for Reprise.

Concerts: The Ultimate Event World Tour with Sammy Davis, Jr., and Dean Martin (later replaced by Liza Minnelli) began at the Oakland Coliseum (March 13). The tour took the trio from coast to coast and abroad; performance at New York's Carnegie Hall in a tribute to Irving Berlin (May 11); with Liza Minnelli, performance at the Waldorf-Astoria Hotel in New York at a Friars Club tribute to Barbara Sinatra (May 14); performance with Sammy Davis and Liza Minnelli at the Shrine Auditorium in Los Angeles at the "Legends of Our Time" convention, which was sponsored by Anheuser-Busch (November 3).

Film: Animated Singing Sword in *Who Framed Roger Rabbit?*

1989

Album: *Frank Sinatra: Gold!* (Capitol).

Honors: Will Rogers Award, The City of Beverly Hills; Great Plate of the Bimillenary of Paris; Frank and Barbara Sinatra named Revlon's first "Unforgettable Couple."

1990

Albums: *Frank Sinatra: The Capitol Collector's Series* (Capitol); *Frank Sinatra: The Capitol Years* (Capitol); *Frank Sinatra: The Reprise Collection* (Reprise).

Concerts: Inaugural concert at the new Knickerbocker Arena in Albany, New York (January 30); performances at Radio City Music Hall in New York (May 13–16). Sinatra cancelled the last four shows of this engagement following the death of his close friend Sammy Davis, Jr.; performances in London, Glasgow, and Stockholm (June); a national concert tour with comedian Don Rickles kicked off at the Cal Expo Amphitheater in Sacramento (August); the Diamond Jubilee World Tour to commemorate his 75th birthday began at the Meadowlands Arena in New Jersey (December 3). Sinatra's opening act was Steve Lawrence and Eydie Gorme.

Film: *Listen Up: The Lives of Quincy Jones.*

Television: *Sinatra 75: The Best Is Yet to Come* (December 17).

Honor: Ella Fitzgerald Lifetime Achievement Award, The Society of Singers.

1991

Recordings: FS recorded "Silent Night" for a special collection to benefit abused children.

Albums: *Sinatra Reprise: The Very Good Years* (Reprise); *Sinatra Sings the Songs of Van Heusen and Cahn* (Reprise).

Concerts: Among its many stops, the Diamond Jubilee World Tour had FS performing among the ruins in Pompeii, Italy (September 26).

Television: *Sinatra: The Voice of Our Time* (March).

1992

Albums: *Sinatra: Music from the Television Miniseries* (Reprise); *Tommy Dorsey and Frank Sinatra: Stardust* (Bluebird/RCA).

Concerts: With Liza Minnelli and Shirley MacLaine, FS performed at the Waldorf-Astoria Hotel to benefit Andrew Stein's bid to become Mayor of New York (January 21); European concert tour (June).

Television: Sinatra: The Music Was Just the Beginning (November 8 and 10).

Honor: Distinguished Lifetime Achievement Award, American Cinema Awards.

1993

Recordings: 30 songs for Capitol.

Albums: Duets (Capitol); *Frank Sinatra: The Columbia Years, 1943–1952—The Complete Recordings* (Columbia).

Concerts: Concert tour of England, Germany, and Sweden (June); performance at the Hollywood Center, a floating casino in Aurora, Illinois (August 19–21); inaugural concert at Foxwoods Resort Hotel and Casino in Ledyard, Connecticut (November 17–21).

Honors: Career Achievement Award, Palm Springs International Film Festival; Capitol Records' first Tower of Achievement Award.

1994

Albums: Duets II (Capitol); *The Essence of Frank Sinatra* (Columbia); *Frank Sinatra: 16 Most Requested Songs* (Columbia); *Frank Sinatra: The V-Discs* (Columbia); *Sinatra and Sextet: Live in Paris* (Reprise); *The Sinatra Christmas Album* (Reprise); *Tommy Dorsey–Frank Sinatra: "The Song Is You"* (RCA Victor).

Concerts: During a concert stop in Richmond, Virginia, Sinatra collapsed on stage (March 6); performance at the Meadowlands Arena in New Jersey (August 2); performance at the Kiel Center in St. Louis (October 21); performance at the United Center in Chicago (October 22); performance at the Fukuoka Dome in Japan—his final concert appearance (December 19–20).

Television: Sinatra Duets (November 25).

Honors: Grammy Legend Award for Lifetime Achievement; first recipient of the Francis Albert Sinatra Tribute, The Arts Center Foundation of New Jersey.

1995

Albums: Frank Sinatra: The Best of the Capitol Years (Capitol); *Frank Sinatra: The Complete Reprise Studio Recordings* (Reprise); *Harry James and His Orchestra, Featuring Frank Sinatra* (Columbia); *I've Got a Crush on You* (Columbia); *Sinatra and Dorsey: Greatest Hits* (RCA Victor); *Sinatra 80th: All the Best* (Capitol); *Sinatra 80th: Live in Concert* (Capitol).

Concert: Performance with Willie Nelson in Palm Springs at the Frank Sinatra Desert Classic golf tournament—his final public performance (February 25).

Television: Cameo in TV movie *Young at Heart* (March 12); *Sinatra: 80 Years My Way* (December 14).

1996

Albums: Everything Happens to Me (Reprise); *Frank Sinatra: The Complete Capitol Singles Collection* (Capitol); *Frank Sinatra Sings Rodgers and Hammerstein* (Columbia); *Swing and Dance with Frank Sinatra* (Columbia).

Television: Entire episode of ABC's *Turning Point* devoted to celebration of his 81st birthday (December 12).

Honor: Grammy for Best Traditional Pop Vocal, *Duets II.*

1997

Albums: *Frank Sinatra and the Red Norvo Quintet: Live in Australia, 1959* (Blue Note); *Frank Sinatra and the Tommy Dorsey Orchestra: Love Songs* (RCA Victor); *Portrait of Sinatra* (Columbia); *Sinatra Sings His Greatest Hits* (Columbia); *The Very Best of Frank Sinatra* (Reprise).

Radio: "Sinatra" on PBS series *This American Life* (April).

Honor: Selected to receive the Congressional Gold Medal. The Senate sponsor of the legislation was Senator Alfonse D'Amato and the House sponsor, Congressman Jose Serrano, both of New York.

1998

Honor: Award of Merit, American Music Awards (January 26).

Selected Bibliography

Frank Sinatra is, simply put, the most "documented" entertainer of the century. As such, it is not feasible to assemble anything like an exhaustive bibliography on his life and work. The following list represents some of the more accessible and revealing pieces published over the past six decades.

BOOKS

Ackelson, Richard W. *Frank Sinatra: A Complete Recording History of Techniques, Songs, Composers, Lyricists, Arrangers, Sessions and First-Issue Albums, 1939–1984*. Jefferson, NC: McFarland, 1992.

Adler, Bill. *Sinatra, the Man and the Myth: An Unauthorized Biography*. New York: New American Library, 1987.

Barnes, Ken. *Sinatra and the Great Song Stylists*. London: Ian Allan, 1972.

Britt, Stan. *Sinatra: A Celebration*. New York: Schirmer, 1995.

———. *Sinatra the Singer*. London: Macmillan, 1989.

Clarke, Donald. *All or Nothing at All: A Life of Frank Sinatra*. London: Macmillan, 1997.

Coleman, Ray. *Sinatra: Portrait of the Artist*. Atlanta: Turner Publications, 1995.

Deacon, John. *The Frank Sinatra Discography*. Crawley, England: Crawley Duplicating, 1961.

Dellar, Fred. *Sinatra: His Life and Times*. London: Omnibus, 1995.

DeStefano, Gildo. *Frank Sinatra*. Venezia: Marsilio, 1991.

Doctor, Gary L. *The Sinatra Scrapbook*. Secaucus, NJ: Carol Publishing Group, 1991.

Douglas-Home, Robin. *Sinatra*. New York: Grosset and Dunlap, 1962.

Dureau, Christian, and L. Christophe. *Frank Sinatra*. Paris: Editions PAC, 1984.

Frank, Alan. *Sinatra*. New York: Hamlyn, 1978.

The Frank Sinatra Songbook. Secaucus, NJ: Warner Brothers Publications, 1989.

Freedland, Michael. *All the Way: A Biography of Frank Sinatra*. New York: St. Martin's Press, 1998.

Friedwald, Will. *Sinatra! The Song Is You: A Singer's Art*. New York: Scribner's, 1995.

Garrod, Charles. *Frank Sinatra*. Zephyrillis, FL: Joyce Record Club Publications, 1989–90.

Gehman, Richard. *Sinatra and His Rat Pack*. New York: Belmont, 1961.

Goddard, Peter. *Frank Sinatra: The Man, the Myth and the Music*. Don Mills, Canada: Greywood, 1973.

Goldstein, Norm. *Frank Sinatra: Ol' Blue Eyes*. New York: Holt, Rinehart and Winston, 1982.

Hainsworth, Brian. *Songs by Sinatra, 1939–1970*. Branhope, England: B. Hainsworth, 1973.

Harvey, Jacques. *Monsieur Sinatra*. Paris: A. Michel, 1976.

Hawes, Esme. *The Life and Times of Frank Sinatra*. Philadelphia: Chelsea House, 1997.

Hodge, Jessica. *Frank Sinatra*. North Dighton, MA: JG Press, 1994.

Holder, Deborah. *Completely Frank: The Life of Frank Sinatra*. London: Bloomsbury, 1995.

Howlett, John. *Frank Sinatra*. New York: Simon and Schuster/Wallaby, 1979.

Irwin, Lew. *Sinatra: A Pictorial Biography*. Philadelphia: Courage, 1995.

Jewell, Derek. *Frank Sinatra: A Celebration*. Boston: Little, Brown, 1985.

Kahn, E. J. *The Voice: The Story of an American Phenomenon*. New York: Harper and Brothers, 1947.

Kelley, Kitty. *His Way: The Unauthorized Biography of Frank Sinatra*. New York: Bantam, 1986.

Kops, Bernard. *Playing Sinatra: A Play*. London: Samuel French, 1992.

Lahr, John. *Sinatra: The Artist and the Man*. New York: Random House, 1997.

Lake, Harriet. *On Stage: Frank Sinatra*. Mankato, MN: Creative Education, 1976.

Levy, Shawn. *Rat Pack Confidential: Frank, Dean, Sammy, Peter, Joey, and the Last Great Showbiz Party*. New York: Doubleday, 1998.

Lonstein, Albert I. *Sinatra: An Exhaustive Treatise*. New York: Musicprint Corp., 1983.

Lonstein, Albert I., and Vito R. Marino. *The Revised Compleat Sinatra*. New York: Musicprint Corp., 1970, 1979, 1981.

Marino, Vito R., and Anthony C. Furfero. *The Official Price Guide to Frank Sinatra Records and CDs*. New York: House of Collectibles, 1993.

Martin, Peter. *Sinatra, The Early Years: An Exclusive Collection of Photographs*. Tiburon, CA: P. Martin/Dodsmith Publishing, 1980.

McKuen, Rod. *Frank Sinatra: A Man Alone*. Hollywood: Cheval Books, 1969.

Mustazza, Leonard. *Ol' Blue Eyes: A Frank Sinatra Encyclopedia*. Westport, CT: Greenwood Press, 1998.

O'Brien, Ed (with Robert Wilson). *Sinatra 101: The 101 Best Recordings and the Stories Behind Them.* New York: Boulevard, 1996.

O'Brien, Ed, and Scott P. Sayers, Jr. *The Sinatra Sessions, 1939–1980.* First Edition. Dallas: Sinatra Society of America, 1980.

The Original Frank Sinatra Scrap Book. NP: Golden State Music Co., 1984.

Peters, Richard. *The Frank Sinatra Scrapbook: His Life and Times in Words and Pictures.* New York: St. Martin's Press, 1982.

Petkov, Steven, and Leonard Mustazza. *The Frank Sinatra Reader.* New York: Oxford University Press, 1995.

Phasey, C. A. *Francis Albert Sinatra Tracked Down.* London: Buckland, 1995.

Pickard, Roy. *Frank Sinatra at the Movies.* London: Hale, 1994.

Ridgway, John. *The Sinatrafile, Part 2.* Second edition. Birmingham: John Ridgway, 1991.

Ringgold, Gene, and Clifford McCarthy. *The Films of Frank Sinatra.* Second edition. Secaucus, NJ: Citadel, 1989.

Rockwell, John. *Sinatra: An American Classic.* New York: Random House/Rolling Stone, 1984.

Romero, Jerry. *Sinatra's Women.* New York: Manor, 1976.

Ruggeri, Paolo. *Frank Sinatra.* Rome: Lato Side Editori, 1981.

Sayers, Scott P., and Ed O'Brien. *Sinatra—The Man and His Music: The Recording Artistry of Francis Albert Sinatra, 1939–1992.* Austin, TX: TSD Press, 1992.

Scaduto, Anthony. *Frank Sinatra.* London: Michael Joseph, 1976.

Sciacca, Tony. *Sinatra.* New York: Pinnacle, 1976.

Shaw, Arnold. *Sinatra: Retreat of the Romantic.* London: W. H. Allen, 1968.

———. *Sinatra: The Entertainer.* New York: Delilah, 1982.

———. *Sinatra: Twentieth Century Romantic.* New York: Holt, Rinehart and Winston, 1968.

Sinatra, Frank. *A Man and His Art.* New York: Random House, 1991.

———. "Tips on Popular Singing." New York: Embassy Music Corporation, 1941.

Sinatra, Nancy. *Frank Sinatra: An American Legend.* Santa Monica: General Publishing Group, 1995.

———. *Frank Sinatra: My Father.* Garden City, NY: Doubleday, 1985.

Taraborrelli, J. Randy. *Sinatra: Behind the Legend.* Secaucus, NJ: Carol Publishing Group, 1997.

Tarantino, Jimmie. *Sacred Sanctuary of Frank Sinatra.* Newark, NJ: Tribune, 1959.

Taylor, Paula. *Frank Sinatra.* Mankato, MN: Creative Education, 1976.

Turner, John Frayn. *Frank Sinatra: A Personal Portrait.* New York: Hippocrene, 1983.

Vare, Ethlie Ann. *Legend: Frank Sinatra and the American Dream.* New York: Boulevard, 1995.

Ventura, Michael. *The Death of Frank Sinatra: A Novel.* New York: Henry Holt, 1996.

Wilson, Earl. *Sinatra: An Unauthorized Biography.* New York: Macmillan, 1976.

Yarwood, Guy. *Sinatra in His Own Words.* New York: Delilah/Putnam, 1982.

Zehme, Bill. *The Way You Wear Your Hat: Frank Sinatra and the Lost Art of Livin'.* New York: HarperCollins, 1997.

BOOKS WITH SUBSTANTIAL MATERIAL ON SINATRA

Balliett, Whitney. "King Again." In *Goodbyes and Other Messages: A Journal of Jazz, 1981–1990*. New York: Oxford University Press, 1991. (This article appeared originally in *The New Yorker*, 4 October 1982.)

Bloom, Ken. *American Song: The Complete Musical Theatre Companion*. 2 vols. New York: Facts on File, 1985.

———. *Hollywood Song: The Complete Film and Musical Companion*. 3 vols. New York: Facts on File, 1995.

Brady, John. "A Collector's Case for the Voice." In *The Revised Compleat Sinatra 1981 Cumulative Supplement*. Ed. Albert I. Lonstein. New York: Musicprint Corp., 1981.

Davis, Francis. "A Man and His Mishegoss." In *Outcasts, Jazz Composers, Instrumentalists, and Singers*. New York: Oxford University Press, 1990.

Deutsch, Armand S. "Me and My One-Nighters with Sinatra." In *Me and Bogie*. New York: Putnam, 1991. (This article originally appeared in *McCall's* under the title "A Night Out with Sinatra," August 1983.)

"Frank Sinatra" [Interview, 1963]. Reprinted in *Playboy Interviews*. Chicago: Playboy Press, 1967.

Friedwald, Will. "Sinatra!" In *Jazz Singing: America's Great Voices from Bessie Smith to Bebop and Beyond*. New York: Collier, 1992.

Furia, Philip. *The Poets of Tin Pan Alley: A History of America's Great Lyricists*. New York: Oxford University Press, 1990.

Giddins, Gary. "Frank Sinatra: An Appreciation." In *Rhythm-a-Ning*. New York: Oxford University Press, 1987. (An earlier version of this piece appeared in *Stereo Review* under the title "The One and Only Frank Sinatra," February 1984.)

———. "The Once and Future Sinatra." In *Riding on a Blue Note*. New York: Oxford University Press, 1981.

Grove, Lee. "Last Night, When We Were Young: Swooning with Sinatra." In *The Revised Compleat Sinatra 1981 Cumulative Supplement*. New York: Musicprint Corp., 1981. (This article originally appeared in *Boston* magazine in 1974.)

Hajdu, David, and Roy Hemming. *Discovering Great Singers of Classic Pop*. New York: Newmarket Press, 1991.

Hamm, Charles. *Yesterdays: Popular Song in America*. New York: Norton, 1979.

Kennedy, William. "Frank Sinatra: Pluperfect Music." In *Riding the Yellow Trolley Car*. New York: Viking, 1993. (This article originally appeared in *The New York Times Magazine* under the title "Under My Skin," 7 October 1990.)

Lees, Gene. "The Sinatra Effect." In *Singers and the Song*. New York: Oxford University Press, 1987.

Pleasants, Henry. *The Great American Popular Singers*. New York: Simon and Schuster, 1974.

Rickard, Graham. "Frank Sinatra." In *Famous Names in Popular Music*. Hove, England: Wayland, 1980.

Salvatori, Dario. *Tu Vuo Fa L'Americano: La Vicenda Dei Grandi Italo-Americani da Frank Sinatra a Madonna*. Naples: Tullio Pironti, 1995.

Saporta, Sol. "Frank Sinatra: Artistry and Ideology." In *Society, Language, and the University: From Lenny Bruce to Noam Chomsky*. New York: Vantage Press, 1974.

Sheed, Wilfred. "The Voice." In *Essays in Disguise*. New York: Knopf, 1990.

Sinatra, Frank. "Foreword." In *The Big Bands*, by George T. Simon. Fourth edition. New York: Schirmer, 1981.

———. "Introduction." In *Las Vegas*, by Tom Campbell. Port Washington, NY: Skyline, 1984.

Talese, Gay. "Frank Sinatra Has a Cold." In *Fame and Obscurity*. New York: Dell, 1981. (This article originally appeared in *Esquire*, April 1966.)

Wilder, Alec. *American Popular Song: The Great Innovators, 1900–1950*. New York: Oxford University Press, 1972.

ARTICLES

"Action in Las Vegas." *Time*, 22 September 1967, 101.

Adler, J. "Frankie and Ronnie." *Newsweek*, 19 January 1981, 20–21.

Allen, Steve. "The Greatest Singer of Them All." *The Village Voice*, 20 June 1995, 6, 8, 15.

Alter, J. "Doonesbury Contra Sinatra." *Newsweek*, 24 June 1985, 82.

Altobell, Don. "Have You Heard Sinatra?" *Audio*, December 1970, 40–42.

Ames, Morgan. "He's Still—Well, Sinatra." *High Fidelity*, February 1975, 114.

Anderson, Jon. "Sinatra Fans Celebrate Birthday in Their Ways." *The Chicago Tribune*, 13 December 1995, Sec. 2C, p. 2.

Aquilante, Dan. "Sinatra Didn't Have to 'Duet.' " *The New York Post*, 2 November 1993, 30.

"Back on Top." *Time*, 10 May 1954, 72–74.

Baker, Glen A. "Sinatra Smooths Aussie Feathers in His $1-Mil Return Engagement." *Variety*, 13 January 1988, 2, 76.

Baker, Russell. "The Ears of the Age." *The New York Times*, 5 March 1994, A23.

Balliett, Whitney. "King Again." *The New Yorker*, 4 October 1982, 142–43.

Baumgold, Julie. "Frank and the Fox Pack." *Esquire*, March 1994, 89–96.

Bellafante, Ginia. "Frank & Co." *Time*, 12 December 1994, 92.

Bennett, Karen. "When You Heard This Star, He Made You Feel Like a Star." *The Philadelphia Inquirer*, 12 December 1995, A23.

Bennett, Tony. "Essentials: Frank Sinatra." *The Guardian*, 24 November 1995, Sec. 2, p. 10.

Benza, A. J. "Frank-ly Atrocious." The New York *Daily News*, 22 October 1995, 30.

———. "Somethin' Stupid in Mag." The New York *Daily News*, 29 October 1995, 32.

Benza, A. J., and Michael Lewittes. "Frankly Speaking." The New York *Daily News*, 21 November 1995, 18.

Bernhard, Sandra. "The Next Page: An Open Letter to Frank Sinatra." *Rolling Stone*, November 1990, 17.

Bernhart, Milt. "Practice Makes Posterity." *The Village Voice*, 20 June 1995, 14–15.

"Best Defense." *Newsweek*, 31 July 1972, 21–22.

Bliven, Bruce. "The Voice and the Kids." *The New Republic*, 6 November 1944, 592–93.

Block, Valerie. "MBNA Card Immortalizes Sinatra in Plastic." *American Banker*, 20 December 1995, 8.

Blumenthal, Bob. "For Sinatra, the Whole Is Greater Than the Parts." *The Boston Globe*, 2 September 1994, 85.

———. "Frank Sinatra: Wasting Away in Duetville." *The Boston Globe*, 13 November 1994, B7.

Bogdanovich, Peter. "Sinatra and Company." *Esquire*, February 1978, 120–23.

Bornfeld, Steve. "Sinatra Fans Boo." *The New York Post*, 3 March 1994, 65.

Borzillo, Carrie. "Frank, Tony Make Modern Rock Inroads." *Billboard*, 25 December 1993, 5, 115.

Bradley, Jeff. "Sinatra." *The Denver Post*, 10 December 1995, F1.

———. "Sinatra Sends Mixed Message on Uneven Twilight CD 'Duets.'" *The Denver Post*, 4 November 1993, E1.

Brennan, Don. "Singing and Swinging by the Sea." *The News Gleaner Magazine*, 17 October 1990, 3–4.

Brown, Paul B. "His Way." *Forbes*, 8 October 1984, 238.

Browne, David. "Frank 'n' Style." *Entertainment Weekly*, 18–25 February 1994, 36–44.

Bryson, John. "Sinatra at Fifty." *Look*, 14 December 1965, 61–74.

Bunch, William. "Start Spreadin' the Word." *The Philadelphia Daily News*, 10 January 1997, 4.

Caen, Herb. "Frankly Frank." *The San Francisco Chronicle*, 11 December 1995, A12.

———. "Hollywood on the Hill." *The San Francisco Chronicle*, 8 November 1992, PWN, p. 1.

Calloway, Earl. "Frank Sinatra 'Duets' Features Young Stars." *The Chicago Defender*, 30 October 1993, 28.

Carlson, T. "Happy 75th to Ol' Blue Eyes." *TV Guide*, 15–21 December 1990, 18.

Carman, Tim. "Live in Paris, Frank Sinatra." *The Houston Post*, 3 April 1994, H19.

———. "Sinatra Makes You Forget Any Questions." *The Houston Post*, 5 October 1994, A18.

Cerio, G. "Frank Analysis." *People Weekly*, 18 December 1995, 89–90+.

Chaffin, Tom. "Sinatra Worked at His Trade—And It Showed." *The Philadelphia Inquirer*, 12 December 1995, A23.

"The Chairman Emeritus." *Time*, 5 April 1971, 58.

"The Chairman Is a Punk." *Time*, 13 September 1993, 85.

"Chairman of the Board." *Newsweek*, 28 October 1963, 60.

"Chairman of the Board." *Time*, 16 July 1965, 62.

"Chairman of the Boors." *Newsweek*, 22 September 1986, 69.

"The Chairman, to the Bored." *Harper's*, December 1990, 24.

Champlin, Charles. "A Life in the Voice." *The Los Angeles Times*, 2 December 1990, CAL, p. 7.

Cheshire, Maxine. "Agnew and Sinatra: A Curious Friendship." *McCall's*, May 1978, 62+.

Christiansen, Richard. "A Season for Sinatra." *The Chicago Tribune*, 10 December 1995, Sec. 14, p. 3.

Citron, Alan. "Sinatra Duets: Capitol Records' Love of Them Is Lovelier the Second Time Around." *The Los Angeles Times*, 8 November 1994, D5.

Clines, Francis X. "As Pizza Maker Knows, Sinatra Still Delivers." *The New York Times*, 10 October 1993, Sec. 1, p. 33.

Cocks, Jay. "The Chairman and the Boss." *Time*, 16 August 1986, 72–73.

———. "A Pair of Kings." *Time*, 21 September 1992, 64.

Connick, Harry, Jr. "A Perfect Singer, Ever Since He Began the Beguine." *The New York Times*, 9 December 1990, H26.

Cook, Richard. "Original Sinatra." *Punch*, 21 April 1989, 50–51.

Coombes, A. "Frank Sinatra." *Ladies' Home Journal*, October 1979, 134–35+.

Corbett, John. "Of Science and Sinatra." *Down Beat*, April 1994, 28–31.

Coughlin, Ruth. "Let's Be Frank, Ol' Blue Eyes: I've Got You Under My Skin." *The Detroit News and Free Press*, 14 December 1995, E1.

"The Crooner Connection," *Time*, 17 August 1992, 52–53.

Cushman, R. "It Was a Very Good Career." *Saturday Night*, December 1995/ January 1996, 105–106+.

D'Amato, (Senator) Alfonse. "Congressional Gold for Ol' Blue Eyes? Yes, Sinatra Has Earned It." The New York *Daily News*, 9 March 1997.

Davidson, Bill. "The Life Story of Frank Sinatra: Blondes, Brunettes and the Blues." *Look*, 11 June 1957, 84+.

———. "The Life Story of Frank Sinatra: Talent, Tantrums and Torment" *Look*, 14 May 1957, 36–42+.

———. "The Life Story of Frank Sinatra: Why Frank Sinatra Hates the Press." *Look*, 28 May 1957, 123–24.

Davis, Francis. "Popular Music: *Duets II* by Frank Sinatra." *Stereo Review*, March 1995, 89.

Davis, Sammy. "How Frank Taught Me Friendship." *Today's Health*, November 1971, 30–33.

DeCurtis, Anthony. "Recordings: Their Way." *Rolling Stone*, 19 May 1994, 97–98+.

"Dedication: Frank Sinatra." *Screen World*, 1991, 3.

Defaa, Chip. "Classic 78 Drops Right in Groove." *The New York Post*, 20 April 1994, 47.

DeLeon, Clark. "Please, Mister, Please; Play Fifty-Two-Oh-Nine." *The Philadelphia Inquirer*, 24 October 1993, B2.

DeLuca, Dan. "RuPaul? Barney? The Duets Could Go On and On." *The Philadelphia Inquirer*, 24 November 1994, C1, C8.

———. "Selling Sinatra." *The Philadelphia Inquirer*, 29 October 1995, G1, G13.

Deutsch, Armand S. "A Night Out with Sinatra." *McCall's*, August 1983, 35+.

Dodd, Susan. "Sinatra" (short story). *The New Yorker*, 16 May 1988, 32–35.

Dollar, Steve. "Doubling Up for Success." *The Atlanta Constitution*, 2 November 1993, E1.

———. " 'Duets' a Blithe Reworking of Beloved Sinatra Standards." *The Atlanta Constitution*, 2 November 1993, E9.

———. "75 Frank Facts." *The Atlanta Constitution*, 11 December 1990, B1.

———. "Sinatra the Showman Charms, Cuts Loose." *The Atlanta Constitution*, 18 August 1993, B11.

Dretzka, Gary. "Tribute to Old Blue Eyes Spans Generations, Styles." *The Chicago Tribune*, 21 November 1995, Sec. 2C, p. 10.

Early, Gerald. "Listening to Frank Sinatra" (poem). *The Prairie Schooner*, 63 (Fall 1989), 108–110.

Ehrlich, H. "Sinatra's English Import." *Look*, 5 March 1968, 71–75.

Elwood, Philip. "Frankly Speaking, or, My Life with The Voice." *The San Francisco Chronicle*, 3 December 1995, C17.

Evanier, D. "Sinatra Line." *National Review*, 24 November 1978, 1492–93.

Evelyn, Maude. "Idol Remembered." *Esquire*, July 1965, 84–85.

Facter, Sue. "Blue Eyes Shining." *USA Today*, 21 November 1995, D2.

Fantel, Hans. "Sinatra's 'Duets' Album: Is It a Music Recording or Technical Wizardry?" *The New York Times*, 1 January 1994, A11.

Feather, Leonard. "Sinatra and MacLaine Offer Contrasting Sets." *The Los Angeles Times*, 19 September 1992, F2.

———. "Sinatra Still Chairman of the Board." *The Los Angeles Times*, 12 February 1991, F2.

———. "Singing the Praises of Frank Sinatra." *The Los Angeles Times*, 5 December 1990, F1.

———. "*Trilogy*—The Voice in Command." *The Los Angeles Times*, 20 April 1980, CAL, p. 3.

Feeney, Mark. "Under Our Skin." *The Boston Globe*, 9 December 1990, A1.

Fein, Art. "A Way with Words." *Variety*, 12 December 1995, S25, S26.

Ferguson, Andrew. "Sinatra at 80: Ring-a-Ding-Don't." *The Weekly Standard*, 11 December 1995, 32–36.

Ferrer, J. M. "Sinatra Special That's Very: Sinatra's Spectacular Revisited." *Life*, 9 December 1966, 24.

"Fifty Years of Teen Idols." *People Weekly*, 27 July 1992, 42–63.

"Fighting Spirit." *People Weekly*, 27 January 1997, 75.

Finck, David. "Sinatra Swings." *The Village Voice*, 20 June 1995, 16.

Fitzgerald, Jim. "Ol' Blue Eyes Doesn't Cut It My Way Now." *The Detroit News and Free Press*, 15 November 1992, G4.

Fotheringham, Allan. "In Which the Scribe Huddles on the Floor, Watches a Master and Thinks of a Mister." *Maclean's*, 29 October 1979, 64.

"Frankie and His Friends." *Time*, 5 February 1973, 34–35.

"Frankie in Madison." *Time*, 25 August 1958, 64.

"Frankie's Robert Soxers." *Newsweek*, 23 December 1946, 61.

"Frank 'n' Stein." *The New Yorker*, 8 February 1993, 33–34.

"Frank Sinatra." *People Weekly*, 27 July 1992, 57.

"Frank Sinatra in Gary." *Life*, 12 November 1945, 45–46+.

"Frank Sinatra: The Classic Interviews." *Down Beat*, February 1994, 31.

"Frank Sinatra—The Man with the Answers." *Vogue*, February 1984, 356–57+.

"Frank Sinatra Receives Ella Fitzgerald Award at Beverly Hills Gala." *Jet*, 24–31 December 1990, 16.

"Frank Sinatra Sings to 7,000 at Stadium." *The New York Times*, 4 August 1943, 14.

Frazier, George. "Frank Sinatra." *Life*, 3 May 1943, 55–62.

Freivogel, William H. "Listening After All These Years." *The St. Louis Post–Dispatch*, 24 October 1994, B17.

Friedwald, Will. "A Sinatra Top 10." *The Village Voice*, 20 June 1995, 12–13.

———. "Sinatra: The Jazz Singer." *Down Beat*, March 1996, 16–21.

"From Beginning to End, Frank Was Sammy's Best Friend and Biggest Fan." *Jet*, 4 June 1990, 26–28.

Fulford, Robert. "Sinatra with Sweetening." *The New Republic*, 18 November 1957, 22.

Gallo, Phil. "Singer's Connection with Listener Spans Generations." *Variety*, 12 December 1995, S2.

Gates, David. "Too Much Togetherness?" *Newsweek*, 8 November 1993, 79.

Gehman, Richard. "The Enigma of Frank Sinatra." *Good Housekeeping*, July 1960, 61+.

Giddins, Gary. "The One and Only Frank Sinatra." *Stereo Review*, February 1984, 52–58.

———. "The Ultimate in Theater." *The Village Voice*, 20 June 1995, 3–4.

Gilmore, Mikal. "The Majestic Artistry of Frank Sinatra." *Rolling Stone*, 18 September 1980, 60.

———. "The Wonder of Sinatra." *Rolling Stone*, 24 January 1991, 47–48.

Gleason, Ralph J. "Frank: Then and Now." *Rolling Stone*, 6 June 1974, 11.

Goldman, Kevin. "Advertising: EMI Unit Pitches Sinatra Album Its Way." *The Wall Street Journal*, 17 November 1993, B10.

Graff, Gary. "Great Pretenders No Threat to the Throne." *The Detroit News and Free Press*, 4 July 1995, C1.

Graham, Jefferson. "Sinatra Turns 75: Through Some Very Good Years, the Crooner Is Still on Top of the Heap." *USA Today*, 10 December 1990, D1.

Graham, Renee. "Sinatra Tribute: Glories Outweigh the Groans." *The Boston Globe*, 14 December 1995, 80.

Green, Tom. "Not the Retiring Kind." *USA Today*, 24 March 1994, D1.

———. "Sinatra Returns and Still Does It His way." *USA Today*, 25 March 1994, D1.

Greene, Bob. "One More for the Road." *The Chicago Tribune*, 19 May 1993, Sec. 5, p. 1.

Gugliotta, Guy. "Rep. Serrano Finds His Way to Honor Sinatra." *The Washington Post*, 14 November 1995, A17.

Gundersen, Edna. "A Chorus of Approval for Sinatra." *USA Today*, 27 October 1995, D2.

———. "Ol' Blue Eyes Still Can Make It Anywhere." *USA Today*, 11 December 1995, A1–A2.

———. "Sinatra Didn't Get to Say It His Way." *USA Today*, 2 March 1994, D2.

———. "Sinatra Doubles Up for More 'Duets.' " *USA Today*, 17 October 1994, D1.

———. "Sinatra Goes from Crooning to Cravats." *USA Today*, 21 February 1995, D1.

Haber, Joyce. "Frank Sinatra's Swan Song—His Way." *The Los Angeles Times*, 15 June 1971, View (Part IV), pp. 1, 16.

Hamill, Pete. "An American Legend: Sinatra at 69." *50 Plus*, April 1985, 26–29, 64–66.

———. "Frankly Magic, but It's a Quarter to Three." *The New York Daily News*, 21 November 1993, 3, 21.

———. "Sinatra: The Legend Lives." *New York*, 28 April 1980, 30–35.

Hamilton, J. "Working Sinatras." *Look*, 31 October 1967, 90+.

Hamlin, Jesse. " 'Duets II' A Bit Too Much." *The San Francisco Chronicle*, 4 December 1994, DAT, p. 39.

———. "Playing Favorites with Sinatra." *The San Francisco Chronicle*, 10 December 1995, DAT, p. 29.

Handy, Bruce. "Another Way." *Time*, 14 April 1997, 98.

———. "Duets III: The Poetry of Frank Sinatra and Friends." *The New York Times Magazine*, 12 November 1995, 116.

Haran, Mary Cleere. "Pal Frank." *The Village Voice*, 20 June 1995, 10.

Harrington, Richard. "Sinatra's 'Duets': Neither Here Nor There." *The Washington Post*, 7 November 1993, G1.

"He Can't Read a Note but He's Dethroning Bing, and Frank Sinatra Is 'Wunnerful' to the Gals." *Newsweek*, 22 March 1943, 62.

Heckman, Don. "Classy Supplements to the Classics." *The Los Angeles Times*, 31 October 1993, CAL, p. 65.

———. "Sinatra's September Songs Still Well Worth Hearing." *The Los Angeles Times*, 14 September 1993, F2.

Heller, Karen. "Before You Grovel, Ask: Would Frank Do It?" *The Philadelphia Inquirer*, 29 September 1991, J3.

"Hellzapoppin', Daddy-O: Mythic Men Behaving Badly." *The New York Times*, 8 June 1997, E7.

Henderson, Harry, and Sam Shaw. "Gift to the Girls." *Collier's*, 17 April 1943, 69.

Hentoff, Nat. "Can Sinatra Still Be Romantic?" *Progressive*, November 1984, 40.

———. "Hokey Tunes 'Bug' Frank."*Down Beat*, 25 March 1953; rpt. *Down Beat*, February 1994, 32.

Hess, David. "Congress Salutes Sinatra with a Gold Medal." *The Philadelphia Inquirer*, 30 April 1997, A3.

Hewitt, Bill. "Frank Takes a Fall." *People Weekly*, 21 March 1994, 46–47.

Hilburn, Robert. "Frank Sinatra." *The Los Angeles Times*, 12 January 1996, F16.

———. "Frank Sinatra on 'Duets' and His Unlikely Partners." *The Los Angeles Times*, 31 October 1993, CAL, p. 6.

———. "He's Gotten Under Their Skin." *The Los Angeles Times*, 21 November 1995, F1.

———. "Looking Back: His Way." *The Los Angeles Times*, 16 November 1995, F1.

Hilzenrath, David S. "Start Spreadin' the Cheese." *The Washington Post*, 7 October 1992, B1.

Himes, Geoffrey. "Ol' Blue Eyes, Without the Sparkle." *The Washington Post*, 30 August 1994, C3.

———. "Sinatra, Ever the Showman." *The Washington Post*, 23 July 1991, C7.

———. "Summing Up Sinatra." *The Washington Post*, 26 December 1990, C7.

Hinckley, David. "Frank & Co. Go Together . . . Like a Horse and, uh, Carriage (sort of)." The New York *Daily News*, 21 November 1995, 31.

———. "Pop's Odd Couplings." The New York *Daily News*, 7 July 1996, 19.

———. "Second Time Around." The New York *Daily News*, 13 November 1994, 42–43.

———. "The Sound of the Sinatra to Come." The New York *Daily News*, 11 September 1994, 31.

"His Stuff." *The New Yorker*, 2 July 1990, 25.

"His Way." *People*, 17 December 1990, 165–66.

Hodges, Ann. "Doing It His Way." *The Houston Chronicle*, 25 November 1994, D1.

Holden, Stephen. "Can Sinatra's Second Act Top the First?" *The New York Times*, 20 November 1994, Sec. 2, p. 45.

———. "Concert: Frank Sinatra." *The New York Times*, 11 December 1983, A116.

———. "Concert: Frank Sinatra Begins Carnegie Series." *The New York Times*, 12 September 1987, I15.

———. "Frank Sinatra Opens and Then Cancels." *The New York Times*, 17 May 1990, C21.

———. "Good, Bad and Good Days in the Life of Frank Sinatra." *The New York Times*, 1 March 1991, C26.

———. "Guide to Middle Age." *The Atlantic*, January 1984, 84–87.

———. "Pop's Patriarch Makes Music Along with His Heirs," *The New York Times*, 31 October 1993, Sec. 2, pp. 1, 34.

———. "A Royal Tribute Without the Guest of Honor." *The New York Times*, 28 July 1995, C3.

———. "The Sinatra Vocalism, Early, Mature and Late." *The New York Times*, 31 December 1990, A11.

———. "They Did It His Way." *The New York Times*, 10 December 1995, Sec. 4, p. 5.

Hollman, Laurie. "Displaying Frank Admiration: In South Philadelphia, Sinatra Is Everywhere." *The Philadelphia Inquirer*, 10 November 1991, B1–B2.

Horton, Robert. "Ol' Blue Eyes." *American Film*, July/August 1988, 51–53.

Hunt, Dennis. "Frank Sinatra." *The Los Angeles Times*, 10 March 1995, F25.

Hunt, George W. "Of Many Things." *America*, 24 November 1990, 386.

Hylton, Jeremy. "Capitol Retrospective Shows Frank Sinatra at His Best." *The Tech*, 3 June 1991, 12, 15.

"Idols Team Up on TV." *Life*, 16 May 1960, 103–104.

Innaurato, Albert. "Frank and Ella." *Opera News*, November 1996, 66.

Jacobson, M. "Frank Talk." *Esquire*, February 1996, 31.

Jefferson, Margo. "Strangeness in the Night." *Vogue*, September 1988, 412.

Jeske, L. "Caught." *Down Beat*, October 1980, 52–53.

Joel, Billy. "Frank Sinatra." *Esquire*, June 1986, 300.

Johnson, Kirk. "A Casino and a Crooner: They Did It Their Way." *The New York Times*, 20 November 1993, A23.

Jones, James T., IV. "Early, Eclectic Sinatra." *USA Today*, 5 October 1993, D1.

———. "Sinatra Box Sets Come Out Swingin'." *USA Today*, 28 November 1990, D1.

————. "Sinatra's Swing 'Song': The Sound of Greatness." *USA Today*, 30 August 1994, D1.

Jubera, Drew. "Chairman Calls Omni to Order." *The Atlanta Journal-Constitution*, 30 January 1994, F28.

Kahn, E. J. "Phenomenon: Just a Kid from Hoboken." *The New Yorker*, 9 November 1946, 36–40+.

————. "Phenomenon: The Fave, the Fans, and the Fiends." *The New Yorker*, 2 November 1946, 37–40+.

————. "Phenomenon: The Voice with the Gold Accessories." *The New Yorker*, 26 October 1946, 36–40+.

Kaltenbach, David. "The Song Is You." *Daytripper*, November 1992, 11.

Kelley, Kitty. "Congressional Gold for Ol' Blue Eyes? No, His Past Is Too Tainted." The New York *Daily News*, 9 March 1997.

————. "A Gold Medal for Ol' Blue Eyes?" *Newsweek*, 2 October 1995, 25.

Kelly, Katy. "Frank Fun Between Sinatras." *USA Today*, 6 February 1996.

Kempton, Murray. "Sinatra: The Lion in Winter." *New York Newsday*, 17 November 1993, 7, 112.

Kennedy, William. "Come Rain, Come Shine." *The Guardian*, 6 December 1990, 21.

————. "Under My Skin." *The New York Times Magazine*, 7 October 1990, 40–41+.

Kerrison, Ray. "Ol' Blue Eyes Still Has the Magic." *The New York Post*, 25 August 1993, 14.

"The Kid from Hoboken." *Time*, 29 August 1955, 52–54+.

King, Larry. "In the Greenroom with Ol' Blue Eyes." *Cosmopolitan*, November 1990, 142–44.

"King of the Birds." *Time*, 22 May 1964, 48.

Kloer, Phil. "Sinatra Special an Embarrassment of Low Notes." *The Atlanta Journal-Constitution*, 25 November 1994, 27.

Knight, Arthur. "Star Time?" *Saturday Review*, 21 November 1970, 56.

Kogan, Rick. "Getting Semi-Tough with Frank Sinatra." *The Chicago Tribune*, 6 November 1992, Sec. 5, p. 1.

————. "Lost Vegas." *The Chicago Tribune*, 25 August 1993, Sec. 5, p. 1.

Kohn H. "Sinatra: The History Beyond the Rumors." *Rolling Stone*, 19 March 1981, 12–14.

Korall, Burt. "A Measure of Sinatra." *Saturday Review*, 15 October 1966, 58–59.

Kram, Mark, Jr. "I Was a Mouse in the Rat Pack." *Philadelphia*, December 1994, 102–105, 145–48.

Kuntzman, Gersh. "Frank Puts Pearl in a Jam." *The New York Post*, 10 November 1993, 29.

————. "From 'Stillborn' to Chairman of the Board." *The New York Post*, 1 December 1995, 3.

Kuntzman, Gersh, and Kyle Smith. "Birthday Boy Sinatra Takes the Cake." *The New York Post*, 1 December 1995, 3.

"L.A. Branch of NAACP Gives Sinatra Achievement Award." *Jet*, 1 June 1987, 56.

Lague, Louise. "Still Doing It His Way." *People Weekly*, 17 December 1990, 65–66.

Lahr, John. "Sinatra's Song." *The New Yorker*, 3 November 1977, 76–95.

Lannon, Linnea. "Sinatra Gives Powerful Performance." *The Detroit News and Free Press*, 10 November 1991, Q4.

Lardne, John. "Synthetic Fun." *The New Yorker*, 2 November 1957, 114–18.

"La Voce and the USO." *Newsweek*, 23 July 1945, 90.

Lawson, Terry. "His Bad Boy Period Past, It's Finally OK to Like Frank." *The Detroit News and Free Press*, 10 December 1995, H1.

Lear, Martha Weinman. "The Bobby Sox Have Wilted, but the Memory Remains Fresh." *The New York Times*, 13 October 1974, Sec. 2, pp. 1, 12.

Leckey, Andrew. "Color Ol' Blue Eyes Green." *The Chicago Tribune*, 9 December 1993, Sec. 6, p. 9.

Leerhsen, Charles. "Still Good and Saucy at 75." *Newsweek*, 17 December 1990, 66–67.

Lees, Gene. "Frank Sinatra: Confessions and Contradictions." *High Fidelity*, March 1969, 120.

———. "The Performance and the Pain." *High Fidelity*, May 1967, 95.

———. "The Sinatra Phenomenon." *High Fidelity*, October 1977, 22–28.

———. "Sinatra—That Certain Style." *Saturday Review*, 28 August 1971, 45, 54.

———. "Underrated Sinatra." *High Fidelity*, June 1969, 109.

Levinson, Aaron. "South Philly Sinatra." *Daytripper*, November 1992, 7.

Leydon, Joe. "Friends, Colleagues Salute Frank Sinatra at Film Festival." *The Houston Post*, 11 January 1993, D2.

Lichtman, Irv. "Carnegie Hall Concerts Honor Sinatra, Songwriters for Crooner's 80th Birthday." *Billboard*, 8 April 1995, 52.

Littwin, Susan. "The Man and the Myth." *TV Guide*, 7 November 1992, 10–14.

Long, Jack. "Sweet Dreams and Dynamite." *American Magazine*, Spring 1943, 41, 143–35.

Lowthar, William. "Sinatra Connection." *Maclean's*, 26 January 1981, 27–28.

———. "Sinatra's Right to Life." *Maclean's*, 5 December 1983, 68.

Lupica, Mike. "Sinatra Belts Out a Home Run." The New York *Daily News*, 21 November 1993, 20–21.

Mallowe, Mike. "The Selling of Sinatra." *Philadelphia*, September 1983, 114–18, 190–99.

Mandel, Howard. "Rock/Pop Recordings: *Duets* by Frank Sinatra." *Audio*, February 1994, 81.

Mann, Dinn. " 'What a Man!' Sinatra Takes a Bow at Tribute." *The Atlanta Constitution*, 12 December 1995, E6.

Manning, Anita. "Chicago School Starts Spreading the Detention Blues." *USA Today*, 22 September 1992, A1.

Marchese, John. "Owning the Name but Not the Fame." *The New York Times*, 30 April 1995, Sec. 1, pp. 45, 49.

Martinez, Al. "Sid Mark, Speaking Frankly." *Philadelphia*, April 1993, 57–62.

———. "Voices in the Night." *The Los Angeles Times*, 4 August 1992, B2.

Marty, Martin E. "Sentenced to Sinatra." *Christian Century*, 11 November 1992, 1047.

Marymont, Mark. "They Did It His Way." *The Philadelphia Inquirer*, 2 November 1993, E1, E6.

McCaffrey, Neil. "I Remember Frankeee." *National Review*, 26 September 1975, 1060–61.

McClintick, David. "Sinatra's Double Play." *Vanity Fair*, December 1993, 50–52, 62–70.

McConnell, F. D. "A Very Good 80 Years." *Commonweal*, 15 December 1995, 18–19.

McDonnell, Terry. "What Would Frank Do?" *Esquire*, June 1991, 27.

McDonough, John. "Early Sinatra: The Great American Voice." *The Wall Street Journal*, 28 September 1994, A16.

———. "80 Years His Way: Homage for the Last Universal Icon." *The Wall Street Journal*, 14 December 1995, A13.

McWilliams, Michael. "New York, New York Throws Ol' Blue Eyes a Birthday Bash." *The Detroit News and Free Press*, 14 December 1995, E4.

———. " 'Sinatra' Is a Frank Portrait of His Rough 'n' Tumble Life." *The Detroit News and Free Press*, 6 November 1992, D1.

Merkin, Richard. "Frank with Relish." *Vanity Fair*, January 1996, 38.

Mieses, S. "Sinatra's Ultimate Song." *Rolling Stone*, 8 November 1984, 91–92.

Miller, Jim. "All-American Music." *Newsweek*, 8 September 1986, 62–63.

———. "Star-Spangled Sinatra." *Newsweek*, 18 October 1982, 109.

Mitchell, Rick. "Duets." *The Houston Chronicle*, 7 November 1993, Z6.

———. "Duets II." *The Houston Chronicle*, 20 November 1994, Z6.

———. "Sinatra Still Making It, Doing It His Way." *The Houston Chronicle*, 5 October 1994, A2.

———. "Song to Be Sung." *The Houston Chronicle*, 2 October 1994, Z8.

Moon, Tom. "Swinging with the 'Saloon Singer,' " *The Philadelphia Inquirer*, 2 November 1993, E1, E5.

Morris, Chris. "At Long Last, Sinatra Is Multiplatinum." *Billboard*, 19 February 1994, 14, 17.

Mortimer, Lee. "Frank Sinatra Confidential: Gangsters in the Night Clubs." *American Mercury*, August 1951, 29–36.

Munson, Kyle. "Ol' Blue Eyes at 80." *The Des Moines Register*, 12 December 1995, 1T.

"My Way vs. Their Way." *Time*, 11 April 1977, 65.

Naughton, Keith. "Old Blue Eyes Set to Help Lido Say Goodbye to Chrysler His Way." *The Detroit News and Free Press*, 23 August 1992, D1.

"New Role for Sinatra-san." *Life*, 3 July 1964, 80+.

Newman, D. "Where the King of the World Goes." *Esquire*, April 1964, 120–21+.

Newquist, Roy. "Sinatra Power." *McCall's*, July 1968, 79, 120–22.

Nieves, Evelyn. "High Hopes in Hoboken." *The New York Times*, 28 November 1993, Sec. 1, p. 52.

———. "Sinatra Library? Hoboken Ho-Ho-Holds Its Breath." *The New York Times*, 22 November 1994, B5.

Nolan, Jim. "His Songs Marked Their Lives." *The Philadelphia Daily News*, 10 January 1997, 5.

Novak, Ralph. "Looking Back on 50 Years of Popular Music, a Critic Has Two Words for Sinatra: 'The Best' " [Interview with John Rockwell]. *People*, 28 January 1985, 80–82.

Nower, Lia. "Sinatra Wows Crowd at Kiel Center." *The St. Louis Post-Dispatch*, 22 October 1994, B2.

O'Connor, John. "Sinatra: The Good, the Bad, the Music." *The New York Times*, 6 November 1992, C28.

———. "The Stars Honor a Legend at 80." *The New York Times*, 14 December 1995, C11.

———. "TV: Expert Pacing and Polish of the Sinatra Show." *The New York Times*, 15 October 1974, 79.

———. "With Sammy Davis, the Spirit Lingers." *The New York Times*, 5 July 1990, C16.

Okrent, Daniel. "The Compact Sinatra." *Esquire*, April 1988, 36.

———. "Frank and Company." *Life*, December 1990, 117–25.

———. "Saint Francis of Hoboken." *Esquire*, December 1987, 211–16.

"Ol' Blue Eyes and Chivas." *Adweek's Marketing Week*, 7 January 1991, 17.

O'Neal, Nan. "A[nheuser]-B[usch] Eyes Sinatra in the 'Night.' " *Advertising Age*, 2 May 1988, 4.

Oulahan, R., and Thomas Thompson. "And Sinatra Tangles with the Law." *Life*, 27 September 1963, 93–95.

Page, Andrew. "A Sunday with Sinatra." *Daytripper*, November 1992, 6–11.

Palmer, Robert. "Sinatra and Martin, Rock Stars." *The New York Times*, 19 May 1977, Pt. III, p. 22.

Papajohn, George, and Patricia Callahan. "Sinatra Still the Life of the Toddlin' Town." *The Chicago Tribune*, 16 May 1993, Sec. 2C, pp. 1–2.

"Paramount Piper." *The New Yorker*, 25 August 1956, 23–24.

Pareles, Jon. "When the Power Costs More Effort." *The New York Times*, 21 April 1994, C21.

Perry, Claudia. "Behind the Legend." *The Houston Post*, 2 October 1994, H6.

———. "Duets Destined for Repetition and Mediocrity." *The Houston Post*, 25 November 1994, G5.

———. "Sinatra's Reworking of Classic Hits Contains Mostly Misses." *The Houston Post*, 1 November 1993, B1.

Philips, Chuck. "Why Ol' Blue Eyes Is Back—And How Capitol Got Him." *The Los Angeles Times*, 29 September 1993, F1.

Picard, John. "Sinatra: A Memoir." *Iowa Review*, Fall 1994, 1–12.

Plagens, Peter. "Stranger in the Night." *Newsweek*, 21 March 1994, 75.

Pleasants, Henry. "Appoggiatura, Tempo Rubato, Portamento—He Uses 'Em All." *The New York Times*, 13 October 1974, Sec. 2, pp. 1, 21.

———. "Some Singer!" *Stereo Review*, March 1982, 104.

Plotz, David. "Can Even Death Stop Ol' Blue Eyes?" *Slate.com*, 4 October 1997. http.www.slate.com.

Pomerantz, Gary. "Stranger in Town: Where's Sinatra Hiding?" *The Atlanta Journal-Constitution*, 30 January 1994, F28.

Pool, Bob. "Heartfelt Thanks." *The Los Angeles Times*, 14 February 1992, B3.

"Pops Tops." *Time*, 27 December 1954, 40.

"The Private World and Thoughts of Frank Sinatra." *Life*, April 1965, 84–96+.

Pryor, Thomas M. "The Rise, Fall and Rise of Sinatra." *The New York Times Magazine*, 10 February 1957, 17, 60–61.

Puig, Claudia. "Is This Really His Life?" *The Los Angeles Times*, 26 July 1992, CAL, p. 6.

Ramirez, Anthony. "A Major Record Album: Only a Phone Call Away." *The New York Times*, 7 October 1993, D1.

Rayman, Graham. "Sinatra Still Packs House." *New York Newsday*, 18 November 1993, 13.

"Refuge from Bobby-Soxers." *Time*, 22 April 1946, 45.

Reich, Howard. "A Bouquet for Sinatra." *The Chicago Tribune*, 26 August 1990, Sec. 13, p. 4.

———. "Come Dance with Him." *The Chicago Tribune*, 23 November 1990, Sec. 5, p. 1.

———. "Drama Shares Stage with Song in Sinatra Show." *The Chicago Tribune*, 3 September 1990, Sec. 1, p. 8.

———. "Fighting Form." *The Chicago Tribune*, 4 November 1993, Sec. 5, p. 8.

———. "A Frank Look." *The Chicago Tribune*, 10 March 1991, Sec. 5, p. 3.

———. "Frank Sinatra Lets New Yorkers Know He's Top of the Heap." *The Chicago Tribune*, 16 May 1990, Sec. 1, p. 22.

———. "His Kind of Show." *The Chicago Tribune*, 24 October 1994, Sec. 1, p. 20.

———. "His Way." *The Chicago Tribune*, 30 April 1991, Sec. 5, p. 3.

———. "His Way Keeps Working: Years Deepen Sinatra's Interpretations." *The Chicago Tribune*, 13 May 1993, Sec. 1, p. 24.

———. "His Way: Sinatra's Half Century on Record." *The Chicago Tribune*, 26 August 1990, Sec. 13, p. 5.

———. "Paris Loves Sinatra in the Summer (of '62)." *The Chicago Tribune*, 27 March 1994, Sec. 13, p. 24.

———. "Seamless Work." *The Chicago Tribune*, 24 November 1994, Sec. 5, p. 15E.

———. "Sinatra at 80." *The Chicago Tribune*, 13 November 1995, Sec. 5, p. 1.

———. "Sinatra Before Swing." *The Chicago Tribune*, 16 October 1994, Sec. 13, p. 20.

———. "Sinatra Croons on Duo Tunes." *The Chicago Tribune*, 11 October 1993, Sec. 1, p. 14.

———. "Sinatra Devotees Get First Hearing of 'Duets' Sequel." *The Chicago Tribune*, 10 November 1994, Sec. 1, p. 32.

———. "Sinatra's Concert a Fitting Tribute to His Kind of Town." *The Chicago Tribune*, 16 July 1991, Sec. 1, p. 18.

Reilly, Patrick M. "Sinatra's Wife and Kids Battle over Frank Inc. While His Health Slips." *The Wall Street Journal*, 26 September 1997, A1, A14.

Reilly, Peter. "Supercharged Sinatra." *Stereo Review*, November 1984, 92.

"Relationships of Sinatra with Blacks That Book About Him Does Not Highlight." *Jet*, 13 October 1986, 56–59, 62.

Renner, Michael J. "Sinatra, 78, Still Does the Best Songs the Best." *The St. Louis Post-Dispatch*, 23 October 1994, D3.

Ressner, Jeffrey. "And Again, One More for the Road." *Time*, 21 March 1994, 72.

Ringle, Ken. "To Be Perfectly Frank: It's Been a Rich, Celebrated, Painful Life. You Can Hear It All in Sinatra's Music." *The Washington Post*, 10 December 1995, G1.

Roberts, Chris. "Vocal Heroes: Fly Me to the Croon." *Melody Maker*, 20 November 1993, 23–24.

Roberts, Jerry. "Surveying the Big Picture." *Variety*, 12 December 1995, S13, S14, S20, S22.

Robins, Wayne. "Twilight Time." *New York Newsday*, 12 June 1993, Pt. II, p. 21.

Rockwell, John. "Pop: Sinatra at Carnegie." *The New York Times*, 10 September 1981, C30.

———. "Sinatra at the Garden Is Superb TV as Well." *The New York Times*, 14 October 1974, 42.

Rosen, Craig. "Capitol Starts Spreading the News." *Billboard*, 30 October 1993, 89.

Rosen, Steven. "A Very Good Year." *The Denver Post*, 27 December 1995, G8.

Roush, Matt. "A Worthy Salute to Sinatra." *USA Today*, 14 December 1995, D3.

Royko, Mike. "How a Photog Got Under Sinatra's Skin." *The Chicago Tribune*, 3 August 1994, Sec. 1, p. 3.

Russell, L. "Frankly Admiring." *People Weekly*, 4 December 1995, 85–86+.

Russell, Rosalind. "Frank Sinatra's $25,000 Weekend." *The Ladies' Home Journal*, January 1967, 48+.

———. "Sinatra: An American Classic." *The Ladies' Home Journal*, November 1973, 26–27.

Ryon, Ruth. " 'Duet' Suits Ol' Blue Eyes." *The Los Angeles Times*, 5 March 1995, K1.

"Sammy and Frank Treat L.A. to Rare Duo Performance." *Jet*, 21 September 1987, 55.

"Sammy Davis, Frank Sinatra and Dean Martin Together Again for Historic Concert Tour." *Jet*, 21 December 1987, 36.

Santosuosso, Ernie. "In Concert, Frank Always Did It His Way." *The Boston Globe*, 9 December 1990, A5.

———. "Slenderized Sinatra Puts on a Spirited Show." *The Boston Globe*, 31 August 1990, 67.

Santurri, Edmund N. "Christian Theology and Frank Sinatra." *The Cresset*, December 1992, 20–23.

Scheck, Frank. "Sinatra 'Duets' Showcase His Familiar Vibrant Voice." *The Christian Science Monitor*, 6 December 1993, 16.

———. "That Sinatra Magic Still Lives." *The Christian Science Monitor*, 23 May 1994, 15.

Schoemer, Karen. "He Did It His Way." *Newsweek*, 20 November 1995, 82–84.

———. "Tried Is True for Sinatra." *The New York Times*, 19 November 1991, C18.

Schulberg, Budd. "Secrets of Sinatra: Inside Tales of His Life and Career." *New Choices*, December 1993/January 1994, 58–63.

Schwartz, Jonathan. "And Now the End Is Near: Sinatra's Last Audition." *Esquire*, May 1995, 80–82.

———. "One More for the Road." *Gentlemen's Quarterly*, December 1993, 114, 117–18.

———. "Sinatra: In the Wee Small Hours." *Gentlemen's Quarterly*, June 1989, 228–31, 281–83.

Seigel, Jessica. "Ol' Blue Eyes Rolls Pair of 7s." *The Chicago Tribune*, 14 December 1992, Sec. 1, p. 20.

Selvin, Joel. "Frank Sinatra Does It His Way on Duet Album." *The San Francisco Chronicle*, 31 October 1993, DAT, p. 33.

Shaw, Arnold. "Puppet, Pirate, Poet, Pawn, and King: A Sinatra Retrospective." *High Fidelity*, August 1971, 65–68.

Shepard, Richard V. "Sinatra Fans on L.I. Relive Winter of '42." *The New York Times*, 10 April 1974, 30.

"Show Biz Legends Reunite on U.S. Concert Tour." *Jet*, 7 March 1988, 56–59.

Shuster, Alvin. "Sinatra Enthralls 3,000 at a Concert in London." *The New York Times*, 9 May 1970, Sec. 14, p. 3.

Sigesmund, B. J. "Is This Frank's Final Bow?" *Newsweek*, 23 December 1996, 72.

Simels, Steve. "Sinatra's *Duets*: Doobie, Doobie, Don't." *Stereo Review*, February 1994, 145.

Simon, George. "What's Wrong with Music!" *Metronome*, February 1948, 15–16, 27.

Simonds, C. H. "For Now." *National Review*, 18 May 1971, 532.

Sinatra, Frank. "The Chairman, to the Bored." *Harper's*, December 1990, 24.

———. "The Haters and the Bigots Will Be Judged." *The Los Angeles Times*, 4 July 1991, B5.

———. "Let's Not Forget We're All Foreigners." *Magazine Digest*, July 1945, 8–10.

———. "Love Song to My Granddaughter." *The Ladies' Home Journal*, September 1974, 97.

———. "Me and My Music." *Life*, 23 April 1965, 86–104.

———. "The Way I Look at Race." *Ebony*, July 1958, 35–44.

———. "We Might Call This the Politics of Fantasy." *The New York Times*, 24 July 1972, 27.

———. "What's This About Races?" *Scholastic*, 17 September 1945, 23.

Sinatra, Tina. "Her Father's Daughter." *Ladies' Home Journal*, December 1993, 46–48.

"Sinatra." *The New Yorker*, 6 April 1987, 32–34.

"Sinatra Appears at Newport Fete." *The New York Times*, 5 July 1965, 8.

"Sinatra Connection." *Newsweek*, 5 February 1973, 28–29.

"Sinatra Fans Pose Two Police Problems and Not the Less Serious Involves Truancy." *The New York Times*, 13 October 1944, 211.

"Sinatra: An Intimate Portrait." *Life*, October 1995, 74–83.

"Sinatra and Pavarotti in Concert." *Harpers Bazaar*, March 1984, 292–93.

"Sinatra: Where the Action Is." *Newsweek*, 6 September 1965, 39–42.

Sobran, Joseph. "The Man Who Was Sinatra." *National Review*, 17 February 1992, 54–55.

"Solid-Gold Sinatra." *Newsweek*, 21 October 1957, 70.

Span, Paula. "The Frank Sinatra Museum, Hoboken's Field of Dreams." *The Washington Post*, 23 December 1993, C1.

———. "Swooning for Sinatra." *The Philadelphia Inquirer*, 3 January 1994, E5, E7.

Sparta, Christine. "Fans Put in Their Bids for a Piece of Sinatra's Life." *USA Today*, 4 December 1995, 2D.

Stearns, David Patrick. "Frank Sinatra, Jr., Chimes in on Tribute to His Father." *USA Today*, 24 July 1995, D4.

———. "In 'Duets,' Sinatra Clashes with Titans." *USA Today*, 2 November 1993, D8.

Stevens, Larry. "Frank Sinatra at 80: Still the Champ!" *Dance and the Arts*, 1 March 1996, 24.

Stewart, Zan. "On the Road with Sinatra." *Down Beat*, June 1995, 39.

Steyn, M. "The Cat in the Hat." *The American Spectator*, February 1996, 44–45.

St. Johns, A. R. "The Nine Lives of Frank Sinatra." *Cosmopolitan*, May 1956, 82–89.

Storm, Jonathan. "Frank Homage." *The Philadelphia Inquirer*, 24 November 1994, C1, C5.

———. "*Sinatra* Portrays a Singer and a Survivor." *The Philadelphia Inquirer*, 8 November 1992, N1, N10.

Strum, Charles. "Sinatra: The Idol, the Institution, the Mini-Series." *The New York Times*, 8 November 1992, Sec. 2, p. 30.

Stryker, Mark. "Under Our Skin." *The Detroit News and Free Press*, 10 December 1995, H1.

Stryker, Mark, and Terry Lawson. "The Best of Sinatra, the Worst of Sinatra." *The Detroit News and Free Press*, 10 December 1995, H9.

"Surrogate." *The New Yorker*, 9 December 1991, 44–45.

Sweeting, Adam. "The Daddy of All Legends." *The Guardian*, 13 November 1995, Sec. 2, p. 6.

"Swooner-Crooner." *Life*, 23 August 1943, 127–28.

"Swoon Song." *Newsweek*, 16 August 1943, 80.

Takiff, Jonathan "Duet Again." *The Philadelphia Daily News*, 16 November 1994, 25–26.

Talese, Gay. "Frank Sinatra Has a Cold." *Esquire*, April 1966, 89–98+.

———. "When Frank Sinatra Had a Cold: A Reflection on the Cause of Today's Common Journalism." *Esquire*, November 1987, 161–66.

"Talk with a Star." *Newsweek*, 6 July 1959, 84.

Taves, I. "Frank Sinatra." *The Women's Home Companion*, May 1956, 38–41+; and June 1956, 34–35+.

Teachout, Terry. "Frank Sinatra." *High Fidelity*, April 1987, 75–76.

———. "Taking Sinatra Seriously." *Commentary*, September 1997, 55–58.

"That Guy Sinatra." *Coronet*, November 1955, 6.

"That Old Sweet Song." *Time*, 5 July 1943, 76.

Theroux, Alexander. "When Songs Were Golden: The Era of Ira Gershwin, Oscar Hammerstein, Alan Jay Lerner and Sinatra." *The Chicago Tribune*, 24 December 1995, Sec. 14, pp. 1, 8.

Thompson, Thomas. "Frank Sinatra's Swan Song." *Life*, 25 June 1971, 70A–74A.

———. "Understanding Sinatra." *McCall's*, October 1974, 18+.

"Tony Bennett Salutes Sinatra His Way, and Brilliantly." *Time*, 21 September 1992, 64.

Tosches, Nick. "The Death, and Life, of the Rat Pack." *The New York Times*, 7 January 1996, Sec. 2, p. 34.

Trebbe, Ann. "Simply Unforgettable." *USA Today*, 29 August 1989, D1.

———. "Sinatra's Message to Moody Michael." *USA Today*, 17 September 1990, D1.

Verna, Paul. "Album Reviews: *Duets II* by Frank Sinatra," *Billboard*, 26 November 1994, 100.

Vogel, Thomas T., Jr. "On Disk: My Epiphany with Blue Eyes." *The Wall Street Journal*, 19 January 1994, A16.

"The Voice." *Newsweek*, 20 December 1943, 94–96.

"The Voice Turns 80." *St. Louis Post-Dispatch*, 14 December 1995, C22.

Voland, John. "The Arrangement: Musical Architects Gave Guidance to 'The Voice.' " *Variety*, 12 December 1995, S4, S8, S14.

Weber, Bruce. "Swooning (and Bidding) for Something of Sinatra's." *The New York Times*, 2 December 1995, A24.

Webster, Emma. "The Sinatras' Greatest Gift." *Variety*, 12 December 1995, S25–S26.

Weinman, Martha. "High Jinks in High Society." *Colliers*, 8 June 1956, 32–33.

Wells, E. "The Rise and Fall and Rise Again of Frank Sinatra." *Good Housekeeping*, August 1954, 56–59+.

Werner, Aaron. "Sinatra: An Appreciation." *Daytripper*, November 1992, 8.

Whitall, Susan. "Totally Frank." *The Detroit News and Free Press*, 6 November 1992, D1.

Whiteside, Johnny. "Players: Constellation of Talent." *Variety*, 12 December 1995, S4, S10.

"Why Sinatra Just Won't Quit." *Time*, 21 March 1994, 72.

Wiener, Jon. "When Old Blue Eyes Was 'Red.' " *The New Republic*, 31 March 1986, 21–23.

Williams, Richard. "Voice of the Century." *The Guardian*, 12 December 1995, Sec. 2, p. 2.

Willman, Chris. "Bono, Barbra, Blue Eyes? Yes, It Works." *The Los Angeles Times*, 31 October 1993, CAL, pp. 6, 65.

———. "Faux Pairings Hurt 'Sinatra Duets.' " *The Los Angeles Times*, 25 November 1994, F24.

———. "Paging Sammy, Dino and Bing." *The Los Angeles Times*, 13 November 1994, CAL, p. 66.

"With *Duets II*, Sinatra Again Woos the Kids." *Time*, 12 December 1994, 92.

"With Sinatra in London." *Newsweek*, 3 November 1958, 48–49.

Wittels, D. G. "Star-Spangled Octopus: How MCA Acquired Frank Sinatra." *The Saturday Evening Post*, 24 August 1946, 20+.

"Words and Music." *Time*, 21 April 1947, 44.

"Worst of Song: *Duets* by Frank Sinatra." *People Weekly*, 27 December 1993, 16.

Wright, Christian Logan. "Sinatra 101." *Mademoiselle*, April 1991, 136.

Zehme, Bill. "And Then There Was One." *Esquire*, March 1996, 86–93.

Zuckoff, Mitchell. "Tribe Hits a Jackpot." *The Boston Globe*, 18 November 1993, 1.

Index

About the Contributors

T. H. ADAMOWSKI is Professor of English at the University of Toronto. His scholarly interests include Faulkner, Lawrence, Mailer, Bellow, and Sartre. He has been a Sinatra fan since he first heard "Angel Eyes" in 1958.

RICHARD APT is a New Jersey-based collector of and dealer in Sinatra-related merchandise, and he is among the most knowledgeable people in the world about things Blue Eyes. His webpage is magnificently designed and well worth checking out at http://www.blue-eyes.com.

BILL BOGGS is a television and radio host and producer. He has won three Emmys for his work as a talk-show host on Fox and Westinghouse TV. He was also the first person to do an in-depth interview with Frank Sinatra on his New York–based program—*Midday with Bill Boggs*—in 1975.

STAN CORNYN has written the liner notes for many of Frank Sinatra's classic Reprise albums, and he has won several Grammy Awards for his work. He stopped writing liner notes around 1970, when he became Executive Vice President of Warner Bros. Records.

GERALD EARLY, a poet and essayist, is the author of more than eight books. They include: *How the War in the Streets Is Won: Poems on the Quest of Love and Faith* (1995) and *One Nation under a Groove: Motown and American Culture* (1995).

WILL FRIEDWALD is the author of the critically acclaimed musical biography of Frank Sinatra, *Sinatra! The Song Is You: A Singer's Art* (1995). His previous book, *Jazz Singing: America's Great Voices from Bessie Smith to Bebop and Beyond* (1992), also contains an excellent chapter on Ol' Blue Eyes.

PHILIP FURIA is Professor and Chair of the Department of English at the University of North Carolina at Wilmington. He is the author of *The Poets of Tin Pan Alley: A History of America's Great Lyricists, Ira Gershwin: The Art of the Lyricist*, and a forthcoming book on the songs of Irving Berlin.

GILBERT L. GIGLIOTTI is Associate Professor of English at Central Connecticut State University. He specializes in the Neo-Latin poetry of colonial and revolutionary America. A longtime fan of Ol' Blue Eyes, he hosts a weekly radio program, "Frank, Gil, and Friends," on WFCS in New Britain and Hartford, Connecticut.

ROGER GILBERT is Associate Professor of English at Cornell University, where he teaches courses in American literature. He is the author of *Walks in the World: Representation and Experience in Modern American Poetry* (1991) and has published essays on topics ranging from contemporary poetics to the Chicago Bulls.

CHARLES L. GRANATA is a Frank Sinatra historian and archivist. Among other musical endeavors, he is a project director and producer for Sony Music/Legacy Recordings, where he is responsible for restoring and reissuing Mr. Sinatra's Columbia-era recordings.

KEN HUTCHINS was instrumental in establishing the Sinatra Internet Mailing List hosted by Temple University. He is a contributor to various Sinatra sites on the World Wide Web. In his day job, he works for the IBM Corporation.

RICHARD IACONELLI, a graduate of Temple University's Annenberg School of Communications and Theater, is a free-lance writer and a lifelong admirer of Frank Sinatra.

LEONARD MUSTAZZA is Associate Dean and Professor of English and American Studies at Penn State University's Abington College in suburban Philadelphia. He is the author of two previous books on Frank Sinatra: *The Frank Sinatra Reader* (with Steven Petkov), published by Oxford University Press in 1995, and *Ol' Blue Eyes: A Frank Sinatra Encyclopedia*, published in 1998 by Greenwood Press.

DANIEL OKRENT is editor of New Media at Time Inc., and the former editor of *Life* magazine. The author of four books, he wrote a regular column on jazz and classic pop for *Esquire* magazine in the 1980s.

EDMUND N. SANTURRI is Professor of Religion and Philosophy and Director of "The Great Conversation Program" at St. Olaf College in Northfield, Minnesota. He is the author of *Perplexity in the Moral Life: Philosophical and Theological Considerations* (1987) and co-editor (with William Werpehowski) of *The Love Commandments: Essays in Christian Ethics and Moral Philosophy* (1992). A longtime Sinatra fan, he previously published an article titled "Christian Theology and Frank Sinatra" in the December 1992 issue of *The Cresset*.

JAMES F. SMITH is Professor of English and American Studies and Head of the Division of Social Science at Penn State University's Abington College. The author of numerous scholarly articles on American culture and popular literature, he is the co-author (with Vicki Abt and Eugene Christiansen) of a landmark study of gambling, *The Business of Risk: Commercial Gambling in Mainstream America*, published in 1985 by the University Press of Kansas.

LLOYD L. SPENCER is a board-certified psychiatrist in practice for more than thirty-five years. He currently serves as Medical Director of Ozark Counseling Services, a community mental health facility, in Mountain Home, Arkansas. He has also taught psychopharmacology and pathophysiology at the Forest Institute of Professional Psychology in Springfield, Missouri. He abhorred "Frankie" in the forties, but has adored "Sinatra" ever since.